ONE WEEK LOAN

This book is due for return on or before the last date shown below.

10 FEB 2014

VALUES IN CRIMINOLOGY AND COMMUNITY JUSTICE

Edited by Malcolm Cowburn, Marian Duggan,
Anne Robinson and Paul Senior

First published in Great Britain in 2013 by

Policy Press
University of Bristol
6th Floor
Howard House
Queen's Avenue
Clifton
Bristol BS8 1SD
UK
Tel +44 (0)117 331 5020
Fax +44 (0)117 331 5367
e-mail pp-info@bristol.ac.uk
www.policypress.co.uk

North American office:
Policy Press
c/o The University of Chicago Press
1427 East 60th Street
Chicago, IL 60637, USA
t: +1 773 702 7700
f: +1 773-702-9756
e:sales@press.uchicago.edu
www.press.uchicago.edu

© Policy Press 2013

British Library Cataloguing in Publication Data
A catalogue record for this book is available from the British Library

Library of Congress Cataloging-in-Publication Data
A catalog record for this book has been requested

ISBN 978 1 44730 035 9 hardcover

The right of Malcolm Cowburn, Marian Duggan, Anne Robinson and Paul Senior to be identified as editors of this work has been asserted by them in accordance with the 1988 Copyright, Designs and Patents Act.

The statements and opinions contained within this publication are solely those of the editors and contributors and not of the University of Bristol or Policy Press. The University of Bristol and Policy Press disclaim responsibility for any injury to persons or property resulting from any material published in this publication.

Policy Press works to counter discrimination on grounds of gender, race, disability, age and sexuality.

Cover design by Policy Press
Front cover image: istock.com
Printed and bound in Great Britain by CPI Group
(UK) Ltd, Croydon, CR0 4YY

Contents

A brief introduction

Malcolm Cowburn

This book is about values; values in action in the making of theory, the shaping of research and the implementation of policies in practice. Robinson (2011, p 4) describes three usages of the word 'value':

1. Used as a verb, *to value* means to esteem or hold in regard.
2. *Value* as a noun refers to the worth, merit or importance placed on, for instance, a particular characteristic or quality.
3. *Values* are also a set of normative beliefs or standards held by a social group.

This book incorporates all of these usages. The first two usages point to estimations, mostly public estimations, of the social worth of criminology and community justice; to use the words first coined by Carrabine et al (2000), they point to the nature of 'public criminology'. However, in line with many of the chapters in this book, the issues of 'social worth' and 'public valuation' are immediately problematic and raise issues of *whose* evaluation of *what*. To be valued as a resource for governmental policy may be to be dismissed as valueless by those who seek to critique government policy and practices. Loader and Sparks (2011) have explored in depth the nuances and contradictions innate in the role of the public intellectual. These issues point directly to the third usage highlighted earlier, the problem of allegiance (or not), first highlighted by Becker (1967) in his article 'Whose side are we on?' This article has provoked and continues to stimulate wide-ranging discussion in the social sciences since its publication (see, eg, Gouldner, 1975; Hammersley and Gomm, 2000; Liebling, 2001; Delamont, 2002; Cohen, 2011). The authors in this volume add their own distinctive contributions to this debate.

The idea for this book emerged from a group of academic staff in one university where criminology is practised (ie taught and researched at theoretical and applied levels); this core group was made up of experienced academics and people new to working in higher education. Some of the group had much experience of applied work in the criminal justice system and some had recently completed research degrees. Experienced and inexperienced writers offered to work together to produce a book that considered the value(s) of criminology and community justice. At this point, The Policy Press became involved and the scope of the book grew and a wider range of authors was recruited. In order to develop coherence without imposing conformity, contributors were asked to reflect on Howard Becker's influential 1967 article.

The present collection is unique because it considers Becker's question from three related perspectives: theory, criminal justice practices, and research and policy. Stan Cohen has noted that the interrelationship of these three areas has been, and is, important to the development of criminological 'knowledge', because this 'knowledge is situated not just or even primarily, in the 'pure' academic world, but in the applied domain of the state's crime control apparatus' (Cohen, 1988, p 67, cited in Loader and Sparks, 2011, p 8). Thus, theorising, research and practices are all inevitably linked to wider political arenas. Stan Cohen died earlier this year (2013), but for over 40 years, he was concerned with the issues of allegiances and rights in criminological practice. Moreover, his work as a social worker and in the human rights movement ensured that this concern was theoretical, political and practical.

These chapters contribute to a developing reflexivity that is becoming increasingly common within criminal justice practice (Robinson, 2011) and criminological literature (Loader and Sparks, 2011; Turner, 2013), and a key part of this reflexivity is to recognise that research, policy and practice are all imbued with values, and that the language used inevitably carries an implicit (e)valuation of people and their actions. The contributions in this book variously reflect on the value(s) of criminology and community justice. In the first section, issues of values and how they relate to and are embodied in epistemology are explored. The second section is concerned with exploring issues in relation to practice or practices; and the final section of this book addresses values in the practice of research and policymaking.

References

Becker, H. (1967) 'Whose side are we on?', *Social Problems*, vol 14, no 3, pp 234–47.

Carrabine, E., Lee, M. and South, N. (2000) 'Social wrongs and human rights in late modern Britain: social exclusion, crime control and prospects for a public criminology', *Social Justice*, vol 27, no 2, pp 193–211.

Cohen, S. (1988) *Against criminology*, New Brunswick, NJ: Transaction.

Cohen, S. (2011) 'Whose side were we on? The undeclared politics of moral panic theory', *Crime Media Culture*, vol 7, no 3, pp 237–43.

Delamont, S. (2002) 'Whose side are we on? Revisiting Becker's classic ethical question at the *fin de siecle*', in T. Welland and L. Pugsley (eds) *Ethical dilemmas in qualitative research*, Aldershot: Ashgate Publishing Ltd, pp 149–63.

Gouldner, A. W. (1975) *For sociology: renewal and critique in sociology today*, Harmondsworth: Pelican Books.

Hammersley, M. and Gomm, R. (2000) 'Bias in social research', in M. Hammersley (ed) *Taking sides in social research*, Abingdon: Routledge, pp 151–66.

Liebling, A. (2001) 'Whose side are we on? Theory, practice and allegiances in prisons research', *British Journal of Criminology*, vol 41, pp 472–84.

Loader, I. and Sparks, R. (2011) *Public criminology?*, Abingdon: Routledge.

Robinson, A. (2011) *Foundations for offender management: theory, law and policy for contemporary practice*, Bristol: The Policy Press.

Turner, E. (2013) 'Beyond "facts" and "values": rethinking some recent debates about the public role of criminology', *British Journal of Criminology*, vol 53, no 1, pp 149–66.

Notes on contributors

Katherine Albertson is a research fellow at the Hallam Centre for Community Justice, Sheffield Hallam University. Katherine has been involved in both the management and collection of fieldwork data on a diverse range of projects across the criminal justice sector. She has extensive experience of interviewing offenders regarding their views on the services provided to support desistance from criminal activity. Over more recent years, mapping, modelling systems and process evaluation have formed significant components of the activities Katherine has been involved in while assessing reducing reoffending initiatives. She has also been involved in qualitative interviews to assist in cost capture activities.

Kevin Albertson is a principal lecturer in the Department of Accounting, Finance and Economics at the Manchester Metropolitan University Business School. He has published widely on economic theory and social policy. Over recent years, he has focused on applying an economic analysis to criminal justice practices, examining formal sanctions and deterrence effects, as well as the emerging trend of privatisation in criminal justice from an economic perspective. He is co-author, with Professor Chris Fox, of the popular textbook *Crime and economics: an introduction* (Routledge, 2012).

Liz Austen is a principal lecturer and criminology programme leader at Sheffield Hallam University. Her doctoral research was focused on young people and risk-taking. Her interests include the application of postmodern theory to crime and deviance, research methodologies, and the sociology of risk.

James Banks is a senior lecturer in criminology at Sheffield Hallam University. He has published in a number of journals including: *Crime, Media, Culture*; *Critical Criminology*; *The Howard Journal of Criminal Justice* and the *European Journal of Crime, Criminal Law and Criminal Justice*. He is currently engaged in research examining the regulation of the online gambling market.

Simon Cottee is a senior lecturer in criminology and criminal justice at Kent University. His research interests are focused on deviance, apostasy and political violence. He is currently working on the Economic and Social Research Council-funded study of Islamic apostasy, 'The apostates: a qualitative study of ex-Muslims in Britain' (RES-000-22-4308).

Malcolm Cowburn is Emeritus Professor of Applied Social Science at Sheffield Hallam University. His three main areas of research interest are sex offenders and sexual violence, prisons and diversity, and research ethics.

Marian Duggan is a senior lecturer in criminology at Sheffield Hallam University. Her research interests span gender, sexuality and hate crime victimisation. She is the author of several publications in these areas, including *Queering conflict: examining lesbian and gay experiences of homophobia in Northern Ireland* (Ashgate, 2012). Marian's current research interests focus on gendered experiences of hate crime and male engagement in 'violence against women' prevention strategies.

Dan Ellingworth is a senior research fellow at the Hallam Centre for Community Justice at Sheffield Hallam University, where his work has focused on quantitative elements of evaluations of various criminal justice initiatives. The main emphasis has been on assessing reconvictions following various offender management programmes delivered both in custody and in the community, including national evaluations of Integrated Offender Management, Intensive Alternatives to Custody and Layered Offender Management. Previously, he has held teaching posts at Sheffield Hallam University and Manchester Metropolitan University, and maintains interests in victimology, youth justice, criminal justice policy and the analysis of large government data sets.

Anthony Ellis is a postgraduate research student and part-time criminology tutor at the University of Sheffield. He is currently writing up his doctoral thesis, which is funded by the White Rose Network. His doctoral research utilised in-depth ethnographic research methods, principally life history interviews and observations, with men involved in violence and crime. His research interests fall broadly into the areas of gender, identity and crime, particularly masculinities and their intersection with violence. He is also interested in how violent victimisation affects men and masculinity.

Stephen Farrall is Director of the Centre for Criminological Research in the School of Law at the University of Sheffield, where he has worked since 2007. His most recent publication is: Farrall, S. and Jennings, W. (2012) 'Policy feedback and the criminal justice agenda: an analysis of the economy, crime rates, politics and public opinion in post-war Britain', *Contemporary British History*, vol 26, no 4, pp 467–88.

Chris Fox is Professor of Evaluation at Manchester Metropolitan University, where he leads the Policy Evaluation and Research Unit (PERU). He is involved in a wide range of evaluation and research projects and is particularly interested in programme and policy evaluation, economic evaluation, and new directions in policy, such as payment by results and Social Impact Bonds. He is leading and contributing to a number of evaluations in the criminal justice system, many with an economic component. He teaches undergraduate and postgraduate modules, including Economics and Crime, Policy Evaluation and Research, and Community Safety. Chris is joint editor (with Tim Bateman) of the journal *Safer Communities*. He is also lead author of the first substantial publication on justice reinvestment: *Justice reinvestment: Can the criminal justice system deliver more for less?* (Routledge, 2013), together with Kevin Albertson and Kevin Wong.

Paula Hamilton is a senior lecturer in criminology and criminal justice. She joined Sheffield Hallam in 2004 from Manchester University, having previously worked as a probation officer in Greater Manchester. Her teaching and research interests lie primarily in the areas of the criminal justice process, penology and criminal justice policy. She is also passionate about introducing students to gender and crime issues, including violence against women and relationships between masculinities and crime. Paula is currently completing doctoral research – a narrative enquiry into how people desist from a previous criminal lifestyle and the role of contemporary rehabilitative interventions in that process.

Jean Henderson has extensive experience as a Probation Officer, and was a regional practice development trainer with the Midlands Probation Training Consortium before joining Sheffield Hallam University in January 2004. She teaches undergraduate criminology modules including Rehabilitation and Punishment, and Violent Crime. Jean is also a key member of the team delivering the professional qualifying degree programme for probation officers, where her specialist areas include values and ethics, understanding and working with risk, and critically reflective practice.

Victoria Lavis is a chartered psychologist and lecturer in psychology at the University of Bradford. Since 2000, her interest has focused on research and knowledge transfer activities in the prisons of England and Wales. Recent collaborative research, funded by the Economic and Social Research Council, explored the response to diversity in a maximum-security male dispersal prison in the North of England. Recent knowledge transfer work has focused on using appreciative inquiry to enhance staff–prisoner relationships in dispersal prisons.

Fergus McNeill is Professor of Criminology and Social Work at the University of Glasgow. His main interests relate to institutions, cultures and practices of punishment and its alternatives.

Claire Moon is senior lecturer in the sociology of human rights in the Department of Sociology and the Centre for the Study of Human Rights at the London School of Economics. She is the author of *Narrating political reconciliation: South Africa's Truth and Reconciliation Commission* (Lexington Books/Rowman and Littlefield, 2008) and has published widely on topics such as transitional justice, truth commissions, post-conflict reconciliation, apologies, reparations (with reference to South Africa and Argentina), war trauma, human rights reporting and forensic knowledge in human rights.

David Moxon is a former senior lecturer in criminology at Sheffield Hallam University. He holds a PhD from the University of Sheffield and has published work on various topics, including the 2011 riots in the UK, illegal drug use among older adults and, following on from his PhD studies, Marxism's relation to criminology.

Craig Paterson is a principal lecturer in criminology at Sheffield Hallam University. Craig received his PhD on electronic monitoring and surveillance in the commercial sector in 2006. His publications span commercial crime control and policing, including two books: *Understanding the electronic monitoring of offenders* (VDM Verlag, 2009) and, with Ed Pollock, *Policing and criminology* (Learning Matters, 2011). His current research interests include private security in criminal justice, police education and restorative policing.

Ed Pollock is a senior lecturer in criminology at Sheffield Hallam University. He joined Sheffield Hallam in 2006 from Nottingham Trent University after completing his PhD, which focused on how the Internet can create an enabling environment for the expression and development of online racial hatred, and facilitate criminal and other harmful activity. His main areas of interest are forensics, hate crime and extremist ideology, sentencing and penology, and policing. His most recent publication, with Craig Paterson, is *Policing and criminology* (Learning Matters, 2011). He is an editor of the *Internet Journal of Criminology* and is a member of the Independent Monitoring Board at HMP Whatton and HMP Leicester.

Gary Potter is a senior lecturer in criminology at London South Bank University where he teaches (among other things) Green Criminology alongside Drugs and Crime. He is a member of the International Green Criminology Working Group and wrote the definition of 'green criminology' for their website (see: greencriminology.org). Even his drug-related research is green: he has written one book on cannabis cultivation (*Weed, need and greed*; Free Association Books, 2010) and co-edited another with Tom Decorte and Simon Bouchard (*World wide weed*; Ashgate, 2011).

Muzammil Quraishi is a senior lecturer in criminology and criminal justice at the University of Salford, Centre for Social Research. He is author of *Muslims and crime* (Ashgate, 2005) and numerous texts on Muslim populations with regards to offending and victimisation. His latest publications include, with Rob Philburn, *Researching racism* (Sage, 2013) and a chapter on 'British Asian Muslims and child sexual exploitation', in S. Hamid (ed) *Young British Muslims: rhetoric and realities* (Routledge, 2013). His research interests include Islamic jurisprudence, religion/ethnicity in prison, colonialism and crime, and comparative criminology. His methodological leanings are towards qualitative ethnographic research informed by the critical race theory perspective.

Stephen Riley is a senior lecturer in law at Sheffield Hallam University. His research interest is the philosophy of law with particular focus on human dignity, justice and the legal person.

Anne Robinson has extensive experience as a practitioner and manager in youth justice. She joined Sheffield Hallam University as a senior lecturer in 2005 and currently leads the programme for probation officer training. She is the author of *Foundations for offender management: theory, law and policy for contemporary practice* (Policy Press, 2011) and *Foundations for youth justice: person-centred approaches to practice* (Policy Press, forthcoming).

Paul Senior is Professor of Probation Studies and Director of the Hallam Centre for Community Justice (HCCJ) at Sheffield Hallam University. He has always operated with one foot in the real world, having held a joint appointment with probation for 17 years and also worked part-time as a freelance consultant and researcher, as well as conducting responsive consultancies in Hong Kong, Singapore and New Zealand. He leads research in the HCCJ on Integrated Offender Management, restorative justice and the reintegration of prisoners back into the community. He has published widely on probation practice, probation training and criminal justice policy issues.

Sunita Toor joined Sheffield Hallam University in March 2006 as a senior lecturer in criminology. Sunita teaches a range of criminological modules at undergraduate and postgraduate levels. Her specialist areas and research interests are criminological theory and philosophies of crime; comparative criminologies; race, ethnicity, culture and crime; Asian criminality, especially focusing on young women, as well as issues pertaining to equalities and diversity within criminology more broadly.

Tammi Walker is a chartered psychologist, an honorary researcher at the University of Manchester and a lecturer in psychology at the University of Bradford. Since 1999, she has undertaken research and clinical practice in HMP Prison Service and Secure Forensic Psychiatric Services. Current collaborative research, funded by the National Institute of Health Research (RfPB), is a pilot randomised controlled treatment trial of a short-term psychological intervention for self-harm in female prisoners in three prisons in England. She is co-author on the recent Department of Health's 'Women's enhanced medium secure services' report. She maintains her long-standing research in self-harm and suicide in prisons, women in prisons, and gender issues in offending.

Kevin Wong has been Deputy Director of the Hallam Centre for Community Justice at Sheffield Hallam University since spring 2010. He previously worked as assistant director at Nacro, a major crime-reduction charity, and has over 25 years' experience of volunteering for, working in and researching the voluntary and community sector. Most recently, he has managed multi-site research projects commissioned by the Home Office and Ministry of Justice, including building voluntary and community sector capacity in offender management, and two community-based criminal justice payment-by-results pilots.

Maggie Wykes is a senior lecturer in criminology at the University of Sheffield and has published on news, culture, violence, gender, justice, body image, paedophilia and internet crime. She is currently involved in comparative research on the prosecution of sexual violence with the Gender, Health and Justice Unit at the University of Cape Town, which is funded by the British Academy.

SECTION ONE

Values of criminological theories

The first section of this book assesses 'sides' and values in relation to a selection of criminological theories that have come a long way from the early classical or positivistic schools of thought. The contributors in this section review, critique and evaluate what has been included and omitted from traditional criminological inquiry, placing a particular emphasis on, or arguing from, subordinated and overlooked perspectives. These chapters demonstrate some of the 'sides' that Becker's (1967) article sought to address while also offering perspectives on newer or emergent areas in criminological theorising, indicating the ever-expanding nature of values within this discipline.

Beginning with Chapter One, Simon Cottee sets the scene by examining the place of morals and values in criminology's traditional judgement of, and suggested responses to, offenders and offending. Drawing on the discipline's failure to account for some of the worst atrocities in history, Cottee suggests that criminologists are (implicitly at least) engaged in a moral positioning of the offender, upon which public responses to offending are based. Therefore, if theorising about crime can be argued to have a direct impact on how crime and criminals are treated, then criminologists must be aware of who they are including or omitting, and how their own values and judgements are imparted to, and received by, the public. In emphasising the diversity of such values, Cottee provides an insightful round-up of the most prominent criminological theories to date, from early positivistic depictions through to more recent cultural incarnations, demonstrating the vast range of values and judgements demonstrated within criminology while also paving the way for several of the chapters to follow.

In Chapter Two, Liz Austen and Malcolm Cowburn present the first in a series of 'sides', examining the social construction of criminological research and theory production through a postmodernist lens. The recognition that knowledge is informed by, shapes and determines understanding and perspectives is demonstrated by reference to several identities addressed within the postmodernist 'umbrella'. These subject positionings are revealed to have emerged as responses to more traditional forms of criminological inquiry, and prove vital for challenging the foundational concepts upon which much criminological thought has been constructed. Indeed, in addressing the issues of presenting different sides of a story within the developing realm of 'public criminology', Austen and Cowburn reiterate the need for criminologists to be aware of the discussions that they are contributing to, and the responses that such perspectives may elicit.

In Chapter Three, David Moxon analyses the challenges facing Marxist criminologists, who, following a recent period of relative silence, appear to be experiencing a revival in terms of a valid, if shifting, theoretical approach in criminology. Applying Becker's questions of 'sides' and 'values' to Marxist criminologists, Moxon demonstrates how the impact of four decades of social change has posed difficulties to Marxists attempting to answer such queries. As a result, he suggests invoking Colin Sumner's notion of 'censure', applying the concept in a manner that shifts the focus of these inquiries to more pressing issues more suited to Marxist analysis. The chapter's discussion of the changing nature of society and developments in class and economic divides illustrates the need for Marxist criminology to reassert itself in relation to Becker's questions if it is to remain relevant in a contemporary environment.

Victoria Lavis and Tammi Walker explore the impact of feminism on criminology in Chapter Four. Invoking key theorists in this area, they address five core areas of perceived tension in relation to the competing values evident in feminism and criminology. These areas cover: theorising from 'real' and 'discursive' positions; focusing on specific versus generalisable theories; whether a 'feminist criminology' is both desirable and achievable; addressing gender essentialism and feminist perspectives on male lawbreaking; and, finally, whether to focus on gender awareness or gender neutrality when engaging in feminist analyses. Ultimately, Lavis and Walker draw on the merits of intersectional approaches to assess how feminist methods can challenge discrimination in the criminal justice system.

Expanding on the theme of gender and criminology, in Chapter Five, Anthony Ellis and Maggie Wykes seek to 'bring back the boys' by interrogating the limitations of theory accounting for men's involvement in crime. Demonstrating how masculinities theories largely focus on the criminal and physical harms of marginalised or socially insecure men, they illustrate the need for a more explicit analysis on theorising the violences of powerful men. The chapter invokes a global perspective, drawing on case studies espousing the nature and impact of men's violence before turning its attention to the crimes of the powerful, with particular reference to men involved in the recent economic crisis. The critique offered in the chapter suggests that criminology needs to go further in addressing the constitutive benefits of crime and violence to powerful masculinities in order to effectively theorise a wider range of harms.

In Chapter Six, Sunita Toor provides an overview of how negative engagements with racial diversity have led to a 'racialisation' of crime in the UK. Several significant domestic and international events have occurred over the past decade, which, in turn, have prompted a disproportionately negative focus on Asian Muslim populations in the West and a growing criminalisation of British Asian Muslim communities in particular. The chapter illustrates how events such as the Salman Rushdie affair, the Bradford Riots and the fallout from 9/11 and 7/7 have increased surveillance of these communities (as opposed to the 'traditional' focus on black populations), homogenising 'Asian' and 'Muslim' within a framework of danger and fear.

In Chapter Seven, James Banks and David Moxon provide an overview and critique of cultural criminology, demonstrating how the discipline continues to expand into new and under-theorised territory while indicating the potential for a unified, macro-approach to criminological theorising. The chapter draws on well-known proponents of the cultural criminological enterprise, relocating the study of crime in a sociological framework before querying why a uniformity of analysis has not yet emerged in this area. One rationale for this is the reactionary nature of cultural criminology; continually taking the 'other' side has led to it being more of a response to macro-level theories than a producer of such theories in its own right.

Finally, in Chapter Eight, Gary R. Potter addresses similar issues in his analysis of green criminology, a more recent development in comparison with the other perspectives in this section, but one that can be seen as occupying the margins of criminology with regards to research and theory production. Illustrating the varied and applicable lessons green criminology can offer the discipline as a whole, the chapter addresses critiques and justifications of the green approach while demonstrating how green criminology's espousal of core value positions is at the heart of the critical criminological enterprise, providing a voice for the powerless while demanding accountability from the powerful.

Reference
Becker, H. (1967) 'Whose side are we on?', *Social Problems*, vol 14, no 3, pp 234–47.

ONE

Judging offenders: the moral implications of criminological theories

Simon Cottee

Introduction

This is from *An intimate history of killing*, Joanna Bourke's controversial and unsettling account of military combat in the 20th century:

> The massacre had begun just after eight o'clock on the morning of 16 March 1968, when 105 American soldiers of Charlie Company, 11th Brigade of the American Division, entered the small village of Son My in the San Tinh District, Quang Ngai Province, on the north-eastern coast of South Vietnam near the South China Sea. By the time Calley and his men sat down to lunch, they had rounded up and slaughtered around 500 unarmed civilians. Within those few hours, members of Charlie Company had 'fooled around' and laughed as they sodomized and raped women, ripped vaginas open with knives, bayoneted civilians, scalped corpses, and carved 'C Company' or the ace of spades on to their chests, slaughtered animals, and torched hooches. Other soldiers had wept openly as they opened fire on crowds of unresisting old men, women, children, and babies. At no stage did these soldiers receive any enemy fire or encounter any form of resistance save fervent pleadings.... After the massacre, the men of C Company burned their way through a few other villages, eventually reaching the seashore where they stripped and jumped into the surf. (Bourke, 1999, p 160)

These gruesome details – and, indisputably, the devil is decidedly in the detail here – are by now notorious, as is the name to which this massacre is commonly referred: My Lai. War crimes and massacres are tangential to the subject matter of criminology. There are historical reasons for this, relating to the circumstances of criminology's birth and its dependence on state patronage (see, especially, Garland, 1994). But there are no good *intellectual* reasons for it. War crimes are moral abominations; but they are also of course *crimes*, and are thereby part of the subject matter of criminology.

I begin with war crimes and massacres not because I want to argue that criminology is deficient in neglecting to address them (although this is certainly the case; see Maier-Katkin et al, 2009), but because they vividly bring into focus and dramatise the problem I want to explore in what follows. The problem centres on how social scientists write about and understand the perpetrators of human suffering and injustice. More specifically, I shall be concerned to explore how criminological explanations – that is, purportedly neutral accounts of why offenders offend – *morally* construct the offender.

I

The conventional 'self-reflexive' wisdom in criminology goes something like this: criminology is a heavily and unavoidably value-laden enterprise. It is shaped by the political or policy interests of those who patronise it. Even those who remain determinedly independent from the criminal justice state cannot escape the hegemony of values: the thematic emphases of their research and the perspectives that they adopt necessarily reflect their moral concerns and sympathies. Furthermore, criminological research *objectively* has implications for policy: it can illuminate the wisdom or otherwise of doing (or not doing) things. All this is now fashionably and forthrightly recognised among contemporary criminologists. But the really interesting and absolutely fundamental question in relation to values is the one least discussed or least acknowledged among them. This is the question of how explanations of offending behaviour *morally frame* the offender. When refracted through the prism of criminological explanation, what does the offender look and feel like to us? Having been enlightened about the sources of their criminality, are we likely to feel *more* or *less* indignant towards them? Those murdering sadistic bastards of 'C Company', how does the criminological narrative shape how we think and feel about *them*? For one thing, it will not contain the description 'murdering sadistic bastards'. The criminological consensus is firm on this: professional criminologists are *not* in the business of condemning, still less verbally abusing, the offender; rather, their aim is to *understand* them. But not so fast: criminologists may *say* this, but this is no guarantee *whatsoever* that their proffered understandings will be free of moral judgement on the matter. So, the question must be asked: what are criminological theories *doing* in respect to the offender? In trying to explain his or her behaviour, do they at the same time somehow shape how he or she looks, in terms of key moral categories (good, bad, evil, etc)? Or, are they perfectly neutral on this issue? Connectedly, how (if at all) do criminological theories impact on the moral sentiments of those who absorb them? Do they leave us emotionally unmoved, or are they doing something to us, like, for example, *tempering* our hostility towards the offender, or, at the other extreme, *intensifying* our moral contempt for them? Who, hypothetically, would the offender rather have as his or her narrative interpreter: a radical Marxist or a rational choice theorist? From which theoretical prism would they look their best?

My own sense is that these questions, despite their importance, exacerbate criminologists. This, I think, is for two reasons. First, for many criminologists, the subject of the criminal offender (as opposed to the *societal reaction* to him or her) is simply not a matter of central intellectual concern (see, especially, Jefferson, 2002, p 145), and, hence, any probing about his or her moral evaluation in criminological theories can be readily dismissed. Second, the idea that criminological theories contain or elicit moral judgements about offenders strikes at the very heart of the criminological psyche. It calls into question the foundational criminological assumption that criminology, however value-laden, is still a serious candidate in the business of producing credible and morally neutral explanations for why or how people offend.

These issues raise some important, indeed fundamental, questions about the criminological enterprise. 'Nothing', Dostoevsky famously wrote, 'is easier than to denounce the evildoer', and criminologists are self-avowedly *not* in that business. But what business, exactly, are they in? Criminological theories, plainly, are designed to enlighten and educate: that is, to provide more or less convincing explanations of why people engage in criminal conduct. But if they contain, or may elicit, certain moral judgements towards the criminal offender, they are also doing something *more* than enlightening and educating: they are, in addition, doing *moral work*. What if the effect of that moral work is to make life difficult for the offender? Ought the criminologist to revise their explanatory scheme in response, or to continue to remain faithful to it because they believe it to be empirically sound? What, more fundamentally, is the *point* of criminology: to *intellectually* enlighten the public about crime or to *morally* edify its responses to criminal offenders? And what happens when these two projects stand in tension with one another? I touch on and leave open these questions in the conclusion.

II

Cesare Lombroso's (1876, pp 435–36) anthropological criminology characterises the offender as a monstrous and genetically abnormal person. Willem Bonger portrays him as a brutalised, egoistic, sordid inadequate (Taylor et al, 1973, pp 222–36). Durkheim thinks he's either a rootless loner (the egoist) or an irrepressible individualist (the anomist) (Giddens, 1971, pp 82–5). Robert K. Merton, reformulating Durkheim, posits that he is a frustrated social climber (Finestone, 1976). Subcultural theory presents him as a belligerent, status-obsessed loser (Cohen, 1955). Labelling theory implies that he is a victim, 'more sinned against than sinning' (Gouldner, 1968, p 122). Marxist criminology (or variants of it) suggests that he is a revolutionary, anti-capitalist insurgent (Young, 1979, pp 14–16). Feminist criminologists portray him as a subjugated but resisting *her* (Smart, 1976). Rational choice theories of crime picture him/her as a self-maximising consumer (Hayward, 2007). Disengagement theories insist that he/she is a banal conformist (Bandura, 1990). Cultural criminology sees him/her as a bored thrill-seeker (Ferrell, 2004). What, morally, I want to ask, is involved in these (caricatured) constructions of the criminal offender? How (if at all) do they shape his or her moral image? Moreover, how (if at all) might they affect our moral feelings towards them and their deserved fate?

The core argument in what follows will be that criminological explanations carry moral implications for the offender. I argue that criminological theories, regardless of the subjective intentions of their exponents, serve to depict the offender in a certain moral light, and, hence, potentially affect how the recipients of these theories feel about the offender and how they ought to be dealt with. This undercuts the self-image of criminologists as explicators, not moralists.

III

The question of values in criminology has recently attracted considerable discussion among criminologists. Invariably taking their cue from Howard S. Becker's (1967) classic article 'Whose side are we on?', they have focused particular attention on the role and influence of the researcher's sympathies in the production of empirical research (see, especially, Liebling, 2001). Another key issue under discussion has been the political implications of criminological research and how empirical findings can be brought more closely to bear on the formulation of criminal justice policy (see, especially, Bottoms and Tonry, 2002). However, missing from this discussion has been the issue of the *moral* implications of criminological research. This is not to say that the issue has been ignored altogether. There is one exception, albeit a large and important one, namely, Stanley Cohen's 1979 paper, 'Guilt, justice, and tolerance: some old concepts for a new criminology' (reprinted in Cohen, 1988, pp 114–46). Cohen's paper is a profoundly acute and penetrating analysis of the moral assumptions of the then new critical criminologies. It is a difficult article to summarise because it is so full of arresting insights and observations. According to Cohen, the critical criminologists of the late 1960s and early 1970s, whether of interactionist or Marxist persuasion, neglected to properly address and clarify the moral conclusions of their theoretical positions. Referring to the labelling theorists, Cohen writes:

> If deviants were not pathological beings driven by forces beyond their control, then surely as rational, responsible beings should they not be punished *more* severely? Ah no, that is not *quite* what we meant. And when we talked about being on the side of the deviant, did this mean we were actually in favor of what he did? Here, our answers were really torturous. (Cohen, 1988, p 115, emphases in original)

Cohen also detects a selective morality in the work of critical criminologists. Towards most forms of deviance (like dope-smoking and political unrest), 'an exceedingly low-minded moral nihilism seemed the order of the day', whereas towards others (like corporate fraud), 'a high-minded moral absolutism prevailed' (Cohen, 1988, p 116).

Reflecting on these themes, Cohen discusses the My Lai massacre and refers to Mary McCarthy's account of the trials of Calley, Medina and others for their involvement in the massacre. McCarthy, Cohen says, sought to refute the argument, prevalent on the Left at the time, that it was rank liberal hypocrisy to blame Calley and his company commander Medina for the atrocity, since the 'real' culprits were President Lyndon Johnson, his advisors and, indeed, the entire culture of violent capitalist imperialism. From the perspective of the Left, Calley and his men were just cogs in a machine over which they had no control. McCarthy challenged this portrayal, arguing that it served to exonerate those directly responsible for the massacre.

Speaking of the new critical criminologists, Cohen intuits in their thinking a logic or style directly borrowed from the leftist dissidents who defended Calley and his men against the army. He writes:

> One constant sociological impulse has been to shift accountability for crime onto higher and higher levels of the social structure. Not just family, neighbourhood, and social-class position but the whole system – capitalism in all its ways – was to blame. And final irony: the very system of social control itself was fatefully implicated in the causal path to crime. (Cohen, 1988, p 126)

Cohen adds that 'each successive theory harboured its own particular implications for the question of guilt but these never surfaced' (Cohen, 1988, p 126). Referring to labelling theory, Cohen observes that 'some political consequences surely followed from the more sentimental (and I believe largely correct) thrust of the theory that most official criminals have been pushed around, railroaded, and generally had a raw deal', but alas, 'we were elusive about these' (Cohen, 1988, p 126). My aim in what follows is to continue the discussion bracingly initiated by Cohen and to clarify some of the issues he raises.

IV

In trying to understand or explain a person's wrongdoing, one is always liable to be charged with either *justifying* or *excusing* it. The charge usually comes from the political Right, although hawkish liberals can also be heard levelling it.

Two points are necessary here. The first is that the social activities of *justifying* and *explaining*, though often confused, must be kept firmly separate. When one *explains* something, one tries to say *why* it happened. One does not need to take a position on whether it was good or bad that it happened; one just tries to establish what caused it. In contrast, when one *justifies* something, one tries to say why it was right that it happened. Since 'Why did X happen?' and 'Was X justified?' are two different questions, and since there is no reason to suppose that the answers to them must be the same, explanations and justifications are completely distinct.

The second point is that to explain criminal behaviour is not *necessarily* to excuse it. An excuse denies agent-responsibility. To excuse someone of a wrong is, hence, to 'let them off the hook', to free them from legal and moral blame. For example, I cannot be blamed for killing my wife if I did so unconsciously, while I was sleeping. An explanation is an account of why something happened or why someone did something. But there will be occasions when an explanation is impossible to distinguish from an excuse (Cohen, 1988, p 129): 'I killed my wife because I lost control of my body while asleep' is an explanation of why I killed my wife, but it is also at the same time an *excuse*, relieving me of any moral and legal blame for the killing. If anything, I am to be pitied: I unwittingly killed a person I deeply admired and loved (if found mildly irritating from time to time). Explanations, in other words, *can* excuse. But they need not, or *not necessarily*: one can explain the events that led to someone committing a crime without denying or minimising their moral and legal responsibility for that crime. Whether or not a criminological explanation functions as an excuse will very much depend on the substance of the explanation offered and how it constructs the circumstances leading to or surrounding the crime under investigation (see Geras, 2002). Do criminological theories *excuse* the criminal offender? Only if they construct the offender's criminal wrongdoing as *inevitable* and *beyond their sentient control*, and thus as something they cannot possibly be held legally and morally accountable for. I do not know of any contemporary criminological theory or approach which does that. However, this does not mean that criminological theories are completely value-free in respect to the offender's moral character and deserved fate. In the following sections, I try to substantiate this.

V

Who is more repellent, morally speaking: William Jefferson Clinton or Mohammed Atta? We all know about Mohammed Atta's criminality. But we do not all know about the criminality of President Clinton. Observe, then, the following bill of indictment, recounted separately and in different contexts, by Noam Chomsky (2001) and Christopher Hitchens (1999, pp 87–103). On 20 August 1998, the Clinton administration authorised the destruction of the Al-Shifa chemical plant in Khartoum, believing it to be a nerve gas facility linked to Osama bin Laden. The administration was wrong: the factory was in fact a producer of medical and pharmaceutical drugs, completely unrelated to the holdings of bin Laden. Only one person was killed in the rocketing of Al-Shifa, but, as Chomsky shows, many thousands died because the people of Sudan had lost its chief source of medicines and pesticides. 'This single atrocity', Chomsky (2001) says, 'destroyed half the pharmaceutical supplies of a poor African country and the facilities for replenishing them, with an enormous human toll'.

According to Hitchens, not only did the destruction of Al-Shifa result in a devastating loss of life, but the Clinton administration could and should have known in advance that Al-Shifa was not a Weapons of Mass Destruction (WMD)-producing facility. They could and should have known because they could have carried out an inspection of the factory. But they chose not to. Furthermore, Hitchens writes, citing Seymour Hersh's account of the incident, 'four of the five Joint Chiefs had been kept in the dark about it, as had Louis Freeh of the FBI, who was then in Africa investigating the ghastly bombings of two neighbouring US Embassies'. The President, in other words, 'acted with caprice and brutality and with a complete disregard for international law' (Hitchens, 1999, pp 93–4).

Can one justifiably compare Clinton's bombing of Al-Shifa with the 9/11 attacks? Both, indisputably, caused terrible destruction and loss of life. Perhaps the overall scale of suffering indirectly caused by the Al-Shifa attack was greater. But surely they are different? Surely President Clinton is not on the same moral plane as Mohammed Atta? The crucial distinction hinges on the question of intent. Clinton, to be sure, was criminally reckless in targeting Al-Shifa for attack, but his *intent* was emphatically not to kill as many innocents as possible, which was clearly what Atta and his fellow jihadists had intended in attacking the World Trade Centre.

President Clinton, then, is not Mohammed Atta, but the *degree* of separation between the two is crucially dependent on how one explains Atta's transformation into a suicidal mass murderer. If one contextualises Atta's behaviour in terms of a history of exploitation, repression and humiliation of Muslims by the West, and sees his actions as 'driven' – this is Gore Vidal's (2002) preferred metaphor – by the weight of that history, the moral distance between Clinton and Atta narrows appreciably.

The significance of this point for criminological explanation cannot be exaggerated. In the aftermath of the 9/11 attacks, a number of highly prominent Anglo-American leftists sought to explain the attacks in terms of America's bloody history of imperialist aggression and exploitation in the Muslim world (for a detailed account, see Cottee and Cushman, 2008). In the words of Tariq Ali (2002, p 2), 'The subjects of the Empire had struck back'. This occasioned a deep split within the Left, and drew vitriolic responses from leftist stalwarts like Michael Walzer, Christopher Hitchens, Norman Geras and Paul Berman, all of whom riposted that to explain the 9/11 attacks in terms of American imperialism was to radically misunderstand the nature of the jihadists' grievances and their reasons for targeting the US. At the centre of the controversy was the issue of moral guilt or moral blame. Were Ali and like-minded leftists *excusing* the 9/11 attackers? This is certainly how their detractors saw it. Shortly after the attacks, Walzer (2001) wrote an article enumerating and demystifying the rationalisations implicit in Ali's construction of 9/11. Hitchens (2001a) was similarly, to use the title of one of his articles, 'Against rationalization', declaring that the 9/11 murderers were fighting not to free Gaza, but 'for the right to throw acid in the faces of unveiled women in Kabul and Karachi' (Hitchens, 2001b). Salman Rushdie (2002, p 392), in his critique of the Left's reaction to 9/11, did not hesitate to point out what he saw as the obvious: that by locating the 'root causes' of the attacks in US foreign policy, the Left had effectively abandoned 'the basic idea of all morality: that individuals are responsible for their actions'. Ali and his fellow comrades vehemently counter-riposted, insisting that they were merely trying to contextualise the attacks, not excuse the people responsible for them.

What this controversy shows is that purportedly explanatory schemes may well embody deep implications for the moral guilt of the offender and whether or not we are inclined to see them as good, bad, not so bad and so on. Mohammed Atta is not President Clinton, but viewed from the perspective of Ali's Third World leftism, he resembles not a monster or crazed fanatic, but a resister of American aggression, 'driven' or 'pushed' by an uncontrollable anger at its violence, a figure perhaps more deserving of pity than contempt.

VI

It is sometimes thought that if one person is responsible for something, no one else can be responsible for it; or that, conversely, if A is partly responsible for something B did, then B's responsibility must be lessened. If someone thought this, then they might see any attempt to allocate a degree of responsibility to A as being tantamount to partially excusing B. But this would be an error. Suppose I relentlessly and rudely impugn my friend's driving skills, and he reacts by punching me. Am I responsible for my friend's violent reaction towards me? I think I am, at least partly: had I not been so insistent and caustic about his failings behind the wheel, he would not have struck me. Does this imply that my friend is not responsible for his violent actions? Of course not: he did not have to hit me and could have chosen not to. It is perfectly legitimate to say, then, that I am partly responsible for my bloody nose, without implying that this diminishes my friend's responsibility in any way. In his discussion of the My Lai massacre, Cohen (1988, p 126, emphasis added) makes a similar point: holding Johnson and his inner circle responsible does not imply excusing the soldiers who committed the atrocities. 'It should be possible to theorize about the "ultimate" or "real" cause of the massacre', Cohen says, '*and still hold that individual participants exercised some real choices at a particular moment*', and, hence, are partly to blame for what they did.

Explanatory contextualising, then, need not be tantamount to excuse-making. But it certainly plays a role in shaping the moral image of the offender. Broadly speaking, the more an explanatory account diminishes the causal role of the offender, the less morally abhorrent he or she looks, and, hence, the less condemnatory we – the audience at whom the account is aimed – feel towards them. We can still *blame* them: it was, after all, their *choice* to commit the offence; they could, had they chosen, have acted otherwise. As Cohen points out in relation to My Lai, not all the soldiers in Charlie Company participated in the slaughter. Norman Geras (1998, p 98), referring to the Holocaust, similarly writes that 'there are always those who refuse and those who resist'. But once we recognise the limited scope of their choices and opportunities, their moral image is somehow enhanced (though not, of course, completely cleansed), and, correspondingly, our feelings towards them become less incensed, less judgemental. Many criminological theories, especially those of a strongly sociological bent, situate the offender within a structural context of radically limited choices and possibilities, and, hence, serve to *improve* the moral image of the offender. Implicit in these theories is the suggestion that criminal conduct, far from being a reflection of the depraved and deep-seated personal character traits of the criminal offender, is in fact a consequence of extraneous societal factors, which caused or 'pushed' them into criminality. Hence, it is social structure, and not some permanent characterological disposition belonging to the offender, which is primarily to blame for their criminal actions. Seeing the offender in this light inevitably softens our attitude towards them. This does not necessarily mean, as many on the political Right argue, that criminological theories serve to *excuse* the offender, but they are certainly doing something morally important in respect to him or her. This is a significant point, and it ought to be better and more widely recognised in criminological circles.

VII

Let me now try to pin down these issues in a more direct and expansive way by considering the literature on disengagement practices and war crimes. I do not have the space to summarise the full range of this literature here (for a useful overview, see Geras, 1998, pp 97–9), and, hence, for the purposes of brevity, I shall concentrate on just one, albeit large and seminal, contribution to it, namely, the work of Albert Bandura (see, especially, 1990) on 'mechanisms of moral disengagement'. Bandura's approach, in line with the wider literature on disengagement (see Kelman, 1973; Bauman, 1989; Browning, 1992), gives causal primacy to the contextual situation in which war crimes occur, playing down the role of the characterological traits of the perpetrators.

One of Hannah Arendt's famous insights is that ordinary people can do extraordinarily bad things. Her evocative phrase 'the banality of evil' was a reference not to the evil that people do, but to the human *authors* of evil, who, she thought, are often boring and mundane. With reference to Adolf Eichmann, Arendt (1963, p 253) spoke of the 'ludicrousness of the man', and noted that, like most others implicated in the Holocaust, he was 'neither perverted nor sadistic … but terribly and terrifyingly normal', without 'diabolical or demonic profundity'. Echoing Arendt, Bandura posits that the perpetrators of war crimes are not on the whole sadistically predisposed, but are ordinary, and indeed otherwise decent, human beings.

Bandura's analysis is based on the following assumptions: that in the course of socialisation, people adopt moral standards that serve as guides and deterrents for conduct; that they apply these standards to how they act and punish themselves when they fail to live up to them; and that the application of moral standards and, hence, the exercise of self-sanctions are *selective* processes, which depend upon how the agent construes the circumstances in which they find themselves. Bandura's central contention is that certain mechanisms exist that serve to temporarily prise or, in Bandura's phrase, *disengage* internal moral control from destructive behaviour, thus facilitating people to commit acts that they would otherwise find reprehensible. Specifically, internal moral control can be disengaged by, variously, 'reconstruing conduct as serving moral purposes, by obscuring personal agency in detrimental activities, by disregarding or misrepresenting the injurious consequences of one's actions, or by blaming and dehumanizing the victims' (Bandura, 1990, p 161). Bandura's core research finding is summarised as follows: 'It requires conducive social conditions rather than monstrous people to produce heinous deeds. Given appropriate social conditions, decent, ordinary people can be led to do extraordinarily cruel things' (Bandura, 1990, p 182).

Returning to My Lai, let us suppose that Calley and his men, as they themselves later testified, were 'only' following the orders of their superiors, whom they felt a strong urge to please and not to disappoint; that they felt an urgent and overwhelming desire to wreak vengeance on the villagers, whom they suspected of harbouring the enemy; and that throughout their military training, they had been exposed to sustained propaganda dehumanising the Vietnamese, whom they now regarded with outright revulsion. Does explaining their behaviour in these terms materialise any implications for the moral guilt of Calley and his men? Does it force us to reconsider our prejudgements about their essential moral selves? And is it likely to affect our feelings towards these killers?

These questions can all be answered in the affirmative. If we immerse ourselves in the gruesome detail of what the men did and refuse to situate their actions within the wider context in which they were acting, we are assailed not only by a sense of incredulity and incomprehension about what occurred, but also by feelings of profound hostility towards the perpetrators. However, if we contextualise their actions in terms of 'conducive social conditions', not only can we better understand what occurred, but we are likely to feel less antipathy towards the perpetrators. From the prism of Bandura's explanatory framework, we are forced to acknowledge their fundamental humanity; to acknowledge that they were acting in accordance with the orders of their superiors; to acknowledge that it was their moral bad luck (see Nagel, 1979, pp 24–38) to have been conscripted in an army and to have found themselves in Vietnam; and to appreciate that had things turned out differently, it could have been us and not them doing what they did. None of this is to suggest that the actions of the perpetrators are any less condemnable (the sadistic murder and torture of innocents is always wrong) or that they ought to be excused (they *chose* to do what they did and could, as some indeed *did*, have acted otherwise). But in seeing them not as monsters, but as *ordinary human agents*, subject to the contingencies of historical circumstances, perhaps we are inclined to think that they are not *fundamentally* or *uniformly* bad, and perhaps, as a corollary, we are also inclined to temper our hostility towards them. Adopting Bandura's viewpoint does not diminish our sense of outrage and repulsion at the *actions* of the perpetrators, but it does, if we take it seriously, encourage us *not* to feel that way towards the *perpetrators* themselves, who, from within Bandura's framework, are pictured not as morally flawed characters, but as characters flawed by the wider circumstances in which they were acting and over which they had no control.

VIII

Criminological theories, I have been arguing, embody strong implications for the moral status of the offender, and may well influence our feelings towards them and their deserved fate. This raises some important questions relating to criminology as an enterprise and the kinds of purposes it should properly serve. If criminological knowledge does indeed shape the moral image and possible reception of the offender, should criminologists worry about this? What should be the criminologist's guiding, driving interest: the truthfulness of their explanatory narratives or the human rights of the offender? And how should they proceed when their fidelity to the former impacts negatively on the life and circumstances of the offender?

The fate of the criminologist, it seems, is not an enviable one. They are doubly alienated: first, from the policy process; and, second, and perhaps more disturbingly, from their own theoretical constructs. Lucia Zedner (2003, p 234) has put this very well: 'Arguably, a major, but rarely contemplated, problem for criminology is less its impotence than the uncontrollable potency of ideas or research findings once in the public domain'. Or, as Stanley Cohen more tersely and memorably expressed it, criminological ideas are as 'slippery as eels' (quoted in Taylor, 2007, p 23).

After publishing *Delinquency and drift*, his critique of positivism in the juvenile court, David Matza (1964) began to receive enthusiastic letters from police chiefs: 'at last', they said, 'someone is coming out clearly in favour of punishment against soft liberal treatment'. The moral of this story is that criminologists have an obligation to clarify the moral implications of their narratives, and that if *they* do not do it, *someone else* will and in possible violation of their intended meaning.

In moral philosophy, there is a fascinating literature, relating mainly to the Holocaust, on the extent (if any) to which ideological belief and cultural membership can excuse wrongdoing (see, especially, Moody-Adams, 1994; Scarre, 1998, 2005; Zimmerman, 2002). Here, the implications of various historical explanations for perpetrator responsibility and guilt are acknowledged and explored, and there is vigorous debate over what considerations need to be taken into account in our moral appraisals of wrongdoers. A fully reflexive criminology (see Nelken, 1994) ought to follow the lead of these moral philosophers, and try to make overt the moral implications of its full range of explanatory models. If criminological theories *do* have implications for the moral status of the offender, as I am suggesting, criminologists must not only clarify these, but also bring them to bear in public debates over how offenders ought to be treated. This is just one of the ways in which criminology, as Garland and Sparks (2000, p 19) put it, can 'engage public discourse' on 'a central issue of our time'.

Acknowledgment

In thinking about the issues treated here, I have greatly benefited from discussions with Norman Geras and owe a heavy debt to his writings on connected themes.

References

Ali, T. (2002) *The clash of fundamentalisms: crusades, jihads and modernity*, London: Verso.

Arendt, H. (1963) *Eichmann in Jerusalem: a report on the banality of evil*, New York, NY: Viking Press.

Bandura, A. (1990) 'Mechanisms of moral disengagement', in W. Reich (ed) *Origins of terrorism: psychologies, ideologies, theologies, states of mind*, Washington, DC: The Woodrow Wilson Centre Press.

Bauman, Z. (1989) *Modernity and the Holocaust*, Ithaca, NY: Cornell University Press.

Becker, H.S. (1967) 'Whose side are we on?', *Social Problems*, vol 14, no 3, pp 239–47.

Bottoms, A. and Tonry, M. (eds) (2002) *Ideology, crime and criminal justice: a symposium in honour of Sir Leon Radzinowicz*, Devon: Willan Publishing.

Bourke, J. (1999) *An intimate history of killing: face-to-face killing in twentieth century warfare*, New York, NY: Basic Books.

Browning, C.R. (1992) *Ordinary men: Reserve Police Battalion 101 and the final solution in Poland*, New York, NY: HarperCollins.

Chomsky, N. (2001) 'Memo to Hitchens', *Counterpunch*, 1 October. Available at: http://www.counterpunch.org/chomskyhitch.html (accessed 1 March 2010).

Cohen, A.K. (1955) *Delinquent boys: the culture of the gang*, New York, NY: The Free Press.

Cohen, S. (1988) *Against criminology*, New Brunswick, NJ: Transaction Books.

Cottee, S. and Cushman, T. (eds) (2008) *Christopher Hitchens and his critics: terror, Iraq and the Left, with an Afterword by Christopher Hitchens*, New York, NY: New York University Press.

Ferrell, J. (2004) 'Boredom, crime and criminology', *Theoretical Criminology*, vol 8, no 3, pp 287–302.

Finestone, H. (1976) *Victims of change: juvenile delinquents in American society*, London: Greenwood Press.

Garland, D. (1994) 'Of crimes and criminals: the development of criminology in Britain', in M. Maguire, R. Morgan and R. Reiner (eds) *The Oxford handbook of criminology*, Oxford: Clarendon Press.

Garland, D. and Sparks, R. (2000) 'Criminology, social theory and the challenge of our times', in D. Garland and R. Sparks (eds) *Criminology and social theory*, Oxford: Oxford University Press.

Geras, N. (1998) *The contract of mutual indifference: political philosophy after the Holocaust*, London: Verso.

Geras, N. (2002) 'Marxism, the Holocaust and September 11: an interview with Norman Geras', *Imprints*, vol 6, no 3. Available at: http://eis.bris.ac.uk/~plcdib/imprints/normangerasinterview.html (accessed 21 March 2010).

Giddens, A. (1971) *Capitalism and modern social theory*, Cambridge: Cambridge University Press.

Gouldner, A.W. (1968) 'The sociologist as partisan: sociology and the welfare state', *The American Sociologist*, vol 3, pp 103–16.

Hayward, K. (2007) 'Situational crime prevention and its discontents: rational choice theory versus the "culture of now"', *Social Policy & Administration*, vol 41, no 3, pp 232–50.

Hitchens, C. (1999) *No one left to lie to: the triangulations of William Jefferson Clinton*, London: Verso.

Hitchens, C. (2001a) 'Against rationalization', *The Nation*, 8 October.

Hitchens, C. (2001b) 'The pursuit of happiness is at an end', *London Evening Standard*, 19 September.

Jefferson, T. (2002) 'For a psychosocial criminology', in K. Carrington and R. Hogg (eds) *Critical criminology: issues, debates, challenges*, Devon: Willan Publishing.

Kelman, H.C. (1973) 'Violence without moral restraint: reflections on the dehumanization of victims and victimizers', *Journal of Social Issues*, vol 29, pp 25–61.

Liebling, A. (2001) 'Whose side are we on? Theory, practice and allegiances in prisons research', *British Journal of Criminology*, vol 41, no 3, pp 472–84.

Lombroso, C. (1876) *L'uomo Delinquente*, Milano: Hoepli.

Maier-Katkin, D., Mears, D.P. and Bernard, T.J. (2009) 'Towards a criminology of crimes against humanity', *Theoretical Criminology*, vol 13, no 2, pp 227–55.

Matza, D. (1964) *Delinquency and drift*, New York: John Wiley & Sons.

Moody-Adams, M.M. (1994) 'Culture, responsibility, and affected ignorance', *Ethics*, vol 104, no 2, pp 291–309.

Nagel, T. (1979) *Mortal questions*, Cambridge: Cambridge University Press.

Nelken, D. (ed) (1994) *The futures of criminology*, London: Sage.

Rushdie, S. (2002) *Step across this line: collected non-fiction 1992–2002*, London: Jonathan Cape.

Scarre, G. (1998) 'Understanding the moral phenomenology of the Third Reich', *Ethical Theory and Moral Practice*, vol 1, pp 423–45.

Scarre, G. (2005) 'Excusing the inexcusable? Moral responsibility and ideologically motivated wrongdoing', *Journal of Social Philosophy*, vol 36, no 4, pp 457–72.

Smart, C. (1976) *Women, crime and criminology*, London: Routledge and Kegan Paul.

Taylor, I., Walton, P. and Young, J. (1973) *The new criminology: for a social theory of deviance*, London: Routledge and Kegan Paul.

Taylor, L. (2007) 'The other side of the street: an interview with Stan Cohen', in D. Downes, P. Rock, C. Chinkin and C. Gearty (eds) *Crime, social control and human rights*, Devon: Willan Publishing.

Vidal, G. (2002) *Perpetual war for perpetual peace: how we got to be so hated*, New York, NY: Thunder's Mouth Press/Nation Books.

Walzer, M. (2001) 'Excusing terror: the politics of ideological apology', *The American Prospect*, 5 November. Available at: http://www.prospect.org/cs/articles?article=excusing_terror (accessed 24 September 2010).

Young, J. (1979) 'Left idealism, reformism and beyond: from new criminology to Marxism', in B. Fine, R. Kinsey, J. Lea, S. Picciotto and J. Young (eds) *Capitalism and the rule of law*, London: Hutchinson.

Zedner, L. (2003) 'Useful knowledge? Debating the role of criminology in post-war Britain', in L. Zedner and A. Ashworth (eds) *The criminological foundations of penal policy: essays in honour of Roger Hood*, Oxford: Clarendon Press.

Zimmerman, M.J. (2002) 'Controlling ignorance: a bitter truth', *Journal of Social Philosophy*, vol 33, no 3, pp 483–90.

TWO

Postmodernism and criminological thought: 'Whose science? Whose knowledge?'

Liz Austen with Malcolm Cowburn

Introduction

In 1991, Sandra Harding published her seminal work on scientific inquiry *Whose science? Whose knowledge? Thinking from women's lives* (Harding, 1991); this chapter borrows part of the title of her book to highlight the challenge to established forms of knowledge that is presented by postmodern thought. The challenge is epistemological and ethical. It involves re-examining the basis of criminological knowledge and how this impacts on the practices of criminal justice agencies. Key to this exploration is the *social construction* of crime. From a postmodern perspective, crime, people who commit crimes, people who suffer as a result of crimes and the legal processes through which crimes are defined and processed are not considered only to have objective characteristics that can be measured and described. They are open to interpretation, and it is interpretation that 'constructs' the science and the knowledge. Postmodernism introduces the possibility of there being many voices that can contribute to understanding. It challenges the authority of positivist-dominated criminology to speak about crime, criminals and victims. It demands a re-examination of criminal justice processes that are underpinned by positivist assumptions and positivist forms of knowledge. In bringing these challenges, postmodernist approaches provide a means whereby the experiences and voices of marginalised groups (eg women, minority ethnic groups, sexual minorities, disabled people and victims of crime) can enter the dominant discourses that shape criminology and community justice.

In doing this, postmodern theory demands that the question first posed by Becker (1967) concerning 'sides' and 'allegiances' in relation to research and (by extension) policy and practice is addressed. By giving voice to groups, their 'side' is more clearly articulated. By problematising the authority of 'scientific' epistemologies, it could be argued that postmodern thought is clearly on the 'side' of the subordinate; the person, group or community that is defined and contained by someone else's knowledge. However, it is not that straightforward. As other chapters in this book show, taking sides is not merely a binary choice. Postmodernism highlights this complexity and the difficulties involved in articulating allegiances and identifying standpoints.

This chapter first outlines some basic tenets of postmodern thought, it then moves on to consider the impact of postmodern thought on theorising crime and deviance. Closely linked to this is *how* criminological research is conducted; the discussion explores this and what it means. The chapter concludes with a reflection on the contribution that postmodernism can make to criminology and community justice.

Criminology, positivism, discourse and the postmodern challenge

> Criminology has many meanings but at its widest and most commonly accepted it is taken to be the scientific understanding of crime and criminals. But such a definition will really not get us very far. For hidden within the term there come many different approaches to 'science' and different disciplines. (Carrabine et al, 2004, p 4)

In their *sociological introduction* to *Criminology*, Carrabine and colleagues point to the disturbance that postmodern thought has caused to the academic discipline of criminology. Prior to the challenge of postmodern thinking, the words 'science' and 'scientific' represented incontrovertible bodies of knowledge underpinned by particular methodological approaches. The science of crime and criminals operated within what was considered to be unproblematic boundaries defined and prescribed by criminal law. Law as a 'grand narrative' or what was 'right' and what was 'wrong' was unchallenged; those transgressing its dictates were uncontroversially identified as 'criminals', and criminals were one of the 'objects' of study for the criminologist. Similarly, the method of studying criminals was also an uncontested activity guided by the methodological principle of science – objectivity. The aim of scientific inquiry was to understand a phenomenon (in this case, crime and the criminal), and a key part of understanding was to identify and explain causation. If this part of the study was accurate and effective, it could then be employed in predicting future events (crimes), and if prediction was successful, it could intervene in the criminogenic process and thus reduce crime. Thus, criminological research could contribute 'positively' to creating social conditions in which the incidence of crime was reduced and criminals were appropriately 'treated' by the criminal justice system (CJS).

Postmodern thought has both challenged the epistemological underpinnings of much criminological research and also threatened the ontological security of the discipline as a 'positively' focused social science. In his seminal text, *The postmodern condition: a report on knowledge*, Lyotard (1984, p xxiv) called for 'incredulity towards meta-narratives' and a rejection of grand theories that offered universal explanations of social phenomena or prescribed social action based on theories. Since that date, postmodernism has grown and diversified.

It is not the intention here to provide a definitive account of postmodernism; to do so may be the activity of a classifying modernist. However, Cheek and Gough (2005, p 302) suggest that 'we can no more provide a straightforward definition of "postmodernism" than stipulate the meanings of "love" or "justice" – these terms are perpetual foci of speculation and debate'. There are many different variations of postmodern thought, from the radical postmodernists (who promote the end of modernity and a hyper-real replacement) to the strategic postmodernists (who reconstruct the notion of modernity) (Lemert, 2005, p 67). A central principle within postmodernism is disenchantment with traditional, modernist and scientific values (Lea, 1993), and, within this, there is a rejection of 'rationality, linearity, progress, and control' (Cherryholmes, 1988, in Cheek and Gough, 2005, p 302). Gergen (2000, p 195) suggests that 'perhaps it is best to view [postmodernism] as pointing to a range of inter-related dialogues on our current condition'. He does, however, go on to reflect on the impact of the prefix 'post' – it invokes a sense of 'rapid transition', 'a creeping sense of fragmentation' and:

> a pervasive sense of erosion in a firm sense of self, the falling away of traditional values, and the loss of confidence in the *grand narratives* of the past – a trust that governments, economic planners, or scientists, for example can lead us to a better future. (Gergen, 2000, p 195, emphasis in original)

In relation to the academic world, Gergen notes that postmodern thought is seen 'set against the modernist faith in the individual mind, rationality, objectivity and truth' (p 195).

As mentioned earlier, these characteristics are central to dominant understandings of criminology and its historical aspirations to positivist knowledge. Reiner (2007, p 347) notes that 'The term "positivism" in histories of criminological theory is used to refer to the project of seeking causal explanations of crime on the methodological and logical model attributed to the natural sciences.' But, as implied earlier, the process of 'seeking' was prescribed and defined. Social science (in this case, criminology) adopted the methodology of the natural sciences (Nicholson, 1995). Key to this methodology is careful systematic observation, from which general laws are elicited. Van Langenhove (1995) has suggested that underpinning the natural science approach to social data is an assumption that analysis of 'facts', collected through systematic observation and measurement, will reveal laws that form the basis of prediction in relation to personal behaviours, social movements and so on. He notes:

> Within the natural sciences model for social sciences, the idea of explanation is copied from the models of explanation used in the classical physical sciences such as inorganic chemistry and Newtonian physics. These models are aimed at generating law–like predictions based on causal relations. (Van Langenhove, 1995, p 14)

However, the process by which data are collected is of crucial importance if 'contamination' is to be avoided. The prime source of contamination is the researcher: her or his personal history, social location, education and beliefs. All of these factors have the potential to introduce 'bias' into the research process and findings, unless they are very consciously noted and excluded. Hammersley and Gomm (2000, p 154) characterise this approach to research as 'foundationalist' (they note that the term 'positivist' has become too 'elastic' to be of any analytical value). Foundationalism refers to a research approach that uses terms like 'validity', 'error' and 'bias'. A key aspect of foundational research is that 'the sources of data are treated as independent of, and as imposing themselves on, the researcher' (Hammersley and Gomm, 2000, p 154). Where error and bias occur, it is because of the 'illegitimate intrusion of external factors, notably the subjectivity of the researcher of the influence of his or her social context' (Hammersley and Gomm, 2000, p 154). Objectivity provides the remedy to these faults. Foundationalist social research may be both quantitative and qualitative, but it particularly influences quantitative approaches. Such research, based on 'hard' data, is particularly influential in social/penal policy circles; sometimes, the mere presence of statistical calculations can appear to '[transform] data into valid conclusions' (Hammersley and Gomm, 2000, p 155). However, the terminology and assumptions of foundationalist research are also found in qualitative work, with assumptions that interviews are aiming to catch and depict the truth or 'reality' of a situation separated from the researcher or the research process (Hammersley and Gomm, 2000, p 155).

Foundational knowledge, however, does not operate in a vacuum; it is inextricably linked to the operation of (political) power. There is not space here to develop fully this relationship, but it is of clear significance for the political location of (some) criminological knowledge. Foucault (1977), for example, has shown how the growth of social-scientific knowledge was used to categorise and discipline subordinate populations within prisons. Wacquant (2001) has developed this analysis further by incorporating a closer ethnic analysis of prison populations to suggest that prisons in the US may be playing a role in sustaining white hegemony in that country (the paper was written before Obama became President, but, in terms of the overall distribution of wealth in the US, black and Hispanic groups are over-represented in the groups living in poverty in 2012[1]).

The challenge of postmodernism to foundational methodologies and, consequently, hegemonic knowledge has been profound. Hammersley and Gomm (2000) suggest that the dominance of foundationalism in social science collapsed during the middle decades of the 20th century and that this has led to the emergence of sceptical and relativist views (including postmodernism). Relativist views assert the locational specificity of the knowledges produced by research (Hammersley and Gomm, 2000, p 156; Harding, 2006, pp 145–56). While the logical validity of these knowledge claims has been questioned (Hammersley and Gomm, 2000, p 157), the effect of considering relativistic knowledges has been to assert the voices of subordinated populations.

Alongside the relativistic response to foundational knowledge, standpoint theory has also provided a robust alternative voice – particularly, but not exclusively, from feminist scholars (see, eg, Harding, 1991, 2006; Lennon and Whitford, 1994; Code, 2006). Standpoint theories have provided the vehicle through which subordinated groupings – for example, women (feminist standpoint), minority ethnic groups (post-colonial theory) and gay and lesbian people (queer theory) – can develop research from a standpoint that does not objectify and interpret their experiences from a hegemonic (ie white, male, middle-class, middle-aged, able-bodied and heterosexual) perspective that is implicitly embodied in natural science methodologies. Hammersley and Gomm (2000, p 158) summarise standpoint theories thus:

> all accounts of the world reflect the social, ethnic, gendered etc position of the people who produced them. They are constructed on the basis of particular assumptions and purposes, and their truth or falsity can only be judged in terms of standards that are themselves social constructions, and therefore relative.

However, the theories and practices are not merely aspects of a cultural perspective, they are created or resist creation within a context of power and resistance. In 1991, Sandra Harding commented that foundational approaches to research:

> fail to grasp that modern science has been constructed by and within power relations in society, not apart from them. The issue is not how one scientist or another used or abused social power in doing his science but rather where the sciences and their agendas, concepts, and consequences have been located within particular currents of politics. How have their ideas and practices advanced some groups at the expense of others? (Harding, 1991, p 81)

Social/criminological research occurs not in a vacuum, but in dynamic relationship to political power. Harding (2006) develops this argument more forcefully in her later work, highlighting, in particular, the relationship between power and not only research methodology, but also the research agenda as embodied in the sources of major funding for research. This is an issue that is returned to later in this chapter. However, in problematising epistemologies and highlighting the links between power and knowledge, postmodern thinking highlights the socially constructed nature of knowledge; a key concept in this process is the notion of *discourse*.

Burr (2003, p 64) has commented that the word discourse 'refers to a set of meanings, metaphors, representations, images, stories, statements and so on that in some way together produce a particular version of events'. Foucault's (1972, p 117) fuller definition of the term is: 'A body of anonymous, historical rules, always determined in the time and space that have defined a given period, and for a given social, economic, geographical, or linguistic area, the conditions of operation of the enunciative function.' Or, more simply, 'practices which form the objects of which they speak' (Foucault, 1972, p 49, cited in Burr, 2003, p 64). However, Bell (1993, p 42) further clarifies Foucault's use of the term and locates discourse within a political context; knowledge and power are inextricably interwoven:

> For Foucault, [discourse] is both less and more than 'language'. It is less in that [it] is not a description of the whole language system ... it is more in that it is not just speaking and writing, but entails social and political relations: one cannot dissociate discourse from a social context where relations of power and knowledge circulate.

Lukes highlights Foucault's concern with power and knowledge, particularly 'expert' knowledges focused on 'solving' social problems (eg crime):

> [Foucault] proposed that there is a deep and intimate connection between power and knowledge, viewing these mechanisms in relation to the various applied social scientific disciplines that, so he argued, render them effective: their effectiveness, in his view, largely derives from the shaping impact on people of experts' knowledge claims. (Lukes, 2005, p 88)

Walker and Boyeskie (2001) have developed this further in relation to criminological thought by highlighting how various criminological discourses have socially constructed 'criminality'. However, they caution against uncritically accepting dominant discourses of crime and criminality that are particularly driven by quantitative approaches: 'unless discourse is understood, the relevance of theory driven research may be lost to obsession with proper methods and/or mesmerising statistical numeration' (Walker and Boyeskie, 2001, p 109). They suggest that postmodern approaches to discourse and discourse analysis point to the importance of an approach that is critically aware of the power of interpretation (hermeneutics) in understanding the 'power of words in research, policy and the language of our field' (Walker and Boyeskie, 2001, p 110). They highlight the power implicit in, for example, Beccaria's (1764) language of 'law' or Foucault's (1977) analysis of insanity and 'unreason' and power.

Nevertheless, 'expert knowledge' is a key component of a discourse that has underpinned much criminological thought since the 19th century; this is the modernist notion of 'progress', which has its roots in the very origin of positivist thought. Auguste Comte (1798–1857) is viewed as one of the founding thinkers of 'sociology'. He linked the development of 'scientific' ways of thinking with social progress and suggested that societies are destined to go through three stages of development: the *theological/religious*, the *metaphysical* and the *positive* stages. The final stage of development was characterised by the predominance of rational thought and the scientific method. It was considered that, eventually, the scientific method would develop and be applicable to all areas of study (the study of the science of humanity being the final stage of development). The key feature of the scientific method is that, by virtue of its rigour and 'objectivity', human problems could be studied and resolved; and, of course, it is from Comte's terminology that the word 'positivist' was derived (Jenkins, 2002, pp 20–2). Thus, the notion of 'progress' is inextricably interwoven with foundationalist/positivist epistemologies; progress was achieved by identifying universal laws that were deemed to apply to 'humanity'. In relation to criminology, Reiner (2007) points to the work of Lombroso, Ferri and the 'moral statisticians' Guerry and Quetelet as being significant early positivist thinkers. As mentioned earlier, the positivist methodological orientation was predominantly (but not exclusively) quantitative and it sought to uncover generalisable laws and predict behaviours and social developments.

Generalisable laws and, particularly, the prediction of behaviours are both central tenets and ongoing aspirations in the assessment of the likelihood that a person convicted of a criminal offence will reoffend. This activity has become a central feature of the activities of many parts of the CJS. In the next section of this chapter, postmodern insights are brought to bear on risk assessment and the likelihood of reoffending.

'The truth, the whole truth and nothing but the truth': a postmodern reflection on risk assessment[2]

Risk assessment is an activity that is central to the operation of criminal justice agencies and also lies at the heart of a foundationalist approach. The probation service has a standardised approach to assessing the risk of reoffending posed by each offender supervised using the Offender Group Reconviction Score (OGRS) and the structured tool, OASys (Offender Assessment System) (Canton, 2011). Since 2001 (with the formation of the National Probation Service), Probation Areas – now Probation Trusts – have employed forensic psychologists to assist in risk-assessing serious offenders. Moreover, forensic psychologists have worked in prisons and developed risk-assessment protocols for a range of offenders for many years (McGurk et al, 1987). Forensic psychology is the dominant discipline within the CJS concerned with the assessment of risk. There is an immense and enduring psychological literature in relation to risk assessment and risk management (for reviews of this literature in relation to sex offenders, see, eg, Beech and Ward, 2004; Bengtson and Långström, 2007). Essentially, the literature is underpinned by foundationalist assumptions, and is concerned with developing more accurate means of predicting the likelihood that a convicted offender will commit another offence.

The literature identifies two different approaches to assessment: actuarial and clinical (Grubin, 1999), or artefact and clinical approaches (Kemshall, 2003). Actuarial approaches use risk factors that have been consistently identified as relevant criminogenic features – typically, these factors are: previous offences, relationship history and criminality (Beech and Ward, 2004; Farrington, 2007) and are described as being *static* (ie they are not amenable to change). Clinical approaches are based on the assessment made by the professional (psychologist, psychiatrist, probation officer) dealing with the individual person who may pose a risk to others. Purely clinical approaches generally include consideration of *dynamic* factors (eg mood, attitudes, physical circumstances – including the availability of victims) affecting the individual under assessment. However, the actuarial tendency in assessing offenders is strong within a broad 'community protection' approach (Kemshall, 2008) and the research literature continues to indicate that a pure actuarial approach is more accurate in predicting reoffending (Bengtson and Långström, 2007). A key feature of much of the psychological literature on risk and risk assessment is its 'scientific' and, therefore, inaccessible (to the lay reader) language. The terminologies, derived from medical, psychological and statistical vocabularies, together create what may be considered to be 'expert' knowledge. A key part of sustaining and developing this form of knowledge is the 'risk analysis professional' (Douglas, 1992, p 11), who operates within 'the favoured paradigm of individual rational choice'. Additionally, Douglas (1992, p 12) notes that the development of risk 'expertise' has led to the development of specialist sub-disciplines that develop their own technical language (ie inaccessible to the general public), which, in its quest for 'objectivity', ignores issues such as 'intersubjectivity, consensus making ... [and] social influences on decisions'. Even the names of some of the instruments (Static – 99, Static – 2002, the Risk Matrix – 2002; cited in Bengtson and Långström, 2007, p 138) imply an abstracted technical world with processes and procedures only to be understood by technical 'experts'. These are characteristics of 'risk' that have been identified in sociological, particularly postmodern, theory. Bauman (1993, pp 200–8), for example, highlights how risk discourses, through technologised approaches to knowledge, create a self-perpetuating highly technical form of knowledge as the only valid way to approach, understand, assess and manage risk. This has the effect of prioritising certain forms of intellectual activity (calculative and mathematical) and certain subjects for inquiry (Bauman, 1993, p 194). The offender and his 'offending behaviour' become the sole concern; other issues related to relationships, social class and other identities become erased and irrelevant to this administrative criminological gaze (Kemshall, 2003, p 69). What this gaze does not see is the various discriminations that occur in criminal justice processes (eg in relation to ethnicity, gender and class).

However, as Robinson (2011, p 107) has observed, although risk prediction is promoted as being an 'objective' and merely 'technical' process, it is not value-free. Moreover, it is also only as 'strong' as the information that is put into the system. Thus, while the foundationalist aspiration of being able to predict reoffending and particularly serious reoffending is sustained through increasingly complex iterations of assessment manuals, it is also brought under critical scrutiny through an examination of both values and practice. Robinson (2011, p 107) comments that 'the choice of tools and the use that is made of them in order to target services and surveillance can be extremely value-laden and potentially politicised'. Douglas (1992) notes that the way that a culture constructs and manages risks provides insights into how that culture is structured and what issues shape its social organisation (Sparks, 2001, p 168). Risk is a political vehicle used widely to legitimate the policies and practices of particular groups at specific times (Douglas, 1992; Sparks, 2001).

However, the process of risk assessment is not mechanistically undertaken by automatons. While actuarial approaches to risk have the potential to oppress socially marginalised groups (Silver and Miller, 2002), Eadie and Canton (2002, cited in Robinson, 2011, p 108) have highlighted the importance and role of professional values and accountabilities in recognising and, in some cases, ameliorating these issues. Effectively, concerns with social justice and values represent a different form of knowledge that may be in conflict with narrow administrative practices.

Contested knowledges, power, resistance and research: the 'dilemmas and predicaments' of the 21st-century criminologist

Ian Loader and Richard Sparks (2011, p 26) have pointed to the 'dilemmas and predicaments' involved in answering 'questions concerning the work criminologists can and should do, the problems that are selected for attention, the methods deployed to solve them, and the audiences towards which such activity is addressed'. This chapter concludes with reflection on these issues from a postmodern perspective and, to do this, it is essential to return to the challenges to foundationalist epistemologies identified earlier. Hammersley and Gomm (2000, p 160) indicate that although, in many ways, foundationalist epistemology and associated methodologies were deemed to have failed by the end of the 20th century, the principal radical alternative approaches (relativism and feminist standpoint theory) were also 'weak' and untenable. They therefore suggested that it was necessary to reconsider, among other things, 'the nature of ... bias as [it] relates to social research' (Hammersley and Gomm, 2000, p 160). This, inevitably, brings discussion back full circle to Becker's statement in relation to bias, power and knowledge: 'we provoke the charge of bias, in ourselves and others by refusing to give credence and deference to an established status order, in which knowledge of truth and the right to be heard are not equally distributed' (Becker, 1967, p 242).

The issue of bias is complex and is defined differently according to the epistemological standpoint of the researcher (Hammersley and Gomm, 2000; Harding, 2006). It is not the intention here to delve deeply into the philosophical and methodological implications of these debates. There is, however, one implication of postmodern deconstruction of foundationalist meta-narratives that is of importance to this chapter; this is the identification of how the relationship between research funders and dominant forms of knowledge shapes the research agenda and inevitably prioritises some forms of knowledge and excludes others. Hammersley and Gomm (2000, p 165) have suggested that 'we live in dangerous times for research'. The agendas of those funding research are driving what is to be researched and how it is to be researched. They suggest that 'the pursuit of knowledge' is subordinated to more applied outcomes defined before any research has occurred. They worry that the increased emphasis on the role of research 'users' is shaping a narrowly utilitarian concept of knowledge. More recent developments in the assessment of research outcomes[3] that give weight to the 'impact' of research have added to these concerns. Similarly, Walters (2009) has examined the nature of research funded and undertaken by the Home Office Research Development and Statistics Directorate (HORDS) and also the Scottish Executive. He has identified 'how Home Office criminology is politically driven; how it provides policy salient information for politically relevant crime and criminal justice issues; [and] how its research agenda is motivated by outcomes that are of immediate benefit to existing political demands' (Walters, 2009, p 207). However, for Walters (2008), it is through the research-funding activities of central governments that some activities are defined as crime while others are ignored. He highlights how the activities of working-class people are more likely to be viewed as crimes, whereas the dishonest activities of middle-class affluent groups may be neglected:

> It is clear that the Home Office is only interested in rubber-stamping the political priorities of the government of the day. If it were concerned with understanding and explaining the most violent aspect of contemporary British Society (notably the modern corporation), it would fund projects that analyse corporate negligence, commercial disasters and workplace injuries – but it doesn't. (Walters, 2008, p 13)

He further outlines other aspects of how funded research knowledge creates a particular version of events – generally designed to serve the interests of the funder.

However, Walters (2009, p 210) suggests that criminology does not have to play the tune demanded by the paymaster. He identifies the development of a 'public criminology that ... takes as part of its defining mission a more vigorous systematic and effective intervention in the world of social policy and social action' (Walters, 2009, p 210). Constitutive penology, 'as an analytical approach to examining the discourses, institutions, philosophies, and practices of punishing' (Barker, 2010, p 237), adopts a similar critical position; Cowling (2006, p 8) notes that the aim of constitutive criminologists is not to 'replace one truth with another'; instead, it is to invoke 'a multiplicity of resistances' 'to the ubiquity of power'. The work of Chong Ho Shon (2002) illustrates these processes by exploring the detail of encounters between the police and citizens; for example, he notes that 'prior research has overlooked instances of language use where the meaning and intention is ambiguous or where a participant subverts the communicative process by saying one thing to mean another' (Chong Ho Shon, 2002, p 151). Edwards and Sheptycki (2009) similarly identify a new form of criminology ('third wave') that acknowledges the politics of research without a partisan approach.

A key part of developing these approaches is to recognise and utilise a wide range of knowledges developed in a variety of subordinated groups. This requires criminology and criminologists to participate in dissemination beyond the university classroom and academic journals. It requires the recognition of diversity and diverse forms of knowledge. It requires recognition and rejection of grand homogenising 'meta-narratives' and the validation of diverse voices. However, for this activity to be effective, it requires a type of academic rigour that is critical and aware of epistemological issues in the construction of knowledge. Although Hammersley and Gomm (2000, p 165) suggest that aligned and campaigning standpoints are not appropriate for research because 'they do not maximise the chances of discovering the truth about the matter concerned, which is the primary responsibility of the researcher', they appear to have readopted foundationalist assumptions about the nature of truth. The work of Sandra Harding (1991, 2006) may provide a postmodern way through the seeming impasse. She argues for what she calls 'strong objectivity' or a pluralist approach to knowledge-building. 'Strong objectivity' requires the researcher to state the ideological and political position from which they make their inquiries and explore the relationship of these to the matter being researched, the method whereby it has been researched, the resultant findings and what others have published (Harding, 1991, p 152). 'Strong objectivity' requires that the knower, the researcher, explicitly theorise his/her effect – as an involved party – on the creation of knowledge.

Postmodernism provides many challenges for criminology, an academic discipline initially built upon foundationalist epistemological assumptions. Through engaging with the challenges, some criminologies have changed. Public criminology recognises the need to incorporate a range of experiences and knowledges. It critically examines the role of research and how this relates to broader criminological/sociological issues, such as the defining and policing of certain acts as criminal. Reflexive criminological practice does require criminologists to ponder on issues of allegiances in all stages of research. However, allegiance or strong objectivity does not automatically equate with a simple taking of sides. As Liebling has noted:

> In my experience it is possible to take more than one side seriously, to find merit in more than one perspective, and to do this without causing outrage on the side of officials

or prisoners, but this is a precarious position with a high emotional price to pay. (Liebling, 2001, p 473)

However, to do this requires the researcher to be able to account fully for how findings have been achieved. Harding (2006, p 156) summarises the challenges and the hopes that postmodernism presents:

> we can be confident that the sciences thought to have advanced the forms of democratic social relations envisioned by the Enlightenment and its heirs today are most likely not the ones that work well to advance the new forms of democratic social relations for which feminisms, multiculturalism and postcolonialisms yearn today. Nor can they engage effectively with the recently appearing new ways of producing scientific knowledge.... The rise of new social values, interests and the relations they direct requires new inquiry practices and principles that can support and in turn be supported by these new forms of, we hope, democratic social relations. Our methodological and epistemological choices are always also ethical and political choices.

Notes

[1] See United States Census Bureau (2012) 'The national data book; the 2012 statistical abstract'. Available at: http://www.census.gov/compendia/statab/2012/tables/12s0711.pdf

[2] This section draws from and develops the work of Cowburn (2010, pp 234–7).

[3] See: http://www.ref.ac.uk/panels/assessmentcriteriaandleveldefinitions/

References

Barker, V. (2010) 'Book review: Bruce A. Arrigo and Dragan Milovanovic, *Revolution in penology: rethinking the society of captives*, Rowman & Littlefield: Lanham, MD, 2009 pp 213', *Theoretical Criminology*, vol 14, p 237.

Bauman, Z. (1993) *Postmodern ethics*, Oxford: Blackwell.

Beccaria, C. [1764] (1963) *On crimes and punishments*, Indianapolis: Bobbs–Merrill.

Becker, H. (1967) 'Whose side are we on?', *Social Problems*, vol 14, pp 239–47.

Beech, A.R. and Ward, T. (2004) 'The integration of etiology and risk in sexual offenders: a theoretical framework', *Aggression and Violent Behavior*, vol 10, pp 31–63.

Bell, V. (1993) *Interrogating incest: feminism, Foucault and the law*, London: Routledge.

Bengtson, S. and Långström, N. (2007) 'Unguided clinical and actuarial assessment of re-offending risk: a direct comparison with sex offenders in Denmark', *Sex Abuse*, vol 19, pp 135–53.

Burr, V. (2003) *Social constructionism* (2nd edn), Hove: Routledge.

Canton, R. (2011) *Probation: working with offenders*, Abingdon: Routledge.

Carrabine, E., Iganski, P., Lee, M., Plummer, K. and South, N. (2004) *Criminology: a sociological introduction*, Abingdon: Routledge.

Cheek, J. and Gough, N. (2005) 'Postmodernist perspectives', in B. Somekh and C. Lewin (eds) *Research methods in the social sciences*, London: Sage Publications Ltd, pp 302–9.

Cherryholmes, C. (1988) *Power and criticism: poststructural investigations in education*, New York, NY: Teachers College Press.

Chong Ho Shon, P. (2002) 'Bringing the spoken words back in: conversationalizing (postmodernizing) police–citizen encounter research', *Critical Criminology*, vol 11, pp 151–72.

Code, L. (2006) *Ecological thinking. The politics of epistemic location*, Oxford: Oxford University Press.

Cowburn, M. (2010) 'Invisible men: social reactions to male sexual coercion – bringing men and masculinities into community safety and public policy', *Critical Social Policy*, vol 30, no 2, pp 225–44.

Cowling, M (2006) 'Postmodern policies? The erratic interventions of constitutive criminology', *Internet Journal of Criminology*. Available at: www.internetjournalofcriminology.com

Douglas, M. (1992) *Risk and blame: essays in cultural theory*, London: Routledge.

Eadie, T. and Canton, R. (2002) 'Practising in the context of ambivalence: the challenge for youth justice workers', *Youth Justice* vol 2, no 1, pp 14–26.

Edwards, A. and Sheptycki, J. (2009) 'Third wave criminology: guns, crime and social order', *Criminology & Criminal Justice*, vol 9, no 3, pp 379–97.

Farrington, D.P. (2007) 'Childhood risk factors and risk-focused prevention', in M. Maguire, R. Morgan and R. Reiner (eds) *The Oxford handbook of criminology*, Oxford: Oxford University Press, pp 602–40.

Foucault, M. (1972) *The archaeology of knowledge and the discourse on language*, London: Routledge.

Foucault, M. (1977) *Discipline and punish: the birth of the prison*, London: Allen Lane.

Gergen, K.J. (2000) *An invitation to social construction*, London: Sage.

Grubin, D. (1999) 'Actuarial and clinical assessment of risk in sex offenders', *Journal of Interpersonal Violence*, vol 14 no 3, pp 331–343.

Hammersley, M. and Gomm, R. (2000) 'Bias in social research', in M. Hammersley (ed) *Taking sides in social research*, Abingdon: Routledge, pp 151–66.

Harding, S. (1991) *Whose science? Whose knowledge? Thinking from women's lives*, Milton Keynes: Open University Press.

Harding, S. (2006) *Science and social inequality: feminist and postcolonial issues*, Urbana and Chicago, IL: University of Illinois Press.

Jenkins, R. (2002) *Foundations of sociology: towards a better understanding of the human world*, Basingstoke: Palgrave Macmillan.

Kemshall, H. (2003) *Understanding risk in criminal justice*, Maidenhead: Open University Press.

Kemshall, H. (2008) *Understanding the community management of high risk offenders*, Maidenhead: Open University Press.

Lea, J. (1993) 'Criminology and postmodernity', in P. Walton and J. Young (eds) *The new criminology revisited*, London: Macmillan.

Lemert, C. (2005) *Postmodernism is not what you think* (2nd edn), Colorado, CO: Paradigm Publishers.

Lennon, K. and Whitford, M. (eds) (1994) *Knowing the difference: feminist perspectives in epistemology*, London: Routledge.

Liebling, A. (2001) 'Whose side are we on? Theory, practice and allegiances in prisons research', *British Journal of Criminology*, vol 41, pp 472–84.

Loader, I. and Sparks, R. (2011) *Public criminology?*, Abingdon: Routledge.

Lukes, S. (2005) *Power: a radical view*, Basingstoke: Palgrave.

Lyotard, J.-F. (1984) *The postmodern condition: a report on knowledge* (trans G. Bennington and B. Massumi), Manchester: Manchester University Press.

McGurk, B., Thornton, D. and Williams, M. (eds) (1987) *Applying psychology to imprisonment*, London: HMSO.

Nicolson, P. (1995) 'Feminism and psychology', in J.A. Smith, R. Harré and L. Van Langenhove (eds) *Rethinking psychology*, London: Sage, pp 122–42.

Reiner, R. (2007) 'Political economy, crime and criminal justice', in M. Maguire, D. Morgan and R. Reiner (eds) *The Oxford handbook of criminology*, Oxford: Oxford University Press, pp 342–80.

Robinson, A. (2011) *Foundations for offender management: theory, law and policy for contemporary practice*, Bristol: The Policy Press.

Silver, E. and Miller, L.L. (2002) 'A cautionary note on the use of actuarial risk assessment tools for social control', *Crime and Delinquency*, vol 48, no 1, pp 138–61.

Sparks, R. (2001) 'Degrees of estrangement: the cultural theory of risk and comparative penology', *Theoretical Criminology*, vol 5, no 2, pp 159–76.

Van Langenhove, L. (1995) 'The theoretical foundations of experimental psychology and its alternatives', in J.A. Smith, R. Harré and L. Van Langenhove (eds) *Rethinking psychology*, London: Sage.

Wacquant, L. (2001) 'Deadly symbiosis: when the ghetto and prison meet and mesh', *Punishment & Society*, vol 3, no 1, pp 95–134.

Walker, J.T. and Boyeskie, J.A. (2001) 'The discourse of criminality: from Beccaria to postmodernism', *Critical Criminology*, vol 10, no 2, pp 107–22.

Walters, R. (2003) *Deviant knowledge: criminology, politics and policy*, Cullompton: Willan Publishing.

Walters, R. (2008) 'Government manipulation of criminological knowledge and policies of deceit', in T. Hope and R. Walters (eds) *Critical thinking about the uses of research*, London: Centre for Criminal Justice Studies, Kings College London.

Walters, R. (2009) 'The state, knowledge production and criminology', in R. Coleman, J. Sim, S. Tombs and D. Whyte (eds) *State, power, crime*, London: Sage, pp 200–13.

THREE

Marxist criminology: whose side, which values?

David Moxon

Introduction

Howard Becker, in his famous article 'Whose side are we on?' (Becker, 1967), suggests that one possible way to avoid 'taking sides' in the research endeavour is to adopt a 'third point of view'. Such a point of view is simply one that is different to those that are under scrutiny. However, for Becker, this also ultimately involves taking a side as it:

> would indeed make us neutral with respect to the two groups at hand, but would only mean that we had enlarged the scope of the political conflict to include a party not ordinarily brought in whose view the sociologist was taking. (Becker, 1967, p 254)

With this, Becker confirms his general argument that it is impossible to remain neutral.[1]

In these passages, Becker uses Marxism as his example of a 'third point of view'. By doing so, he unintentionally raises questions that demand renewed attention from Marxist criminologists: whose side are they on, and what values guide their work? These questions are intensely problematic for Marxist theory today. Revisiting them in a contemporary context is vital given the current feeling, alluded to by Downes and Rock (2007, p 232) and evidenced by recent work by Cowling (2008), that Marxist criminology may be on the cusp of renewal.[2]

In what follows, the two questions will be explored and the difficulty Marxism has in answering them will be outlined. In response to the first question, it will be contended that due to the massive social changes that have occurred over the last four decades or so, the class that Marxism is 'for', the class that supposedly will ultimately vindicate the theory in practice, no longer exists in any coherent form. As a result, it has become increasingly difficult for Marxists to provide a robust response to Becker's first question. As for the second question, the suggestion will be that the very structure of Marxist theory renders it extremely challenging to definitively specify which values it should be guided by, or which ones it should promote. Thus, attempting to answer Becker's second question, or questions like it, is a long-standing and intractable problem for Marxists.

Marxism's fall from prominence in the discipline of criminology (see Taylor, 1999a; Russell, 2002) is partly down to its inability to answer such fundamental questions as these convincingly. Of course, it is also related to the more general demise of Marxism, and its continued political association with the brutal state socialist regimes of the former Eastern Bloc. Yet, a way forward for Marxist criminology does exist. It involves the continued development of Sumner's notion of 'censure' (see, eg, Sumner, 1976, 1990a, 1994; see also Moxon, 2011). Sumner sees crime and deviance as ideological censures; behaviours that offend the worldview or interests of the dominant groups in society are marked off and designated as 'criminal' or 'deviant'. Of course, all groups in society censure, but only the powerful have the means to institutionalise their censures and make them binding on the rest of society.

The concept of censure not only has the potential to revitalise Marxist criminology, but also involves a shift in focus that renders the questions posed by Becker of less immediacy for Marxists. Instead, the priority becomes the interrogation of the ideological underpinnings of censures: why is certain behaviour deemed unacceptable by certain groups, and what are the processes by which such sectional censures are disseminated, accepted or resisted? Answering these questions does not require the specification of which values one supports or whose side one is taking. Yet, ultimately, adoption of the censure perspective can only delay engagement with Becker's questions. A Marxism that cannot or is unwilling to address the issues that Becker raises is one that has turned full circle, from a perspective with an avowed aim to not only interpret, but also change, the world, to one that is content to sit limp and disengaged on the sidelines of academia.

The next two sections of the chapter will explore the difficulties Marxism has in answering the questions called to mind by Becker. First, the question of 'sides' will be addressed and, second, the question of 'values'. Following this, the idea that censure represents the best way forward for Marxist criminology will be developed, and some of the theoretical consequences of the position will be outlined. Finally, it will be suggested that while such a project renders Becker's questions of less immediate significance, they remain lurking in the background and Marxist criminology must confront them again very soon or fade into insignificance.

Whose side are Marxists on?

On the face of it, Marxists can provide a relatively straightforward answer to the question of whose side they are on. Broadly speaking, Marxists can be said to be on the side of the proletariat, the working class; as Becker himself says, Marxism's focus is on the 'workers' (1967, p 245).

For Marx and Engels, the proletariat were a class forced to sell their labour in order to survive (see, eg, Marx and Engels, 1968, pp 41–2). Their definition remained largely unproblematic for well over a century. Marxist and Marxist-influenced criminologists frequently discussed issues of crime and deviance in class terms. For instance, Willem Bonger, the first Marxist criminologist, refers to both the 'proletariat' and 'lower proletariat' in his 1916 work *Criminality and economic conditions* (Bonger, 1969). Later, Taylor, Walton and Young (1973) adopted the labels 'working class', 'lower working class', 'skilled working class' and 'middle class'. Moreover, there was little doubt as to 'whose side' Taylor, Walton and Young were on; they recast the working-class deviant as an almost heroic, proto-revolutionary actor, deliberately offending the norms of an oppressive society. For them, the criminal or deviant was not 'a passive, ineffectual, stigmatised individual', but a 'decision maker who often actively violates the moral and legal codes of society' (Taylor et al, 1973, p 147).

Of course, the classical Marxist notion of large, opposed class blocs has always been something of a caricature. Yet, the notion was at least *plausible* in the modernity of the 20th century, and even more so in Marx's time when the working class often formed a visibly homogeneous bloc on the factory floor:

> Masses of labourers, crowded into the factory, are organised like soldiers. As privates of the industrial army they are placed under the command of a perfect hierarchy of officers and sergeants. Not only are they slaves of the bourgeois class, and of the bourgeois State; they are daily and hourly enslaved by the machine, by the overlooker, and, above all, by the individual bourgeois manufacturer himself. The more openly this despotism proclaims gain to be its end and aim,

the more petty, the more hateful and the more embittering it is. (Marx and Engels, 1968, pp 41–2)[3]

Yet, even as Taylor, Walton and Young were creating the new criminology, the old certainties of class and class structure in industrial capitalist society were beginning to unravel. Late modern capitalism has transformed the nature of what was the working class such that it can no longer constitute an unproblematic focus for Marxism. The decline of traditional extractive and heavy industry and the concomitant decentralisation of populations and employment are critical in this; 'occupational communities' have largely eroded (Lash and Urry, 1987, p 102), and there is often little security in the tertiary, short-term, part-time work that does exist. As such, 'working life is saturated with uncertainty' (Bauman, 2000, p 147) and we have witnessed what has been provocatively called 'the death of the social' (Rose, 1996). With this, the social basis for the formation of class consciousness has all but disappeared. As Savage, Bagnall and Longhurst (2001) found, people remain aware of class terminology and are able to talk about class as a socio-political issue, but are increasingly less willing to place *themselves* within a particular class. It seems that consumption has replaced production as the measuring rod by which individuals judge themselves and others, and, indeed, as the defining characteristic of advanced Western societies (Lasch, 1979; Bauman, 1998). This allows for an 'intensive differentiation' between individuals who may once have considered themselves members of the same class (Crook et al, 1992, p 131). Consumerism renders patterns of inequality much more 'fluid'; society resembles 'a mosaic of multiple status identities rather than a small number of enclosed social capsules'. Personal standing now largely relies on 'one's status accomplishments in the sphere of consumption, one's access to codes'. This includes 'the products one uses, the places one goes, the leisure pursuits in which one engages, the clothes one wears', as opposed to work and ownership (Crook et al, 1992, pp 132–3).

What, then, of the very concept of class itself? Cohen maintains that the traditional Marxist formulation, where one's 'class' is their objective position within the relations of production, is still of value: 'A person's class is established by nothing but his objective place in the network of ownership relations, however difficult it may be to identify such places neatly' (Cohen, 1978, p 73).[4] This may be so, but the real issue of course is that it is becoming increasingly difficult to 'neatly identify' the place-holders of class. This problem is surely intensifying despite the many attempts to refine the basic notion of the working class. One early and important attempt at this was made by Dahrendorf (1959), who suggested that Marx's concept of class, reliant as it was on property ownership or the lack thereof, was historically relative and had been transcended. He suggested a new schism between a 'command class' and an 'obey class', and a new view of class conflict as the struggle between those with authority and those without. More recent are the efforts by Poulantzas (1973, 1978) and Wright (1978, 1985) to develop increasingly sophisticated and differentiated notions of class, and Laclau and Mouffe's (1985) more fundamental and self-consciously 'post-Marxist' recasting. Nevertheless, by the beginning of the 1980s, Hobsbawm (1981) asked whether the 'forward march of labour' had been 'halted', and Gorz (1982, p 69) was sufficiently confident to bid farewell to the working class and point to the emergence of a 'post-industrial neo-proletariat'.[5]

The dissolving of the traditional working class has been noted in the criminological field by, among others, those with Marxist-influenced backgrounds (Taylor, 1999b; Young, 1999, 2007). The picture generally painted is of a fraction of relatively well-paid but insecurely employed and alienated workers beholden to consumerism and attempting to maintain their advantage over a fraction who are largely excluded from employment and consumption spheres, but who are still seduced by consumer desires. Those in the latter, essentially de-proletarianised group, tend to be the focus of the criminal justice agencies and make up the bulk of the prison population in advanced Western nations (see Bauman, 1992, p 51; Wacquant, 2009).[6] In addition, the impact of globalisation has been noted, in particular its promotion of rampant consumerism at the same moment as its intensification of global inequalities (Cowling, 2008; Young, 2008).

Where does this leave us in attempting to answer the question of whose side Marxism is on? It seems clear that the working class as traditionally conceived no longer exists. It is unclear what exists in its place. Is it a post-industrial neo-proletariat, or a plethora of class fractions and positions, or a liquid mass of individualised and depoliticised consumers, or an excluded de-proletarianised rump, or all of this and more? Could one simply argue instead that late-modern Marxism is on the side of the oppressed? Possibly, but this simply begs the question of who exactly 'the oppressed' are: are they one or more of the above groups? Or are they people from minority ethnic groups, or women, or homosexuals? Are they the insecurely employed or the unemployed, or the sweatshop workers of the developing world? Are they those who live on deprived council estates, or those in the slums of the world's megacities? Only one thing seems to be certain in all of this: the class that Marxism is 'for', the class that supposedly will ultimately vindicate the theory in practice, no longer exists in any coherent form, if, indeed, it ever did. There are no easy answers to Becker's first question for today's Marxist.

What values are central to Marxism?

If Marxism struggles to satisfactorily answer Becker's first question, then perhaps an even graver problem reveals itself once the second question is addressed. The very structure of Marxist theory has frustrated attempts by Marxists to explicate a coherent moral position, a concept of justice, or to promote particular values and ends and the appropriate means for pursuing them. Indeed, as Anderson (1980) has suggested, Marxist theory has tended towards the active avoidance of moral discourse, as such ventures have been held to intrude upon the project of causal understanding.

For Lukes (1985), these difficulties arise from a 'paradox' within Marxist theory. On the one hand, Marxism claims that there is no objective moral truth; morality, and by extension values, are instead held to be a form of ideology, social in origin and serving class interests. On the other hand, Marxist writing, including Marx's own, abounds in moral judgements; Lukes (1985, pp 8–26) provides examples aplenty. Furthermore, few socialist leaders have been proletarian in origin, so could scarcely be said to have been acting in line with their own class needs (Lukes, 1985, p 3). Lukes suggests that this paradox can be resolved by drawing a distinction between the morality of *recht*, which Marxism condemns as anachronistic, and the morality of emancipation, which it 'adopts as its own' (Lukes, 1985, p 29). Rights, for Marx, were a means of stabilising production relations, and emancipation would allow those very relations to be transcended. Yet, despite this, Marxism has consistently failed to provide an adequate blueprint for the society that emancipation will create. This is because Marxism's desire to remain rooted in the material conditions of the day has blunted its utopian edge and prevented it from specifying in any detail what the 'good society' might look like; any attempt to do so could be condemned as an idealist fantasy. In addition, Marxism fails to specify the appropriate means to achieve its ill-defined goal, and, as a consequence, the possibility of offering moral resistance to measures taken in its name has been blocked (Lukes, 1985, p 141).

Lukes concludes that Marxism is a version of long-range and perfectionist consequentialism that, problematically, lacks the mechanisms to judge consequences (Lukes, 1985, pp 141–5). It is also morally blind to all that has no bearing on its project, and cannot condemn any action that promotes its desired outcome (Lukes, 1985, p 146). As such, in many respects, the theory is normatively bankrupt. Clearly, answering Becker's second question is no straightforward task for Marxism.

These issues are brought into yet sharper relief when questions of value, justice and morality are directly addressed by Marxists. There has been considerable debate as to whether Marx thought capitalism an unjust social system. A range of positions on the issue have developed. There are those, relying on an assortment of evidence from Marx's writings, who claim that he did not feel that capitalism was unjust (Tucker, 1969; Wood, 1981). Conversely, there are those, utilising a similarly broad array of textual evidence, who claim that he did consider capitalism unjust (Husami, 1978; Cohen, 1983; Elster, 1985). Other positions include those of Young (1981), who argues that Marx felt that the worker is treated justly as a seller of labour power but is robbed in the production process due to the extraction of surplus value, and Brenkert (1983), who feels that the moral indignation expressed by Marx concerns not justice, but freedom. Famously, Geras (1985, 1992) argues that Marx did consider capitalism unjust, but that he did not think that he thought this. White (1996) agrees with this and suggests that Marx based his tacit position on a 'needs principle'. However, McCarney argues that there is no confusion or contradiction in Marx's position whatsoever. For McCarney (1992, p 36), Marx:

> takes capitalist exchange and distribution to be just and capitalist exploitation to be neither just nor unjust, falling as it does outside the domain of the category of justice. Whatever objections may be made to this position, it is logically and conceptually in good order. It does not need, or deserve, to be described as equivocal, confused or inconsistent.

Miller (1984) suggests that Marx felt capitalism to be *neither* just nor unjust, which is broadly in line with Sayers (1994), who notes that Marx makes no appeal to trans-historical values, his critique of society being an entirely immanent one. Finally, Lukes feels that the four basic positions on the issue (that capitalist relations are just, that they are unjust, that they are just in one respect and unjust in another, and that they are neither just nor unjust) are not only all plausible interpretations of Marx's writings, but are actually reconcilable and hierarchically organised; 'the answer, I believe, is that Marx maintained all these positions and that he brought all these perspectives to bear at once' (Lukes, 1985, p 59).

What is the poor Marxist criminologist to make of this in attempting to answer Becker's second question? Given that it is the very structure of Marxist theory itself that leads to these difficulties, any espousal of particular values is likely to be highly contentious. What, then, is to be done?

A way forward for Marxist criminology

As suggested in the introductory section, one of the reasons for Marxism's decline in criminology is its inability to convincingly answer Becker's questions. The question of whose side Marxists are on has been rendered increasingly problematic as a result of the epochal social changes of the past 30 years or so, and the question of which values are central to Marxism has proved a persistent and contentious source of theoretical blockage. Recognition of such intractable difficulties demonstrates the distance travelled since Marxist criminology's golden age of the 1970s, when a confidence in mission characterised what could then be quite plausibly described as the 'movement'. Perhaps the best example of this is provided by Quinney, whose criminology aimed for no less than the 'development of a new consciousness – a critical philosophy', which would render possible the collapse of capitalist society, a solution to the crime problem and 'a whole new way of life' (Quinney, 1973, p 1). Such confidently expressed sentiments make startling reading for the jaded Marxist of today. Indeed, Quinney's work is shot through with the feeling that such cataclysmic changes are not only possible, but imminent.

Yet, the culmination of Marxist work in criminology in the 1970s and early 1980s was not the creation of the good society, but, instead, the thorough deconstruction of the criminological field (Sumner, 1976, 1994; O'Malley, 1987, 1988), a good few years before 'postmodern' themes were brought to bear on it.[7] Sumner in particular was influential in showing how the categories of 'crime' and 'deviance' are ideological ones. As I have argued at length elsewhere (Moxon, 2011), it is the continuation of this project and its application to the contemporary that should provide the basis for any renaissance in Marxist criminology.

For Sumner, 'crime' and 'deviance' are not valid groups; they are 'hopelessly inadequate as empirical descriptors of social behaviour' (Sumner, 1990a, p 26). Indeed, 'the search for a general concept [such as crime or deviance] to encompass such widely varying practices, problems and situations was itself logically misguided' (Sumner, 1994, p 310). The behaviours that these categories cover are too diverse to be amenable to explanation by single all-encompassing aetiological theories. The only common aspects of 'deviant' or 'criminal' behaviours are that they are purposive behaviours, and that they have been labelled as deviant or criminal.[8]

According to Sumner, those actions marked off as being 'criminal' or 'deviant' are the ones that offend various aspects of the ideology or worldview of those in positions of power and authority. That hegemonic ideology itself is borne of class conflict, in the interaction between consciousness and practical experiences (Sumner, 1979; Sumner and Sandberg, 1990). In short, 'the "social" world, the realm of society, does not just produce offensive behaviours but also perceptions of offensiveness and thus crime and deviance are always doubly socially constructed' (Sumner, 2004a, p 6).

All groups of people develop censures, but in class societies, the economically dominant class has the greatest capacity to assert its censures, for instance, through the legal system and its control of media and communication (Sumner, 1976, p 170; 1990a, p 27). The sectional censures of the dominant class are thus able to become social censures, widely accepted and internalised even by subordinate classes (Sumner, 1976, p 170). In this way, censures have an important role in the reproduction of hegemony. The 'daily censure of crime attempts to unify and publicise the hegemonic bloc's vision of its nation and morality' (Sumner, 1990b, pp 47–9); offenders are marked off from non-offenders, good symbolically marked off from evil.

Furthermore, for Sumner, the processes that have led to the erosion of the great class blocs of modernity also mean that the concept of censure's time has come. As the 'social' disintegrates in late modernity, and shared understandings are increasingly scarce, so the real nature of 'deviance' and 'crime' as political constructs is progressively exposed. Gradually, crime and deviance are revealed:

> as the dominant censures of the day, reflecting dominant economic, political and cultural interests and preferences and targeting the groups, individuals and acts offending those interests and preferences. A particular censure of crime or deviance, and the level of its enforcement, may approximate to some democratically shared 'social' value to some degree, and may even contribute to some poorly defined social health, but as a whole censures and their enforcement tend to reflect the antisocial interests of capital, patriarchy and ethnicities. (Sumner, 2004a, p 28).

The concept of censure not only has the potential to revitalise Marxist criminology, but, more importantly for our present purposes, it also involves a shift in focus that renders the questions posed by Becker of less immediacy for Marxists. The interrogation of the ideological underpinnings of censures becomes the priority: why is certain behaviour deemed as unacceptable by certain groups? What ideologies colour censorious opinions, judgements and statutes? What are the historical conditions of the emergence of particular censures and the process of their elevation to fully social status? What are the processes by which such sectional censures are disseminated, accepted or resisted?[9] Becker's questions do not lie at the heart of such a project.

The censure approach: two consequences

The adoption of the censure perspective by Marxists entails a number of theoretically significant consequences, of which two are worthy of note here. First, the adoption of the notion of censure takes Marxism beyond the remit of 'criminology' and the study of 'crime' as traditionally conceived. Once attention is directed towards censures, Marxism need no longer be hamstrung by adherence to categories, such as 'crime', created by the state. This is because it rejects the category of 'crime' as an ideological term covering a variety of different behaviours with no common element, other than their labelling as 'crime' and their purposive nature.[10] Indeed, according to Sumner (1990c, p 2):

> Any criminology which ignores the social roots and contested character of the criminal justice system, by taking the state definitions of crime as adequate definitions of types of behaviour, is not only antediluvean but also discreditable as a dominant ideological arm of the state.

Further still, to accept state definitions of crime:

> Is to convey the sectional and historical tools of the state into universally valid behavioural concepts. It is to take the state as God of all knowledge and to assume that even popular assent to legislation automatically transforms context bound political judgement into universal truth. (Sumner, 1994, pp 301–2)

Thus, it is 'precisely by theorising in its own terms and not in those provided by a criminological discourse' (O'Malley, 1987, p 82) that

Marxism can aid the understanding of crime and criminal justice systems. If this project is pursued and issues of crime and criminal justice systems are collapsed into a more general Marxist framework, then the entire notion of a 'Marxist criminology' can itself be considered a 'myth' (O'Malley, 1988, p 75).

Second, the adoption of the notion of censure by Marxists readily allows for a dialogue with other perspectives. Although Sumner initially developed the concept of censure within a self-consciously Marxian framework (Sumner, 1976), more recently, he has stressed how there could be different political 'takes' on the general theory (Sumner, 2004b),[11] and there is nothing inherent in its formulation that prevents its articulation with other theories, themes and ideas in the criminological canon. This is important, for, as Tierney (2010, pp 334–5) suggests, fragmentation and cross-fertilisation are emblematic of contemporary criminological theory; 'self contained theoretical clusters' are increasingly rare. Today, 'critical' criminology 'is characterised by degrees of diversity and fragmentation, partly resulting from the dissolution of its explicit links with Marxist social theory' (Tierney, 2010, p 361). Yet, Marxist traces and echoes can be seen in the work of critical criminologists who are not expressly Marxist in orientation, such as left realists, cultural criminologists, feminist criminologists, green criminologists and theorists of punishment, globalisation, white–collar and corporate crime, and moral panics and the media. As Downes and Rock (2007, p 324) argue: 'it is more difficult than in the past … to see where Marxism begins and ends'. Petty, dogmatic, self-imposed factionalism is clearly self-defeating in such a context.

Such factionalism is even more nonsensical when, as Roemer (1988, p 124) suggests, the central thrust of Marxist theory is now widely adopted by social theorists of all hues: 'it is questionable what it means to take a specifically Marxist approach to history when the materialist axiom, the cornerstone of the Marxist approach, has become central to almost all contemporary social thought'. Indeed, as Elster (1986, p 5) argues, there is an inevitable paradox that Marxism, like any theory, must face: if it is not plausible, then it will simply disappear, but if it is plausible, then it is likely to be subsumed into the mainstream of social science and cease to be specifically Marxist. As such, the decline of explicitly Marxist work in critical criminology is, in one sense, a result of the fundamental theoretical plausibility of the materialist perspective.[12]

Conclusion: the persistence of Becker's questions

It is clear that Marxism has immense difficulty in providing robust answers to the questions raised by Becker. The erosion of the traditionally conceived classes of modernity has made it increasingly difficult for Marxists to specify whose side they are on, and the contradictions inherent in the theory itself make the espousal of particular values a daunting and divisive task. An adoption of the censure perspective not only offers Marxist criminology a productive way forward, but also renders Becker's questions of less immediate importance.

Rather than worry about the taking of sides or the specification of values, Marxism can instead proceed as a form of immanent critique. In an increasingly divided world where a multitude of opposed groups are angrily censuring each other across chasms of misunderstanding (Sumner, 2012) and the nation state is increasingly governing the poor through its criminal justice policy, an engaged and reinvigorated Marxism is required more urgently than ever. Marxism's most pressing task is to expose the interests and mores behind censures and to analyse the mechanisms that allow some censures to become institutionalised and binding upon even those who do not share them. This might well require Marxists to step outside of the familiar confines of criminology as well as engage with insights from other traditions, as the censure perspective allows.

Yet, this does not quite get Marxists off the hook. As Sumner (2004b) himself has argued:

> at the end of the day, there is no alternative but to face up to the painful task of deciding whether we still need to censure certain things, whether we still need to assign blame to our enemies, and to explore the vision of the world which delivers either another alternative set of censures or a mode of dispute resolution which can avoid blaming others.

In fact, according to Sumner (2004b), 'the fundamental need analytically is for a renewed normative jurisprudence, something which has become rather unfashionable, to specify what we censure and whether that censure needs to be expressed through the principles and concepts of the criminal law'. So, the censure perspective prioritises other issues, but Becker's questions, difficult as they are for Marxists to answer, will not go away. They remain in the background, quietly demanding renewed attention once the time is right.

Notes

[1.] As Hammersley (2000, p 13) argues, the subtleties of Becker's position are often ignored; 'he does not argue that sociologists should set out to be partisan.... [P]aradoxically, he sees research as contributing to the achievement of Leftist political goals precisely by concentrating exclusively on the task of pursuing the truth for its own sake'.

[2.] Of course, not all of Marxism is the same, though it is not unusual for it to be treated as though it is, particularly by its critics. That said, as the issues dealt with in this chapter cut across the variety of Marxisms that have been developed over the years, for convenience's sake, the chapter will deal with 'Marxism' as a whole.

[3.] Of course, even the physical proximity of workers as described in this passage is no guarantee of the formation of a class consciousness. See Nichols and Armstrong's (1976) study of the problems involved in creating a homogeneous working-class bloc, even in a single factory.

[4.] Cohen was responding to Thompson who, in *The making of the English working class* (Thompson, 1963), contended that the working class effectively created itself when the conditions were ripe.

[5.] Even Marx and Engels themselves made an attempt to develop a more nuanced, differentiated view of class structure with their notion of the 'lumpenproletariat' (see Engels, 1956, p 14; Marx, 1963, p 75; Marx and Engels, 1968, p 44).

[6.] Note how this picture broadly follows the split between the proletariat and their 'lumpen' cousins initially proposed by Marx and Engels.

[7.] As Callinicos (1989) has argued, postmodern ideas, for all their iconoclasm and purported novelty, have been around for many years, and can even be traced to works by Marx, Durkheim and Weber.

[8.] For a similar argument, see Smart (1990).

[9.] Previous work in this vein includes Thompson's (1975) analysis of the development of the crimes of trespass and theft in *Whigs and hunters* (see Sumner, 1994, pp 298–300) and Hall et al's (1978) *Policing the crisis*.

[10.] As noted earlier, an identical argument applies to the category of 'deviance'.

[11.] Indeed, Sumner's own work was heavily indebted to symbolic interactionist sociology from the outset (see Moxon, 2011).

[12.] Despite this, there is still value in retaining the Marxist label, for it situates one's work in an intellectual tradition and identifies its heritage. As Wright (2003, p 19) puts it: 'what was really at stake to me was the nature of the constituency or audience to whom I wanted to feel accountable'.

References

Anderson, P. (1980) *Arguments within English Marxism*, London: Verso.

Bauman, Z. (1992) *Intimations of postmodernity*, London: Routledge.

Bauman, Z. (1998) *Consumerism, work and the new poor*, Buckingham: Open University Press.

Bauman, Z. (2000) *Liquid modernity*, Cambridge: Polity.

Becker, H. (1967) 'Whose side are we on?', *Social Problems*, vol 14, no 3, pp 234–47.

Bonger, W. (1969) *Criminality and economic conditions*, Bloomington, IN: Indiana University Press.

Brenkert, G. (1983) *Marx's ethics of freedom*, London: Routledge & Kegan Paul.

Callinicos, A. (1989) *Against postmodernism: a Marxist critique*, Cambridge: Polity.

Cohen, G.A. (1978) *Karl Marx's theory of history: a defence*, Oxford: Clarendon Press.

Cohen, G.A. (1983) 'Review of Wood's Karl Marx', *Mind*, vol 92, pp 440–5.

Cowling, M. (2008) *Marxism and criminological theory: a critique and a toolkit*, Basingstoke: Palgrave Macmillan.

Crook, S., Pakulski, J. and Waters, M. (1992) *Postmodernization: change in advanced society*, London: Sage.

Dahrendorf, R. (1959) *Class and class conflict in industrial society*, London: Routledge & Kegan Paul.

Downes, D. and Rock, P. (2007) *Understanding deviance: a guide to the sociology of crime and rule breaking* (5th edn), Oxford: Oxford University Press.

Elster, J. (1985) *Making sense of Marx*, Cambridge: Cambridge University Press.

Elster, J. (1986) *An introduction to Karl Marx*, Cambridge: Cambridge University Press.

Engels, F. (1956) *The Peasant War in Germany*, Moscow: Progress Publishers.

Geras, N. (1985) 'The controversy about Marx and justice', *New Left Review*, vol 150, pp 47–85.

Geras, N. (1992) 'Bringing Marx to justice: an addendum and rejoinder', *New Left Review*, vol 195, pp 37–69.

Gorz, A. (1982) *Farewell to the working class: an essay on post-industrial socialism*, London: Pluto Press.

Hall, S., Critcher, C., Jefferson, T., Clarke, J. and Roberts, B. (1978) *Policing the crisis: mugging, the state and law and order*, London: MacMillan.

Hammersley, M. (2000) *Taking sides in social research: essays on partisanship and bias*, London: Routledge.

Hobsbawm, E. (1981) 'The forward march of labour halted?', in M. Jacques and F Mulhern (eds) *The forward march of labour halted?*, London: Verso.

Husami, Z. (1978) 'Marx and distributive justice', *Philosophy and Public Affairs*, vol 8, pp 27–64.

Laclau, E. and Mouffe, C. (1985) *Hegemony and socialist strategy: towards a radical democratic politics*, London: Verso.

Lasch, C. (1979) *The culture of narcissism*, New York, NY: W.W. Norton.

Lash, S. and Urry, J. (1987) *The end of organised capitalism*, Cambridge: Polity Press.

Lukes, S. (1985) *Marxism and morality*, Oxford: Clarendon Press.

Marx, K. (1963) *The Eighteenth Brumaire of Louis Bonaparte*, New York, NY: International Publishers.

Marx, K. and Engels, F. (1968) 'Manifesto of the Communist Party', in K. Marx and F. Engels, *Selected Works*, London: Lawrence and Wishart.

Miller, R. (1984) *Analyzing Marx*, Princeton, NJ: Princeton University Press.

McCarney, J. (1992) 'Marx and justice again', *New Left Review*, vol 195, pp 29–36.

Moxon, D. (2011) 'Marxism and the definition of crime', *In-Spire Journal of Law, Politics and Societies*, vol 5, no 2, pp 102–20.

Nichols, T. and Armstrong, P. (1976) *Workers divided*, London: Fontana.

O'Malley, P. (1987) 'Marxist theory and Marxist criminology', *Crime and Social Justice*, vol 29, pp 70–87.

O'Malley, P. (1988) 'The purpose of knowledge: pragmatism and the praxis of Marxist criminology', *Contemporary Crises*, vol 12, pp 65–79.

Poulantzas, N. (1973) *Political power and social classes*, London: New Left Books.

Poulantzas, N. (1978) *State, power, socialism*, London: New Left Books.

Quinney, R. (1973) *Critique of legal order: crime control in capitalist society*, Boston, MA: Little, Brown and Company.

Roemer, J. (1988) *Free to lose: an introduction to Marxist economic philosophy*, Cambridge, MA: Harvard University Press.

Rose, N. (1996) *Inventing our selves: psychology, power and personhood*, Cambridge: Cambridge University Press.

Russell, S. (2002) 'The continuing relevance of Marxism to critical criminology', *Critical Criminology*, vol 11, pp 113–35.

Savage, M., Bagnall, G. and Longhurst, B. (2001) 'Ordinary, ambivalent and defensive: class identities in the northwest of England', *Sociology*, vol 35, no 4, pp 875–92.

Sayers, S. (1994) 'Moral values and progress', *New Left Review*, vol 204, pp 67–85.

Smart, C. (1990) 'Feminist approaches to criminology, or postmodern woman meets atavistic man', in L.R. Gelsthorpe and A.M. Morris (eds) *Feminist perspectives in criminology*, London: Routledge and Kegan Paul.

Sumner, C. (1976) 'Marxism and deviancy theory', in P. Wiles (ed) *The sociology of crime and delinquency in Britain. Volume two: the new criminologies*, London: Martin Robertson.

Sumner, C. (1979) *Reading ideologies: an investigation into the Marxist theory of ideology and law*, London: Academic Press.

Sumner, C. (1990a) 'Rethinking deviance: towards a sociology of censure', in C. Sumner (ed) *Censure, politics and criminal justice*, Buckingham: Open University Press.

Sumner, C. (1990b) 'Reflections on a sociological theory of criminal justice systems', in C. Sumner (ed) *Censure, politics and criminal justice*, Buckingham: Open University Press.

Sumner, C. (1990c) 'Introduction: contemporary socialist criminology', in C. Sumner (ed) *Censure, politics and criminal justice*, Buckingham: Open University Press.

Sumner, C. (1994) *The sociology of deviance: an obituary*, Buckingham: Open University Press.

Sumner, C. (2004a) 'The social nature of crime and deviance', in C. Sumner (ed) *The Blackwell companion to criminology*, Oxford: Blackwell.

Sumner, C. (2004b) 'Social censure and political domination', paper delivered at the University of Turin, 12 March.

Sumner, C. (2012) 'Censure, culture and political economy: beyond the death of deviance debate', in S. Hall and S. Winlow (eds) *New directions in criminological theory*, London: Routledge.

Sumner, C. and Sandberg, S. (1990) 'The press censure of "dissident minorities": the ideology of parliamentary democracy, Thatcherism and "policing the crisis"', in C. Sumner (ed) *Censure, politics and criminal justice*, Buckingham: Open University Press.

Taylor, I. (1999a) 'Crime and social criticism', *European Journal of Crime, Criminal Law and Criminal Justice*, vol 7, no 2, pp 180–96.

Taylor, I. (1999b) *Crime in context: a critical criminology of market societies*, Cambridge: Polity.

Taylor, I., Walton, P. and Young, J. (1973) *The new criminology: for a social theory of deviance*, London: Routledge and Kegan Paul.

Thompson, E.P. (1963) *The making of the English working class*, London: Victor Gollancz.

Thompson, E.P. (1975) *Whigs and hunters: the origin of the Black Act*, London: Allen Lane.

Tierney, J. (2010) *Criminology: theory and context* (3rd edn), Harlow: Pearson.

Tucker, R.C. (1969) *The Marxian revolutionary idea*, New York, NY: W.W. Norton.

Wacquant, L. (2009) *Punishing the poor: the neoliberal government of social insecurity*, Durham, NC: Duke University Press.

White, S. (1996) 'Needs, labour and Marx's conception of justice', *Political Studies*, vol XLIV, pp 88–101.

Wood, A. (1981) *Karl Marx*, London: Routledge & Kegan Paul.

Wright, E.O. (1978) *Class, crisis, and the state*, London: New Left Books.

Wright, E.O. (1985) *Classes*, London: Verso.

Wright, E.O. (2003) 'Falling into Marxism; choosing to stay', in S. Turner and A. Sica (eds) *A disobedient generation*, Thousand Oaks, CA: Sage Publications.

Young, G. (1981) 'Doing Marx justice', in K. Neilsen and S.C. Patten (eds) *Marx and morality*, Guelph, Ontario: Canadian Association for Publishing in Philosophy.

Young, J. (1999) *The exclusive society: social exclusion, crime and difference in late modernity*, London: Sage.

Young, J. (2007) *The vertigo of late modernity*, London: Sage.

Young, J. (2008) 'Vertigo and the global Merton', *Theoretical Criminology*, vol 12, no 4, pp 523–7.

FOUR

A contemporary reflection on feminist criminology: whose side are we on?

Victoria Lavis and Tammi Walker

Introduction

This chapter critically considers the ways that the changing values of feminism have impacted upon its contribution to criminology. It draws upon Becker's (1967) suggestion, revisited by Morris, Woodward and Peters (1998) and, more recently, by Liebling (2001) and Cohen (2011), that researchers should ask themselves whose 'side' they are taking when they conduct research. The question of 'sides', who takes them and when, forms the central theme of the chapter, as it mirrors the concerns raised by both modernist and postmodernist feminist researchers. These concerns relate not only to the value bases of research (Roman and Apple, 1990; Oakley, 2000; Noddings, 2003), but also to the practice of power that underpins research and theory generation (Wolf, 1992; Davis, 2008).

This chapter interrogates five value-related tensions that affect feminist criminology today. Inherent within these tensions are concerns about what and how to research and theorise women's criminality and fears regarding the dangers of essentialising female lawbreaking. There are calls for a feminist criminology that can challenge not only sexism, but also other discriminatory practices within the criminal justice system. Chesney-Lind (2006) and Burgess-Proctor (2006), among others, have argued that although age, class, sex, race and gender have been applied to understanding crime, such theorising has failed adequately to explore the impact of these minoritising factors intersecting. The chapter closes by considering how the values within feminism and the intersectional influences and contributions that age, class, sex, sexuality, race and gender have upon crime can contribute to the future developments of criminological theorising.

Feminist criminology: introducing five value-based tensions

Feminist criminology is one of many approaches to researching and theorising crime and criminal justice. It is concerned with attending to the complex interplay of social, structural and individual factors that constitute and reconstitute gender, gender relations and those who commit crime (Miller and Mullens, 2009). While feminist criminology contains many different strands or standpoints (Hartsock, 1983; Harding, 1986, Heckman 1997), these cohere around a number of central tenets that place gender and gender relations at the heart of their theorising. They critique traditional systems of knowledge generation as biased towards male experience (Spender, 1981) and seek to explore and theorise women's experience in its own right, rather than as a deviation from a male 'norm' (Daly and Chesney-Lind, 1988).

We have identified five value-based areas of tension facing feminist criminology, which form the bases of discussion within this chapter. While it may be argued that these tensions represent merely the 'tip of the iceberg', they have a particular salience to the current climate within the UK, where consideration of equalities and diversities is infusing changes to the law, social life and crime, for example, in the influence of the Race Relations (Amendment) Act 2000 and the Equality Act 2010 on wider social policy and the criminal justice system. Of these five tensions, two principal areas underlie the remaining three. The first questions the primary aim of feminist criminology and it is inextricably driven by epistemological and ontological questions. Feminist criminologists have argued for a focus on research and theory generation based on the experiences of 'real' women (Carlen, 1983, 1986; Carrington, 1990, 1998; Chesney-Lind, 1999). However, others highlight the importance of how women are constructed within criminological and legal discourse, and the need to make visible and to challenge the structures, discourses and associated practices that position and oppress women (Young, 1994, 1996). This debate is linked to a second area of contention arising from differences in the underlying and sometimes competing values of feminism and criminology. Feminism, as a wider discipline, is primarily concerned with asking questions about gender and its intersections with race, sex and class (Fine, 1992; Miller and Mullens, 2009). In contrast, criminology is tasked with the production of generalisable theories of crime that can inform an understanding of causes and interventions (Daly, 2006).

Crucially, these two primary frictions have contributed to three, further, value-based tensions. First, there is debate regarding whether a 'feminist criminology' is achievable or desirable and if this is the right way forward to consider the relationship between gender and crime (Smart, 1976; Young, 1994). Concurrent to this tension are concerns about how far feminist criminology should seek to research and theorise male lawbreaking (Daly, 2006) and the potentially negative consequences of essentialising women's criminal activity (Carlen, 1994) if it does not. The final tension in the chapter explores whether criminology should continue to pursue gender-neutral theories of crime and criminality, thus maintaining objectivity (or, as Rich [1980] critiqued, 'male subjectivity') and sidestepping questions of bias, or, alternatively, explore what can be afforded by pursuing 'gender-aware' theorising. Before moving on to interrogate these tensions it is important to consider how they relate to Becker's question about whose side we are on.

Feminism within criminology: the taking of sides

Becker (1967) suggests that what is troubling about the question 'Whose side are we on?' is the subjective concern that research may be accused of being biased, unbalanced or unscientific. He outlines two circumstances in which such accusations might be made, drawing a distinction between *apolitical* and *political* situations. These two situations have relevance to both the historical and current position of feminism within criminology. Becker proposed that accusations of bias are most likely to occur in situations where research seeks to give credence to the perspective of a subordinate group within a hierarchy. If, for the purpose of this argument, the discipline of criminology is taken to be a 'hierarchy', where different theoretical approaches are afforded varying levels of dominance and credibility, then this definition captures neatly the historical project of feminist research within criminology.

Daly (2008, p 9) asserts that during the 1970s and early 1980s, the general aim of first-wave feminist criminology was to make the feminine visible within the criminological frame, to ask 'Where are girls, women, and gender in theories of crime, victimisation, and justice?' Encompassed in this aim was the major task of amending the lack of empirical understanding and knowledge on female offending and criminalisation (Stanko, 1990). In response to accusations of 'amnesia of women' (Gelsthorpe, 2004, p 4), some criminologists during this period sought to address the imbalance by 'inserting' women into existing criminological theories. However, this practice served only to conceal women within the trajectory of theories established to describe the criminality of men (Gelsthorpe, 2004). This first-wave research, it might be argued, reflects Becker's *apolitical* situation: the voice of the subordinate (women) was being attended to, but, as yet, the different 'segments or ranks' within the hierarchy of criminology were 'not organised for conflict' (Becker, 1967, p 241). However, as Evans (1995) has noted, second-wave feminism emerged with the expressed goal of striving for equality, making it clear that feminist criminology would not be *apolitical* in its agenda. Subsequent bodies of feminist research developed, focusing on the misrepresentation of women offenders, critiquing theories of criminality developed from and validated on men (Smart, 1976; Campbell, 1981), and illustrating the limited relevance of such theorising for explaining women's crime (see, eg, Smart, 1976; Leonard, 1982). Consequently, Gelsthorpe (2004) argues, feminist criminology embarked upon an explicitly 'political project'. This project included making evident women's victimisation (principally in the area of sexual assault and domestic violence), highlighting discriminatory practices within the criminal justice system and drawing attention to the experiences of female victims of crime and to female victims' experiences of the criminal justice system (Walklate, 2001). Indeed, as it has developed, through its second and now third waves, feminism has sought not only to highlight what is made invisible within mainstream theories, but also to determine the way that criminology as a discipline might progress. In doing so, it seems placed firmly within Becker's articulation of *politicised* situations, which he suggests occurs when 'the parties to the hierarchical relationship engage in organised conflict, attempting either to maintain or change existing relations of power or authority' (Becker, 1967, p 241). Indeed, it is perhaps the very politicised nature of feminism within criminology that gives rise to the tensions discussed in this chapter.

Tension one: the 'real' and the 'discursive'

Becker (1967) acknowledged the centrality of the questions of ontology that drive research and theory generation, arguing that researchers need to attend to 'openly conflicting definitions of reality' (Becker, 1967, p 244), in particular, the likelihood that the knowledge and findings arising from their research would inevitably problematise some definitions, thereby conferring different value statuses. Such tension is clearly evident in the diversity of ways in which feminist theorising has intersected with criminology. Taking a linear approach, it is possible to identify two distinct strands of feminist criminological research: the first focusing on what Carlen (1987) terms *real women*, documenting and theorising from women's actual lived experiences; and the second focusing on making visible and challenging the structures, discourses and associated practices that allegedly position and oppress women, and exploring how women negotiate and resist these. The former identifies with an explicitly realist ontological position, while the second is underlain by a constructionist epistemology wherein realism becomes contested and open to critique.

Daly (2004) reflects on these two strands, arguing that the focus on researching and theorising from the lives of 'real women' was a logical extension of early feminist research that had 'challenged the Androcentrism of the field, as scholars filled knowledge gaps about women law-breakers, victims and criminal justice workers' (Daly, 2004, p 47). It encompassed research into, for example, violence against women, women's experiences of imprisonment (Carlen, 1983, 1987), cultural differentiation in youth justice (Carrington, 1990) and female gang culture (Chesney-Lind, 1999). However, Daly suggests that by the 1990s, the shift within feminism towards a concern with knowledge production and the emergence of postmodernism engendered a focus on how women were constructed within criminological and legal discourse. One example of this is Alison Young's (1990, 1994, 1996) work illuminating the impact of culture on the representation of crime and constructions of criminality. This distinction between the *real* and the *discursive*, sometimes referred to as the 'intellectual double shift' (Daly and Maher, 1998, p 1), is not merely a function of changing paradigms, it represents an ongoing area of tension for feminist criminology. Miller and Mullen (2009, p 219) argue that 'Gender operates not just within the practices and organisation of social life, but also within the discursive fields by which women (and men) are constructed or construct themselves'. The distinction is also exemplified in Smart's (1995, p 231) argument that while it is necessary to explore 'woman' as constructed within legal and criminological discourse, a discourse analysis of 'the raped woman is of little value unless we are also talking to women who have been raped'.

Such a tension strikes at the heart of feminist values and the unapologetically political aims of advancing social justice for women, engendering social change and representing human diversity (Eichler, 1986). Consequently, it makes relevant Becker's (1967, p 239) point that when research is politicised, 'judgements of who has a right to define the nature of reality that are taken for granted in an apolitical situation become matters of argument'.

Tension two: the competing values of feminism and criminology

These 'matters of argument' to which Becker refers extend beyond the ontological to the differences in the underlying and sometimes competing value bases of feminism and criminology. As already noted, feminist values arise from its concern with interrogating gender, the gender order and gender relations (Connell, 2002), how gender intersects with race, sex, sexuality and class (Maher, 1997; Daly and Maher, 1998), how it constructs women's and men's behaviour, and what part men and women play in this construction (Weedon, 1987). In contrast, criminology has been primarily focused upon the production of generalisable theories of crime (Daly, 2006), with the effect that theories generated from researching men are assumed to accurately account for female crime and female lawbreakers. Miller and Mullen (2009, p 219) articulate the effect of these differences, suggesting that they 'have led, at times, to erroneous charges of polemic bias in feminist research. In fact, the theory/praxis relationship amongst feminist scholars is not strikingly different in practice from the parallel reality that policy goals also drive much criminological theory and research'.

The foundations of such bias can be understood in relation to Becker's 'hierarchy of credibility', where 'members of the highest group have the right to define the way things really are' (Becker, 1967, p 241), since feminist research knowledge casts doubt on the 'official line' of criminological theory. However, the accusation of bias does not come merely from outside the feminist academy. For example, despite espousing the value of representing human diversity, feminism has not always been successful in addressing intersections between gender and other minoritising differences. This was notably highlighted by Crenshaw (1993, p 1242) when she argued that:

> Feminist efforts to politicise experiences of women and antiracist efforts to politicise experiences of 'people of colour' have frequently proceeded as though the issues and experiences which they detail occur on mutually exclusive terrains. Although racism and sexism readily intersect in the lives of real people, they seldom do in feminist and antiracist practices.

Moreover, the explicitly political nature of feminist inquiry has also been a problematic value for some feminist researchers. Haack (2003, p 15), for example, questions the distinction between what she terms 'politicised inquiry' and 'honest inquiry', suggesting that politicised feminist epistemologies can constrain scientific inquiry. What is troubling, she suggests, is not the notion of politicised inquiry, but the implication inherent within it: that 'genuine, honest inquiry is neither possible nor desirable' (Haack, 2003, p 15). Her comments speak to Becker's concerns that there is danger in assuming that 'the man (or woman) at the top knows *best*' (Becker, 1967, p 234; emphasis added) and suggests, in contrast to Becker, that while feminist criminologists are aware that there are sides to be taken, the decision about which side to take is complex and troubling.

Tension three: is a feminist criminology desirable and achievable?

The third tension relates to the status of feminist criminology within the discipline and has been the subject of debate, without resolution, for more than two decades. As far back as 1976, Smart asserted that criminology as a discipline might be immune to feminist critique, with the result that feminist criminology might become seen as a discrete and token area within the discipline. Her prediction is redolent of Becker's arguments about the 'hierarchy of credibility' that exists within any system or discipline grouping. If, as earlier in this chapter, criminology is taken to be the 'system', then Smart's comments position feminist criminologists as in danger of subordination within the system. This positioning is significant given Becker's suggestion that it is the members of the 'highest group' in any system who have the power to generate credibility and shape the 'values' of the system. The impact of this, he suggests, is that 'We are, if we are proper members of the group, morally bound to accept the definition imposed on reality by the superordinate group in preference to the definitions espoused by subordinates' (Becker, 1967, p 241).

Indeed, Daly (2006) argues that by the early 1990s, Smart's initial fears had developed further. At question was whether criminology was even a helpful starting point for beginning to explore the question of gender and crime and whether a 'feminist criminology' was possible, or even desirable, given the epistemological and theoretical gap between the two disciplines. Smart's concerns were not isolated, as a number of prominent feminists writing on criminology have critiqued the two disciplines as fundamentally incompatible (see, eg, Stanko, 1993; Young, 1994). However, occupying a precarious position within a hierarchy is not unfamiliar to feminists working within any discipline or system. Indeed, it can be argued that feminists are perhaps better placed than most supposedly subordinate groups, since at the heart of their value structure is the aim to recognise and give voice to those previously unheard or actively silenced, and to generate knowledge and theory that makes credible what others have marginalised (Cosgrove and McHugh, 2000). This buoyancy is perhaps evident in Gelsthorpe's (1997, p 1) suggestion that while:

> Doubts are still expressed in conference halls, institutional corridors and class rooms (if not in academic papers) as to whether there is such a thing as feminist criminology ... reports of its death or non existence have been greatly exaggerated.

Indeed, Walklate (2004), writing some 17 years after Smart's initial concerns were voiced, signposted the impact of feminism, in particular, liberal feminism, upon criminology. She suggests that as a result of feminist research, there is now 'a her-story of women researching within criminology and a her-story of work addressing female offending behaviour' (Walklate, 2004, p 48). Moreover, the election of Lorraine Gelsthorpe as President of the British Criminological Society in 2011 would also seem to indicate that feminist criminology is not only successfully resisting any attempts at relegation to the subordinate, but also well placed to actively impact upon the future shaping of criminology.

Tension four: gender essentialism and the inclusion of male lawbreaking in feminist criminology

Proposals about the future 'shape' of criminology and the position of feminist criminology within the discipline hierarchy, however, are intimately bound up in a fourth tension: the extent that feminist criminology should focus exclusively on female crime and criminality or whether its remit should also encompass male lawbreaking behaviour. This complex tension exemplifies Becker's question about 'Whose side are we on?' and his arguments about how and when charges of bias are made. Brown (1986, p 35) has highlighted the range of problems that arise when feminist criminologists take a side that centres solely on the 'women and crime' question. One of the risks she identifies is effectively illustrated in theorising on imprisonment. The more the issues around women's imprisonment are treated as separate, the further mainstream criminology (or male criminology) is left to its own methods, untouched by feminist reproach, and is therefore assumed to be accurate and inclusive when it discusses criminality. Thus, in Becker's terms, the 'status quo' or current 'hierarchy' of (male–dominated) theories is reinforced and supported by the absence of critique from within its own 'ranks'.

Brown identifies a further danger associated with the 'woman and crime' perspective to criminology that is linked to its very label. The exclusive exploration of 'woman' in this body of work postulates that it is possible to substitute the biological classification of sex with the socio–cultural category of gender. For example, women's criminal activity is not located within biology; rather, it is explained by reference to the ways that women who fail to meet stereotypical expectations of femininity are stigmatised and then fall foul of the criminal justice system (Walklate, 2004). In other words, Walklate (2004, p 14) notes, this approach assumes 'that it is possible to replace biologically rooted understandings (sex) with socially rooted ones (gender). Expressed in this way it is a position that hints at essentialism'. Thus, in excluding theorising of male crime, feminist criminology falls foul of its own accusation of 'gender essentialism', particularly those strands of feminist criminological theory that seek to imply that there is a universal 'women's experience' or 'men's experience' waiting to be uncovered and theorised (Rice, 1990). Thus, as Becker identifies, it lays itself open to the accusation of bias not based on 'failures of technique or method but on conceptual defects ... of seeing things from the perspective of only one party to the conflict' (Becker, 1967, p 245).

Carlen (1994) has further questioned gender essentialism and asserts that focusing exclusively on the experience of 'women' serves to create a premise that the causes and responses to female criminality are inherently different to those of men. Taking imprisonment as her starting point, she argues that the focus of the research gaze on women's prisons has been extremely dispersed, with assertions of theoretical innovation having primarily concentrated on 'adding in' demands in relation to class and race (Rice, 1990) or emphasising the capacity of women's 'resistance' to oppression, for example, highlighting the many modes of resistance within women's prisons (Shaw, 1992). Theorising and conceptualising about imprisonment in this manner, Carlen purports, has led to prioritising and privileging female gender constructs that are no longer a reasonable or sufficient point for understanding imprisonment. Rather, she asserts that:

> Class, gender, race, and racism should still be studied in relation to imprisonment. And the views of prisoners and prison officers should be taken seriously. None the less,

let us for a time; at least, give empirical research priority to the prison's overwhelming power to punish. (Carlen, 1994, p 137)

In doing so, she highlights and privileges concern about the 'punitive power' of prisons, arguing that rather than focusing on the gender-specific needs of women and male prisoners separately, there is a need to study prisons primarily as forms of punishment. Thus, her arguments illustrate how focusing on taking 'one' side or 'another' can divert researchers from theorising and addressing issues that impact on all prison stakeholders, regardless of their supposedly gender 'superordinate' or 'subordinate' status.

Tension five: gender-aware criminology or gender-neutral theorising

Thus, it appears that the future for criminology and feminism within the wider discipline is rooted in the development of theorising and research that can offer an integrated approach to understanding and accounting for the experiences of men and women, both real and discursive. While this seemingly addresses the question of whose side criminology is taking, there remains considerable debate regarding whether such integrated theorising should be 'gender-neutral' or 'gender-aware' (Gelsthorpe, 1997).

The gender-neutral hypothesis seeks predominantly to apply traditional theories (eg social disorganisation and anomie/strain theory), developed to explain male criminality, to women. However, this has created a 'generalisability problem' (see Daly and Chesney-Lind, 1988), as criminologists have tested theories derived from all-male samples to see if they apply to women (Warren, 1981; Zietz, 1981). Steffensmeier and Allan (1996, 2000) argue that gender-neutral theories provide explanations of less serious forms of female and male criminality, and for differences in such crime categories. However, Miller and Mullens (2009) maintain that the weakness of such theories is that they fail effectively to account for the precise ways that there are gender differences in the type, frequency and context of criminal behaviour.

Steffensmeier and Allan (1996) maintain that it is possible to develop a unified theoretical framework for explaining gender differences in crime that would be compatible with gender-neutral theories provided that it accommodates four key components. The framework should describe both male and female criminality and the 'context' of offending, especially in terms of serious forms of crime. Routes and pathways into crime are a further element and, lastly, the framework should explore the extent that gender differences in crime derive from a complex interaction of social, historical, cultural, biological and reproductive differences. In this way, their framework would be *gender-aware*: incorporating gender norms, moral development, social control, sexuality, access to criminal opportunity and motivation.

Feminists, like Daly (2006), have critiqued theories that purport to be gender-neutral while simultaneously inclusive of a gendered approach as illogical and a contradiction in terms. Daly proposes that if feminist criminology is to expand, then it must draw upon both criminology, through its theories of crime, and on feminism, through its theories of sex and gender. This proposition informs her conceptual schema of four interrelated elements upon which criminology could build theories of gender and crime: *gender ratio of crime, gendered pathways, gendered crime* and *gendered lives* (Daly, 1998, p 94–9). Miller and Mullins (2009), drawing on Daly's notion of *gendered lives*, argue that compared with other aspects of feminist criminology, this is the most challenging as it requires a focus on gender beyond the study of crime. Daly (2006) highlights Maher's (1997) systematic examination of women drug users' complex lives in New York City drug markets in the late 1980s and early 1990s as exemplifying the scope, depth and benefits of the possible application of a *gendered lives* approach, while simultaneously illustrating the need to attend to the intersections of gender, race and class.

As these newer strands of criminological theorising extend and develop, seeking to navigate the tensions and facilitate a more mutually agreeable approach, it is relevant to note Becker's caution regarding the 'problem of infinite regress'. There can, he argues, be no perfect solution that adequately accounts for all aspects of criminality, all perpetrators of crime. Rather, he invites us to 'meet the demands of our science by always making clear the limits of what we have studied, marking the boundaries beyond which our findings [or, in this case, theorising] cannot safely be applied' (Becker, 1967, p 247).

Intersectionality: exploring the possibilities for feminist criminology

In summarising the arguments presented thus far, the chapter has drawn on Becker (1967) to suggest that the place of feminism within criminology and its ability to shape the future direction of criminology's value base and subsequent theorising is intimately tied to its politicised nature and the position it can claim within a hierarchy of credibility.

Moreover, it has argued that accusations of bias and questions about whose side, individually and collectively, feminist criminologists take in their research have been levelled by critics within both feminism and the wider discipline. The chapter has demonstrated that an integrated approach to accommodating male and female experience of crime and lawbreaking is widely recognised as both desirable and necessary. However, such theorising must be able to account for social divisions wider than gender alone. Drawing initially on Eichler (1986), Crenshaw (1991) and, later, the work of Carlen (1994), it has been suggested that if feminism is to maintain its underlying values to represent human diversity, an integrated approach must also be able to account for the ways that categories of social divisions are expressed, represented and subjectively experienced. This last section of the chapter considers the utility of intersectionality as a means of navigating some of the tensions discussed. It aims to illustrate how such an approach might provide a means for feminism to negotiate its status within criminology.

As indicated at the outset of the chapter, some feminist criminologists (see, eg, Burgess–Proctor, 2006; Chesney-Lind, 2006) have argued that while social divisions such as age, class, sex, sexuality, race and gender have been individually applied to understanding crime, such applications have failed to adequately account for the ways that these minoritising factors intersect. Indeed, Walklate (2004) articulates that the margins or intersections between race, class, age, gender and sexuality have been 'blind spots' within criminology. One way that the interface between systems of oppression has begun to be theorised in wider disciplines is through 'intersectionality'. The term, while a key feature of feminist theorising since the early 1990s (see Crenshaw, 1991; Collins, 1998; Acker, 1999; Yuval-Davis, 2006), is still emergent in its application within criminology (see, eg, George, 2001; Brewer and Heitzeg, 2008; Cherukuri et al, 2009). Davis (2008, p 68), acknowledging the extension from Crenshaw's original conceptualisation, characterises intersectionality as 'the interaction between gender, race, and other categories of difference in individual lives, social practices, institutional arrangements and cultural ideologies and the outcome of these in terms of power'. She notes that 'other categories of difference' include (although this is not intended to be an exhaustive list) sexuality, disability status, nationality, immigration status and faith. Davis also notes the confusion, both within and external to the feminist academy, regarding the status of the 'intersectionality' concept, illustrating how it has been discussed variously and conflictingly as theory, heuristic device and/or a constituent of social, ideological or cultural structures.

This diversity is reflected in some exponents arguing its merits as a means of making sense of individual experience and identity while others argue that it is more properly an element of social structures and/or cultural discourse (Prins, 2006). If this diversity of application is construed as *flexibility* rather than confusion, it would seem to offer the possibility to bridge the gap between the *real* and *discursive* strands of feminist criminological research. To suggest this is not to ignore the debates that have taken place regarding the plurality of ways that intersectionality has been applied and developed (see Walby et al, 2012), but rather to subscribe to the view outlined by Davis (2008, p 69) that it is 'precisely the vagueness and open-endedness of "intersectionality" [that] may be the very secret to its success'. Embracing intersectionality holds the potential for feminist criminologists to theorise and engage with the differences that exist within and among women and men in relation to crime and criminality. Thus, it bears relevance to the lives of real people while at the same time enabling consideration of the ways that women and men are constructed and oppressed by discourse (see, eg, Bredstrom's [2006] discussion of the relevance of intersectionality to feminist HIV/AIDS research). Indeed, as Phoenix (2006, p 187) suggests:

> It foregrounds a richer and more complex ontology than approaches that attempt to reduce people to one category at a time. It also points to the need for multiple epistemologies. In particular, it indicates that fruitful knowledge production must treat social positions as relational.

Yuval-Davis (2006, p 201) argues that intersectionality holds the promise of 'a major analytic tool that challenges hegemonic approaches to the study of stratification as well as reified forms of identity politics'. However, she cautions that this promise is dependent upon a thorough consideration of social divisions in their organisational, intersubjective, experiential and representational forms. Indeed, she cautions against what she refers to as the 'additive' application of intersectionality, suggesting that at an ontological level, each social division manifests differently. This caution is notable if the historical pitfall of criminology – the accusation that the challenge of accommodating difference has been met by an 'add and stir' approach (Chesney-Lind, 2006) – is to be avoided. Thus, the application of intersectionality must take account of the mutually constitutive interrelationships between categories of social division and how these link with the material structures and power differentials that contribute to criminality.

Baca Zinn and Thornton Dill (1996) suggest that the power of intersectionality is achieved by theorising gender and each individual's social location as socially constructed through the intersection of race, class, gender and other inequalities; thus, all people are therefore theorised as experiencing *both* oppression *and* privilege. Daly and Stephens (1995) refer to this as the '*both/and*' concept. This approach is resonant of Liebling's (2001) arguments in her consideration of taking sides in research. Drawing on Becker, she asks why it is less acceptable to offer appreciative understanding of those who manage prisons than of prisoners, as if somehow those who wield power (warders) are not themselves subject to the power of others (governors) who are themselves subject to higher power relations. Adopting a 'both/and' concept has resonance with Liebling's (2001, p 473) comment on her own experience that 'it is possible to take more than one side seriously, to find merit in more than one perspective, and to do this without causing outrage on the side of officials or prisoners'.

Moreover, intersectionality seems to have wide appeal, for example, recent work by Steffensmeier et al (1998) illustrates how young black men come to be treated most harshly at the point of sentencing because their race, age and gender combine to create a social location at the margins of multiple, intersecting minority groups. This would seem to demonstrate that intersectionality offers a 'location' for theorising crime that can draw together otherwise diverse factions within criminology. Additionally, given its relative infancy in development and application to social theory and criminology (Walby et al, 2012), scope is offered for feminist criminologists to shape intersectionality as it further develops as a concept. For example, Walby et al (2012, p 228), in their critique of intersectionality, identify the question of 'how to address the relationship between structural and political intersectionality without reducing political projects to social structures?' as currently unaddressed. Feminist criminology would appear well placed to contribute to the further exploration of such an issue.

In drawing the chapter to a close, we return to Becker's article and the solution that he proposes to the 'Whose side are we on?' question. He concludes that researchers should:

> Take sides as [their] personal and political commitments dictate, use [their] theoretical and technical resources to avoid the distortions that might introduce into [their] work, limit [their] conclusions carefully, recognise the hierarchy of credibility for what it is and field as best [they] can

the accusations and doubts that will surely be [their] fate. (Becker, 1967, p 247)

We contend that intersectionality represents a 'theoretical resource' that may enable feminist criminology to hold to its values: advancing social justice, identifying and critiquing the power relations that occur where multiple social inequalities intersect, illustrating how those power relations are resisted and challenging the systems that create and maintain this inequality. In doing so, they do not uphold intersectionality as a universal panacea for the tensions discussed in the chapter, but rather suggest that it offers the means to negotiate the complexity these afford.

References

Acker, J. (1999) 'Rewriting class, race and gender. Problems in feminist rethinking', in M. Feree, J. Lorber and B. Hess (eds) *Revisioning gender*, London: Sage, pp 44–69.

Baca Zinn, M. and Thornton Dill, B. (1996) 'Theorising difference from multiracial feminism', *Feminist Studies*, vol 22, pp 321–31.

Becker, H. (1967) 'Whose side are we on?', *Social Problems*, vol 14, no 3, pp 239–47.

Bredström, A. (2006) 'Intersectionality?: a challenge for feminist HIV/AIDS research', *European Journal of Women Studies*, vol 13, no 3, pp 229–43.

Brewer, R. and Heitzeg, N. (2008) 'The racialisation of crime and punishment criminal justice, color blind racism and the political economy of the prison industrial complex', *American Behavioural Scientist*, vol 51, no 5, pp 625–44.

Brown, B. (1986) 'Women and crime: the dark figures of criminology', *Economy and Society*, vol 15, no 3, pp 355–402.

Burgess-Proctor, A. (2006) 'Intersections of race, class, gender and crime: future directions for feminist criminology', *Feminist Criminology*, vol 1, no 27, pp 27–47.

Campbell, A. (1981) *Girl delinquents*, Oxford: Basil Blackwell.

Carlen, P. (1983) *Women's imprisonment: a study in social control*, London: Routledge & Kegan Paul.

Carlen, P. (1986) 'Women and crime: the dark figures of criminology', *Economy and Society*, vol 15, no 3, pp 355–402.

Carlen, P. (1987) 'Introduction: gender, crime and justice', in P. Carlen and A. Worrall (eds) *Gender, crime and justice*, Milton Keynes: Open University Press.

Carlen, P. (1994) 'Why study women's imprisonment? Or anyone else's?', *British Journal of Criminology*, vol 34, pp 131–40.

Carrington, K. (1990) 'Aboriginal girls and juvenile justice: what justice? White justice', *Journal for Social Justice Studies*, vol 3, no 1, pp 1–18.

Carrington, K. (1998) *Who killed Leigh Leigh?*, Sydney: Random Press.

Cherukuri, S., Britton, D. and Subramaniam, M. (2009) 'Between life and death: women in an Indian state prison', *Feminist Criminology*, vol 4, no 3, pp 252–74.

Chesney-Lind, M. (1999) *Female gangs in America*, Chicago, IL: Lake View Press.

Chesney-Lind, M. (2006) 'Patriarchy, crime and justice: feminist criminology in an era of backlash', *Feminist Criminology*, vol 1, no 1, pp 6–26.

Cohen, S. (2011) 'Whose side were we on? The undeclared politics of moral panic theory', *Crime Media Culture*, vol 7, pp 237–43.

Collins, P. (1998) 'The tie that binds: race, gender, and US violence', *Ethnic and Racial Studies*, vol 21, no 5, pp 917–38.

Connell, R. (2002) *Gender*, Cambridge: Polity Press.

Cosgrove, L. and McHugh, M. (2000) 'Speaking for ourselves: feminist methods and community psychology', *American Journal of Community Psychology*, vol 28, pp 815–38.

Crenshaw, K. (1991) 'Mapping the margins: intersectionality, identity politics, and violence against women of color', *Stanford Law Review*, vol 43, no 6, pp 1241–99.

Crenshaw, K. (1993) 'Beyond racism and misogny', in M. Matsuda, C. Lawrence and K. Crenshaw (eds) *Words that wound*, Boulder, CO: Westview Press.

Daly, K. (1998) 'Gender, crime and criminology', in M. Tonry (ed) *The handbook of crime and punishment*, New York, NY: Oxford University Press, pp 85–108.

Daly, K. (2004) 'Different ways of conceptualising sex/gender in feminist theory and their implications for criminology', in M. Chesney-Lind and L. Pasko (eds) *Girls, women and crime*, Thousand Oaks, CA: Sage.

Daly, K. (2006) 'Feminist thinking about crime and justice', in S. Henry and M. Lanier (eds) *The essential criminology reader*, Boulder, CO: Westview Press.

Daly, K. (2008) 'Feminist perspectives in criminology: a review with Gen Y in mind', in E. McLaughlin and T. Newburn (eds) *The handbook of criminal theory*, London: Sage.

Daly, K. and Chesney-Lind, M. (1988) 'Feminism and criminology', *Justice Quarterly*, vol 5, pp 497–538.

Daly, K. and Maher, L. (1998) 'Crossroads and intersections: Building from feminist critique', in K. Daly and L. Maher (eds) *Criminology at the crossroads: feminist readings in crime and justice*, New York, NY: Oxford University Press, pp 1–17.

Daly, K. and Stephens, D. (1995) 'The "dark-figure" of criminology: towards a black and multi-ethnic feminist agenda for theory and research', in N. Hahn Rafter and F. Heidensohn (eds) *International feminist perspectives in criminology: engendering a discipline*, Philadelphia, PA: Open University Press.

Davis, K. (2008) 'Intersectionality as buzzword: a sociology of science perspective on what makes a feminist theory successful', *Feminist Theory*, vol 9, no 1, pp 67–85.

Eichler, M. (1986) 'The relationship between sexist, non-sexist, woman-centred and feminist research', *Studies in Communication*, vol 3, pp 37–74.

Evans, J. (1995) *Feminist theory today: an introduction to second wave feminism*, Thousand Oaks, CA: Sage.

Fine, M. (1992) *Disruptive voices: the possibilities of feminist research*, Ann Arbor, MI: The University of Michigan Press.

Gelsthorpe, L. (1997) 'Feminism and criminology', in M. Maguire, R. Morgan and R. Reiner (eds) *The Oxford handbook of criminology* (1st edn), Oxford: Oxford University Press, pp 511–34.

Gelsthorpe, L. (2004) 'Back to basics in crime control: weaving in women', *Critical Review of International Social and Political Philosophy*, vol 7, no 2, pp 76–103.

George, S. (2001) 'Why intersectionality works', *Women in Action*, no 2, pp 1–7.

Haack, S. (2003) 'Knowledge and propoganda', in C. Pinnick, N. Koertge and R. Almeder (eds) *Scrutinising feminist epistemology: an examination of gender in science*, Piscataway, NJ: Rutgers University Press, pp 7–19.

Harding, S. (1986) *The science question in feminism*, Ithaca, NY: Cornell University Press.

Hartsock, N. (1983) *Money, sex and power*, New York, NY: Longman.

Heckman, S. (1997) 'Truth and method: feminist standpoint theory revisited', *Signs*, vol 22, no 2, pp 341–65.

Leonard, E. (1982) *Women, crime and society*, New York, NY, and London: Longman Inc.

Liebling, A. (2001) 'Whose side are we on? Theory, practice and allegiances in prisons research', *British Journal of Criminology*, vol 41, pp 472–84.

Maher, L. (1997) *Sexed work: gender, race and resistance in a Brooklyn drug market*, Oxford: Clarenden Press.

Miller, J. and Mullens, C.W. (2009) 'The status of feminist theories in criminology', in F. Cullen, J. Wright and K. Blevin (eds) *Taking stock: the status of criminological theory (Advances in Criminological Theory, volume 15)*, New Brunswick, NJ: Transaction, pp 397–417.

Morris, K., Woodward, D. and Peters, E. (1998) '"Whose side are you on?" Dilemmas in conducting feminist ethnographic research with young women', *Social Research Methodology*, vol 1, no 3, pp 217–30.

Noddings, N. (2003) *Caring: a feminine approach to ethics & moral education* (2nd edn), Berkeley, CA: University of California Press.

Oakley, A. (2000) *Experiments in knowing: gender and method in the social sciences*, Cambridge: Polity Press.

Phoenix, A. (2006) 'Interrogating intersectionality: productive ways of theorizing multiple positioning', *Kvinder, Køn & Forskning*, vol 2, no 3, pp 21–30.

Prins, B. (2006) 'Narrative accounts of origins: a blind spot in the intersectional approach?', *European Journal of Women's Studies*, vol 13, no 3, pp 277–90.

Rice, M. (1990) 'Challenging orthodoxies in feminist theory: a black feminist critique', in L. Gelsthorpe and A. Morris (eds) *Feminist perspectives in criminology*, Buckingham: Open University Press, pp 59–69.

Rich, A. (1980) 'Compulsory heterosexuality and lesbian existence', *Signs*, vol 5, no 4, pp 631–60.

Roman, L.G. and Apple, M.W. (1990) 'Is naturalism a move away from positivism? Materialist and feminist approaches to subjectivity in ethnographic research', in E. Eisner and A. Peshkin (eds) *Qualitative inquiry in education*, New York, NY: Teachers College Press, pp 38–74.

Shaw, M. (1992) 'Issues of power and control: women in prison and their defenders', *British Journal of Criminology*, vol 34, no 4, pp 438–53.

Smart, C. (1976) *Women, crime and criminology: a feminist critique*, London: Routledge and Kegan Paul.

Smart, C. (1995) 'Feminist approaches to criminology – or postmodern woman meets atavistic man', in C. Smart (ed) *Law, crime and sexuality*, London: Sage.

Spender, D. (1981) *Man made language*, London: Routledge and Kegan Paul.

Stanko, E. (1990) *Everyday violence: how women and men experience sexual and physical danger*, London: Pandora.

Stanko, E. (1993) 'Ordinary fear: women, violence and personal safety', in P. Bart and E. Moran (eds) *Violence against women: the bloody footprints*, London: Sage.

Steffensmeier, D. and Allan, E. (1996) 'Gender and crime: toward a gendered theory of female offending', *Annual Review of Sociology*, vol 22, pp 459–87.

Steffensmeier, D. and Allan, E. (2000) 'Looking for patterns, gender, age and crime', in J. Shelley (ed) *Criminology: a contemporary handbook*, Belmont, CA: Wasdworth.

Steffensmeier, D., Ulmer, J. and Kramer, J. (1998) 'The interaction of race, gender and age in criminal sentencing: the punishment cost of being young, black and male', *Criminology*, vol 36, pp 763–93.

Walby, S., Armstrong, J. and Strid, S. (2012) 'Intersectionality: multiple inequalities in social theory', *Sociology*, vol 46, pp 224–40.

Walklate, S. (2001) 'Fearful communities?', *Urban Studies*, vol 36, pp 929–39.

Walklate, S. (2004) *Gender, crime and criminal justice*, Cullompton: Willan.

Warren, M. (1981) *Comparing female and male offenders*, London: Sage.

Weedon, C. (1987) *Feminist practice and poststructuralist theory*, Oxford: Blackwell.

Wolf, M. (1992) *A thrice told tale: feminism, postmodernism, and ethnographic responsibility*, Stanford, CA: Stanford University Press.

Young, A. (1990) *Femininity in dissent*, London: Routledge.

Young, A. (1994) 'Feminism and the body of criminology', in D. Farrington and S. Walklate (eds) *Offenders and victims: theory and policy*, London: British Society of Criminology and ISTD.

Young, A. (1996) *Imagining crime*, London: Sage.

Yuval-Davis, N. (2006) 'Intersectionality and feminist politics', *European Journal of Women's Studies*, vol 13, no 3, pp 193–209.

Zeitz, D. (1981) *Women who embezzle or defraud*, New York, NY: Praeger.

FIVE

Bringing the boys back home: re-engendering criminology

Anthony Ellis and Maggie Wykes

Introduction

This chapter explores the price paid by the theoretical omission and/ or obfuscation of men in work on crime and particularly work on violence. We focus on violence because although men dominate in most categories of offending, it is violence where masculinity is so obviously implicated and yet masculinity per se remains elusive within the vast literature of criminological treatises on violence. We write this chapter at a crucial point in history for the discipline. Recorded crime rates indicate that crime, particularly in the UK, has decreased in recent years, despite the onset of the worst economic recession in decades. Some criminologists have busied themselves considering the reasons for the 'crime drop', often paying homage to the *impact* of administrative criminology and its success in designing out criminal opportunities. Yet, they seem to have completely missed, or perhaps *disavowed* (Hall, 2012a), the glaringly obvious: levels of harm across the globe remain high, even if they do not show up in the statistics. For instance, if crime-measuring instruments were able to record the various harmful behaviours and (mal)practices that plunged the global economic system into recession, perhaps the 'crime drop' may not have been so dramatic.

With this context in mind, we take a much broader approach to harmful violence, exploring the violences of both the powerful and the powerless and acknowledging that in both instances most actors are male. We cover a lot of ground in this chapter and recognise that our coverage of some of the issues we allude to is brief. But the purpose is to be suggestive of how a moral criminology with 'values' (Becker, 1967) might right the wrongs of decades spent ignoring or poorly theorising men's place in crime. In doing this, the chapter delineates men's place in violence globally, critically reviews feminist work on violence and evaluates the contribution made by some masculinities research in order to argue that men must become the focus for theoretical work in order to properly address the damages caused by their offending and to change the ongoing reproduction of gendered roles and identities that sustain those levels of harm. We finish the chapter by returning to the notions of 'morality' and 'values' introduced by Becker (1963, 1967) and their potential implications for the current context in which criminology operates.

Masculinities, crime and violence: an overview

As far back as the mid-20th century, criminologists acknowledged that men commit far more crime than women, dominating incidents of more serious and violent crimes. Yet, this was acknowledged implicitly rather than explicitly, and in ways that did not directly address men's gender. The legacy of biological positivism left the discipline clinging to biologically assumed differences between men and women that manifested in specific sex roles, which largely naturalised men's propensity for aggression (Smart, 1976). The advent of feminism served as the much-needed catalyst for a critical interrogation of the concepts of sex and gender and their relationship with offending. It was during the early 1990s that the first significant advancements were made in the study of masculinities and crime. Developments since have generated a substantial body of literature on the topic. And yet, gender within criminology continues to be associated with women rather than with questions of men and what men actually do (Collier, 2004). The study of gendered 'men' who offend remains, to an extent, relatively marginal and nascent.

Early contributions were located within the broad theoretical frameworks of hegemonic masculinity, and violence and crime as forms of structured action. Connell's (1987, 2005) seminal works on gender relations and power posited that there are a plethora of masculinities constituted via their interaction with other social structures (namely, class and race), but that at any given time there is one that occupies an ideologically dominant, hegemonic, position. Hegemonic masculinity reinforces 'the legitimacy of patriarchy, which guarantees the dominant position of men and the subordination of women' (Connell, 2005, p 77). On violence, Connell argued that physical coercion is an important resource that is not incompatible with the establishment and exercise of hegemony (Connell, 1987).

Messerschmidt (1993, 1997) was the first scholar to develop a general theory that linked masculinities to violent and criminal behaviour.

Heavily influenced by Connell's work, he suggested that committing violence or crime represented situational attempts by men to perform and 'do' masculinity when other, more legitimate, resources for gender performance may be limited by socio-structural constraints. Towards the end of the 1990s and into the new millennium, a wave of critical writings emerged in opposition to hegemonic masculinity and structured action approaches (Collier, 1998, 2004; Hood-Williams, 2001; Hall, 2002; Jefferson, 2002). Although multifaceted in their criticisms, a lynchpin of these critical writings was the observation that socio-structural approaches lacked a discriminatory mechanism for distinguishing between men who commit violence and crime and those who do not. Without doubt, there exists 'plenty of support for the view that masculinity and gender relations are socially structured and varied' (Treadwell and Garland, 2011, p 624). But whether theoretical approaches to crime that rely solely on structural accounts of masculinity can adequately explain most violent crimes, which are committed by a minority of men – not all men (see Hood-Williams, 2001; Hall, 2002) – remains questionable.

These criticisms paved the way for a paradigmatic shift within the literature from structures to psyches (Hood-Williams, 2001), a shift that was spearheaded by British criminologist Tony Jefferson. Jefferson (2002) argued that, as a concept, hegemonic masculinity had generated an over-socialised view of men. In contrast, Jefferson offered a more psychoanalytic reading of male subjectivity, focusing on men's individual biographies and their psychic investments in masculine discourses. Through a series of psychoanalytic readings of the biography of the convicted rapist and former world heavyweight boxing champion Mike Tyson (Jefferson, 1996, 1998), Jefferson began to assemble a theoretical framework that drew attention towards men's inner feelings of anxiety and vulnerability, and how these emotions can shape violent masculinities.

Later, Gadd and Jefferson's (2007) psychosocial criminology synthesised their earlier works into a more general theoretical approach to understanding offender motivation, which attempts to account for both the social world and the discursive realm encountered by the subject, as well as their psychic inner world of 'unconscious as well as conscious processes' (Gadd and Jefferson, 2007, p 4). Their approach to men's violence overcomes 'the idea of masculinity seen only as a manifestation of power' (Gadd and Jefferson, 2007, p 185), and with a more psychoanalytically informed reading of men's violence, reveals inner feelings of powerlessness that drive outbursts of physical aggression. The 'psyches' approach to explaining men's criminality has not escaped criticism; feminist criminologists have argued that the shift sidesteps issues of men's agency and responsibility for violence (Howe, 2008) and has generated forms of analysis that are devoid of the potential for political activism (Collier, 2004; Wykes and Welsh, 2009), so negating the possibility of change.

Despite criticisms of the shift towards psyches, recent contributions from critical branches of criminology also identify subjectivity as mutually constituted at the nexus of individual psychology and the social world. However, in contrast, these more recent contributions 'account for the economic, socio-political and hegemonic-cultural macro-contexts in which relations are forged' (Hall, 2012a, p 194). Winlow and Hall's (2006, 2009; see also Winlow, 2012) more recent works focus on socially and economically marginalised men, who, in the vast majority of cases, constitute the '*highly specific sub-groups of the category "men"*' (Hood-Williams, 2001, p 43, emphasis in original) that perpetrate most violent crimes and have often been identified within criminological scholarship as the group of men most disadvantaged by the social, political and economic transformations that took place towards the end of the 20th century.

Winlow and Hall conceptualise marginalised masculinities as products of historic transformations in the fabric of capitalism's political economy, reproduced and embodied within successive generations of working-class men through the durable, visceral habitus. Gendered aspects of the visceral habitus frame the self-identities of working-class men, who tend to be socialised within climates of marginality and insecurity, where there is a heightened risk of experiencing interpersonal violence and intimidation. These authors rightly stress that working-class masculinities are not inherently violent; it is only a minority who commit violence frequently. So, 'it is not violence itself that is valued but the ability to retain some sense of dignity and respect in the face of it' (Winlow and Hall, 2009, p 288) that matters most to some men who hail from marginal backgrounds.

Although the cultural injunctions Winlow and Hall (2009) discuss are largely defensive in nature, they can become justifications employed by a minority of persistently violent men raised in circumstances of acute and immediate insecurity. Physical and psychological abuse may loom large in the biographies of violent men. It is the humiliation and indignity of being physically dominated, the memory of those traumatic emotions, and the fear they may be experienced again that are often harnessed during explosions of violent rage (Winlow and Hall, 2009; Winlow, 2012). Emotion and memory shape the masculinities of violent men, who use their reputations and potential for violence as a means of narcissistic self-elevation within cultures that valorise the stoic maintenance of self-dignity in the face of external hostilities and threats (see also Treadwell and Garland, 2011).

Such perspectives, however, assume a particular view of male violence as limited to just inflicting or avoiding *criminal, physical harm*. In many ways, this accepts a rather *conservative* definition of violence, which inhibits extrapolation to sexual violence, psychological violence and, we would argue, economic and state violence, whether these latter two are 'legal' or not; the violence of the powerful should be just as central in an account of men and violence as the violence of the insecure and marginalised. So, with critical awareness of this theoretical context, the remainder of the chapter addresses the current and diverse forms of harm currently being perpetrated by men in a global context; in other words, what are we talking about when we talk about men and violence? Then, perhaps, we can consider how (or, indeed, whether) criminology should respond, and, if so, from which value standpoint (Becker, 1967).

Men's violence in a global context

The current costs of men's violence are vast, varied and global in scope. Domestic abuse, for example, covers many cruelties that remain secret, but domestic violence injuries alone have serious financial implications for states, as well as physical damage to women's bodies (including foetal morbidity) and mental health. According to Home Office figures, injuries caused by domestic abuse cost the UK National Health Service (NHS) in the region of £1.2 billion a year (Derbyshire Police, 2006); while, in Australia, 'Domestic violence was the main reason homeless people sought out crisis accommodation' (*The Age*, 2005).

The misogyny of men's violence is not always recognised: in 2007, Amnesty International reported that 'More than 60 million women are "missing" from the world ... as a result of sex-selective abortions and female infanticide' (Amnesty International, 2007). In England and Wales, misogyny is evident with high levels of reported rape and low conviction levels. The Home Office records a litany of reasons for high attrition rates, including a 'tendency to concentrate on issues affecting the credibility of victims' (Home Office, 2010, p 21). Similar trends have been uncovered in South Africa, where work on violence against women has developed quickly since democratisation; yet, there is little, if any, evidence of a downturn in offending or improvement in prosecutions:

"in South Africa you have judges sending women to jail for stealing a loaf of bread to feed her baby, but men who gang rape women, who murder lesbians, who beat their wives to death, they walk the streets as free men." (Tshidi, aged 31, from Cape Town, quoted in Action Aid, 2009)

These examples are despite the introduction of new laws (eg Criminal Law [Sexual and Related Matters] Amendment Act 2007 in South Africa; and the Sexual Offences Act 2003 in England and Wales). In England, the failure of the criminal justice system to deal with 'rape ... encapsulates the sheer inadequacy of the law in relation to gendered violence and the deeply gendered assumptions that surround legal responses to it' (Wykes and Welsh, 2009, p 111).

Interpersonal violence committed by men is often directed at those closest to them: their wives, partners, children and, sometimes, themselves. In the summer of 2010, the former nightclub doorman, Raoul Moat, attempted to kill his ex-partner, killed her new partner and blinded a police officer after his release from a short prison term for abusing a child. Moat finally committed suicide after a manhunt in the wilds of Northumbria, England. The journalistic coverage mobilised some extraordinarily revealing narratives of masculinity within the national media and raised theoretical issues about masculine identity and subjectivity (Ellis et al, 2012). Only a month before Moat's rampage, Derrick Bird, a white, middle-aged taxi driver from Cumbria with no prior history of violence, shot dead 12 people before committing suicide (BBC, 2010).

Gregory (2012) has documented and analysed homi-suicides in the UK, where men kill their children, a current or ex-partner, and then themselves. She suggests that the imminent loss of propriety over intimates represents a challenge to masculinity that can only be resolved through lethal violence towards others and then upon themselves. Such intimate violences by men against partners and/or children and/or selves are not uncommon globally. In Australia, they have led to bitter argument, with claims that 'some high profile fathers' rights groups have been trying to use these terrible murder cases to promote their agenda of showing men as victims of the current family law system' (Johnston, 2012). In the US, Ramsland (2012) theorises in *Psychology Today* that:

A sense of failure can overwhelm certain men, especially those who cannot tolerate humiliation. It's not an option for them to allow a part of themselves to continue, so children may become collateral damage. This way, they can be certain that they have exercised the ultimate form of control.

The theme of humiliation identified by Ramsland resonates strongly with Winlow and Hall's (2009) work discussed earlier, but their approach tends to focus more on violence between men as often being about *retaliating first* to pre-empt such painful humiliation and shame. It goes nowhere near accounting for the possibility of a father murdering his own children being termed *collateral damage*.

Certainly, some men's violence specifically targets other men, often with very high levels of physical damage. The UK experienced a dramatic increase in rates of lethal interpersonal violence during the late 20th century, with both offenders and victims 'almost exclusively ... men of working age living in the poorest parts of the country' (Dorling, 2004, p 186). In Northern Ireland, survey and prosecution data reveal that young men are over-represented as both perpetrators and victims in violent incidents, and have higher than average mortality rates due to homicide or assault (McCready et al, 2006).

In-depth ethnographic work currently being conducted in marginalised communities in the north of England on male-to-male violence (Ellis, forthcoming) suggests that complex motivations and moralities lie behind the facade of both actualised and potential violence. The research indicates that perpetrators harbour acute feelings of cynicism, insecurity and paranoia. They recognise, and understand, the moral injunctions against violence, yet display a righteous vindication with regard to their own violence, in what they perceive is a dangerous and merciless social world. Empathy is in short supply and they often see little point in trying to resolve disputes with words; the old adage rings true for these men: *actions speak louder*. But perpetrating violence is not the full story for these men, as victimisation looms large within their biographies. Newburn and Stanko (1994) have rightly argued that criminology has consistently failed to account not just for men's offending, but for their victimisation, and the possibility that men who are persistently violent are also highly likely to succumb to serious violence themselves. Making sense of 'the realities of the lives of some – especially young – males' (Newburn and Stanko, 1994, p 154) has not been a priority for a discipline that struggles to acknowledge gender as a crucial variable.

Existing work on men's violence consistently finds that they target their abuse at externalised objects and individuals. Violent men often thrust themselves into extremely insecure situations where there is a heightened possibility that they themselves will be victimised. We suggest, somewhat speculatively and tentatively, that this represents an almost inverted model of self-harm, in which they have little regard for those they are intent on harming, but neither do they care much about themselves. Indeed, self-harm may be an appropriate way of explaining such risky violence. As intimated by Edwards (2006), being masculine is actually defined, fundamentally, by varied violations against the self and the committing of violations against others. Among women, self-harming behaviours are associated *psychosocially* with poor self-esteem, fear of adult life (or fear of failure in adult life) and pressure from unrealistic representations of gender in culture (Wykes and Gunter, 2005). While such pressures may relate to women harming themselves, they may also help explain men's engagement in high-risk violence with men; the impetus may not be so very different.

Another area of violence (largely unacknowledged as male) is mass street or public violence, often, but not always, described as *gang-derived*.[1] Here, youth, race, terror, religion, class (Wykes and Welsh, 2009) and – after the 2011 street riots in the UK – *consumerism* are blamed for violence. Hall (2012b) quotes Zizek (2011) to conclude that capitalism has created the riotous *beast* in order, of course, to justify controlling it. However, he expresses this rather more floridly:

> This powerful energy is become [*sic*] increasingly untethered and free-ranging, and in the absence of politics and shared symbolic order,[2] we must resign ourselves to the continuation of the situation as described, the latent objectless anxiety of a slowly disintegrating pseudo-pacification process punctuated by unpredictable eruptions of the barbarism of order in a downward spiral towards a fractious society of enemies. (Hall, 2012b, p 161, note added)

Certainly, the riots smacked of an intense desire and obsession with the symbolic capital imbued in consumer items, but what is missing from Hall's account is a clear acknowledgement that the perpetrators were mostly men (nearly 90% of arrests), mostly adult (80% over 18; nearly 30% over 25) involved all races (35% black and 40% white) and most of those arrested had previous 'form' (85%). Hall, though, focuses on the unemployment of some 40% and the benefits claims of a further 35%[3] as the key explanation for *riot* and seems to suggest that somehow 'core working class values' would have turned a riot into a revolution (Hall, 2012b, p 156). The potential for a socialist-based politics to create positive change is debatable, however, considering its divisive impact, historically, in splitting the miners into two camps during the 1984/85 British strike (Waddington et al, 1991) and largely excluding whole swathes of black workers and women from unionised politics in the decades before. Moreover, it continues a tendency to a victimological model of disempowered masculinity, one that is also current in South Africa, where: 'Massive unemployment, poverty, easy access to weapons and the lingering effects of the racial oppression of apartheid have been cited as reasons for the persistently high levels of violent crime' (Aljazeera, 2012).

Such a model never engages with the fact that women are subject to all these too but rarely turn to dangerousness as a result. Nor are such violences just part of interpersonal grudges, street wars or 'domestics': rape in war; torture and humiliation; enslavement; human sacrifice; forced circumcision; extortion; protection rackets – the list of victims and harms is endless. We can see these as *wrong* simply because in one jurisdiction or another they are labeled *crimes* and criminologists duly study them; but it is not just poor, disenfranchised, ill-educated or *othered* men who harm and damage.

The violences of the powerful

There is violence beyond variables, statistics, criminal justice policy and practice, and, therefore, so very often beyond criminology, which is caught in the web of positivist epistemology that pays its salaries, funds its research, publishes its articles and pats its back. There are the violences of the powerful often justified by *law, economics* or *security* (the US and the UK invading Iraq included all three but rather downplayed *economics*) and much more subtle symbolic forms of violence – 'a violence of language, a violence that hides behind smiles, handshakes, business deals and expressions of sincerity' (Winlow, 2012, p 203). Examples are the CEOs of the transatlantic investment banking system, who have overseen, and been party to, some of the worst excesses of corporate greed and dishonesty in Western capitalism's history, inflicting endemic and catastrophic levels of systemic violence upon the global population at large. Yet, this is not *crime*. In Britain, 'The Treasury said it was unsure whether or not powers existed to prosecute any traders' (Murphy and Goodway, 2012), while a letter to *The Guardian* precisely makes our point: 'It is clear that finance capital continues to act purely to make huge profits, legally or illegally. The banking system is not a support to the real economy but a criminal conspiracy against it' (Davies, 2012).

Equally, in the air-conditioned corridors of the corporate stratosphere, we find the aggressive intimidatory practices of business conglomerates such as News International, which is part of the global Murdoch news empire, and whose use of predatory journalistic practices has been exposed recently in the phone-hacking scandal. The true extent of these practices, both in terms of quantity and harm, is only beginning to enter the public domain via the 2012 Leveson Inquiry. These corporations exercise a real stranglehold on our politics, whose own criminality was dramatically exposed in the recent MPs' expenses scandal. Despite the very wide news coverage, there was still reluctance to accept that this was crime:

> MPs faced judgment over the expenses scandal and the prospect of criminal charges loomed. More than half the Commons was ordered to repay a total of £1.1 million to the taxpayer – though astonishingly, dozens of MPs had failed to cough up even as an official audit was made public. (Wright and Chapman, 2010)

Of the MPs implicated, by September 2011, only 'four MPs and two members of the House of Lords have so far been jailed as a result of the expenses scandal' (Evans, 2011). The longest sentence served was six months. Moreover, increasingly, our public services are privately provided, with companies like G4S running prisons alongside their private security operations, but failing to fully deliver contracted security for the 2012 Olympics in London. CEO Nick Buckles was called to a parliamentary committee to explain his company and was met with outrage: 'amateur', 'humiliating', 'disaster' and 'unacceptable' were just some of the words used (Hoggart, 2012). Yet, Hoggart adds, Buckles 'plans to keep his £57m management fee'. It takes a letter from a member of the public rather than a criminologist or journalist to point out the *moral* if not *criminal* underbelly here:

> Is G4S being paid nearly £300,000 million for supplying 10,000 security guards for the duration of the Olympics?[4] Is that nearly £30,000 per guard? It would be interesting to know how much of the £30,000 is being allocated to overheads and equipment. (Jones, 2012)

Instead, the morality of paying eye-wateringly large sums to a corporation unable to fulfil its basic contractual obligations remains unaddressed. Rather, this is joked about by Hoggart, writing in *The Guardian* with deeply class-ridden references to the CEO's 'silly mullet hair do' and his tan (Hoggart, 2012). That these and similar actions globally are not seen as serious crime, and, indeed, violence in the worst sense, is an achievement of capital cultural hegemony par excellence. More, that they are not seen as acts largely enabled and controlled by men demonstrates the massive falsification of consciousness that patriarchy continues to purvey. Criminology is largely blind, or turning a blind-eye, in both areas.

The men, and the very few women, who sit atop the global economic order are neo-liberal capitalism's *undertakers* (Hall, 2012a), the movers and shakers. They represent those who are prepared to 'do what is necessary' in the furtherance of their own interests and to ensure the reproduction of the *hallowed* system, even at the expense of the lives and livelihoods of those who are less fortunate (see Hall, 2012a). Although there is difference in their methods (more subtle forms of violence and harm as opposed to directly physical), they nonetheless appear on the same continuum as those men who perpetrate *real* physical violence in locations of acute marginality, in that they are also about power, fear, shame, humiliation and status. So, it is surely the job of a moral criminology to bring gender into the analysis of violence in all its manifestations and wherever it is perpetrated throughout the social order.

The (im)morality of criminology

Yet, despite the consistent evidence of violence as masculine, there still remains resistance within criminology to focusing on men. This is not to deny the progress that has been made recently within the discipline thanks to the efforts of a small number of criminologists and their theoretical and empirical works. These developments, though, remain quite marginal within the discipline's corpus, having yet to be fully developed into theoretical frameworks capable of critically engaging with men's offending throughout the social order. Rather, emphasis within the masculinities and crime literature is predominantly on socio-economically marginalised men. In many other analyses, gender has been somewhat diluted by genuine and very pertinent criminological work on other identity variables. There is little work on masculinity per se as opposed to black masculinity, working-class masculinity or homosexual masculinity, disregarding work on areas such as youth, terrorism, white-collar crime, state crime, gangs, street violence and drugs that does not discuss masculinity or often even acknowledge that this is men's crime. Feminist work in all its many rich and complex manifestations retains, and perhaps rightly so, an emphasis on the place of women in crime and criminal justice, thereby inevitably focusing theory upon victims. As a result, much theory diverts from, obfuscates or just ignores the 'elephant in the room' of the gender crime nexus that aligns differently sexed bodies so differently but so discreetly to different crime roles and, by doing so, necessarily reproduces that gendered nexus. It must be important to query the efficacy and, indeed, morality of any concern with crime that negates, obfuscates or denigrates the sex variable.

Yet, in practice, that is what has happened. Despite a century of positivistic counting and labelling according to every possible variable that can be assigned to a human body, criminology has still not fully theorised the relationship between masculinity and crime, perhaps because it has learnt its own lesson too well: studying crime and seeking the causes of crime in men is always problematised, because, of course, not all men offend *and so it goes*. But exchange crime for violence and things change: violence defined by the World Health Organization (WHO) is a broad continuum of abuses and harms:

> The intentional use of physical force or power, threatened or actual, against oneself, another person, or against a group or community, that either results in or has a high likelihood of resulting in injury, death, psychological harm, mal-development, or deprivation. (WHO, 2012)

Critically revisiting Becker's (1963) concept of the *moral entrepreneur* as the 'crusading reformer who feels that the existing rules of society have failed to address some pressing evil' (Snyder, 2010, p 166), we argue that the application of legitimate rules itself may well be manifestly *evil* and is frequently violence and/or violation exercised normally, regularly, systematically and un-reflexively by men, just as violences and/or violations are labelled *deviant by* moral entrepreneurs. Violence is the exercise of power par excellence, from the use of it by capital and states, legitimately, in war, torture, policing, social control, economic exploitation, profiteering and punishment, to the oppressive legitimated control of powerful men against threats to their status. Such control of the public is barely acknowledged as *control* but includes the criminalisation, emasculation, impoverishment and disenfranchisement of, and occasionally negotiation with, men (and sometimes women) who challenge authority. In private, there are more personal controlling, hidden, unacknowledged and often un-criminalised intimate abuses, from emotional cruelty to so-called *honour killing*, depriving victims of identity, autonomy, action and, ultimately, life. These, and indeed all harms, are *overwhelmingly* committed by men.

So, by elevating *violence* to a variable, we cannot ignore the service it offers men. Although not all men act in an overtly harmful way, crime, and particularly violence, whether real or symbolic, is a constituent of masculinity. Crime operationalises the power of the state to describe, protect and legitimate normal masculinities, gender roles and relations through law by discursively marking out *others*. Crime is also the illegitimatised attempt to exercise power by *others*, normally *othered* men, who pose the greatest threat to power, but sometimes women. In both instances, through law and crime, discursively and in practice, there is *violence* in the constitution of masculinity. This somewhat turns on its head a frequent claim in criminology that masculinity has some causal or probable relationship to crime per se and violence in particular, because we argue rather that crime and especially violence is rather constitutive and continuously reconstitutive of masculinity or masculinities, regardless of their legitimacy.

In writing this chapter, we are aware that we might be 'traduced on the one hand as a nihilist and on the other as a law and order ideologue' (Howe, 2008, p 218), as if we were arguing for no laws against disempowered people or more laws against violences of all kinds. We are not. Simply, we would like to consider the theoretical implications of giving primacy to violence in all its guises rather than giving primacy to criminals, and suggest that criminologists *bring the boys back home* to crime and criminology, but to a rather different place. Not to try to do so would leave things just as they are, and have been, which is neither *moral* nor *entrepreneurial*; which returns us finally to Becker (1967), our 'values' and his question: 'Whose side are we on?'. This question is as pertinent now as it was then, particularly given the current context that criminology has failed to adequately engage with and theorise, as we have described in this brief chapter. Criminology must consider its 'values' and ask of itself 'Whose side is it on?'. Perhaps for too long now, and maybe still, criminology has been afraid of the answer.

Notes

[1.] We acknowledge that gangs – even their very existence – are a contentious area in criminology (Sanchez-Jankowski, 2003), but, for this chapter, that very attention to gangs in academia as well as the media is sufficient to consider how *gang theory* has contributed to understanding masculinity and violence.

[2.] As if it were ever thus.

[3.] Data taken from House of Commons (2011).

[4.] Beginning 27 July for two weeks.

References

Action Aid (2009) 'Hate crimes: the rise of "corrective" rape in South Africa'. Available at: http://www.actionaid.org.uk/doc_lib/correctiveraperep_final.pdf

Aljazeera (2012) 'South Africa rape video suspects in court', 19 April. Available at: http://www.aljazeera.com/news/africa/2012/04/201241918010275165.html

Amnesty International (2007) 'Statistics'. Available at: http:// www.domestic-violence-norwich.org.uk/index.php?page=statistics

BBC news (2010) 'Profile: Cumbria gunman Derrick Bird', 2 November. Available at: http://www.bbc.co.uk/news/10216923

Becker, H. (1963) *Outsiders: studies in the sociology of deviance*, New York, NY: The Free Press.

Becker, H. (1967) 'Whose side are we on?', *Social Problems*, vol 14, no 3, pp 239–47.

Collier, R. (1998) *Masculinities, crime and criminology*, London: Sage.

Collier, R. (2004) 'Masculinities and crime: rethinking the "man question"?', in C. Sumner (ed) *The Blackwell companion to criminology*, Oxford: Blackwell.

Connell, R.W. (1987) *Gender and power: society, the person and sexual politics*, Cambridge: Polity.

Connell, R.W. (2005) *Masculinities*, Cambridge: Polity.

Derbyshire Police (2006) [online] 2 June. Available at: www.derbyshire.police.uk/news/572.html

Dorling, D. (2004) 'Prime suspect: murder in Britain', in P. Hillyard, C. Pantazis, S. Tombs and D. Gordon (eds) *Beyond criminology: taking harm seriously*, London: Pluto.

Edwards, T. (2006) *Cultures of masculinity*, London: Routledge.

Ellis, A. (forthcoming) 'An ethnography of men, violence and social change in the north of England', unpublished PhD thesis, University of Sheffield.

Ellis, A., Sloan, J. and Wykes, M. (2013) '"Moatifs" of masculinity: the stories told about "men" in British newspaper coverage of the Raoul Moat case', *Journal of Crime, Media, Culture*, vol 9, no 1, pp 3–21.

Evans, M. (2011) 'Expenses MPs and their sentences: how long each served', *The Telegraph*, 20 September. Available at: http://www.telegraph.co.uk/news/newstopics/mps-expenses/8776160/Expenses-MPs-and-their-sentences-how-long-each-served.html#

Gadd, D. and Jefferson, T. (2007) *Psychosocial criminology: an introduction*, London: Sage.

Gregory, M. (2012) 'Masculinity and homicide-suicide', *International Journal of Law, Crime and Justice*, vol 40, no 3, pp 133–51.

Hall, S. (2002) 'Daubing the drudges of fury: men, violence and the piety of the "hegemonic masculinity" thesis', *Theoretical Criminology*, vol 6, no 1, pp 35–61.

Hall, S. (2012a) *Theorizing crime and deviance: a new perspective*, London: Sage.

Hall, S. (2012b) 'Consumer culture and the meaning of the urban riots in London', in S. Hall and S. Winlow (eds) *New directions in criminological theory*, London: Routledge.

Hoggart, S. (2012) 'Taxi for Mr Buckles: MPs savage G4S boss over Olympics chaos', *The Guardian*, 18 July.

Home Office (2010) 'Government response to the Stern Review'. Available at: http://www.homeoffice.gov.uk/publications/crime/call-end-violence-women-girls/government-stern-review?view=Binary

Hood-Williams, J. (2001) 'Gender, masculinities and crime: from structures to psyches', *Theoretical Criminology*, vol 5, no 1, pp 37–60.

House of Commons (2011) 'The August 2011 riots: a statistical summary', House of Commons Research Paper. Available at: http://www.parliament.uk/briefing-papers/SN06099

Howe, A. (2008) *Sex, violence and crime: Foucault and the 'man' question*, Oxon: Routledge-Cavendish.

Jefferson, T. (1996) 'From "little fairy boy" to "the complete destroyer": subjectivity and transformation in the biography of Mike Tyson', in M. Mac An Ghaill (ed) *Understanding Masculinities*, Buckingham: OUP.

Jefferson, T. (1998) 'Muscle, "hard men" and "Iron" Mike Tyson: reflections on desire, anxiety and the embodiment of masculinity', *Body and Society*, vol 4, no 1, pp 77–98.

Jefferson, T. (2002) 'Subordinating hegemonic masculinity', *Theoretical Criminology*, vol 6, no 1, pp 63–88.

Johnston, P. (2012) 'Fathers who kill', *ABC*, 1 March. Available at: http://www.abc.net.au/local/stories/2012/03/01/3443583.htm

Jones (2012) Letter in *The Guardian*, 18 July.

McCready, S., Harland, K. and Beattie, K. (2006) 'Violent victims? Young men as perpetrators and victims of violent crime', Centre for Young Men's Studies, Research Update No 1, University of Ulster/Youth Action Northern Ireland.

Messerschmidt, J. (1993) *Masculinities and crime: critique and reconceptualization of theory*, Maryland, MD: Rowman and Littlefield.

Messerschmidt, J. (1997) *Crime as structured action: gender, race, class and crime in the making*, London: Sage.

Murphy, J. and Goodway, N. (2012) 'Bankers in fixing scandal "let off"', *London Evening Standard*, 28 June.

Newburn, T. and Stanko, E.A. (1994) 'When men are victims: the failure of victimology', in T. Newburn and E. Stanko (eds) *Just boys doing business: men, masculinities and crime*, London: Routledge.

Ramsland (2012) 'Fatal fathers: homicidal fathers view children as extensions of themselves', *Psychology Today*, 8 February. Available at: www.psychologytoday.com/blog/shadow-boxing/201202/fatal-fathers/comments

Sanchez-Jankowski, M. (2003) 'Gangs and social change', *Theoretical Criminology*, vol 7, no 2, pp 191–216.

Smart, C. (1976) *Women, crime and criminology: a feminist critique*, London: Routledge.

Snyder, G.J. (2010) 'Howard Becker (1928–)', in K. Hayward, S. Maruna and J. Mooney (eds) *Fifty key thinkers in criminology*, Abingdon: Routledge.

The Age (2005) 'Homeless flee domestic violence: study', 11 February. Available at: www.theage.com.au/news/Breaking-News/Homeless-flee-domestic-violence-study/2005/02/11/1108061832504.html

Treadwell, J. and Garland, J. (2011) 'Masculinity, marginalization and violence: a case study of the English Defence League', *British Journal of Criminology*, vol 51, pp 621–34.

Waddington, D., Wykes, M. and Critcher, C. (1991) *Split at the seams? Community, continuity and change after the 1984–85 coal dispute*, Milton Keynes: OUP.

WHO (World Health Organization) (2012) 'World report on violence and health'. Available at: www.who.int/violenceprevention/approach/definition/en/index.html

Winlow, S. (2012) 'All that is sacred is profaned: towards a theory of subjective violence', in S. Hall and S. Winlow (eds) *New directions in criminological theory*, London: Routledge.

Winlow, S. and Hall, S. (2006) *Violent night: urban leisure and contemporary culture*, Oxford: Berg.

Winlow, S. and Hall, S. (2009) 'Retaliate first: memory, humiliation and male violence', *Crime, Media, Culture*, vol 5, no 3, pp 285–304.

Wright, S. and Chapman, J. (2010) 'Shaming of the 389 greedy MPs who went too far', *The Daily Mail*, 5 February. Available at: http://www.dailymail.co.uk/news/article-1248648/MP-expenses-Shaming-389-greedy-politicians-went-far.html

Wykes, M. and Gunter, B. (2005) *The media and body image*, London: Sage.

Wykes, M. and Welsh, K. (2009) *Violence, gender and justice*, London: Sage.

Zizek, S. (2011) 'Shoplifters of the world unite' in *London Review of Books*, 19 August. Available at: www.lrb.co.uk/2011/08/19/slavoj-zizek/shoplifters-of-the-world-unite

—

SIX

New 'racisms' and prejudices? The criminalisation of 'Asian'

Sunita Toor

Introduction

Historically, discourses in the area of race and crime have focused on the criminalisation and criminality of Britain's black communities, constructing a racialised 'black'–'white' dichotomy. Other minority ethnic communities, such as those who identify as 'Asian', have been less subject to scrutiny. Two things have altered this terrain. First, in the era of late modernity, 21st-century Britain is a milieu of racial, ethnic and cultural hybridity, intersectionality and change. Emergent racisms, prejudices, folk devils and moral panics have transformed and widened racialised perspectives on crime to include other minority ethnic groups. Second, several events (both before and following the attacks on 9/11) have indicated a form of criminalisation specific to British Asians, namely, Pakistani and Bangladeshi Muslims. This chapter reflects on these issues in order to assess whether such developments have led to the formulation of *new* racisms, prejudices and folk devils or if they are illustrative of a regurgitation of *old* discourses in the race, ethnicity, culture and crime debate.

The analysis of 'race' and 'racisms' in this chapter is positioned in the context of existing work on race issues in criminology but with a specific slant on 'sides' and 'values' in relation to the experiences of British South Asian Muslims. The political imperatives of global and British discourses on Islam have made it necessary to ask whose values are favoured and, more interestingly, whose side is to be taken (Becker, 1967). In this sense, the political discourse has bought to the fore – and even encouraged – the criminalisation of Britain's South Asian Muslim population to such a degree that questions are raised regarding the values and mores of these communities, even whose perspective is seen as more 'credible'. As Becker (1967, p 240) states: 'in case of deviance, the hierarchal relationship is a moral one … the subordinate parties are those who, it is alleged, have violated that morality'. So, to what degree is the criminalisation of Britain's South Asian Muslim communities a construct of political machinations and media discourse or a valid portrayal of the criminal facts? The chapter addresses this by discussing the factors and discourses that have contributed to the criminalisation of Britain's South Asian Muslim communities.

In this analysis, *criminalisation* is the act of labelling a community, or indeed its members, as 'criminal' due to its perceived associations and engagement with certain illegal and deviant activities. Adding a culturally specific racial and ethnic framework to this, the chapter argues that there has been a *racialisation* of crime in the UK, and that this has played a significant role in the criminalisation of Britain's South Asian Muslim communities. Racialisation refers to the processes by which specific understandings of race, ethnicity, culture and faith are used to construct a distinct categorisation of Britain's Asian population. This form of racialisation sees a merging and intersection of race and ethnicity, where a distinct racial group – in this case, Asian – is identified, with the focus then falling on specific ethnicities within this racial group, specifically those from the Pakistani and Bangladeshi communities whose faith is Islam. This systematic form of racialisation stigmatises particular South Asian Muslim communities, constructing them as socially and criminally problematic. In this sense, it is often 'members of the highest group' (Becker, 1967) who are able to define how this process of racialisation takes place, as their perspective is regarded as the most credible and valid. As a consequence, the racialisation of Britain's South Asian Muslim communities imposes distinct labels and typologies of identity on this group, placing them in a disadvantageous and disempowered position, which has led to a shift in focus towards members of these groups.

Thoughts on the category 'Asian'

Demographic statistics for 2012 indicated that 14% of Britain's population were non-white, with 7.5% of these being of Asian origin (ONS, 2012). The official usage of the category 'Asian' encompasses a diverse range of people from the Indian subcontinent, such as people from India, Pakistan, Bangladesh and East Africa. However, these are very distinct groups, constituting an array of different cultures, religions, ethnic groups and histories, which renders the term 'Asian' somewhat defunct as a meaningful category. Modood (1990a) differentiates 'Asian' groups according to moralistic philosophies or religious imperatives, where Indians and East African Indians are regarded as 'achievers' and those from Pakistan and Bangladesh as 'believers'. To non-Asians, Brah (1996) highlights how a generalised category is used to represent this group through overtly negative imagery as 'outsiders … undesirables'. The Asian label can act to reproduce and embed prejudices, rather than diminish them. In this way, the category can be used to determine hierarchies in society, in terms of constructing a relationship with the 'Asian' as the 'other'. Similarly, reports (specifically media reports) regarding the rise of Asian/Muslim criminality homogenise these identities through consistently failing to clearly identify perpetrators. The terms 'Asian' and 'Muslim' are used interchangeably, with little regard demonstrated for their very different meanings, not least due to the fact that not all Muslims are from the Indian subcontinent, as the Muslim faith encompasses a diverse range of people from many countries.

The start of the 21st century saw a heightened focus on all things Asian, albeit in a negative sense, through events such as the terrorist attacks of 9/11 and 7/7. The world watched in horror as two planes hijacked by Al-Qaida terrorists on a suicide mission flew into the Twin Towers in New York. The impact of this event is overwhelming in terms of the Western world's response to terrorism; 9/11 became the point at which the threat of Islamic terrorism became global and real. Subsequently, other such atrocities have taken place elsewhere in Madrid, Bali, Casablanca and Istanbul as well as in the UK, where the 7/7 London bombings in 2005 had a significant impact on Britain's Asian communities. The European Monitoring Centre on Racism and Xenophobia (2005, p 3) reported that in the 'immediate period after the attacks there was a temporary and disturbing increase in faith related hate crimes across the UK'. The same report highlights the huge sense of vulnerability and fear of victimisation felt by Muslims across Europe in a heightened era of Islamophobia.

Without a doubt, global terrorism has fuelled Islamophobia and consequently constructed new stereotypes of Muslims and British Asians as deviant extremists and dangerous aliens to Western cultures. In line with this, Miles and Brown (2003, p 166) argue that 'many of the stereotypes and misinformation that contribute to the articulation of Islamophobia are rooted in a particular perception of Islam', one that deems that Islam validates and promotes terrorism. The perceived synergy between Islam and terrorism is continually reaffirmed in mass media images of Britain's South Asian Muslim communities. In addition, key government officials, such as the former Home Secretary John Reid, inform us of the 'threat' being 'enduring – the struggle will be long and wide and deep' (Manningham-Buller, 2006, p 1). Such sentiments were further grounded by Peter Clarke, the head of the Anti-Terrorist Branch of the Metropolitan Police, who described the threat of Al-Qaida-related terrorism as 'real, here, deadly'. Thus, Islam is regarded as contributing to an era of British citizens living with heightened fears of terrorist attacks.

The 'Asian' and 'Muslim' way of life was brought into sharp focus as contrasting with Western ideals. The once-held perception of British Asians constituting submissive, peaceful, tight-knit, family-oriented and law-abiding communities has transformed since the late 1990s (Webster, 1997; Alexander, 2000; Wardak, 2000). Hence, in 21st-century Britain, 'Asian-ness' has been erroneously homogenised in mainstream discourse to be synonymous with 'Islam', which is represented in overtly negative images of religious fanaticism and terrorism (McGhee, 2003). The depiction of Britain's South Asian Muslim communities has most certainly been determined by key events, such as the 9/11 and 7/7 suicide bombings by extremists acting in the name of Islam. However, these events need to be analysed in line with other significant factors, such as the growth of the young British Asian population , socio-economic deprivation, increased victimisation, globalised fear of Islam, as well as political and media discourses, which have all played a role in determining the image of 21st-century Britain's South Asian Muslim communities.

In the sections that follow, a history of developments in Britain's South Asian Muslim communities is presented that demonstrates how negative aspects have been apparent over the past two decades. The analysis of several key events provides an overview of how integrating notions of race, ethnicity, culture and religion alter the dynamics of criminalisation.

The social construction of Britain's South Asian Muslim communities

Analyses of racial criminalisation date back to the 1970s, where the development of 'moral panics' theorising was instantly applicable to young black men and their perceived involvement in street crime (Hall et al, 1978; Cohen, 1980 [1972]). Pearson (1983, p x) sees this practice as being a more explicit illustration of traditionally implicit British responses, where 'the English have been blaming their violence on someone else for a century or more'. As Werbner (2005, p 6) states, the purpose of foreign folk devils is to aid the construction of a 'threat to the purity and order of the nation, the ethnos, seen as a moral community'. Hence, the immigrant other, the outsider, presents both a threat to the moral fabric of British society and a useful scapegoat. Interpretations and misrepresentations of British South Asian Muslims focus largely on aspects of culture, religion, gender and socio-economic factors.

Asian cultures were once heralded as providing strong moral values and principles for their young, with Asian communities referred to as the 'model minority' (Back and Keith, 1999, p 133). Jack Straw, during his time as Home Secretary (1997–2001), commented on the distinguishing features of Asian communities as being tight-knit, insular, hard-working and law-abiding, with a core focus on family, community and faith embedding strong moral imperatives. Although these characteristics are not alien to British society, they can exacerbate perceptions of 'them and us' with regards to reduced interaction. Many scholars (Watson, 1977; Ballard, 1994; Alexander, 2000) have referred to second- and third-generation Asian young people as 'caught between two cultures' (Mac an Ghaill and Haywood, 2005, p 7). It is in this vacuum of duality that Asian young people strive to negotiate their identities with their parents' culture and expectations, amid divergent imperatives arising from their exposure to, and engagement with, wider British society.

Religion is a prime identifier of British Asians and has played a core role in the areas of criminalisation and Islamophobia. Alexander (2000, p 15) refers to 'Muslims' as the 'new blacks' in British society in terms of their 'association of cultural alienation, deprivation and danger that comes with that position'. Previously pejorative discourses with racialised connotations focused exclusively on black populations; now, the focus is on religious affiliation, laden with religious classifications and postulations. Alexander (2000, p 218) refers to one aspect of the crisis of Asian masculinity being 'captured potently in the spectre of a reactive religious fundamentalism', which positions young Muslim men in 'the firing line as Public Enemy Number One'.

Nevertheless, the gendered nature of the criminalisation of Britain's South Asian Muslim communities has been quite distinct. While Asian young men are perceived as problematic and deviant, women are rendered invisible. When Asian females are afforded attention, there is a tendency to perceive them as victims of extreme, patriarchal cultural traditions, with a particular focus on domestic abuse and honour crimes and killings. As a result, a cultural juxtaposition exists whereby the victimisation of Asian females has contributed to the criminalisation of Asian males. On the one hand, Asian women are perceived as law-abiding, insular and vulnerable victims at the hands of their male patriarchs, while, on the other hand, Asian males are seen as violent subjugators, inflicting abuse on their female counterparts in an effort to uphold cultural control. Hence, it is the cultural principles that precipitate this victimisation. This can be clearly observed with honour crimes, which are undertaken in the name of defending a family's 'izzat' (honour). Honour crimes are committed to redeem the shame that has been brought upon the family's reputation and social standing by the behaviour of a female member. The power of honour and ensuring a family's spotless status is imperative to understanding the victimisation of Asian females, who are seen as being the carriers of 'izzat'.

Mama's (2000) study of black female victims of domestic violence found that some men justified their abusive behaviour through traditional and religious imperatives. Such justifications were based on ensuring that women acted according to the cultural and idealised norm of the dutiful wife, which also pertains to white British women. However, the victimisation of Asian females differs in that their culture is depicted as being alien from Western norms and values. In addition, Choudry (1996) highlights how Pakistani women find it difficult to seek help for their abuse due to their lack of personal freedom, language barriers, cultural obligations and restraints, along with uncertainty about their immigration status and rights (Parmar and Sampson, 2005). Moreover, Ahmad and Sheriff (2003) highlight that many Muslim women feel that organisations may censure their culture and religion and so feel reluctant to seek help.

Socio-economic factors also impede women's ability to access services, and can have a wider impact on Asian communities. Both Anwar (1996) and Modood (1990a) indicate that Bangladeshi and Pakistani communities are the most disadvantaged populations in Britain. This is further supported by the Joseph Rowntree Foundation's study, *Poverty and ethnicity in the UK* (Platt, 2007), which found that Bangladeshis, followed by Pakistanis, experience the greatest levels of poverty of any ethnic group. The criminalisation of lower-income groups has precedents in British society, so it is unsurprising that this has been extended to Pakistani and Bangladeshi young people. Scholars such as White (1996) and Goldson (2007) have emphasised how the processes of criminalisation focus on specific marginalised groups in society. Criminology has highlighted the role of class in determining stereotypes and attaching labels to specific groups as the criminal other (Hall et al, 1978). In line with this analysis, White and Cunneen (2006, p 18) state:

> Predominantly young men with an over-representation of youth drawn from minority ethnic communities, low income, low educational achievement, poorly paid and/or

casualised employment (if any) and strained familial relations, are the standard defining characteristics of children and young people most frequently found in juvenile detention centres and custodial institutions.

Moreover, this criminalisation is embedded by 'structural transformations in global political economy' (White and Cunneen, 2006, p 19), which reinforces negative imagery regarding certain segments of the population. A BBC *Panorama* programme entitled 'Underclass in Purdah' (BBC, 1993) portrayed the Bradford Pakistani and Bangladeshi Muslim communities as experiencing many socio-economic and cultural problems. The programme opens by stating that: 'Britain's new underclass is Asian and it is Muslim. A once tightly knit community is now in crisis, with drug abuse, crime and family breakdown on the increase' (BBC, 1993).

The programme highlighted the widening gap between first- and second-generation Muslims as a crucial problem leading to an increase in crime in their community. However, this is established against a backdrop of great social deprivation and poverty. Socio-economic factors were also seen to be instrumental to the Bradford riots in 2001. *The Cantle Report* (Cantle, 2001) focused on the milieu in which the riots occurred, which was marked by dire social and economic conditions and where the local Asian community felt an intense sense of geographical, cultural and political marginalisation. These factors, alongside others, have contributed to a growing criminalisation of Britain's South Asian Muslims during the latter part of the 1980s and continuing into the 1990s. Several events have illustrated how this criminalisation developed: the Salman Rushdie affair, the Bradford riots and the role of the media.

The Salman Rushdie affair

Modood (1990b) highlights how Muslim groups (referring specifically to those of Pakistani and Bangladeshi origin) have become more assertive, politically active and organised as a consequence of the Rushdie affair. In 1988/89, Salman Rushdie's novel, *The Satanic verses* (Rushdie, 1988), caused outrage among most of the leaders of Britain's two million Muslims. Rushdie's book was considered to be a great blasphemy of Islam; many Muslims argued that it slandered their faith and conveyed a hatred of Islam as Rushdie lashed out at the Prophet and his family. What followed changed the nature of responses to Muslims, and consequently Asians, in British society, marking the beginning of a visible and political Muslim presence in British discourse.

On Tuesday, 31 January 1989, a rally in London's Hyde Park involved 8,000 Muslims, many of whom were burning copies of the highly controversial novel. Banners at the rally proclaimed, 'Rushdie is a son of Satan!' and 'Kill the bastard!' (Ruthven, 1990, p 2). Salman Rushdie had committed one of the worst crimes against Islam; he had not only blasphemed it, but had also attacked Islamic identity, and therefore his punishment was to be his life. Ayatollah Ruhollah Khomeini later used a broadcast on Radio Teheran to order 'all zealous Muslims to execute' Salman Rushdie:

> In the name of God Almighty … I would like to inform all the intrepid Muslims in the world that the author of the book entitled *The Satanic Verses*, which has been compiled, printed and published in opposition to Islam, the Prophet and the Koran, has been sentenced to death. (*The Guardian*, 8 November 1990, p 21)

This was a time when all 'zealous' Muslims, worldwide, emphasised their religious and political strength. The display of enraged Muslims protesting en masse had never before been witnessed in British society and, along with the death sentence proclaimed on Salman Rushdie by Ayatollah Khomeini, was to be a historical and significant moment. Religious fanaticism became associated with the Muslim faith, with its followers increasingly considered a potentially dangerous population. No longer were Asian communities (in particular, Pakistanis and Bangladeshis) or Muslims considered 'passive' immigrant settlers. Instead, the event led to widespread awareness of Britain's 'quiet' minority group (Pakistani and Bangladeshi Muslims) as potentially dangerous to the fabric of British society.

The burning of *The Satanic verses* (in 1989) and the Muslim-led rallies against the book were based on religious certitude. The protest by Muslims signified how they felt their faith and Islamic identity had been blasphemed by Salman Rushdie and accepted by white British society, who allowed the book to be published, and also the legal system, which refused to prosecute Rushdie on blasphemy charges. For Ruthven (1990), the Rushdie affair was symptomatic of a crisis based on the divide between Western and Muslim countries; between secular and religious cultures. Britain's Muslim population became intensely aware of their cultural and religious difference from white, Western,

British society, and the associated discrimination and disadvantage this brought.

The Bradford riots

The 1995 riots in Bradford also contributed to negative images of the Pakistani and Bangladeshi Muslim communities. The riots were not based on religious sentiment, but were a conflict between the police and Pakistani/Bangladeshi males, in the context of a 'severe loss of confidence in the police' along with provocative and unreasonable police action (Bradford Congress, 1996). The Bradford Congress (1996) documented that the key trigger to the 1995 riots in the Manningham area of Bradford was police intervention against a 'noisy group' of young Asian males playing football in the street.

The riots represented the pinnacle of issues regarding criminality by Pakistani and Bangladeshi young men. They were considered the faction of the Muslim population who were out of control, living on the edge of society and to be fully subsumed members of a criminal class. The 'cultural gap' within this Muslim community, the conflict between the elders and the youth, was seen as being the cause of the riots and the corresponding criminality. Senior police officers in the area were all too ready to place the blame on the Pakistani and Bangladeshi community, as a series of commentators believed the young people were 'rising up as much against society and elders as against the police.... They have lost in some way their ties with their old religion and their country, yet they feel themselves alienated within Western culture' (Wilkinson, *The Times*, 12 June 1995, p 1).

However, we must recognise the socio-economic problems associated with the Pakistani and Bangladeshi community in Bradford. The decline of industry in the region led to more than half of the Pakistani and Bangladeshi young men in the area being unemployed, with few opportunities of gaining employment in the future (*The Guardian*, 15 July 1995, p 20). It can be argued that issues of cultural conflict within the Pakistani and Bangladeshi community have been facilitated by socio-economic disadvantage, as second- and third-generation young people are reluctant to believe solely in the Islamic faith, which promises that 'Allah will provide'. Many of these young people have become disaffected by the opportunities available to them in British society, and therefore seek their own rewards.

There has been a growing awareness of the involvement of Asian males in criminal activities. FitzGerald (1995) identified that crime rates among minority groups, particularly Asians, were rising. FitzGerald (1998, p 171) later confirmed this view by stating that:

> Pakistanis and Bangladeshis are much younger than the black groups and larger numbers than previously are just about now hitting the peak period for offending.... We are, therefore, likely to see an upsurge in rates of criminal activity among these groups for years to come – although it will continue to be masked as long as it is subsumed within an omnibus 'Asian' category.

However, for Chaudhury (1995, p 4), such demographic evidence cannot be used to predict a rise of criminality among Pakistani and Bangladeshi communities, as he argued:

> There's always been a higher proportion of teenagers among certain Asian groups, so if we were to have an explosion in crime among them then we would have had it by now. It has not happened. What is happening is that as time goes by we will see changes. We will have young people of Asian origin not being so locked into traditional ways and communities.

The rising criminality of Pakistani and Bangladeshi young men, emphasised by the Bradford riots, identified internal community conflicts between the first and second generations, and also between those of strong and weak Islamic faith. Some of the young men were engaged with, and supported, the sex work and drug trade in a red-light area of Manningham Lane, Bradford, whereas many others, those of strong Islamic faith, strongly opposed such activities, protesting and acting as vigilantes by confronting and driving out the prostitutes in the area. There was a definite divide within the Pakistani and Bangladeshi community, based on cultural, religious and generational conflict. However, it would be inaccurate to assume that this was the entire basis for the riots, as Pakistanis and Bangladeshis were in conflict with the police, similar to African-Caribbean young men 20 years earlier. Hence, in similar vein, the media criminalised Pakistani and Bangladeshi young men as a consequence of the riots.

It is the East meets West scenario, as was identified with the Rushdie affair in 1989, a clashing of cultures, cultural hybridity, a crisis of identity, that was considered to be at the heart of the riotous and deviant behaviour of Pakistani and Bangladeshi young men. In contrast to the Bradford riots of 1995, the 2001 disorders in Oldham, Burnley and

Bradford appeared to be a 'confused series of well-publicised violent "racist" clashes and attacks against people and property involving Asian and white young people' (Webster, 2007, p 103).

It was believed and feared by the Asian communities that the British National Party (BNP) and/or the National Front were planning to march in these Asian areas. The racial tensions and array of deprived socio-economic factors within these localities were well documented as the causes that led to the riots. Ironically, the 2001 riots occurred before 9/11 and yet the image of riotous, assertive, aggressive and political Asian young people had already been embedded. Numerous commentators and reports on the riots discussed the breakdown of 'community cohesion', 'segregation', a lack of faith in the police, the abandonment of multicultural policies at a local level and deteriorating race relations as all contributing to the riots (Kundnani, 2001; Ouseley, 2001; Ritchie, 2001; Cantle, 2002; Denham, 2002; McGhee, 2003; Webster, 2003; Burnett, 2004; Worley, 2005).

Bradford has been described as a 'racial tinderbox' (Bakare, 2011), where the Asian community are estranged from the local white working-class communities. This was starkly seen a decade after the 2001 riots as the English Defence League marched through Bradford in August 2010. Ouseley's (2001) vision of a harmonious community in Bradford is a long way from the reality, as the white and Asian communities live in a disparate and segregated manner. However, the racial tensions are not purely based on white–Asian or white–black dichotomies. Darcus Howe's (2004) documentary called *Who you callin' a Nigger?* clearly portrayed the multi-ethnic dimensions of racism in Britain, as he focused on the intra-Asian and intra-black racisms that have manifested throughout minority ethnic communities. In addition, he highlights the conflict and prejudices that exist between distinct minority ethnic communities. Such divergence was seen in the Handsworth riots of 2005 between the African-Caribbean and Pakistani communities. The riot began as a consequence of rumours of the rape of a 14-year-old Jamaican girl by a Pakistani shopkeeper. Hence, the nature of urban disorder has developed in line with multi-ethnic growth in Britain.

The role of the media

Mass media technologies have been used both to expand terrorist agendas and to criminalise British Asians and Muslims alike. Since the mid-1990s, a wide range of media tools have highlighted problematic issues within the Asian community. From the World Wide Web and news broadsheets to film and television, there have been continual professions of anti-Muslim sentiment. The power and influence of these various forms of communicative media has been intrinsic in the criminalisation of Islam.

The growth of mass media technologies has opened and widened the terrorist net in terms of infiltration and obtaining support for its activities; 'Al-Qaida itself says that 50% of its war is conducted through the media' (Manningham-Buller, 2006, pp 1–2). This is indeed demonstrated by video footage of Osama bin Laden and the chilling video wills of British suicide bombers. Such material has been downloaded onto the internet and translated into numerous languages, ensuring mass coverage. Furthermore, Islamic propaganda via satellite television has also made its mark on a massive, global level.

British film and TV has also contributed to the imagery of religious fanaticism, cultural and religious conflict among Britain's Muslim communities, as well as the growth of criminality among Asian young people. *My son the fanatic* (in 1997) was one of the first contemporary portrayals of a second-generation Pakistani young man turning to fundamentalist Islam. The converted young man is part of a group of vigilantes who set about trying to 'clean up' the local area from Western evils, such as drugs and prostitution. More recent examples of British representations of British Muslims have similarly shown young, second-generation Pakistanis being highly discontent with Western, British society, namely, their sense of marginalisation coupled with their political consciousness and sense of religious/cultural victimisation.

The highly controversial Channel 4 film, *Britz* (in 2007), depicts a second-generation British Muslim woman as a suicide bomber. *Britz* tells the story of a brother and sister, Sohail and Nasima, as they are 'pulled in different directions by their conflicting personal experiences in post-9/11 Britain' (Channel 4, 2007). Sohail, a law student, signs up with MI5. His sister, a medical student, becomes Britain's first female suicide bomber. Nasima's motivations were based on her sense of political marginalisation as well as the appalling stigma she felt was imposed upon British Muslims as fundamentalists endorsing terrorist and extremist activities. Such sentiments are portrayed in Ed Husain's (2007) fictional book, *The Islamist*, where a young man turns to extremism as a consequence of his treatment as a Muslim post-9/11.

Islamophobia has also been fuelled by fascist political parties such as the BNP, who have produced an array of propaganda that focuses on the 'threat of Islam'. Such propaganda propagates strong statements from Enoch Powell's 'rivers of blood' speech, where immigrants, in this case, Muslims, are depicted as Islamic extremists and welfare scroungers who are infiltrating British society. In the wake of the global terrorist attacks in New York and London, such discourses have deeply stigmatised British Muslims.

Conclusion

The 21st century has witnessed a change in British rhetoric regarding its Asian communities. As highlighted earlier, there has been a process of criminalisation of Asian Muslims in Britain, which is grounded in key events over the past two decades. The responses to this new folk devil have been in the form of extensive draconian policies, such as the Terrorism Act 2000, Anti-Terrorism, Crime and Security Act 2001, Prevention of Terrorism Act 2005, Terrorism Act 2006 and Identity Card Act 2006, that are purported to aid the fight against global and primarily Islamic terrorism.

In terms of a new racism, it would appear that not only have Asians, especially Muslims, become the modern day folk devil, but also their culture and faith have been criminalised. Moreover, Asian cultures and faith, specifically Islam, have been racialised to the extent that this has led to an obtuse stigmatisation of female victims as well as the criminalisation of Asian young men. Asian cultures and faiths are tarnished as being alien, deviant, tyrannical, extremist and oppressive. It is this racialisation that distinguishes the experience of criminalisation of British Asians from other minority ethnic groups.

References

(NB: References preceded by ★ informed the discussion in the chapter rather than being cited directly.)

Ahmad, F. and Sheriff, S. (2003) 'Muslim women of Europe: welfare needs and responses', *Social Work in Europe*, vol 8, no 1, pp 2–10.

Alexander, C. (2000) *The Asian gang: ethnicity, identity and masculinity*, London: Berg Publisher.

Anwar, M. (1996) *British Pakistanis: demographic, social and economic position*, Coventry: University of Warwick

★Appignanesi, L. and Maitland, S. (1989) *The Rushdie file*, London: Fourth Estate.

★Bagguley, P. and Hussain, Y. (2003) 'The Bradford "riot" of 2001: a preliminary analysis', in C. Barker and M. Tyldesley (eds) *Ninth international conference on alternative futures and popular protest*, Manchester: Manchester Metropolitan University. Available at: http://www.leeds.ac.uk/sociology/people/pb.htm

Back, L. and Keith, M. (1999) *New ethnicities and old racisms*, London: Zed Books.

Bakare, L. (2011) 'A decade after the riots, Bradford is still uneasy about race relations', *The Guardian*, 7 July. Available at: www.guardian.co.uk/commentisfree/2011/jul/07/bradford-riots-race-relations

Ballard, R. (1994) *Desh Pardesh: the South Asian presence in Britain*. London: C. Hurst and Co.

BBC (1993) *Panorama: underclass in Purdah*, 29 March, VHS.

Becker, H. (1967) 'Whose side are we on?', *Social Problems*, vol 13, no 3, pp 239–47.

Bradford Congress (1996) *The Bradford Commission Report: the report of an inquiry into the wider implications of public disorders in Bradford which occurred on 9, 10 and 11 June 1995*, London: Stationery Office.

Brah, A. (1996) *Cartographies of diaspora: contesting identities*, London: Routledge.

Britz (2007) [TV movie] Channel 4, 31 October.

Burnett, J. (2004) 'Community, cohesion and the state', *Race and Class*, vol 45, no 3, pp 1–18.

Cantle, T. (2001) *Community cohesion: a report of the independent review team*, The Cantle Report, London: Home Office.

Chaudhury, V. (1995) 'Violence in Britain: enter the Rajamuffins', *The Guardian*, 19 September, p 4.

Choudry, S. (1996) *Pakistani women's experiences of domestic violence in Great Britain*, Home Office Research Findings 43, London: HMSO.

Cohen, S. (1980 [1972]) *Folk devils and moral panics*, London: Paladin.

Denham, J. (2002) *Building cohesive communities: a report of the Ministerial Group on Public Order and Community Cohesion*, London: Home Office.

European Monitoring Centre on Racism and Xenophobia (2005) *The impact of 7 July 2005 London bomb attacks on Muslim communities in the EU*, Vienna: EUMC.

FitzGerald, M. (1995) 'Asians and crime', Paper presented to the British Criminology Association Conference, University of Loughborough.

FitzGerald, M. (1998) 'Race and the criminal justice system', in T. Blackstone, B. Parekh and P. Sanders (eds) *Race relations in Britain: a developing agenda*, London: Routledge.

Goldson, B. (2007) 'Child criminalisation and the mistake of early intervention', *Criminal Justice Matters*, vol 69, no 1, pp 8–9.

★Goodey, J. (2001) 'The criminalization of British Asian youth: research from Bradford and Sheffield', *Journal of Youth Studies*, vol 4, no 4, pp 429–50.

Hall, S., Critcher, C., Jefferson, T., Clarke, J.N. and Roberts, B. (1978) *Policing the crisis: mugging, the state and law and order*, London: Palgrave Macmillan.

Husain, E. (2007) *The Islamist*, London: Penguin Books.

*Kalra, S.V. (2002) 'Extended view: riots, race and reports: Denham, Cantle, Oldham and Burnley inquiries', *SAGE Race Relations Abstracts*, vol 27, no 4, pp 20–30.

Kundnani, A. (2001) 'From Oldham to Bradford: the violence of the violated', Institute of Race Relations news service, 1 October. Available at: www.irr.org.uk/news/from-oldham-to-bradford-the-violence-of-the-violated/

Mac an Ghaill, M. and Haywood, C. (2005) *Young Bangladeshi people's experiences of transition to adulthood*, York: Joseph Rowntree Foundation. Available at: www.jrf.org.uk/system/files/1859352723.pdf

Mama, A. (2000) 'Women abuse in London's black communities', in K. Owusu (ed) *Black British culture and society*, London: Routledge, pp 89–110.

Manningham-Buller, E. (2006) 'The international terrorist threat to the UK', speech by the Director of the Security Service, Dame Eliza Manningham-Buller, Queen's College, London, 9 November. Available at: https://www.mi5.gov.uk/home/about-us/who-we-are/staff-and-management/director-general/speeches-by-the-director-general/the-international-terrorist-threat-to-the-uk.html

McGhee, D. (2003) 'Moving to "our" common ground: a critical examination of community cohesion discourse in twenty-first century Britain', *Sociological Review*, vol 51, no 3, pp 376–404.

Miles, R. and Brown, M. (2003) *Racism*, London: Routledge.

Modood, T. (1990a) 'Muslims, race and equality in Britain: some post Rushdie affair reflections', *Third text*, vol 4, no 11, pp 127-34.

Modood, T. (1990b) 'British Asian Muslims and the Rushdie affair', *Political Quarterly*, vol 61, no 2, pp 143–60.

*Oldham Independent Review (2001) 'Oldham Independent Review: one Oldham, one future', panel report, Oldham.

ONS (Office for National Statistics) (2012) *Ethnicity and National Identity in England and Wales, 2011*, London: ONS.

Ouseley, H.G. (2001) *Community pride not prejudice*, The Ouseley Report, Bradford: Bradford City Council.

Parmar, A. and Sampson, A. (2005) 'Tackling domestic violence: providing advocacy and support to survivors from Black and other minority ethnic communities', Home Office Development and Practice Report 35, London: Home Office. Available at: http://ndvf.org.uk/files/document/1120/original.pdf

Pearson, G. (1983) *Hooligan: a history of respectable fears*, London: Macmillan.

Platt, L. (2007) *Poverty and ethnicity in the UK*, York: JRF.

Ritchie, D. (2001) *One Oldham one future: Oldham independent report*, Coventry: Institute of Community Cohesion.

Rushdie, S. (1988) *The Satanic verses*, New York, NY: Viking Press.

Ruthven, M. (1990) *A Satanic affair: Salman Rushdie and the rage of Islam*, London: Chatto & Windus.

Wardak, A. (2000) *Social control and deviance: a South Asian community in Scotland*, Aldershot: Ashgate.

Watson, H.S. (1977) *Nations and states: an enquiry into the origins of nations and the politics of nationalism*, London: Methuen.

Webster, C. (1997) 'The construction of British "Asian" criminality', *International Journal of the Sociology of Law*, vol 25, no 1, pp 65–86.

Webster, C. (2003) 'Race, space and fear: imagined geographies of racism, crime, violence and disorder in Northern England', *Capital & Class*, no 80, pp 95–122.

★Webster, C. (2004) 'Policing British Asian communities', in R. Hopkins Burke (ed) *Hard cop/soft cop: dilemmas and debates in contemporary policing*, Cullompton: Willan Publishing.

Webster, C. (2007) *Understanding race and crime*, Berkshire: Open University Press.

★Webster, C. (2009) 'Young people, race and ethnicity', in A. Furlong (ed) *International handbook on youth and young adulthood*, London: Routledge.

★Webster, C. (2012) 'The construction of British Muslim criminality and disorder', in P. Wetherly, M. Farrar, S. Robinson and Y. Valli (eds) *'Islam' in 'the West': key issues in multiculturalism*, Basingstoke: Palgrave.

Werbner, P. (2005) 'The translocation of culture: "community cohesion" and the force of multiculturalism in history', *The Sociological Review*, vol 53, no 4, pp 745–68.

★Wetherly, P., Farrar, M., Robinson, S. and Valli, Y. (eds) *'Islam' in 'the West': key issues in multiculturalism*, Basingstoke: Palgrave.

White, R. (1996) 'Racism, policing and ethnic youth gangs', *Current Issues in Criminal Justice*, vol 7, no 3, pp 302–13.

White, R. and Cunneen, C. (2006) 'Social class, youth crime and justice', in B. Goldson and J. Muncie (eds) *Youth crime and justice*, London: Sage.

Who you callin' a nigger? (2004), directed by Krishnendu Majumdar, with Darcus Howe, TV documentary, Channel 4, 9 August.

Worley, C. (2005) '"It's not about race. It's about community": New Labour and "community cohesion"', *Critical Social Policy: A Journal of Socialist Theory and Practice in Social Welfare*, vol 25, no 4, pp 483–96.

SEVEN

The value(s) of cultural criminology

James Banks and David Moxon

Introduction

Concerned with crime, deviance, modes of social control and related phenomena, cultural criminology positions itself as a response to the abject failure of a mainstream criminology unprepared for the arrival of late modernity (Ferrell et al, 2008). Critical of approaches dominated by ill-developed theory, deterministic methods and statistical testing, cultural criminology has sought to recreate a sociologically inspired criminology that exposes the structures, representations and power relations that underpin crime, inequality and criminal justice. A heady mix of a variety of sociological and criminological traditions, phenomenology, naturalism, interactionism, critical criminology, subcultural theory and postmodern thought constitute and animate this kaleidoscope. Defining cultural criminology has proved somewhat of a challenge for its proponents, who highlight that it is 'less a definitive paradigm than an emergent array of perspectives' (Ferrell, 1999, p 396). As such, it may be best understood as an 'ongoing adventure; a journey that provides new vantage points from which to view the landscape of contemporary culture' (Hayward and Young, 2007, p 103). Nevertheless, from this maelstrom of ideas, perspectives and methodologies, a number of key themes and values may be distinguished.

The chapter begins by outlining some of these key themes and values. Cultural criminology focuses upon, among other things, media representations of crime and deviance, the notion of transgression and its commodification, crime as a source of leisure, and groups on the margins of society. Methodologically, ethnographic approaches are given priority. Exploring and explaining 'crime and deviance' through the eyes of the 'transgressor' is a key feature of cultural criminology and has attracted accusations of researcher bias, romanticism and sympathy for the individuals studied. Nevertheless, a unified response to

Becker's (1967) question 'Whose side are we on?' is unlikely, as cultural criminologists employ and maintain a diverse range of perspectives, values and theoretical traditions.

The second part of the chapter demonstrates how the positions that cultural criminology offers have a long history within the discipline of criminology, and it briefly traces their lineage. Cultural criminologists themselves would not deny this point and, indeed, are quite open in acknowledging their influences. However, we suggest that their influences go back much further than the often-cited post-war work on the sociology of deviance and subcultures. Cultural criminology's novelty, such as it is, lies in its combination of often distinct and divergent elements of previous criminology and their deployment in a contemporary context.

We end by making two observations on the nature of cultural criminology. First, we suggest that, thus far, cultural criminology's self-consciously eclectic deployment of concepts and values from across the criminological canon has not resulted in a unified vision that transcends its constituent theories. While such a project has not been on the cultural criminological agenda, as the perspective matures, this may be one potential avenue of development. Second, within its arsenal, cultural criminology has the weaponry to develop a contemporary understanding of the structural determinants, or what Reiner (2012) calls the 'political economy', of crime. Yet, too often, cultural criminological work is narrowly focused on the micro-level, and thus its utility is narrowed. Moving beyond these (often self-imposed) boundaries is the next challenge for the movement as a whole.

Mapping the contours of cultural criminology

Central to the cultural criminological enterprise is the 'placing of crime and its control in the context of culture: that is viewing both crime and the agencies of control as cultural products – as creative constructs' (Hayward and Young, 2012, p 113). Cultural meanings arise from interactional processes and, as such, crime, deviance, transgression and control are seen as products of human creativity. Of particular interest is how the multiplicity of electronic media communications plays a central role in this construction. Exploring the 'story' of crime and its control as told by the numerous mediated texts and images that create, recreate, reflect and refract the late-modern world is a core component of the cultural venture. Stylised, glamorised, visceral images of crime, criminality and deviance have become central to the cinematic experience; 'reality TV' police shows dominate prime-time viewing, while Rockstar's video game *Grand Theft Auto* has sold 117 million copies worldwide. For cultural criminologists, such televisual, filmic and news media imagery, literature, comic books, computer games and high-end art constitute the experience of crime, self and society. And this commodification of crime and transgression is one of the key features of late modernity.

Indeed, cultural criminologists suggest that the notion of transgression has emerged as a desirable consumer decision, with crime sold as a fashionable cultural symbol (Ferrell et al, 2008). In particular, the rebranding of crime has created a product that is immediately seductive to youth audiences by fusing designer chic with images of criminality and street gang iconography (Hayward, 2004a). However, such imagery can also signify danger and deviance and can evoke fear in others. As Hayward and Yar (2006) recognise, labels and motifs that are valorised by young people also operate as overt signifiers of deviance. Thus, style may simultaneously act as a badge of resistance and be stigmatic. The mediated emergence of the 'chav' may best exemplify this intersection between consumption and style, marginality and social control (Hayward and Yar, 2006). Ridiculed because of their consumer choices, this pejorative label attached to white young people has became synonymous with anti-social behaviour, overbreeding and the seedy belly of the black economy. Much maligned, the 'chav' is marginalised, stigmatised and criminalised because they are deemed aesthetically bankrupt (Ferrell et al, 2008). Indeed, the construction of identity through commodities, with consumption a perceived 'right', can also lead to a 'relative deprivation of identity' for those denied participation (Hayward, 2004b, p 150).

Moreover, the thrill and excitement of transgression itself is increasingly a desirable commodity; 'Crime has been seized upon: it is packaged and marketed to young people as a romantic, exciting, cool and fashionable cultural symbol. It is in this cultural context that transgression becomes a desirable consumer choice' (Fenwick and Hayward, 2000, p 44). Crime and deviance, then, function as leisure options for both those with few other avenues of pleasure, and those who are seeking something 'authentic' and 'real', as opposed to the artificial thrills often offered by the legitimate leisure economy; hedonism and the pursuit of excitement are frequently embedded in acts of transgression. As such, cultural criminologists have analysed the phenomenology of acts in order to better 'tell the story of crime' (Hayward and Young, 2004, pp 270–1). Critical of administrative criminology's construction of the offender as an instrumentally motivated rational decision-maker, cultural criminologists seek to uncover and illuminate the feelings of anger, humiliation, joy and boredom that energise crime and criminality. For Presdee (2000), the carnival of crime represents a release from rationality, embodied in risky acts that thrill, energise and challenge authority.

Exploring those clusters of like-minded individuals on the edge of 'conventional' society has been a major strand of a cultural criminology heavily indebted to works on youth culture and subcultures. Employing *verstehen*-oriented research methodologies, cultural criminologists have used the concept of edgework to examine subcultural groupings' engagement in a variety of illicit acts, from illegal motorbike racing, street fighting and fire-starting to graffiti writing and base jumping (Ferrell, 2001; Ferrell et al, 2001; Librett, 2008). As Lyng (1990, p 857) identifies, edgework activities involve a 'clearly observable threat to one's physical or mental well being or one's sense of an ordered existence'. Consistent within this body of work is the construction of the edgeworker as the transgressor in the illicit act. The groups constituted by such individuals engage in creative, skilful and expressive acts that provide a retreat from the alienating nature of late-modern society. Motivated by the desire for exhilarating experiences that contrast with the monotony of day-to-day life, an 'explosive mix of risk and skill' (Ferrell et al, 2008, p 72) underpins extreme and often illicit voluntary risk-taking, which offers an antidote to the 'unidentifiable forces that rob one of individual choice' (Lyng, 1990, p 870). Sensation-seeking of this type attempts to 'recapture, if momentarily, the lost immediacy of the self-made human experience' (Ferrell, 2004, p 293).

Favouring an ethnographic research orientation, cultural criminologists seek to present a 'sociology of the skin' that unravels the 'lived meanings' (Ferrell, 1997, p 3) of the communities under study through the experiential immersion of the researcher. Responding to the dominance of an orthodox criminology that gives primacy to quantitative data and statistical analysis, they have sought to become 'submerged in the situated logic and emotion' (Ferrell and Hamm, 1998, p 8) of the research subject. Ethnographic methods are considered key to enabling an understanding of the criminal dynamics that motivate and provide meaning to their performance. Cultural criminologists assert that this 'methodology of attentiveness' (Ferrell and Hamm, 1998, p 10) provides researchers with a unique opportunity to explore the contested nature of crime, criminality and criminal justice in the little theatres that constitute everyday life (Ferrell et al, 2008). Methodological engagement with the subjects of study is considered fundamental to an approach that seeks to better understand the structure of inequality and injustice that shapes crime, its control and wider society. It is in this light that the studies of the tiny groups of 'edgeworkers' previously mentioned make sense. Cultural criminologists have also employed immersive ethnographic techniques to study communities as diverse as 'dumpster divers' (Ferrell, 2002), terrorists (Hamm, 2002) and online football supporters (Zaitch and De Leeuw, 2010).

In sum, cultural criminology seeks to reassert a sociologically inspired criminology that can adequately engage with crime and criminal justice in a late-modern world. Culture is placed centre stage, with consumerism, materialism, style and resistance key features of an approach that sees the act of crime as a creative construct. In a 'media-saturated' world (Ferrell and Sanders, 1995), cultural understandings of crime, criminals, deviance and deviants are in constant flux, whereby meaning is continuously constructed, reconstructed, interpreted and reinterpreted. The creative and interactive processes that shape crime and its control are also central to an approach that seeks to understand the phenomenology of the transgressive act. Uncovering the emotions and meanings attached to illicit acts, which are energised by, and generate feelings of, omnipotence, fear, anger and hurt, are key to explaining why individuals may engage in vandalism, theft, destruction and so on. Ethnographic research approaches are employed by researchers seeking to illuminate the lived meanings of deviant groups who operate at the margins of conventional society.

The pre-history of cultural criminology

While cultural criminologists characterise their project as a 'loose federation of outlaw intellectual critiques' (Ferrell, 2007, p 99), it is clear that many of the tenets of cultural criminology have long been a feature of the wider criminological enterprise. Indeed, many of the ideas promoted by cultural criminology have formed part of the mainstream of sociological criminology for well over a century. Cultural criminologists cheerfully acknowledge their debt to their forerunners and generally trace their lineage back to 'the intellectual energy that occurred in the sociology of deviance' (Hayward and Young, 2012, p 114) from the mid-1960s onwards. However, in addition to this, it is possible to see the traces of, among others, Merton, the Chicago school, Gramsci, Durkheim and Marx in the work of cultural criminologists (Presdee, 2004). Our aim here is to sketch just how widely cultural criminology draws upon themes and ideas from the criminological canon, and, thus, how it is informed by the same values as its predecessor perspectives.

Cultural criminology's overall view of crime as a creative construct is clearly influenced by notions of the contingent and the subjective contained within phenomenology and symbolic interactionism, now often referred to under the umbrella heading of social constructionism (Downes and Rock, 2007, p 197). Central here is the notion of labelling, which is most concisely outlined in the famous and oft-quoted passage from Becker (1963, p 4, emphasis in original):

> Social groups create deviance by making the rules whose infraction constitutes deviance, and by applying those rules to particular people and labelling them as outsiders. From this point of view, deviance is *not* a quality of the act the person commits, but rather a consequence of the application by others of rules and sanctions to an 'offender'. The deviant is one to whom the label has been successfully applied; deviant behaviour is behaviour that people so label.

Where cultural criminology has advanced the agenda is in its analyses of the role of contemporary media in constructions of crime and deviance. These analyses focus on computer games and the like, in addition to more conventional concerns with television and film. Analyses of the media are not new within criminology; *Policing the crisis* (Hall et al, 1978) famously outlined the media's role in promoting the moral panic surrounding 'mugging', but the application by cultural criminologists of such ideas to the evolving media landscape is certainly of immense value.

Similarly, cultural criminology's idea of transgression as an increasingly commodified consumer product that confers identity and status resonates with much contemporary sociological analysis, most notably in the criminological arena, with Hall, Winlow and Ancrum's (2008) landmark *Criminal identities and consumer culture*. The riots in England during August 2011, characterised by widespread looting, also produced analyses on these lines. For example, Moxon (2011) identifies how the rioting and looting 'can only be fully comprehended if they are analysed in the context of a society that is becoming increasingly consumerist in its orientation'. Here, the 'opportunistic materialism' (Sumner, 2011) of looters represents conformity to a free-market consumerist society rather than rebellion. Furthermore, this focus is not without precedent in the criminological canon. Indeed, the vision of capitalism, and specifically consumer-led capitalism, as inherently criminogenic is a staple of criminological thought. This ranges from Merton's (1938) idea of ever-expanding consumer desires being unable to be satisfied through socially and legally approved means (picked up by Young's [2003, 2007] notion of 'bulimia'), to the Dutch Marxist Willem Bonger's (1969 [1916]) appreciation that capitalism engenders an egoism and greed right across society, though, of course, it is the egoism and greed of the poor that is more likely to be criminalised. In the early 1970s, Phil Cohen (1972) charted the manner in which the post-war split between an upwardly mobile working class and those left to the declining heavy industries found its representation in the distinct styles of the mods and the rockers. Later *Resistance through rituals* (Hall and Jefferson, 1976) expanded this mode of analysis to account for a whole host of other subcultural groups. Cultural criminology's focus on the meaning of commodities, identity and style must be seen in the light of a considerable pre-existing body of work.

The idea that crime and deviance can serve as a leisure pursuit is also a familiar idea that can be traced back at least as far as 1844 to Friedrich Engels' *The condition of the working class in England* (1987). Engels wrote of the young people of Sheffield's regular Sunday pursuits of sexual liaisons, drinking, dog fighting, gambling, prostitution and arson with the disparaging and condemnatory tone peculiar to Victorian moralists (Engels, 1987, p 216). More recently, as Katz's (1988) seminal work has identified, there are moral and sensual pleasures in 'doing evil' that can underpin deviance. Katz is an avowed influence on cultural criminologists, as is the British strand of subcultural theory, which also posited the deviance-as-leisure perspective. David Downes' work, in particular, has clear echoes in the work of cultural criminologists. He suggested that young working-class people in the UK, with their clear sense of class position and relatively low life expectations, did not suffer from 'strain' or 'status frustration' like their US counterparts, but instead responded to school and work through 'dissociation' (Downes, 1966). In such a context, delinquency became a 'hedonistic response to the anomic strains of dull English life' (Downes and Rock, 2007, p 132). Hargreaves (1967) came to similar conclusions and while he found his 'delinquescents' slightly more oppositional than Downes's, they too were essentially reacting against boredom rather than creating an alternative, 'inverted' set of values, as Albert Cohen (1955) had discovered in the US. Matza's idea of delinquency as willed but intermittent behaviour underpinned by values not dissimilar to conventional ones (Matza and Sykes, 1961; Matza, 1964, 1969) is also clearly of relevance to the cultural project.

Indeed, such is the importance of subcultural theory to the cultural criminological project that it has been suggested that the latter does not depart substantially from the former (Newburn, 2007). This idea is brought into sharp relief when one considers the cultural criminologists' focus on those groups existing 'at the edge' of society and how this is the continuation of a well-established line of work. Over the last five decades or so, a host of sociologically minded criminologists and criminologically minded sociologists have studied a dazzling assortment of subcultural groups. This includes, inter alia, teds (Jefferson, 1976), mods (Cohen, 1972; Hebdige 1976), rockers (Cohen, 1972), skinheads (Clarke, 1976), hippies (Willis, 1976), drug users (Young, 1971; Pearson, 1987), older drug users (Waters, 2009), members of the northern soul scene (Wilson, 2007), football hooligans (Armstrong, 1998), clubbers (Redhead, 1997), bouncers (Hobbs et al, 2003) and working-class entrepreneurs in the informal economy (Hobbs, 1988). Of course, symbolic interactionism, itself following the lead of Chicago sociology, also had a penchant for the study of 'the little social worlds that constitute a society' (Downes and Rock, 2007, p 159) and 'outsider' groups (Becker, 1953). One is reminded of Gouldner's (1962, p 209) famous passage about the symbolic interactionists who were 'at home in the world of hip, Norman Mailer, drug addicts, jazz musicians, cab drivers, prostitutes, night peoples, drifters, grifters and skidders, the cool cats and their kicks'. Seen in this light, the cultural criminologists' fascination with illegal motorbike racers, street fighters, fire-starters, graffiti artists and base jumpers seems less outré and more part of a long and venerable tradition.[1]

In similar fashion, the privileging of ethnographic research methods, which is at the methodological heart of the cultural criminological project, can also be traced back through the history of the discipline. At the birth of 'industrialised' sociology (Downes and Rock, 2007, p 47), the Chicago scholars promoted the epistemological view of knowledge as grounded, of truth as local and situated. How else, then, to attain knowledge or truth without small-scale, in-depth analyses of particular groups and subgroups; Park enjoined his Chicago scholars to go out and get the 'seat of [their] pants dirty in real research' (Park, quoted in McKinney, 1966, p 71). Of course, the lead of the Chicago sociologists was followed by symbolic interactionists and, later, subcultural theorists. As Becker (1998, p 53) put it when discussing the 'so-called labelling theory revolution', it 'directs us to understand how the situation looks to the actors in it, to find out what they think is going on so that we will understand what goes into the making of their activity'. Once again, it is clear just how far the values of cultural criminology are part of the fabric of mainstream sociological criminology.

Two observations on the cultural criminological project

Cultural criminology, then, is rooted in long traditions familiar to any student of criminology. Where does this leave the enterprise? In the first place, it is of course vulnerable to many of the same criticisms that have been levelled against those perspectives that have influenced it. However, a clutch of specific criticisms have also been mounted against cultural criminology. Of particular note are O'Brien's (2005) concerns about cultural criminologists' general imprecision about the concept of 'culture' and the unhelpful dichotomy that is sometimes set up between culture and subculture. O'Brien also registers unease at cultural criminology's political rather than analytical orientation. Cultural criminology's tendency to romanticise crime has also been commented upon (Tierney, 2010, pp 357–8). But, besides this, given the manner in which cultural criminology embraces a plethora of long-standing themes and ideas from the criminological canon, we would make two observations regarding its future direction.

First, we would suggest that cultural criminology has yet to produce a unified vision that transcends its constituent theories. Of course, this has not been a primary aim of a perspective that celebrates its diversity and eclecticism. Yet, at root, some of the elements that go into the cultural criminological stew are only dubiously compatible. Many of the theories that cultural criminology mines make distinctive contributions that rest upon fundamentally different conceptions of the social world (Wright and Randall, 1978). For example, it is no easy task to reconcile the functionalist perspectives of, say, anomie theory with the more conflict-oriented Marxist and radical elements. Thus, one potential challenge for a maturing cultural criminology might be to produce a coherent and robust theoretical position that can form the basis for future analysis. Of course, this is no straightforward task, and many cultural criminologists may not even see such an end as desirable. Indeed, one might even argue that cultural criminology is *defined* by its theoretical bricolage and utilisation of varied perspectives. Yet, without some kind of rigorous synthesis, cultural criminology will simply repeat the mistakes of the past and will not move beyond its component perspectives. Furthermore, there is a risk of incoherence if fundamentally different perspectives are not somehow dialectically reconciled into a new whole or wholes.

Second, it is important that the cultural criminological project takes full account of macro-level, structural factors in its exploration of contemporary criminality. One of the most penetrating criticisms of cultural criminology is that it tends to neglect economic and structural factors (Reiner, 2012, p 304). Indeed, as Sumner (2004, p 25) suggests, 'economics and politics, and the "social"' are not high on the cultural agenda, and 'to talk of capitalism, state and class is ... distinctly unfashionable'. Yet, without at least some consideration of these issues, the cultural criminological project is inherently partial and self-limiting.

For Reiner, the concept of 'political economy' should be central to analyses of crime, but this does not require the sidelining of other factors. He suggests that the notion of political economy:

> is intended to signify a broader approach than simply spotlighting the significance of the economic, let alone economic determinism. The economic must be seen as part of a complex set of interdependencies with individual, moral, cultural and other social dimensions. It is this dialectical interplay of levels of analysis that the label 'political economy' is intended to convey. (Reiner, 2012, p 302)

In short, 'political economy stands for a holistic approach ... verstehen and structural processes are each necessary elements of explanation, complementary not contradictory' (Reiner, 2012, p 328). Such an approach is evident in the classic works on political economy by writers such as Smith, John Stuart Mill and Marx (with whom the term 'political economy' became largely associated).

One issue with the Marxian work that dominated the 1970s in the wake of *The new criminology* (Taylor et al, 1973) was that it tended to bracket off an 'existentialist appreciation of the "seductions of crime" from the perspectives of offenders and more generally downplay[ed] cultural, interpretive and symbolic dimensions' (Reiner, 2012, p 304).[2] Cultural criminology, with its determination to foreground the cultural, interpretive and symbolic, can therefore be seen as part of the long reaction against such trends. Yet, there is a sense that this, in turn, has gone too far, and there is now 'an unjustifiable neglect of structural and macro-social dimensions' (Reiner, 2012, p 304). This is problematic, for, as Reiner suggests, 'without the holistic sensibility that political economy connotes it is impossible to explain patterns and trends in crime and control' (Reiner, 2012, p 304).

The irony is that cultural criminology is already in possession of concepts that allow for just such a holistic approach. Most notable is Young's (2003, 2007) notion of 'bulimia', which, as noted earlier, is a development of Merton's anomie. Indeed, Young has talked persuasively of the need for analysis to properly reconcile agency and structure in his famous discussion of Katz and Merton. As he puts it:

> I think Katz throws the baby out with the bathwater, simply to invert the conventional wisdom by highlighting agency and rejecting structure. Our job is to emphasize both structure and agency and trace how each constitutes the other.... The theory of bulimia which I have proposed involves incorporation and rejection, cultural inclusion and social exclusion, as with Merton, but it goes further than this, emphasizing that this combination of acceptance followed by rejection generates a dynamic of resentment of great intensity. *It is Merton with energy, it is Katz with structure.* (Young, 2003, p 408, emphasis in original)

Yet, too often, cultural criminological work emphasises Katz (and agency) at the expense of Merton (and structure). The manner in which this lacuna is addressed over the coming years will ultimately define cultural criminology's own legacy to future generations of criminologists.

Conclusion

None of this is intended to diminish the value of cultural criminology. The values that inform and shape cultural criminological research are certainly diverse and, at times, incoherent and incompatible. However, its attempt to apply long-standing ideas to the contemporary world, updating them in the process, is of huge value, as is the way it shines a light on what would otherwise be ignored capsules of the social world. Such research has been criticised for its romantic, sympathetic and biased depiction of criminals, deviants and transgressors. Yet, in its defence, it may be 'something of a solution to say that over the years each "one-sided" study will provoke further studies that gradually enlarge our grasp of all the relevant facets of [crime, deviance and modes of social control]' (Becker, 1967, p 247). Furthermore, its reassertion of a sociologically informed criminology offers an important counterpoint to administrative criminology. That said, one does wonder whether the cultural criminologists' railing against administrative criminology (Young, 2011) has more relevance in the US than in the UK, where criminologists of a sociological bent are still well represented, at least in the academy. Indeed, one need not be a cultural criminologist to remain unconvinced by the administrative project.

Moreover, cultural criminologists' cheerful acknowledgement of their influences does make one question their eagerness to portray their project as one of intellectual rebelliousness. As we have shown in this chapter, the values and ideas that drive cultural criminology are a long and established part of the sociological criminological mainstream. What is novel in the cultural project is the style, the self-conscious and knowing bricolage, the flair and the breathless flamboyance, rather than the substance.

Thus, it is important not to get too carried away. Cultural criminology simply does what much good criminology has been doing for many years by locating crime and the responses to it within cultural dynamics, often at the micro scale. Yet, in the final analysis, cultural criminology can appear a little overambitious at times; it deploys a vast range of intellectual resources but not always in a systematic, robust fashion. And, at the same time, it often sidelines political economy to its own detriment, even though it has developed the resources to engage more fully with it. One would hope that these tensions can be resolved.

Notes

[1.] Indeed, when Becker (1967) asks 'Whose side are we on?', the cultural criminologist may well respond that he is on the side of the 'outsider'.

[2.] *The new criminology* (Taylor et al, 1973) itself attempted to avoid this with its call for a 'fully social theory' of crime; the best example arguably remains Hall et al's (1978) *Policing the crisis*, with its consideration of macro, middle range and micro levels (Reiner, 2012, p 303).

References

Armstrong, G. (1998) *Football hooligans: knowing the score*, Oxford: Berg.

Becker, H. (1953) 'Becoming a marihuana user', *American Journal of Sociology*, vol 59, pp 235–42.

Becker, H. (1963) *Outsiders: studies in sociology of deviance*, New York, NY: The Free Press.

Becker, H. (1967) 'Whose side are we on?', *Social Problems*, vol 14, no 3, pp 234–47.

Becker, H. (1998) *Tricks of the trade: how to think about your research while you're doing it*, Chicago, IL: University of Chicago Press.

Bonger, W. (1969 [1916]) *Criminality and economic conditions*, Bloomington, IN: Indiana University Press.

Clarke, J. (1976) 'The skinheads and the magical recovery of community', in S. Hall and T. Jefferson (eds) *Resistance through rituals: youth subcultures in post-war Britain*, London: Hutchinson, pp 99–102.

Cohen, A.K. (1955) *Delinquent boys: the culture of the gang*, New York, NY: The Free Press.

Cohen, P. (1972) *Sub-cultural conflict and working class community*, Working Papers in Cultural Studies No 2, Birmingham: University of Birmingham.

Downes, D. (1966) *The delinquent solution: a study in subcultural theory*, London: Routledge and Kegan Paul.

Downes, D. and Rock, P. (2007) *Understanding deviance: a guide to the sociology of crime and rule breaking* (5th edn), Oxford: Oxford University Press.

Engels, F. (1987) *The condition of the working class in England*, London: Penguin.

Fenwick, M. and Hayward, K. (2000) 'Youth crime, excitement and consumer culture: the reconstruction of aetiology in contemporary theoretical criminology', in J. Pickford (ed) *Youth justice: theory and practice*, London: Cavendish.

Ferrell, J. (1997) 'Criminological verstehen: inside the immediacy of crime', *Justice Quarterly*, vol 14, no 1, pp 3–23.

Ferrell, J. (1999) 'Cultural criminology', *Annual Review of Sociology*, vol 25, pp 395–418.

Ferrell, J. (2001) *Tearing down the streets: adventures in urban anarchy*, Basingstoke: Palgrave.

Ferrell, J. (2002) *Empire of scrounge*, New York, NY: New York University Press.

Ferrell, J. (2004) 'Boredom, crime and criminology', *Theoretical Criminology*, vol 8, no 3, pp 287–302.

Ferrell, J. (2007) 'For a ruthless cultural criticism of everything existing', *Crime, Media, Culture*, vol 3, no 1, pp 91–100.

Ferrell, J. and Hamm, M. (1998) 'True confessions: crime, deviance and field research', in J. Ferrell and M. Hamm (eds) *Ethnography at the edge: crime, deviance and field research*, Boston, MA: Northeastern University Press, pp 2–19.

Ferrell, J. and Sanders, S. (1995) *Cultural criminology*, Boston, MA: Northeastern University Press.

Ferrell, J., Milovanovic, D. and Lyng, S. (2001) 'Edgework, media practices and the elongation of meaning: a theoretical ethnography of the Bridge Day event', *Theoretical Criminology*, vol 5, no 2, pp 177–202.

Ferrell, J., Hayward, K. and Young, J. (2008) *Cultural criminology: an invitation*, London: Sage.

Gouldner, A. (1962) 'Anti-minotaur: the myth of a value-free sociology', *Social Problems*, vol 9, no 3, pp 199–213.

Hall, S. and Jefferson, T. (eds) (1976) *Resistance through rituals: youth subcultures in post-war Britain*, London: Hutchinson.

Hall, S., Critcher, C., Jefferson, T., Clarke, J. and Roberts, B. (1978) *Policing the crisis: mugging, the state and law and order*, London: MacMillan.

Hall, S., Winlow, S. and Ancrum, C. (2008) *Criminal identities and consumer culture*, Cullompton: Willan.

Hamm, M.S. (2002) *In bad company: America's terrorist underground*, Boston, MA: Northeastern University Press.

Hargreaves, D. (1967) *Social relations in a secondary school*, London: Routledge and Kegan Paul.

Hayward, K. (2004a) *City limits: crime, culture and the urban experience*, London: Glasshouse.

Hayward, K. (2004b) 'Consumer culture and crime in late modernity', in C. Sumner (ed) *The Blackwell companion to criminology*, Oxford: Blackwell.

Hayward, K. and Yar, M. (2006) 'The "chav" phenomenon: consumption, media and the construction of a new underclass', *Crime, Media, Culture*, vol 2, no 1, pp 9–28.

Hayward, K. and Young, J. (2004) 'Cultural criminology: some notes on the script', *Theoretical Criminology*, vol 8, no 3, pp 259–73.

Hayward, K. and Young, J. (2007) 'Cultural criminology', in M. McGuire, R. Morgan and R. Reiner (eds) *The Oxford handbook of criminology* (4th edn), Oxford: Oxford University Press.

Hayward, K. and Young, J. (2012) 'Cultural criminology', in M. McGuire, R. Morgan and R. Reiner (eds) *The Oxford handbook of criminology* (5th edn), Oxford: Oxford University Press.

Hebdige, D. (1976) 'The meaning of mod', in S. Hall and T. Jefferson (eds) *Resistance through rituals: youth subcultures in post-war Britain*, London: Hutchinson, pp 87–98.

Hobbs, D. (1988) *Doing the business: entrepreneurship, the working class, and detectives in the East End of London*, Oxford: Oxford University Press.

Hobbs, D., Hadfield, P., Lister, S. and Winlow, S. (2003) *Bouncers: violence and governance in the night-time economy*, Oxford: Clarendon Press.

Jefferson, T. (1976) 'Cultural responses of the teds: the defence of space and status', in S. Hall and T. Jefferson (eds) *Resistance through rituals: youth subcultures in post-war Britain*, London: Hutchinson, pp 81–6.

Katz, J. (1988) *Seductions of crime: moral and sensual attractions in doing evil*, New York, NY: Basic.

Librett, M. (2008) 'Wild pigs and outlaws: the kindred worlds of policing and outlaw bikers', *Crime, Media, Culture*, vol 4, no 2, pp 257–69.

Lyng, S.G. (1990) 'Edgework: a social psychological analysis of voluntary risk taking', *American Journal of Sociology*, vol 95 (January), pp 851–86.

Matza, D. (1964) *Delinquency and drift*, New York, NY: Wiley.

Matza, D. (1969) *Becoming deviant*, Englewood Cliffs, NJ: Prentice Hall.

Matza, D. and Sykes, G. (1961) 'Juvenile delinquency and subterranean values', *American Sociological Review*, vol 26, no 5, pp 712–19.

McKinney, J.C. (1966) *Constructive typology and social theory*, New York, NY: Appleton-Century-Crofts.

Merton, R.K. (1938) 'Social structure and anomie', *American Sociological Review*, vol 3, pp 672–82.

Moxon, D. (2011) 'Consumer culture and the 2011 riots', *Sociological Research Online*, vol 16, no 4.

Newburn, T. (2007) *Criminology*, Cullompton: Willan.

O'Brien, M. (2005) 'What is *cultural* about cultural criminology?', *British Journal of Criminology*, vol 45, no 5, pp 599–612.

Pearson, G. (1987) *The new heroin users*, London: Basil Blackwell.

Presdee, M. (2000) *Cultural criminology and the carnival of crime*, London: Routledge.

Presdee, M. (2004) 'Cultural criminology: the long and winding road', *Theoretical Criminology*, vol 8, no 3, pp 275–85.

Redhead, S. (1997) *Subcultures to clubcultures: an introduction to popular cultural studies*, Oxford: Blackwell.

Reiner, R. (2012) 'Casino capital's crimes: political economy, crime and criminal justice', in M. McGuire, R. Morgan and R. Reiner (eds) *The Oxford handbook of criminology* (5th edn), Oxford: Oxford University Press.

Sumner, C. (2004) 'The social nature of crime and deviance', in C. Sumner (ed) *The Blackwell companion to criminology*, Oxford: Blackwell.

Sumner, C. (2011) 'Riots, aggravated shopping and 30 years of opportunism', *CrimeTalk*. Available at: www.crimetalk.org.uk/archive/section-list/38-frontpage-articles/427-riots-aggravated-shopping-and-30-years-of-opportunism-.html (accessed 14 February 2010.

Taylor, I., Walton, P. and Young, J. (1973) *The new criminology: for a social theory of deviance*, London: Routledge and Kegan Paul.

Tierney, J. (2010) *Criminology: theory and context* (3rd edn), Harlow: Pearson.

Waters, J. (2009) 'Illegal drug use among older adults', unpublished PhD thesis, University of Sheffield.

Willis, P.E. (1976) 'The cultural meaning of drug use', in S. Hall and T. Jefferson (eds) *Resistance through rituals: youth subcultures in post-war Britain*, London: Hutchinson, pp 106–18.

Wilson, A. (2007) *Northern soul: music, drugs and subcultural identity*, Cullompton: Willan.

Wright, C.W. and Randall, S.C. (1978) 'Contrasting conceptions of deviance in sociology: functionalism and labelling theory', *British Journal of Criminology*, vol 18, no 3, pp 217–31.

Young, J. (1971) *The drugtakers: the social meaning of drug use*, London: Paladin.

Young, J. (2003) 'Merton with energy, Katz with structure: the sociology of vindictiveness and the criminology of transgression', *Theoretical Criminology*, vol 7, no 3, pp 389–414.

Young, J. (2007) *The vertigo of late modernity*, London: Sage.

Young, J. (2011) *The criminological imagination*, Cambridge: Polity.

Zaitch, D. and De Leeuw, T.A.J. (2010) 'Fighting with images: the production and consumption of violence among football supporters on the Internet', in K. Hayward and M. Presdee (eds) *Framing crime: cultural criminology and the image*, London: Routledge.

EIGHT

Justifying 'green' criminology: values and 'taking sides' in an ecologically informed social science

Gary R. Potter

Introduction

The question 'Whose side are we on?' (Becker, 1967) is arguably more fundamental and more nuanced for green criminology than elsewhere in the study of crime. More nuanced because green criminology focuses on environmental problems, therefore considering conflicts between humanity and nature alongside the dimensions of social conflict normally implicated in the question. More fundamental because the consideration of value positions inherent in the question is essential to the very definition of green criminology, shaping not only the remit of the field and the approaches taken within it, but also its relationships with the parent subject 'criminology' and the politically charged label 'green'.

In green criminology, broadly defined as 'criminological work that focuses ... on environmental harm' (White, 2008, p 6), an obvious assumption is that concern for environmental issues is a value that influences, if not defines, those working in the field. It is inferred that green criminologists are on the 'side' of nature. This leaves green criminology open to criticism for being overly ideological and overtly political, and therefore particularly prone to accusations of bias. Further, the perceived focus of green criminology – prioritising a concern for nature over social problems and often moving well beyond legal definitions of 'crime' – leads to accusations that it is not really the proper business of *criminology* at all. At the very least, concerns over the value positions inherent within green criminology have contributed to its remaining a niche specialism, kept apart from (and sometimes shunned by) the criminological mainstream.

This chapter examines value positions within green criminology. Primarily, the aim is to explore these positions and consider how they have shaped this field. A further aim, however, is to rise above the ideologically charged 'values' questions to draw out lessons applicable to criminology as a whole. The central contention is that despite the facts that (a) the values of individual researchers inevitably shape their work, and (b) much green criminology is unashamedly ideological, green criminology should not be dismissed as fundamentally politicised or biased. On the contrary, when we strip away the value positions to the bare science that underpins green criminology, we are left with an important observation: a green perspective can contribute greatly to our general understanding of crime. However, there is no inherent need to distance ourselves from ideological perspectives: green criminology fits squarely within a criminological tradition that centralises value positions and wilfully takes sides, supporting the vulnerable against the unchecked power of state and corporate institutions.

What is green criminology?

It helps to begin with a consideration of what green criminology actually *is*, as debates over the definition, remit and even the label attached to this area of study illustrate the centrality of value questions to green criminology. We saw earlier a definition that spoke of a focus on environmental harm. In a similar vein, green criminology has been defined as 'the analysis of environmental harms from a criminological perspective, or the application of criminological thought to environmental issues' (Potter, 2012a). Such definitions make it clear that the 'green' in green criminology pertains to the environment. These definitions also agree in implying that there is something in criminology that can usefully be applied to environmental issues. However, while such definitions encompass the majority of green criminological work, they are not exhaustive. At the very least, both are problematic in their simplicity, presupposing a common understanding of what a criminological approach might be while also talking about a semantically ambiguous environmental *harm* rather than environmental *crime*. They are also somewhat narrow in approach, in that they imply a green criminology that focuses on environmental harm *as* crime, rather than recognising a broader range of ways that green issues may relate to criminology, such as looking at environmental harm as a *cause* of crime (Stretesky and Lynch, 2004; Lynch and Stretesky, 2007; Potter, 2012b) or considering the environmental impact of the mechanisms of the criminal justice system (Lynch and Stretesky, 2010).

Even where definitions do agree that green criminology entails the study of environmental harm, this still leaves the question of the sorts of environmental harm we might be talking about. To help illustrate the answer, we can turn to two established typologies of green crime. First, we can draw on White's (2005; 2008, p 99) distinction between 'brown', 'green' and 'white' issues, where: 'brown' incorporates 'dirty' issues, including pollution and the disposal of hazardous waste; 'green' issues include loss of wildlife, habitats and bio-diversity, logging and deforestation, loss of ozone layer, global warming, and so on; and 'white' covers genetic modification, the development of pathogens, animal testing and other scientific experiments and technological developments involving life forms. This essentially outlines a range of examples of how human interaction with the natural world causes harm to the environment that might be labelled as 'crime'.

A second useful typology is Carrabine et al's (2009) distinction between primary and secondary green crimes. Primary green crimes are those that result in 'direct (primary) damage and destruction caused to environment and species' (Carrabine et al, 2009, p 394). Secondary, or symbiotic, green crime is defined 'as growing out of illegal or negligent government or corporate activity, which can even include the flouting of rules set by such bodies themselves to regulate environmentally sensitive activities' (Carrabine et al, 2009, p 394). Examples include 'state violence against oppositional groups' and 'hazardous waste and organized crime' (Carrabine et al, 2009, pp 394–6). This category of secondary green crimes adds a whole new dimension: we are no longer concerned only with environmental harm *as* crime, but also with other crimes related to attempts to regulate environmental harm. Together, these categories encompass much of the work of green criminologists to date, including well-established examples like illegal logging or pollution (both primary green crimes) and organised crime involvement in disposing of hazardous waste or the trade in endangered species (secondary green crimes). However, it should be noted that this still fails to encompass all examples of what might be considered as green criminological work.

Value positions within green criminology

The preceding discussion begins to illustrate the range of issues that green criminologists may study. When taken together with our earlier definitions, we see a degree of common agreement, but also some differing views, on what does and does not fall within the remit of green criminology. Some of the difference in opinion here reflects the different value positions, as well as different areas of interest, of individual academics. While it is fair to say that most people who work within the field of environmental criminology have some interest in 'green' issues reflecting some personal value position, the nature of these value positions and the ways in which they influence the work of individual scholars vary widely. This is acknowledged within the literature in two key areas of debate that illustrate the relationship between value positions and understandings of what 'green criminology' encompasses. One of these reflects wider debates over what it is to be 'green'; the other reflects broader criminological discussion about the definition of crime and the proper subject matter of the criminologist. We will explore this second issue first.

Traditionally, the focus of criminology has been restricted to those acts that are labelled as crimes. Within the area of environmental harm, this is often problematic. For example, while some logging of old-growth forests is illegal, most is not. Yet, the environmental damage caused by legal and illegal logging is similar. If we are concerned with environmental harm, why focus on one and not the other (White, 2008)? Even when environmental harms are defined as crime, this may vary by jurisdiction. However, much green harm is transnational in nature: a particular pollutant may be illegal in one country, but that does not help those who ingest pollutants produced in other countries that are then transferred across national borders. More generally, criminal law (where it does apply) struggles, for many reasons, to achieve prosecutions in cases of environmental victimisation (Williams, 1996). Given these problems, many green criminologists focus on environmental *harm* rather than the more narrowly defined environmental *crime*. There are undoubtedly value positions influencing the individual criminologist's decision on how widely or narrowly to interpret their remit of studying crime. The value-free criminologist may focus only on those environmental harms criminalised under state or international law. Others may choose to take sides reflecting value positions, studying how legal environmental damage causes harm to certain (usually disadvantaged) members of society on the one hand, or how regulating some environmentally harmful practices restricts the profit-making opportunities of corporations on the other.

If value positions influence how we might interpret 'criminology', they are also central to how we interpret 'green'. An established framework here is the typology of eco-philosophical perspectives initially set out by Halsey and White (Halsey and White, 1998; White, 2008). They identify three ways to conceptualise the relationship between humans and nature. An anthropocentric perspective 'emphasizes the biological, mental and moral superiority of *humans* over all other living and non-living entities' (White, 2008, p 349; emphasis in original). From this perspective, nature is to be utilised for the benefit of mankind, and notions of harm and victimisation are limited to the experiences of people. Alternatively, biocentrism 'views human beings as simply "another species" to be attributed the *same* moral worth as other organisms' (White, 2008, p 352; emphasis in original). Here, humanity's utilisation of nature should have consideration for the harm done to individual life forms and wider ecosystems. A biocentric criminology may consider non-human entities as victims and, as such, engages with debates about animal (and even plant) rights (Benton, 1998; Beirne, 1999, 2007). Ecocentrism is a more nuanced perspective, seeing 'humans and their activities [as] inextricably integrated with the rest of the natural world' (Steverson, 1994, pp 71–2). Here, humans are one species among many, but with certain unique characteristics. We can interact with (ie exploit) our environment on a scale that can have global consequences. What is more, we are aware of how our actions impact on nature and we have the capacity for moral reasoning. As such, moral behaviour for mankind, from this perspective, is that which promotes a balance between human and non-human interests; harmful behaviour is that which upsets the balance: 'Ecocentrism therefore attempts to strike the balance between the instrumental and intrinsic conceptions of non-human nature espoused by anthropocentrists and biocentrists respectively' (White, 2008, p 356).

These three perspectives point to different understandings of what green criminology might focus on, and why. An anthropocentric approach will consider examples of environmental harm leading directly to human suffering (ie environmental victimisation), such as through exposure to pollutants or loss of access to land or resources. Biocentrically oriented criminologists may study harms to animals, or environmental damage for its own sake, with little or no regard to human suffering. An ecocentric criminology may consider a more complex notion of harm as that which upsets both the present and future well-being of both the human and natural worlds, recognising how the interactions between the two render them ultimately inseparable.

Elsewhere, the ideological dimensions of the 'green' in green criminology have been linked to discussions around the remit of 'criminology'. Lynch and Stretesky (2003) consider two broad interpretations of 'The meaning of green'. On the one hand, there is the green perspective of the environmental justice movement, where the concept of environmental harm is informed by ecological science. On the other hand is the 'corporate reconstruction of green' (Lynch and Stretesky, 2003, pp 87–9), where the agenda is shaped by corporate 'greenwashing' (Greer and Bruno, 1997) and the concept of environmental harm is informed by legal and political frameworks. Here, the 'green' corporation, for example, is that which complies with environmental protection regulations rather than that which minimises environmental harm. Where the latter meaning of green encourages a green criminology that focuses on law-breaking, the former calls for a broader criminological remit focusing on harm.

Lynch and Stretesky argue for an unashamedly ideological or political interpretation of 'green' – a green criminology that challenges the social structures and powerful actors (eg the corporations and governments who cause the most environmental damage) that dictate which harmful activities do or do not get labelled as crime in the first place. However, where they embrace the 'green' in green criminology, precisely because of the political and ideological overtones inherent in the word, others reject it for the same reasons. For example, Halsey (2004) specifically argues 'Against "green" criminology' on the grounds that criminology has neither the intellectual framework nor the remit to deal with the extra-legal nuances encountered in the study of environmental harm. Elsewhere, 'environmental criminology' seems to be the preferred term for those who want to avoid overly political or ideological overtones and 'green criminology' a deliberate choice for those who want to emphasise those allegiances, although many authors use the two terms more or less interchangeable (Walters, 2006; White, 2008, pp 6–8). A further alternative label is 'eco-crime' (Walters, 2006), sidestepping the political connotations of green. The term eco-crime tends to be used for those acts that are clearly defined as crime under the law (Walters, 2006), so avoiding the arguments over the remit of criminology. A related, and final, formulation to consider here is White's (2009a, 2011) concept of an 'eco-global criminology', where 'eco' emphasises the *scientific* basis of ecology rather than the ideological connotations of green, and 'global' acknowledges the fact that so many environmental harms are transnational in both commission and impact.

It becomes clear that value positions in the form of eco-philosophical perspectives and in interpretations of the role of the criminologist are central to green criminology, influencing individual scholars' perspectives on both the remit of the subject area and appropriate intellectual approaches to particular problems. This is further reflected by the observation that green criminology is not underpinned by a particular theoretical position, but is best seen instead as taking a 'green perspective' (South, 1998). This lack of cohesion in the field of environmental criminology, as well as the implicit and explicit taking of sides, has led to a variety of criticisms levelled at green criminology. Many of these have already been hinted at, but are worth setting out clearly.

Criticising green criminology

As we have seen, green criminology is neither a rigidly defined subject area nor a universally accepted label. Different contributors have different views of what it should and should not encompass and should or should not be called. Regardless, green criminology *in general* is subject to criticism from both within and beyond its own intellectual community. We can summarise a number of these criticisms as occurring in four (overlapping) arguments.

First, there is the argument that environmental harms, especially those *not* legally defined as crime, are simply beyond the remit of criminology. Taking a green perspective is clearly based on values that are taken as justifying a criminological analysis that moves beyond strict definitions of crime. But acknowledging this undermines the claim that green criminology is criminology at all: if the focus of analysis is not crime, we are beyond our remit, hence Lynch and Stretesky's observation that many criminologists who do work in this area stick squarely with legal definitions of environmental crime precisely '*because* they see it as "value free"' (2003, p 229, emphasis added).

Second, where it is recognised that some of the subject area is indeed criminological, it is suggested that there is no need for a distinct green criminology as these crimes fall within the remit of established criminology. For example, the problem of illegal industrial pollution can be dealt with by the well-established field of corporate crime, especially as the explanations for exceeding pollution or waste production limits are, like corporate fraud and industrial health and safety breaches, so often explained by reference to the drive for profit inherent in the capitalist structures of modern society (White, 2008, pp 144–78). Likewise, studies of the illegal trade and transportation of industrial waste or endangered species might best be seen as studies of organised crime, broadly similar to other types of illegal trafficking, such as of drugs (South and Wyatt, 2011).

Third, even if the idea of a specialist green criminology is accepted, it is still seen as a niche area where its focus renders it of little interest to mainstream criminology's more established notions of '*The problem of crime*' (Muncie and McLaughlin, 2001). In particular, the left-realist criticisms of left-ideologist criminology apply: green criminology does not deal with the lived experience of those who are most often the victims of crime (eg Young, 1992, 2006). Those people who live in fear of crime or who actually experience theft and violence as part of their everyday lives deserve a criminology that will improve their situation, not one that focuses on abstract environmental problems of little direct relevance to the majority of the public.

Fourth, because of the apparent centrality of particular ideological and political positions – the overt taking of sides – green criminology is manifestly *not* value-free, and therefore undermines the ideals of a social *science*. With reference to Becker's original discussion of the 'Whose side?' question, the argument is that the exponents of green criminology have not successfully dealt with their value positions in a way that is sufficient to avoid allegations of bias. In these last two criticisms green criminology may have its place, but not as part of the criminological mainstream.

Justifying green criminology

While there is some merit in the criticisms just outlined, they fail to understand the full implications of a green perspective within criminology. They are also somewhat blind to the development of (mainstream) criminology as a whole: it can be shown that green criminology fits firmly within well-established criminological traditions. Once the full implications of a green perspective in criminology are understood, it becomes clear that green criminology can contribute to our understanding of crime in general – beyond its perceived narrow focus on environmental harm.

We can point to a long tradition of critical engagement with the concept of 'crime' by social scientists, and a widening of the focus of criminology stemming from this. Strict legal definitions of crime have been challenged by many esteemed social scientists at least since the late 19th century. Durkheim (1964 [1893]) saw crime as the 'violation of the collective conscience' and Sellin (1938) saw it as a 'product of conduct norms': in neither case was an understanding of what crime is necessarily embodied in the law. Box (1983), examining how the harmful behaviours of the powerful are often not considered crimes, recognises crime as 'ideological censure'. Becker (1963) famously pointed out that crime is a social construct dependent as much on the successful application of the label 'crime' to an act as the commission of the act itself. The recognition that 'crime' is socially constructed, and that the focus on the social and legal processes that lead to it being constructed are therefore the legitimate focus of the sociologist of crime, is well established.

We can easily highlight other areas of criminological endeavour that, critics have argued, are not focused on the 'real' and everyday crimes that are most central to an understanding of the crime problem. Consider Tappan's (1947) criticisms of the then-emerging criminological focus on white-collar criminals. Tappan argued that criminologists have no right to focus on acts that have not been officially labelled as crime: to do otherwise undermines the legal principles of due process and the presumption of innocence. Even if debates remain as to whether criminology should consider actions that do not come to be labelled as crime, there is no doubt that the study of white-collar and corporate crime is now firmly accepted as within the remit of criminology. More generally, radical and critical traditions within criminology have long pushed back the boundaries of a narrowly focused 'administrative criminology' to question not just why and how crime happens, but why and how certain activities become labelled as 'crimes' in the first place while other, often more harmful, activities do not. Critical criminology goes further, asking why it is that those at the bottom of the social hierarchy tend to bear the brunt of the workings of the criminal justice system, and considers how crime and social conflict relate to social inequalities and social hierarchies more generally (see, eg, Scraton, 1987; Scraton and Chadwick, 1991).

Green criminology was conceived firmly and explicitly within these radical and critical traditions. Michael Lynch (1990) was the first to call for a 'green' criminology with the specific and deliberate use of the word 'green', with all its connotations, emphasising the overlap between the concerns of environmental activists and those of radical social scientists, including, in particular, a Marxist criminological perspective. Both traditions 'are, at some level, in opposition to the ideological foundation of capitalism' (Lynch, 1990, p 1), which is seen as a major driver in both social inequality and environmental damage. Further, it becomes clear that environmental victimisation is not equally spread across populations, but is disproportionately felt by those at the bottom of the social structure (Bovenkerk, 2003; see also the studies that make up Part Two of Rob White's [2009b] collected anthology). Regardless of a care for the environment itself or for non-human life forms, green criminology follows the radical tradition of siding with the least powerful members of society. Taking a biocentric rather than anthropocentric perspective still follows this tradition, but adds non-human entities into the 'social' hierarchy.

It is not just against the common enemy 'capitalism' that environmentalism and socialism become allied, but also in their recognition of how environmental problems overlap with – and exacerbate – existing social inequalities. Indeed the 'red–green alliance' in politics is well established: most Green Parties are also parties of the left and it has been argued that an ecological perspective *is* a socialist perspective (Pepper, 1993). This focus on social inequality remains central to much green criminology, particularly within concepts such as 'environmental racism', where it is recognised that non-white populations are disproportionately exposed to environmental harm (Pinderhughes, 1996; Stephens, 1996; Lynch and Stretesky, 2003; Pellow, 2004). Tying this back to the previous paragraphs, the 'green criminology perspective … tends to begin with a strong sensitivity toward crimes of the powerful, and to be infused with issues pertaining to power, justice and democracy' (White, 2008, p 14).

There are further radical traditions in criminology that we can identify as precedents that help justify a green criminology. Some established strands of criminological thought go so far as to reject 'crime' as the preferred unit of analysis entirely. Commentators such as Cohen (1993, 2001) and Schwendinger and Schwendinger (1970) have suggested that the concept of human rights might be a more objective basis for criminology than state-defined crimes, thus avoiding the problems inherent in states having the power to define crime in the first place. Hillyard and Tombs (2004) go further, suggesting that we reject the notion of crime and, indeed, criminology completely and instead opt for an analysis of social *harms*, whether or not these harms are regulated under the criminal law. These positions may not be widely accepted by all criminologists, even those in the radical and critical traditions, but they are at least taken seriously: all those cited in this paragraph are well respected within the criminological mainstream. Green criminology can clearly be seen to fit into these traditions: concerns over environmental rights or animal rights can be seen as logical extensions to a human rights perspective; focus on environmental harm fits with a focus on social harms.

Even if our concept of criminology is to be rooted in legal constructions of crime, the discipline should be taking a greater interest in the environment. Increasingly, environmental harms are subject to legal regulation in some form or another, and often it is the criminal law itself that is being used to restrict certain environmentally damaging acts. Within the UK, the government of Tony Blair was notorious for creating new crimes (ie expanding the scope of the criminal law to restrict an increasingly wide variety of behaviours). It was reported by the website politics.co.uk that in 10 years in power, 3,605 new offences were created. The government department that created the largest number of new crimes in this period, at 852, was the Department for the Environment, Food and Rural Affairs – more than either the Home Office, which we would associate most readily with criminal legislation, or the Department for Business, Enterprise and Regulatory Reform, which would cover corporate and financial offences. The trend is reflected elsewhere, and the fastest-growing area of international law is also environmental regulation (Sands and Galizzi, 2004). This message is clear: even if criminologists are to be concerned only with legally defined crime, then they should become interested in the environment.

This does not defeat the left-realist criticism that criminology should focus on those crimes that most affect the public and dominate the workings of the criminal justice system. But there are three responses here. First, a criminology that focuses on street crime over other types of crime is as guilty of taking a value position as one that focuses on environmental crime over other types. A value-neutral position would be to see all criminal law as equally subject to criminological focus. Second, as discussed earlier, studies of environmental harms demonstrate that it is often the poorest or most marginalised sections of society (whether globally, nationally or locally defined) that are most likely to be victims. The fact that such groups may not be aware of their status as environmental victims, or that they may still see 'normal' crime as a more pressing concern, does not mean that *we* should ignore it. Quite the contrary: if populations are not even aware of the harms they suffer, this is itself a reason for prioritising the study of those harms.

Third, and perhaps most significantly, environmental harm is increasingly implicated in the *causation* of those very same 'real' crimes that more traditional criminologists would have us focus on. There is not the space here to give a complete overview of the ways that environmental harm may *cause* crime, but we can point to a few examples. Theft and violent crime stem from competition and conflict over resources (consider recent food riots around the world, the incidence of theft and looting after natural disasters, or the repression, genocide and enforced repatriation that has been associated with land and resource grabs in some parts of the world). Conflict over the *enforcement* of existing environmental protection also leads to violence, as in the example of illegal gold-miners in Peru rioting in 2012 because government clampdowns on their environmentally harmful activities left the miners unable to support their families. Other crimes are committed by protesters who increasingly feel the need to resort to direct action (including violence to property and people and acts that may be labelled as eco-terrorism) to have their concerns for the environment heard – and the criminalisation, by governments, of acts of protest that previously fell within the law. Then there are crimes committed by government agencies or corporate interests *against* environmental protesters or local populations. Further to these, we can also recognise that those who are the victims of environmental harm may become more likely to commit 'normal' crimes at later points in their lives: dispossessed peoples (those who have lost their lands or traditional ways of life) are often associated with poverty and addiction, which are themselves implicated in much criminality (as any criminologist would recognise); extreme environmental conditions relate to particular types of crime – such as hot weather and violent crime (eg Simister and Van de Vliert, 2005), or shortage of key resources and domestic violence (Wachholz, 2007); and exposure to certain pollutants has been linked to criminality more generally (eg Stretesky and Lynch, 2004; Lynch and Stretesky, 2007), whether through positivistic models of pollution changing the brain chemistry and, hence, behaviour, or through neo-classical understandings of how exposure to pollution is often one form of deprivation among many, with multiple deprivation itself being a key explanatory factor in patterns of crime.

The recognition of the many ways that environmental harm relates to 'real' crime *other* than those instances where the harm itself is defined as crime points us towards our rebuttal of two other criticisms: that we do not need a dedicated green criminology or that an overtly green criminology is too ideological to meet the requirements of a science. First, it is a distinct green perspective in criminology that is responsible for exposing all the ways that environmental harm relates to crime. Second, although a green perspective implies particular ideological and political allegiances, it is fundamentally a scientific approach as well. Ecological science demonstrates that human and natural systems are neither separate nor separable, particularly in our globalised late-modern world. Humans interact with – and are dependent upon – their environment in many ways, and ecological systems take no account of social boundaries, whether geographical borders or class/power/wealth positions. Indeed, for many social theorists who conceptualise a late-modern 'risk society' as the successor of the class-based society of modernity (eg Giddens, 1991; Beck, 1992), the creation of and exposure to environmental harms become one of the main features of modern living. This is because environmental harm tends to become social harm. Often, this is predictable, which leads to questions as to whether those who allow such harms to happen should be held accountable for this. Other times, given the fact that environmental systems tend to be chaotic, resulting social harms are unpredictable. However, this unpredictability is itself predictable: experience tells us that unchecked environmental damage often does lead to unexpected consequences. This is why many green criminologists and other environmental scholars call for a centralisation of the 'precautionary principle' when regulating environmental harm (for further discussion, see White, 2008, pp 54–83) or allowing environmentally damaging practices. Again, it seems legitimate to ask whether moral, and even legal (eg through negligence or recklessness), allegations of accountability and culpability can or should be levelled against those powerful actors who cause environmental damage or allow such damage to occur.

Conclusions: moving towards the mainstream

There is little doubt that green criminology is an area of intellectual inquiry that is heavily laden with value positions, and that within green criminology, there is the clear taking of sides, but this is no reason to sideline it from the criminological mainstream or to criticise the work emerging under its umbrella as being so biased or political as to undermine its scientific credentials. If we take the 'green' label as a label that centralises the ideological value positions within the subject area, then green criminology can be seen to follow within established critical and radical traditions. An anthropocentric green criminology in this tradition concerns itself with human suffering borne out of environmental harm, and particularly how such suffering tends to disproportionately impact on the poorest and least powerful sections of society. A biocentric green criminology can also be seen to fit within these traditions, viewing animals and other non-human entities within, but further down, the same hierarchies of power we find within human social structures.

Of course, allying green criminology with existing radical and critical traditions does not amount to an argument for green criminology to enter the criminological mainstream: radical and critical approaches are defined, to an extent, by their very opposition to mainstream perspectives. But we can go further in recognising that green criminology has much to contribute when we move away from an interpretation of 'green' as an ideological position. At the very least, a recognition that the criminal law is increasingly used to try to limit environmental harm demonstrates that a value-free administrative criminology needs to increasingly consider green issues. But this is only part of the argument. 'Green' does not have to be a politically laden word: a green perspective can be an ecological perspective in the strict scientific sense. A true understanding of an ecological perspective is that a social science that tries to focus on the human world in isolation from nature does so artificially and naively: we cannot completely separate the social and natural worlds. While there is still, clearly, a wide range of ideological positions *within* green criminology, there is nothing inherently ideological about taking a green perspective. We might, for example, disagree about being anthropocentric, biocentric or ecocentric, but all three perspectives agree that we must consider the impacts of environmental harm beyond the immediate and obvious. To return to the initial question, while some green criminologists may take the sides of particular social or even non-human groups (and with good reason), the general tendency of a green perspective is to recognise that taking account of the environment is to be on *everybody's* side.

References

Beck, U. (1992) *Risk society: towards a new modernity*, London: Sage.

Becker, H. (1963) *Outsiders: studies in the sociology of deviance*, New York, NY: The Free Press.

Becker, H. (1967) 'Whose side are we on?', *Social Problems*, vol 14, no 3, pp 239–47.

Beirne, P. (1999) 'For a nonspeciesist criminology: animal abuse as an object of study', *Criminology*, vol 37, pp 117–47.

Beirne, P. (2007) 'Animal rights, animal abuse and green criminology', in P. Beirne and N. South (eds) *Issues in green criminology: confronting harms against environments, humanity and other animals*, Cullompton: Willan.

Benton, T. (1998) 'Rights and justice on a shared planet: more rights or new relations?', *Theoretical Criminology*, vol 2, no 2, pp 149–75.

Bovenkerk, B. (2003) 'Is smog democratic? Environmental justice in the risk society', *Melbourne Journal of Politics*, vol 29, pp 24–38.

Box, S. (1983) *Power, crime and mystification*, London: Tavistock.

Carrabine, E., Cox, P., Lee, M., Plummer, K. and South, N. (2009) *Criminology: a sociological introduction* (2nd edn), Oxford: Routledge.

Cohen, S. (1993) 'Human rights and crimes of the state: the culture of denial', *Australian and New Zealand Journal of Criminology*, vol 26, no 2, pp 97–115.

Cohen, S. (2001) *States of denial: knowledge about atrocities and suffering*, Cambridge: Polity Press.

Durkheim (1964 [1893]) *The division of labour in society*, New York, NY: Free Press.

Giddens, A. (1991) *The consequences of modernity*, Stanford, CA: Stanford University Press.

Greer, J. and Bruno, K. (1997) *Greenwash: the reality behind corporate environmentalism*, New York, NY: Apex Press.

Halsey, M. (2004) 'Against "green" criminology', *British Journal of Criminology*, vol 44, no 4, pp 833–53.

Halsey, M. and White, R. (1998) 'Crime, ecophilosophy and environmental harm', *Theoretical Criminology*, vol 2, no 3, pp 345–71.

Hillyard, P. and Tombs, S. (2004) 'Beyond criminology?', in P. Hillyard, C. Pantazis, S. Tombs and D. Gordon (eds) *Beyond criminology: taking harm seriously*, London: Pluto Press.

Lynch, M. (1990) 'The greening of criminology: a perspective on the 1990s', *Critical Criminologist*, vol 2, pp 1–5.

Lynch, M. and Stretesky, P. (2003) 'The meaning of green: contrasting criminological perspectives', *Theoretical Criminology*, vol 7, no 2, pp 217–38.

Lynch, M. and Stretesky, P. (2007) 'Green criminology in the United States', in P. Beirne and N. South (eds) *Issues in green criminology: confronting harms against environments, humanity and other animals*, Cullompton: Willan.

Lynch, M. and Stretesky, P. (2010) 'Global warming, global crime: a green criminological perspective', in R. White (ed) *Global environmental harm: criminological perspectives*, Cullompton: Willan.

Muncie, J. and McLaughlin, E. (2001) *The problem of crime* (2nd edn) , London: Sage/Open University Press.

Pellow, D. (2004) 'The politics of illegal dumping: an environmental justice framework', *Qualitative Sociology*, vol 27, no 4, pp 511–25.

Pepper, D. (1993) *Eco-socialism: from deep ecology to social justice*, London: Routledge.

Pinderhughes, R. (1996) 'The impact of race on environmental quality: an empirical and theoretical discussion', *Sociological Perspectives*, vol 39, no 2, pp 231–48.

Potter, G.R. (2012a) 'What is green criminology?'. Available at: http://greencriminology.org/?page_id=584 (accessed 15 November 2012).

Potter, G.R. (2012b) 'Pushing the boundaries of (a) green criminology: environmental harm as a cause of crime', *The Green Criminology Monthly* Available at: http://greencriminology.org/?p=1081 (accessed 15 November 2012).

Sands, P. and Galizzi, P. (2004) *Documents in international environmental law* (2nd edn), Cambridge: Cambridge University Press.

Schwendinger, H. and Schwendinger, J. (1970) 'Defenders of order or guardians of human rights?', *Issues in Criminology*, vol 5, no 2, pp 123–57.

Scraton, P. (1987) *Law, order and the authoritarian state: readings in critical criminology*, Milton Keynes: Open University Press.

Scraton, P. and Chadwick, K. (1991) 'Challenging the new orthodoxies: the theoretical imperatives and political priorities of critical criminology', in K. Stenson and D. Cowell (eds) *The politics of crime control*, London: Sage.

Sellin, T. (1938) *Culture, conflict and crime*, New York, NY: Social Science Research Council.

Simister, J. and Van de Vliert, E. (2005) 'Is there more violence in very hot weather? Tests over time in Pakistan and across countries worldwide', *Pakistan Journal of Meteorology*, vol 2, no 4, pp 55–70.

South, N. (1998) 'A green field for criminology? A proposal for a perspective', *Theoretical Criminology*, vol 2, no 2, pp 211–33.

South, N. and Wyatt, T. (2011) 'Comparing illicit trades in wildlife and drugs: an exploratory study', *Deviant Behavior*, vol 32, pp 538–61.

Stephens, S. (1996) 'Reflections on environmental justice: children as victims & actors', *Social Justice*, vol 23, no 4, pp 62–86.

Steverson, B. (1994) 'Ecocentrism and ecological monitoring', *Environmental Ethics*, vol 16, no 1, pp 71–88.

Stretesky, P. and Lynch, M. (2004) 'The relationship between lead and crime', *Journal of Health and Social Behaviour*, vol 45, no 2, pp 214–29.

Tappan, P. (1947) 'Who is the criminal?', *American Sociological Review*, vol 12, pp 96–102.

Wachholz, S. (2007) '"At risk": climate change and its bearing on women's vulnerability to male violence', in P. Beirne and N. South (eds) *Issues in green criminology: confronting harms against environments, humanity and other animals*, Cullompton: Willan.

Walters, R. (2006) 'Eco-crime', in E. McLaughlin and J. Muncie (eds) *The Sage dictionary of criminology*, London: Sage.

White, R. (2005) 'Environmental crime in global context: exploring the theoretical and empirical complexities', *Current Issues in Criminal Justice*, vol 16, no 3, pp 271–85.

White, R. (2008) *Crimes against nature: environmental criminology and ecological justice*, Collumpton: Willan.

White, R. (2009a) 'Introduction: environmental crime and eco-global criminology', in R. White (ed) *Environmental crime: a reader*, Cullompton: Willan.

White, R. (2009b) *Environmental crime: a reader*, Cullompton: Willan.

White, R. (2011) *Transnational environmental crime: toward an eco-global criminology*, London: Routledge.

Williams, C. (1996) 'An environmental victimology', *Social Justice*, vol 23, no 4, pp 16–40.

Young, J. (1992) 'Ten points of realism', in J. Young and R. Matthews (eds) *Rethinking criminology: the realist debate*, London: Sage.

Young, J. (2006) 'Left-realism', in E. McLaughlin and J. Muncie (eds) *The Sage dictionary of criminology*, London: Sage.

SECTION TWO

Values in criminal justice

These chapters move on to consider the values embedded in criminal justice practices and in the organisational or political structures that help shape them. The attempt is not to be exhaustive, but to provide comment on major areas of criminal justice and penal policy. The authors of the first five chapters highlight tensions and barriers, but also look for possibilities and potential to develop policy and practice so that values and principles are more transparent and more open to healthy and constructive challenge. The final two consider issues of justice and inherent values more broadly, in the one case, exploring the divide between public and private actors and interests and, in the other, questioning the nature of state reparation and its actual, rather than its claimed, impacts.

In Chapter Nine, Fergus McNeill and Stephen Farrall consider the role of probation officers – and of helping relationships more generally – in assisting individuals to desist from crime. The research literature talks about desistance as a journey, a process of change; individuals do not 'become good' overnight but typically practise new ways of being and relating to others over time. The authors argue that where probation officers and others espouse positive virtues and values, this can engender hope and belief in the capacity to change. They ask what might be needed in terms of practitioner qualities and characteristics and in terms of organisational and systemic change to transform penal practice.

In Chapter Ten, Jean Henderson also confronts questions about the probation service's culture and priorities, and the importance of holding strong professional values in the current penal climate, dominated by concerns about risk and public protection. She explores the challenge for new and learning practitioners in this environment and considers the impact of the structural and other changes ahead which mean that 'probation services' will not be the sole preserve of the probation service. Can professional values help guard against fragmentation and inconsistencies as more organisations enter the offender management marketplace?

Developing the theme of professional education, Craig Paterson and Ed Pollock use Chapter Eleven to reflect upon the values of community policing and why the police service in the UK, compared to our

European neighbours, has experienced resistance to incorporating these values into street-level policing. They point to the traditional role of training rather than education as a basis for police work in the UK and consider how a more academic approach might facilitate greater flexibility and reflexivity in the value base for policing practice.

Muzammil Quraishi uses the growing population of Muslim prisoners to examine the institutional efforts of the prison service to respond to ethnic and religious diversity. The prison service was ahead of many organisations in the community in recognising that prejudice and discrimination on the grounds of ethnicity and religion may be closely intertwined. Despite many positive initiatives, research with the 'subordinate' population of Muslim prisoners seems to suggest that, overall, their experiences in prison are still more negative than those of white prisoners. In Chapter Twelve, the author questions why this might be the case and particularly asks why official policy focuses to the extent that it does on the risk of religious extremism when studies indicate a quite different range of concerns for Muslim prisoners about their day-to-day life in custody.

In Chapter Thirteen, Stephen Riley considers the shifting boundaries between the public and the private in criminal justice. Citing the availability of new technologies and social media, the privatisation of criminal justice services previously delivered by public sector agencies, and use of 'bad character' evidence in court proceedings as examples, he reflects upon the implications for the social and the personal, and how the changing public–private divide affects the limits necessarily placed on the role of the state.

Victims are receiving increasing attention within criminal justice, and particularly the victims of 'hate crime'. However, experiences of victimisation and official responses are variable, particularly as the protections afforded by the Equality Act 2010 apply only to those who possess one or more of the 'protected characteristics' stipulated in law. Marian Duggan, in Chapter Fourteen, shows how the victimisation of two socially marginalised groups is ignored or considered invalid, and how they are perceived as threats to society rather than being subject to threat themselves. She argues that the current legislation is framed around identities, not vulnerability, and this provides inadequate redress for disenfranchised individuals or groups in contrast to those who have access to more powerful advocates and whose experiences are acknowledged, not discounted.

The final chapter in this section also addresses victimisation, but from an international perspective. Claire Moon examines two cases where victims of atrocities, in Argentina and under apartheid South

Africa, refused state reparation and offers of monetary compensation. In doing so, she questions the nature of reconciliation and exposes its function as social control: accepting reparation in these two cases meant also accepting the states' narratives of events, which these victims collectively resisted. The author highlights the coercive potential of state reparation and how it can be used to distort the nature of responsibility and blame. Far from being an unalloyed good and automatically 'on the side of' the victims, it can be used to silence them and to pervert, rather than promote, justice.

NINE

A moral in the story? Virtues, values and desistance from crime

Fergus McNeill and Stephen Farrall

Introduction

In this chapter, we draw on theories of desistance and research into desistance to argue that ceasing to offend is a process that involves the development of the motivation, capacity and opportunities to live well, in both a moral and a prudential sense. We present an argument that supporting people to desist from crime is likely to require forms and styles of penal practice that model ways of being and becoming 'good', and that central to such practice are questions of the legitimacy of criminal justice processes and of the moral performance of practitioners. In developing these arguments, our aim is to contribute to policy and practice debates about how best to configure and deliver key penal institutions and practices, particularly those associated with sentencing and sanctioning. However, since those institutions and practices inevitably reflect and refract their social, political and cultural contexts, the question of how to support the acquisition of virtues in the process of desistance inevitably forces us back to questions about the values, virtues and vices of society itself.

The relationship between virtue and necessity – between the moral and the prudential – has been much debated in moral philosophy. Although some philosophers draw a clear distinction between the two, for example, in Immanuel Kant's insistence that only actions motivated by a sense of duty can be morally praiseworthy, others regard the two concepts as overlapping. Indeed, Aristotle's account of ethics implies that we cannot truly flourish as human beings unless we live well in the moral sense, so being a good or virtuous person is inevitably good *for* a person: virtue is a necessity if we are to live a life that is good for us.

The relationship between necessity and virtue is also frequently discussed in literature. Although the origins of the phrase 'to make a necessity of virtue' may be unclear, its most famous use was by

Shakespeare in *Two gentlemen of Verona*. The scene in question finds our hero Valentine, having been banished (unjustly) by the Duke of Milan, wandering in a forest, where he is set upon by other outlaws. But although these outcasts are living beyond the law, and beyond the state, they seem somehow to know virtue (and beauty) when they see it. Moreover, seeing virtue, they seek it and willingly submit to it:

> First Outlaw:
> ...
> But to the purpose – for we cite our faults,
> That they may hold excus'd our lawless lives;
> And partly, seeing you are beautified
> With goodly shape and by your own report
> A linguist and a man of such perfection
> As we do in our quality much want –
>
> Second Outlaw:
> Indeed, because you are a banish'd man,
> Therefore, above the rest, we parley to you:
> Are you content to be our general?
> To make a virtue of necessity
> And live, as we do, in this wilderness?
>
> Third Outlaw:
> What say'st thou? wilt thou be of our consort?
> Say ay, and be the captain of us all:
> We'll do thee homage and be ruled by thee,
> Love thee as our commander and our king....
>
> Valentine:
> I take your offer and will live with you,
> Provided that you do no outrages
> On silly women or poor passengers.
>
> Third Outlaw:
> No, we detest such vile base practises.
> Come, go with us, we'll bring thee to our crews,
> And show thee all the treasure we have got,
> Which, with ourselves, all rest at thy dispose.[1]

Shakespeare's observations on human character were often acute, sometimes anticipating the development of subsequent social science, but is it reasonable to suppose that experiencing virtue and even beauty can have a similar effect on contemporary 'outlaws', on people who have offended? While it seems unlikely that such exposure to virtue could be a *sufficient* condition in and of itself for producing positive change, there are reasons to suggest that it might nonetheless be a *necessary* one.

In a recent film about desistance from crime, one of the most compelling moments features Bobby Cummines OBE, founder of UNLOCK, the National Association of Reformed Offenders. Cummines explains the starting point of his desistance process in a way that resonates with the Shakespearean scene:

> I was lucky. I had a good probation officer and a good education officer in prison who said to me 'You're worth more than that' and gave me a bit of belief in myself. And also, in a way, being banged up all that time, and seeing people that was kind to me, and there was prison officers as well, and people when I came out that were really supportive of me, and they were just decent people. And I saw the beauty of society, and the beauty of those people in society, cause my world was an ugly world. We didn't trust no-one, we injured each other – it was a violent and terrible dark place I was in and life meant nothing. But to see these people that was really there for no other reason than they was nice people – I saw the beauty of society, and I wanted to be part of that beauty. I wanted to be part of *that* society, not the society I was in.[2]

This seems to be a contemporary example of exposure to virtue and beauty prompting and supporting change, but it is only one example. To explore the evidence for and arguments about the role of virtue in supporting desistance further, we begin with a brief overview of some research about the process of desistance from crime itself, examining the relationship between the moral and the prudential in the desistance process. Next, we move on to our substantive focus on what we know from research about how desistance is best supported, exploring what role the virtues and values of practitioners may play in the process. We conclude the chapter by suggesting some of the ways in which the cultural, social and political contexts of contemporary criminal justice might militate against the modelling of virtue by criminal justice practitioners, and thus the acquisition of virtue by those they supervise and aim to support.

Desistance from crime: prudence or morals?

In the 1980s, reflecting wider trends in sociology, Clarke and Cornish (1985) suggested that ex-offenders made a rational decision to cease offending. Clarke and Cornish (1985, pp 172–3) touched on desistance only briefly, producing a hypothetical decision tree to show how a burglar may decide to stop burgling. Notably, they were not arguing that burglars suddenly become moral or virtuous; rather, their model implied a shift in their calculations about their best interests – in other words, a shift in prudential thinking. While Clarke and Cornish did not present any data to support their theoretical model of desistance, one study that did was that by Cusson and Pinsonneault (1986). The data came from qualitative interviews with 17 ex-robbers. The influential factors identified by the authors included: shock (such as being wounded in a bank raid); growing tired of doing time in prison; becoming aware of the possibility of longer prison terms; and a reassessment of what is important to the individual. All of these factors are described in terms of a 'decision' to give up crime; but only the last of them perhaps invokes what we might immediately recognise as 'morality-based' or 'meaning-based' reasons for going straight.

Similar findings have been reported by other researchers: Leibrich (1993, pp 56–7), Shover (1983, p 213) and Cromwell et al (1991, p 83) all note that desisters experienced a period of re-evaluation before desisting. But, of course, while it is true that many individuals (especially those with prolonged engagement in crime) may make decisions to stop offending, it is not clear that these decisions are always 'seen through', or that these decisions alone are sufficient for desistance. A change in the way that one weighs up one's choices (whether morally or prudentially) does not always produce a change in behaviour (as anyone who has every tried to stick to a diet, an exercise regime or any form of religious observance can attest).

A contrasting theory, which emerged in the late 1980s and early 1990s, was that proposed by Gottfredson and Hirschi (1990). Their general theory of crime was intended to account for all crimes, at all times, and extended to include other risky behaviours. Their argument was that those people who are most likely to offend are often found to be impulsive risk-takers who exhibit low levels of self-control. The origins of low social control, they argue, lie in the poor parenting and socialisation practices employed (or not employed) by many offenders' parents. The suggestion is that the 'criminal propensity' of any one individual is instilled early in their lives, but remains relatively stable across their life course. This propensity can be eroded or cemented over time; socialisation is a lifelong process. But even when socialisation does make an individual less impulsive, low-control individuals remain as *relatively* low-control individuals in comparison with their same-age peers. The somewhat depressing conclusion of Gottfredson and Hirschi's position is that life events such as marriage, child-rearing and employment make little difference to criminality, since criminality is determined by self-control, which itself is determined by early childhood experiences.

Gottfredson and Hirschi argued that while criminality remains relatively stable over the life course, the opportunities to commit crimes over time become less and less frequent. Thus, reductions in offending reflect changes in opportunity structures. Such a deterministic stance is, of course, somewhat at odds with rational choice perspectives, and it seems to take *individual* morality out of the picture altogether. That said, it is worth noting that morality may still be in play here, in the sense that the determining social and cultural contexts of individual offending (ie restricted 'opportunity structures') can be cast as the result of our collective moral and political choices. In any event, Gottfredson and Hirschi's arguments caused much debate in criminology, with a recent review of the competing theories of desistance (Ezell and Cohen, 2005, p 259) finding little to support the key tenets of their theorising.

Taking a somewhat different approach, Sampson and Laub's (1993) theory of age-graded social control explores the notion of the bond between an individual and society. The bond is made up of the extent to which an individual has emotional attachments to societal goals, is committed to achieving them through legitimate means, believes these goals to be worthy and is able to involve themselves in the attainment of such goals. Although these are not the terms that they choose, we could conceive of their account as being one that elucidates the acquisition of the virtues of good citizenship (see also Farrall and Calverley, 2006, ch 6). After all, our social bonds in a sense both reflect and construct the reciprocal rights and responsibilities that full membership of a social group or community entails.

Sampson and Laub's theorising posits that engagement in offending is more likely when this bond is weakened or broken. In addition to this, they argue that at various points during the life course, formal and informal social institutions help to secure the bond between the individual and society. For example, for adolescents, school, the family and peer groups influence the nature of the bond between many young people and their wider communities, while employment, marriage and parenthood operate in a similar way for adults. These institutions, and the relationships between individuals that they encourage, help the formation of those social bonds in and through which social control is generated. Thus, one of their key insights is that avoidance of crime is the result of relationships formed for reasons *other than* the control of crime.

Sampson and Laub argue that changes in the individual's relationship with these various institutions are an inevitable feature of modern life, and, as such, are key to understanding engagement in offending over the life course. While much continuity in an individual's life can be observed, key events can trigger changes in an individual's bond to society and, hence, pattern of offending. Similarly, because many relationships endure over time, they can accumulate resources that can help sustain conventional goals and conformity (eg emotional support between marriage partners; Laub et al, 1998). In contrast to Gottfredson and Hirschi, who see low levels of self-control as the end of the matter, Sampson and Laub argue that levels of criminal propensity are open to influence, and that these influences are often the result of informal social control. Furthermore, unlike rational choice theorists, who see desistance as the result of a decision, Sampson and Laub's approach enables one to view desistance as the result of a process that stretches over time and is not based purely on calculative (or prudential) decision-making, but is rather organic and relational.

More recently still, Maruna (2001, p 8) aimed to 'identify the common psychosocial structure underlying [ex-offender's] self-stories, and therefore to outline a phenomenology of desistance'. In this respect, he argued that 'to desist from crime, ex-offenders need to develop a coherent, pro-social identity for themselves' (Maruna, 2001, p 7). He found that desisters among his sample displayed an exaggerated belief that they could control their own futures in some way, and, in addition, a zealous sense of purpose to their 'new' lives. The persisters, on the other hand, 'shared a sense of being doomed or fated to their situation' (Maruna, 2001, p 11). Desistance, then, was bound up in a process by which ex-offenders came to see themselves as essentially 'good' people who, often through little fault of their own (Maruna, 2001, p 12), acted in 'bad' ways. These previous 'bad' ways and the former 'bad' identity, rather than being something to be ashamed of, Maruna argues, are employed by desisters as a means for remaking the sense of their lives and as the basis for making a positive contribution to society (Maruna, 2001, p 12): from offender, to desister, to 'wounded healer'. This process of reconstruction of a moral or virtuous story about oneself – where the 'real me' is a morally good person – is particularly pertinent for our purposes here.

Giordano et al (2002) outlined a four-part 'theory of cognitive transformation', which integrates some of these themes. In their account, the desistance process involves: a 'general cognitive openness to change' (which might involve both prudential and moral reappraisal); exposure and reaction to 'hooks for change' or turning points (which may link to social bonds); the envisioning of 'an appealing and conventional 'replacement self'' (which suggests narrative transformation); and a transformation in the way the actor views deviant behaviour (which implies a reappraisal of attitudes and perhaps values) (Giordano et al, 2002, pp 999–1002). In relation to openness to change, several other scholars researching desistance (eg Cusson and Pinsonneault, 1986; Farrall and Bowling, 1999) have noted that a period of reflection and reassessment of what is important to the individual would appear to be a common feature of the initial process of desistance. We have already noted that, in itself, this is insufficient (Giordano et al, 2002, p 1001; Farrall, 2002, p 225); what is also needed is the exposure to some opportunity to change, and the individual identifying this change as offering a potential 'way out' and then acting upon this. This leads on to the third stage in Giordano et al's schema, the individual's ability to imagine or conceive of themselves in a new (and conventional) role doing new things. The imagined better self or good self must be both credible and authentic to the would-be desister. Finally, the process is completed, they argue (Giordano et al, 2002, p 1002), when old behaviours are no longer seen as desirable or relevant. Giordano et al (2002, p 1003), following work on the relationship between agency and structure (eg Farrall and Bowling, 1999), argue that 'the actor creatively and selectively draws upon elements of the environment in order to affect significant life changes'. In this way, they work towards a model of desistance that draws agency and structure together (see also Maruna and Farrall, 2004; Farrall et al, 2011).

From this brief account of some theoretical perspectives on desistance, we can see that although criminologists have tended to examine the process through psychological or sociological perspectives, moral dimensions of desistance are not difficult to discern. This is hardly surprising since desistance is by definition about moving from behaviours that are routinely morally condemned (at least by many people and institutions) to behaviours that are (at least) expected of and (often) celebrated in 'good citizens' (being a good parent, a good neighbour, a hard worker). Yet, few desistance scholars have engaged directly with moral philosophy or ethics.

A notable exception is to be found in the work of Tony Bottoms and Joanna Shapland, which has drawn on concepts from Aristotle's ethics to make sense of and theorise empirical research on desistance from crime. Bottoms and Shapland (2011), for example, have used Aristotle's concept of '*akrasia*' (weakness of will) in accounting for the fact that even the very persistent offenders involved in their Sheffield desistance study express (and appear to hold) strikingly conformist goals and values. Far from being 'wicked' people (which, for Aristotle, means people who explicitly reject 'the good'), the *akrates* (weak-willed people) know what is right but are often unable to resist temptation. More to the point, they note that the young men in their study often had very many temptations to resist. Bottoms and Shapland (2011) cast these temptations as obstacles to desistance that arise from the social and cultural contexts and conditions in which their research participants lived.

For Aristotle, being and becoming a good person is about the development and embodiment of virtues or qualities of character. There are two *intellectual* virtues that we require to live the good life; these rest alongside more easily recognisable *ethical* virtues (like courage or temperance). The intellectual virtues are *sophia* (which is usually translated as wisdom and combines discernment and knowledge) and *phronesis* (which is sometimes translated as 'practical wisdom' and sometimes as prudence). The pursuit of wisdom and happiness requires both of these virtues; *phronesis* facilitates *sophia*. In a much-quoted passage, Aristotle writes:

> Whereas young people become accomplished in geometry and mathematics, and wise within these limits, prudent young people do not seem to be found. The reason is that prudence [*phronesis*] is concerned with particulars as well as universals, and particulars become known from experience, but a young person lacks experience, since some length of time is needed to produce it. (*Nicomachean Ethics*, 1142a[3])

In other words, knowledge of and commitment to certain values and aspirations is not sufficient in and of itself to produce a life lived in conformity with those values and aspirations. Abstract knowledge of what is good is not enough to *be* good. Being or becoming good takes time and practice; we need to work out what it means day by day, and that both requires and facilitates the development of practical wisdom. Perhaps most importantly for our purposes, Aristotle holds that *phronesis* is both necessary *and* sufficient for being virtuous, since it is impossible to be both *akratic* and *phronetic*; to be both weak-willed and practically wise (or prudent). Desistance from crime, we might suggest, then, is fundamentally about moving from an *akratic* to a *phronetic* state; from weakness of will to practical wisdom. It is about making well-informed decisions based on imperfect knowledge; about weighing up pros and cons and rights and wrongs. But such decision-making – and the development of practical wisdom – as we have already noted earlier, is not easy, and for most people involved in persistent offending, it is made much harder by the practical and social obstacles that they face. Putting it another way, it is not easy being or becoming virtuous in a vicious place, or when vicious people surround you, or where people or institutions treat you viciously. On the other hand, not least in the light of the experience of Bobby Cummines reported earlier, it may be easier to become virtuous for those who are exposed to virtuous people and institutions.

Virtues in the making: supporting desistance

What, then, can be done to support transitions towards virtue? Perhaps, slightly surprisingly, there has been relatively little research that has adopted insights from desistance and focused on how probation or social work supervision has helped probationers cease offending. One of the earliest studies was that undertaken by Julie Leibrich (1993). Leibrich interviewed 48 men and women who had been supervised by probation officers in New Zealand and who had remained conviction-free for about three years after the start of their probation order. Very few of the people Leibrich interviewed spontaneously reported that probation supervision had been of help in terms of their desisting from crime (Leibrich, 1993, p 172), and half of the sample reported that they had not got anything out of the sentences (Leibrich, 1993, p 182). Those who felt that they had got something out of the experience tended to emphasise the chance to talk things through with someone (Leibrich, 1993, pp 182–4). In short, from this early foray, probation supervision did not appear to be a particularly large element in accounts of change away from crime.

In the UK, the first tentative steps towards injecting insights from desistance research into a consideration of the impact of probation supervision were taken by Rex (1999). Although Rex's study lacked data on whether or not the probationers in her sample ($n = 60$) had actually ceased offending or not, her study did throw some much-needed light onto both what happened during supervision sessions and how it contributed to desistance. For some, simply being on probation was enough of a deterrent for them to cease offending (Rex, 1999, p 369); for others, getting help on how to solve problems in their lives was more important (Rex, 1999, p 373). However, practical assistance was not readily forthcoming and probationers often had to rely on their own social networks to meet their employment and housing needs (Rex, 1999, p 374). From Rex's study, one takes the message that displaying an interest in the lives of the probationers is an important first step towards building the sort of relationship that will foster and promote desistance (Rex, 1999, p 375). Significantly, probation officers' concern for probationers as people tended to underlie the development of loyalty (an important virtue, of course) among probationers.

Farrall's studies of the desistance/persistence of almost 200 men and women on probation in England (Farrall, 2002; Farrall and Calverley, 2006) have provided rather more substantive findings. Initially at least, his findings were rather downbeat; while tackling problems relating to accommodation, family relationships and employment were key to assisting desistance from crime, few probation officers appeared willing to engage in assisting probationers with their efforts. This was despite the fact that when officers did assist probationers with these problems, they were more likely to be successfully resolved (Farrall, 2002, pp 160–3). However, such findings did not lead Farrall to conclude that, in probation, 'nothing works'; rather, he emphasised the fact that successful desistance was the product of individual motivation, social and personal contexts, probation supervision and the meanings that people hold about their lives and their behaviours. However, although a follow-up study of members of the same sample (Farrall and Calverley, 2006) produced, in general, similar findings, it also started to uncover some ex-probationers who had become more willing to *retrospectively* attribute more influence to their experience of supervision (see Farrall and Calverley, 2006, pp 42–67). Whereas previously probation's input had been dismissed, some ex-probationers were starting to see the value of what they had taken from probation. At the time of writing, a further follow-up of this sample is being conducted, and initial findings suggest a greater degree of awareness and acceptance on the part of former probationers that the period of supervision had played an important role in their desistance (Farrall, 2011).

Drawing on these empirical studies, and on desistance scholarship more generally, McNeill (2006), in advancing a 'desistance paradigm', has sought to outline ethical arguments for such an approach. One strand of ethical argument in McNeill's (2006) article concerns the virtues that practitioners may have to display in order to support desistance. Virtue-based approaches to ethics (including professional ethics) have experienced something of a resurgence in recent years (Pence, 1991). While professional education in many fields involves attention to questions of ethics and values, and engages with codes of ethics or values, virtue ethics suggests a shift in focus. It moves us away from the question 'What ought I to do?' or 'What principles must I adhere to?' to the question 'What sort of person should I be?'. As McNeill (2006, p 52) noted:

> One of the merits of desistance research is that by asking offenders about their experiences both of attempting desistance and of supervision, progress is made towards answering the question that a would-be 'virtuous' offender manager might ask: What sort of practitioner should I be? The virtues featured in responses from desisters might include optimism, hopefulness, patience, persistence, fairness, respectfulness, trustworthiness, loyalty, wisdom, compassion, flexibility and sensitivity (to difference), for example.

In the context of an ongoing study of the meaning of quality in probation supervision, led by Joanna Shapland at the University of Sheffield, the opportunity has arisen (indirectly) to explore what sorts of virtues probation practitioners identify as being crucial to their work. In an extensive review of the extant literature (Shapland et al, 2012), it was noted that different approaches to thinking about quality reflect different ways of conceiving of 'the good'. One strand in the probation literature implicitly or explicitly defines quality principally in terms of its consequences: good practice is whatever practice is associated with delivering the required outcomes, often cast as reductions in reconviction. This approach is broadly utilitarian (as advocated by Jeremy Bentham and John Stuart Mill); it is concerned with maximising utility or bringing about the greatest good for the greatest number. However, even in the era of 'outcomes', utilitarian approaches are usually moderated somewhat by another way of thinking about quality, one that stresses adherence to certain inviolable ethical standards. Moral philosophers refer to such an approach as 'deontological' or duty-based; an approach commonly associated with Immanuel Kant. Thus, for example, while we might eliminate all *re*offending by executing all offenders, we might consider it wrong – either because the harms caused would outweigh the harms prevented (a utilitarian calculation) or because it would violate the principle of proportionality (a deontological concern).

There is, however, a third approach to quality, based on developing a virtue-based conception. Intriguingly, although fieldwork did suggest a utilitarian concern with goals and outcomes, it also revealed a clear appreciation of the importance of the values, characteristics and skills that probation staff see as being crucial to quality supervision (see Robinson et al, forthcoming). In essence, these findings suggest a focus not so much on the merits of any specific technical approach to securing outcomes or adhering to principles, but rather on *the kind of people* that are capable of and responsible for doing the best-quality probation work. According to the respondents, such people were characterised by a combination of (largely soft/relational) skills, professional training (for those qualified staff) and experience accrued on the job, coupled with the values, personal experiences and qualities that participants brought with them, which were seen as equipping people for quality probation work. It is not difficult to see the links here with Aristotle's insistence on the intellectual virtues of *sophia* and *phronesis* working in concert with the kinds of moral practice virtues suggested by McNeill (2006).

If it makes sense to suggest that those supporting the development of virtues in others must possess and display the virtues themselves, the question remains as to exactly how and under what circumstances virtue can be transmitted from the supporter to the supported. Perhaps that question is best left to developmental psychologists, but what seems clear, not just from desistance research, but from other research as well, for example, on the moral performance of prisons (Liebling, and Arnold, 2004), is that it is only within relationships that model the kinds of virtues described earlier that the formal authority conferred on the worker by the court is likely to be rendered *legitimate* in the mind of the 'offender'. Indeed, without such legitimacy, it seems that the exercise of power runs the risk of both representing and generating viciousness (see Sparks et al, 1996; McNeill, 2009, 2010).

McNeill and Robinson (2012) have recently argued that community sanctions face particular legitimacy problems, arising from several of their features. In particular, their purposes are perennially contested, and are often cast somewhat differently in pursuit of external legitimacy (eg with sentencers, the public and politicians) and in pursuit of internal legitimacy (with those subject to such sanctions). For the latter 'audience', the fluid or liquid legitimacy of community sanctions is a function of their changing forms and shapes; of the ways in which they are negotiated, constructed, contested and reconstructed by the actors involved. The lived reality of being on a community sentence is relationally constructed, not architecturally bounded (as in the prison). This liquid quality can allow legitimacy to 'flow in' (when the relationship is working well and trust and loyalty have been established), but also to 'ebb away' (when promises are broken, services fail to materialise or enforcement is perceived as unjust).

It is possible, of course, to exaggerate the extent to which this liquid quality is particular to community sanctions. The lived realities of being policed or imprisoned (or subject to any form of regulatory authority) are also inevitably relationally constructed. In many contexts within criminal justice (and beyond), therefore, the capacity to exercise authority legitimately seems likely to be a key virtue for practitioners (see Crawford and Hucklesby, 2012).

Conclusions: probation, virtue and necessity

We have argued that it makes sense to think of desistance from crime as involving the acquisition of intellectual and moral virtues, and that supporting the acquisition of virtue probably requires the demonstration of intellectual and moral virtues. Moreover, we have suggested that such demonstration is likely to be impossible in the absence of relationships characterised by legitimacy, not least in the exercise of potentially coercive power. But, important though they are, penal practice virtues cannot be insulated from their wider cultural, political and social contexts. The transmission or communication of virtue does not happen in a vacuum.

An appreciation of these dynamics is apparent in Antony Duff's penal communications theory (Duff, 2001, 2003). Duff (2003) has argued that probation staff can and should act as moral mediators between offenders, victims and the wider community. This moral mediation speaks, at least to us, not just to seeking change in the offending citizen; not just to the development of personal virtue. Equally, it begs a series of complex questions about our collective virtues. If personal virtue is partly about the development of good citizenship, then collective virtue is about the character of the polity to which we all belong, for better or worse. In this regard, Duff (2003) argues that the existence of social injustice, and, in consequence, the denial of citizenship to some, creates profound moral problems for the punishing polity. The response must be 'a genuine and visible attempt to remedy the injustices and exclusion that they [ie some offenders] have suffered' (Duff, 2003, p 194). Duff (2003, p 194, emphasis added) suggests that this implies that:

> The probation officer ... will now have to help the offender
> negotiate his relationship with the polity against which he
> has offended, but by whom he has been treated unjustly and
> disrespectfully: she must speak for the polity to the offender
> in terms that are censorious but also apologetic – terms that
> seek both to bring him to recognise the wrong he has done

and to express an apologetic recognition of the injustice he has suffered: *and she must speak to the polity for the offender,* explaining what is due to him as well as what is due for him.

This is an appealing and, in most respects, compelling account of what probation could and should be. But even the recognition of social injustice (and the promise to do something about it?) falls some way short of exposing more fundamental questions about the values and virtues of society. Richard Sennett (1998, 2006) suggests that 'the new capitalism' has produced a 'corrosion of character': 'work' or 'craft' no longer provides a 'stable sense of identity or security'; rather, the incessant demands for flexible labour, professions and organisations that can respond to rapid changes in deregulated and globalised markets require us to discount and abandon our pasts and to continually reinvent ourselves. The ethical effects of this sort of 'liquid modernity' (Bauman, 2000) arise from the ambiguities, uncertainties and insecurities that it entails – and the materialism, consumption and opportunism that it celebrates. In this context, Jock Young (2007) has argued that crime is not so much the product of being insufficiently socialised into mainstream values as it is the product of being *too* immersed in them (while at the same time excluded from the means to succeed under these materialistic terms). The social and moral problems which Sennett, Bauman and Young identify suggest that new or late capitalist societies have devalued virtue and *phronesis* (prudence) so far as to make them not so much necessities as liabilities.

Returning to the Bobby Cummines quotation from *The road from crime*, some recognition of the wrongs done to 'offenders', and some human concern for them as struggling fellow citizens, seems likely to be a necessity if we are to engage with people in a process of change. If we do not show people virtue and *phronesis* (prudence) in the ways that we treat people (*especially* when they offend us), we are unlikely to convince them of the 'beauty of society' and to draw them towards the good citizenship of the good society. But important though it is that practitioners model virtue, the deeper problem is that we live in a society that too often celebrates and models the viciousness that criminal sanctions invite and require 'offenders' to abandon. The paradox for practice is that virtue is as necessary at the social and political level as it is at the individual level, and that to seek to model and support it in practice compels us to engage in politics, since we depend on one another's virtues to build the sort of polity in which we can thrive together.

Notes

[1] William Shakespeare, *Two gentlemen of Verona*, Act IV, Scene I (abridged). Available at: http://www.shakespeare-literature.com/Two_Gentlemen_of_Verona/13.html/necessity (accessed 30 April 2012).

[2] *The road from crime* (directed by Eamonn Devlin, 2012), funded by European Social Research Council Award No ES/I029257/1. For more information, see: http://blogs.iriss.org.uk/discoveringdesistance/documentary/

[3] Available at: www.perseus.tufts.edu/hopper/text?doc=Perseus%3Atext%3A 1999.01.0054%3Abekker+page%3D1142a

References

Bauman, Z. (2000) *Liquid modernity*, Cambridge: Polity Press.

Bottoms, A. and Shapland, J. (2011) 'Steps towards desistance among male young adult recidivists', in S. Farrall, M. Hough, S. Maruna and R. Sparks (eds) *Escape routes: contemporary perspectives on life after punishment*, Abingdon: Routledge.

Clarke, R.V. and Cornish, D.B. (1985) 'Modeling offender's decisions: a framework for research and policy', in M. Tonry and N. Morris (eds) *Crime and justice: an annual review of research*, Chicago, IL: University of Chicago Press.

Crawford, A. and Hucklesby, A. (eds) (2012) *Legitimacy and compliance in criminal justice*, Abingdon: Routledge.

Cromwell, P.F., Olson, J.N. and Avary, D.W. (1991) *Breaking and entering*, London: Sage.

Cusson, M. and Pinsonneault, P. (1986) 'The decision to give up crime', in D.B. Cornish and R.V. Clarke (eds) *The reasoning criminal*, New York, NY: Springer-Verlag.

Duff, A. (2001) *Punishment, communication and community*, New York, NY: Oxford University Press.

Duff, A. (2003) 'Probation, punishment and restorative justice: should altruism be engaged in punishment?', *The Howard Journal*, vol 42, no 1, pp 181–97.

Ezell, M. and Cohen L. (2005) *Desisting from crime*, Oxford: OUP.

Farrall, S. (2002) *Rethinking what works with offenders*, Cullompton: Willan Publishing.

Farrall, S. (2011) 'The long-term impact of probation supervision: is it still detectable after 15 years?', Ministry of Justice Offender Engagement Seminar, London, 27 September.

Farrall, S. and Bowling, B. (1999) 'Structuration, human development and desistance from crime', *British Journal of Criminology*, vol 39, no 2, pp 252–67.

Farrall, S. and Calverley, A. (2006) *Understanding desistance from crime*, Crime and Justice Series, London: Open University Press.

Farrall, S., Sharp, G., Hunter, B. and Calverley, A. (2011) 'Theorizing structural and individual-level processes in desistance and persistence: outlining an integrated perspective', *Australian and New Zealand Journal of Criminology*, vol 44, no 2, pp 218–34.

Giordano, P.C., Cernkovich, S.A. and Rudolph, J.L. (2002) 'Gender, crime and desistance: toward a theory of cognitive transformation', *American Journal of Sociology*, vol 107, pp 990–1064.

Gottfredson, M.R. and Hirschi, T. (1990) *A general theory of crime*, Stanford, CA: Stanford University Press.

Laub, J.H., Nagin, D.S. and Sampson, R.J. (1998) 'Trajectories of change in criminal offending: good marriages and the desistance process', *American Sociological Review*, vol 63, pp 225–38.

Leibrich, J. (1993) *Straight to the point: Angles on giving up crime*, Otago, New Zealand: University of Otago Press.

Liebling, A. and Arnold, H. (2004) *Prisons and their moral performance: a study of values, quality and prison life*, Oxford: Oxford University Press.

Maruna, S. (2001) *Making good: how ex-convicts reform and rebuild their lives*, Washington, DC: American Psychological Association Books.

Maruna, S. and Farrall, S. (2004) 'Desistance from crime: a theoretical reformulation', *Kölner Zeitschrift für Soziologie und Sozialpsychologie*, no 43, pp 171–194.

McNeill, F. (2006) 'A desistance paradigm for offender management', *Criminology and Criminal Justice*, vol 6, no 1, pp 39–62.

McNeill, F. (2009) 'Helping, holding, hurting: recalling and reforming punishment', the 6th annual Apex Lecture, at the Signet Library, Parliament Square, Edinburgh, 8 September. Available at: https://pure. strath.ac.uk/portal/files/521675/strathprints026701.pdf

McNeill, F. (2010) 'Supervision in historical context: learning the lessons of (oral) history', in F. McNeill, P. Raynorand and C. Trotter (eds) *Offender supervision: new directions in theory, research and practice*, Cullompton: Willan.

McNeill, F. and Robinson, G. (2012) 'Liquid legitimacy and community sanctions', in A. Crawford and A. Hucklesby (eds) *Legitimacy and compliance in criminal justice*, Abingdon: Routledge.

Pence, G. (1991) 'Virtue theory', in P. Singer (ed) *A companion guide to ethics*, Oxford: Blackwell.

Rex, S. (1999) 'Desistance from offending: experiences of probation', *The Howard Journal*, vol 38, no 4, pp 366–83.

Robinson, G., Farrall, S., McNeill, F., Priede, C. and Shapland, S. (forthcoming) *Understanding 'quality' in probation practice: findings from a study in England & Wales*.

Sampson, R.J. and Laub, J.H. (1993) *Crime in the making: pathways and turning points through life*, London: Harvard University Press.

Sennett, R. (1998) *The corrosion of character: the personal consequences of work in the new capitalism*, New York, NY, and London: W.W. Norton and Co.

Sennett, R. (2006) *The culture of the new capitalism*, New Haven, CT, and London: Yale University Press.

Shapland, J., Bottoms, A., Farrall, S., McNeill, F., Priede, C. and Robinson, G. (2012) 'The quality of probation supervision: a literature review', Centre for Criminological Research, University of Sheffield. Available at: http://www.sheffield.ac.uk/polopoly_fs/1.159010!/file/QualityofProbationSupervision.pdf

Shover, N. (1983) 'The later stages of ordinary property offender careers', *Social Problems*, vol 31, no 2, pp 208–18.

Sparks, R., Bottoms, A. and Hay, W. (1996) *Prisons and the problem of order*, Oxford: Clarendon Press.

Young, J. (2007) *The vertigo of late modernity*, London: Sage.

TEN

The value of values in probation practice?

Jean Henderson

Introduction

Probation values have proved somewhat elusive in recent years. While the National Offender Management Service (NOMS) and Probation Trusts have values statements, it is evident that there has been limited discussion of what they mean for practice. The key question posed in this chapter is what value a clear understanding of a professional value base for practice and the different strands to the values debate have in supporting the professional development of probation practitioners. Here, the particular focus is on practitioners undertaking the qualifying programmes for probation officers (often now termed 'offender managers' [OMs]).

The theme running throughout the chapters in this book is that of 'sides'. Becker (1967) and, more recently, Liebling (2001) both reference the notion of 'sides' and analyse the implications of whose 'side' you might be 'on' as a researcher of crime and criminal justice agencies, respectively. Although the roles discussed in this chapter are not those of researchers, there is much in their work that is relevant to the debate about probation values and their context that may offer a differing perspective, and one that helps to illuminate the relationships between the organisation, practitioners and those under supervision. The issue of 'sides' has never been more pertinent to the consideration of the values for professional practice than in the current political context (MOJ, 2013). This chapter explores the current debates about values, the different levels at which values need to be considered and how they impact on professional development. It also explores how theorising about 'sides' may support the learner in developing their understanding and identifying a value base for professional practice in turbulent times.

Where are we now with 'probation values'?

The debate about values in probation occurs in the context of an increasingly challenging environment, both outside and within the service. The broader economic and political climate of penal policy has seen a shift towards a more pecuniary approach to the measurement of performance and success, and a progressively more punitive emphasis in criminal justice interventions (MOJ, 2012a, 2012b, 2013). Growing resource pressures, the introduction of a competitive market and the complex demands on Probation Trusts to deliver public protection *and* value for money, all contribute to the various demands on practitioners. These are compounded by challenges from academia to the 'What Works' approach (Mair, 2004; Brayford et al, 2010), which was championed and heavily resourced through accredited programmes of intervention over the last decade (Chapman and Hough, 1998; McGuire, 2000).

Any discussion of values for practice in the criminal justice context needs to take account of the 'different levels' at which values operate, these being: the structural/political values that shape penal policy; organisational values; values for professional practice and conduct; and the personal values that the individual practitioner brings to their role (Lancaster, 2008; Robinson, 2011). It is perhaps the difference between these values, the way in which they are interlinked and influence each other, and the tensions between them that together form a complex – and, at times, abstract and conceptual – minefield for the learner (Thompson, 2012).

The removal of probation training from within the professional social work qualification in the mid-1990s marked the shift away from a social work value base (Nellis and Gelsthorpe, 2003; Whitehead and Statham, 2006). This value base had many useful concepts, but not all could be easily imported into contemporary probation practice and, in some cases, they were misused to disguise poor practice, particularly in relation to consistency and anti-discriminatory practice (ADP) (Faulkner, 2008). However, cutting the ties with social work meant moving away from a stated code of ethics and an academic body of literature that supported practitioners through their learning and a developmental process in relation to understanding values (Senior, 1984). While values and ADP have been embedded within the previous and current professional probation qualification frameworks, they have not been accompanied with the same wealth of entry-level academic literature to support professional learning and continuing professional development (CPD) as is available to other human service professions. This clearly carries the inherent risk of misunderstanding and disengagement with the necessary debates in respect of values and ethics in relation to professional practice in the offender management context.

In a small-scale study, Deering (2010) found evidence to suggest that the values of trainee probation officers on the Diploma in Probation Studies (DiPS) programme that replaced social work training were still more consistent with a traditional social work value base than anticipated. This may be explained by the values informing career choices. For some trainees, there was a dichotomy between perceptions of their own professional values and those required by organisational and political governance, thus creating potential for dissonance between the professional and their organisational context. The increased focus on the 'utility' of learning for practice (Millar and Burke, 2012), which reflects the shifting priorities of the organisation, may well serve as a further barrier to the discourse on values for effective offender management, and may reduce opportunities for acculturation into professional values systems. There are a number of risks in allowing this situation to flourish, not least the development of a culture of 'subterranean' values, which could militate against open and reflective debate about ethical practice and its underpinning values within the workplace, and most certainly would not support a healthy professional culture. Indeed, this could allow for misunderstandings and misinterpretations to take hold without the benefit of professional challenge, discussion or open examination in supervision, thus undermining accountable practice and, indeed, legitimacy (Gelsthorpe, 2007; Canton and Eadie, 2008).

The contemporary literature specifically on probation values is not yet plentiful, although there is a growing body of academic debate and analysis (Nellis, 2005; Gelsthorpe, 2007; Faulkner, 2008; Canton, 2011; Millar and Burke, 2012). There is a broader literature that explores the history of the service and the changing culture of the organisation and probation values (Vanstone, 2004; Whitehead and Statham, 2006; Senior, 2007; Mair and Burke, 2012). This offers detailed accounts of the past, but attention to the future is understandably circumspect given the volatile futures envisaged (Raynor, 2012). The constant state of flux within probation has not offered the stability necessary to support the development of a coherent and established literature on values for learners. Also, until recently, much of the literature has focused primarily on the debate at a political and organisational level (eg Nellis, 2005; Gelsthorpe, 2007; Senior, 2007; Lancaster, 2008). Although useful critical analysis, this has not always been easily accessible for those practitioners at earlier stages of their professional learning journey who are trying to navigate the maze of complex ethical decision–making inherent in the OM role.

Nonetheless, the literature on professional probation values is growing. However, much of this is written for an academic audience (Gelsthorpe, 2007), and practice-based guidance has been somewhat lacking until recently. Thankfully, this is a changing picture (Canton, 2007, 2011; Robinson, 2011), and the body of work that is available does provide a basis for debate about the nature of values and their importance to offender management practice in the contemporary context.

Developing an understanding of values for professional practice

It is important to begin the professional learning journey with an exploration of personal values. Developing a reflexive approach to understanding personal values and the impact of the self on the dynamics of the supervisory process is a necessary foundation for practice. Without this insight, it is difficult to explore professional values and for OMs to challenge their own beliefs and practice wisdom and the impact these might have on those under supervision. It is the starting point for the exploration of key concepts around values such as respect, discrimination/anti-discrimination, fairness, decency and public protection, rights, and accountability (Canton, 2007;Thompson, 2012).

At earlier stages in the career of the OM, it is perhaps easier to engage learners in thinking around respect, ADP, inclusion and human rights, as they are often responsible for working with individuals deemed to pose a lower risk to the community and who have committed less emotionally challenging offences. It is here that an understanding can be developed that will support the progression to exploring values and ethics in more complex cases requiring learners to consider the supervision of individuals convicted of sexual and violent offences and other serious crimes. This transition, in itself, poses certain challenges to the inexperienced. It leads to the question of whether it is equally easy to empathise with all supervisees or, what Becker (1967) would term, subordinates. Liebling (2001) suggests that, to a great extent, 'folk heroes' have tended to take centre stage in debates about the rights and powerlessness of the subordinate group in research. The reality of probation practice is, nevertheless, that practitioners have to confront the challenge posed to values of working with those most vilified by society for their offences – not just the 'folk heroes', the positively mythologised, but the 'demonised' as well. Both notions need to be challenged in order to practise in an ethically sound and accountable fashion.

A clear understanding of values is essential if practitioners are to avoid being drawn into a generalised 'fear of the bogeyman' (Maruna, 2001), resist the temptation of 'othering' (Young, 1999, 2003) and avoid ascribing a 'master status' of offender to those with whom they work (Whyte and Graham, 2010). It is suggested that the process of 'othering' impacts particularly on those with immigrant status, who are drug users or who commit serious, particularly sexual, offences (Young, 1999), and that it manifests in assumptions made about specific minority ethnic groups (Hudson and Bramhall, 2005). This reinforces the importance of an anti-discriminatory value base, as outlined by Canton (2011), as a means to guard against processes that can implicitly and unconsciously influence practice and frustrate efforts to promote change in supervisees by damaging working relationships. This is increasingly important at a time of social and organisational uncertainty. Professionals do not exist in a 'values vacuum' and at times of wider social uncertainties, they will also be susceptible to the same influences, beliefs and values as the rest of society. The temptation to shore up the sense of self to overcome ontological insecurity (Young, 2007), to bolster the sense of 'us' and the sense of solidarity offered by positioning some groups as 'the other', can be extremely persuasive (Garland, 1990). A sound knowledge and value base that enables the practitioner to reflect on their practice decisions and the nature of professional relationships with those under supervision can operate as a safeguard against unfair discrimination and promote defendable decision-making (Kemshall, 2008).

There is a need to recognise that the lifelong learning journey requires the practitioner to step out of his or her comfort zone in order to critically interrogate personal values and reconcile these with values for professional practice. For some, this may present a considerable emotional as well as academic challenge, particularly where a mismatch or tension between personal and professional values occurs. In these situations, it is not so simple as 'leaving your own values at the door of the office'; they need to be explored using a reflexive approach so as to identify and resolve the tension within an ethical framework for professional practice. Without this reflexivity, the practitioner may find it difficult to overcome either the fear of 'the other', which could promote an excessively and unfairly punitive approach to practice, or the temptation to buy into the mythologising of some types of crime, which can lead to unchallenging sympathy and collusion rather than the appropriate expression of empathy within a challenging professional relationship.

Practitioners are experiencing considerable organisational upheaval, which is more likely to add impetus to such factors than to challenge them. It could be posited that, in addition to the ontological insecurity suggested by Young (1999) as a feature of contemporary society, the pace of organisational change in values, as well as structures, could perhaps create a climate of *professional ontological insecurity*, a crisis of meaning and security in purpose for the practitioner. Clearly stated professional values are one means to work through this, and provide guidance for the practitioner, encouraging insightful and informed practice.

Professional values

Professional values for probation practice should centre around the moral basis for practice, with a focus on justice and decency in the way in which OMs work with supervisees, rather than representing the instrumental aims of the organisation (Canton, 2011). Values are closely associated with the actions and behaviour of professionals (Canton, 2007; Robinson, 2011; Robinson and Ugwudike, 2012). They are necessary as 'probation officers require a clear value base to enable them to formulate intelligent and balanced judgements and make decisions in complex situations' (Whitehead and Statham, 2006, p 167). Values constitute a set of normative beliefs (Robinson, 2011) that shape the acceptable parameters for a professional community of practice. The increasing complexity of offender management and the nature of decisions that can have considerable impact on liberty and safety need to be taken in an informed and ethical manner. OMs work with people, and, as such, professional values militate against inhumane, discriminatory and unjust practice (Nellis, 2005). While practitioners may, at times, feel somewhat powerless as 'subordinates' within the organisation, an understanding of core values encourages consideration of the hidden dynamics of power within the supervisory relationship. Understanding how power can influence supervision is key to working effectively, using authority appropriately, maintaining legitimacy and engaging supervisees in the aims of supervision (Raynor et al, 2010).

For decades, probation officers were perceived as being on the 'side' of the offender, and this may have been reflected in the individual practice of a minority of officers in the last decade. To a great extent, the legitimate function of advocacy for the disadvantaged has been interpreted as 'taking the offenders' side', and the lack of legitimate responsibility for victims added to the belief in the popular imagination and that of other criminal justice organisations that probation has little regard for victims. There is significant pressure for the probation service and OMs to demonstrate that they are 'on the side of' the victim and community, and not that of 'offenders', almost as though these are competing and incompatible 'sides' (Gelsthorpe, 2007; Faulkner and Burnett, 2012). Of course, a more nuanced understanding quickly unveils the fact that victims and offenders are not mutually exclusive groups (Whitehead and Statham, 2006). Thus, rather than 'sides', a more helpful approach to conceptualising the approach to supervisees is a holistic one informed by humanistic values that take into account the totality of the supervisees' experience, including experiences of victimisation (Miller and Burke, 2012).

Values are not set in stone and are subject to debate, interpretation and gradual change to accommodate the changing role of the professional. Nonetheless, it is core concepts such as respect, decency, dignity, rights, reasonableness, fairness, commitment to ADP and, arguably, the belief in the individual's capacity to change that should be at the heart of debates about professional probation practice (see, among others, Nellis and Gelsthorpe, 2003; Nellis, 2005; Gelsthorpe, 2007; Canton, 2007, 2011). The formation of a clear professional value base for practice requires reflexive consideration of the meaning of key concepts: how they might be used; how they might inform – and be informed by – practice; and how they might contribute to the overall aims of reducing reoffending by promoting individual change, public protection and work within the wider community. Values cannot be imposed on practice; they need to grow from professional knowledge, research and debate in both the practice and academic spheres (Gelsthorpe, 2007; Canton, 2011).

Developments in professional knowledge

Developments in academic research on the process of change and the ways in which individuals travel their personal journeys on 'the road from crime' (*Road from crime*, 2012) are presenting a significant challenge to the established 'What Works' orthodoxy of probation practice (Porporino, 2010). Albeit at a theoretical stage at present, and with practice implementation still requiring more consideration, this growing body of knowledge indicates the value of a more positive probation practice that is strengths-based and forward-looking in supporting change and individual efforts towards desistance (McNeill et al, 2010). Interventions designed on the existing cognitive behavioural theoretical premise are not being dismissed as erroneous; rather, the new research expands horizons in theorising about desistance from crime, and suggests that the Risk Need Responsivity model is not the all-encompassing model of change once hoped for (Ward and Maruna, 2007). Elements of this previous approach are still viewed as valid interventions, but emerging research suggests that these should be used within a broader context of understanding the change process, one with a more cogent positive value base in relation to the supervisee (Ward and Maruna, 2007).

Values have always underpinned probation practice, and have been particularly pertinent to the understanding of elements of practice such as pro-social modelling and motivational interviewing (Cherry, 2010). The risk with such models and methods of intervention is that effectiveness and fairness in delivery are contingent on a sound understanding of professional values and ethical practice. The conflict between this established professional knowledge and the increasingly punitive 'squeeze' on professional practice creates an uneasy and complex tension for the professional trying to reconcile research-informed practice and the pressure from 'superordinate' political powers to fulfil the demands of populist punitiveness (Bottoms, 2007) and its values, which have more to do with retribution than rehabilitation and change. Such beliefs are imbued with notions of 'offenders' as being somehow different to the rest of society, and inevitably support interventions with a punitive and exclusionary focus which demand that the professional distances him or herself and adopts an approach that is demonstrably not 'taking the side of' the supervisee (Maruna, 2001). It is as if, for practice to be accountable, there needs to be a demonstrably symbolic punitive element in supervision to prove that the OM is not colluding with the 'offender'. What the evidence from desistance-focused research is demonstrating, however, is that more inclusive and reintegrative practice by OMs is more likely to support long-term normative change (Bottoms, 2001). It is only with a confident understanding of values that the practitioner can resist the pull of populist punitiveness and an ideological approach to practice. While these may inform organisational policy and values, professional values, in contrast, serve to maintain the integrity and professionalism of the practitioner.

Desistance scholars are developing a new approach to the consideration of professional values that explores virtue ethics as a basis for probation practice (see Chapter Nine, this volume). This approach fits well with both the concept and the sophisticated application of pro-social modelling (Cherry, 2010). They recognise the difficulty for individuals in changing their lives in a frequently hostile world, but turn their attention to the *behaviour of the OM* rather than the aspirations for professional practice as indicated in values statements. They indicate that longitudinal research is clearly suggesting that a practice based on values is helpful in promoting change and that, importantly, *how* these values are expressed as part of the OM's communication and relationship is significant. The relational element of supervision has the potential to be extremely powerful (Stevens, 2013); this approach, however, suggests that this can be greatly diminished if OMs do not embrace professional values and ethics into their being as well as engaging in 'values talk' (Lancaster, 2008).

The pressure on practitioners to navigate the complex positions within probation between punitive, managerial and rehabilitative penal discourses and values further indicates that the discourse on professional values is central to the delivery of both ethical and effective practice (Nellis, 2005; Canton, 2007; Goldhill, 2010). The pendulum can, of course, swing in the opposite direction and practitioners, enthused by the positive messages coming from research about a strengths-based approach to practice, might misinterpret research findings and believe that this signifies a return to a heavy emphasis on a Kantian value base (Lancaster, 2008) and an easing back on considerations of risk. This would be an incorrect reading of the emerging desistance research; risk is not avoided and consideration of risk is located within the theorising about change (McNeill and Weaver, 2010). The impending challenge that faces both academics and practitioners, however, is to identify appropriate practice frameworks to support the desistance process that acknowledge the importance of public protection. Open clarification of professional values can serve to counteract the 'subterranean' practice referred to earlier, the place where misunderstandings and misinterpretation might flourish. The resulting outcome is greater attention to an honest and openly accountable practice to all and a professional environment within which to support the developing initiatives in practice.

The changes in National Standards (NOMS, 2011a) have significantly shifted the balance from a prescribed practice to one with greater professional autonomy. While this might be anticipated to be a welcome return to the freedom of professionalism for the experienced practitioner, for many more recently qualified practitioners, this shift has been experienced as one causing significant levels of anxiety, particularly given fears of a 'blame culture' in human services (Kemshall, 1998; Scott, 2010; Fitzgibbon, 2011). These greater levels of discretion can remind practitioners not only of their professional responsibilities and accountabilities, but also of their vulnerabilities as workers, and may create anxieties about their existing practice knowledge and wisdom, in turn increasing a sense of powerlessness within the organisation.

It is conceivable that, unless supported by robust developmental opportunities and the encouragement of a professional values discourse, this could further any sense of *professional ontological insecurity* and uncertainty for both managers and practitioners – again suggesting the importance of a shared and widely discussed understanding of professional values. Reflection at this level is crucial for understanding both the 'murky waters of practice' (Schön, 1983) and ethically sound defendable decision-making (Kemshall, 2008). Such decision-making lies at the heart of professional practice.

Given the importance of values, why has 'values talk' among probation professionals diminished (Lancaster, 2008)? It can perhaps be explained in the uneasy relationship between practice and organisational and policy imperatives. OMs are employees of Probation Trusts (and may increasingly become employees within the voluntary and private sector). They are answerable to the organisation, to NOMS, to the MOJ, to the government, to the courts and to the general public, and are also accountable to the people they supervise (Canton and Eadie, 2008).

Organisational values

The history of the probation service has been discussed extensively elsewhere. What is of note in terms of values, however, is the changing focus as the organisation has developed. Originally guided by the tradition of 'advise, assist and befriend', its values primarily gave expression to the nature of the working relationship between probation officer and the offender/supervisee. The organisation was more aligned to the professional values of practitioners. From the 1990s, however, organisational values shifted in focus to encompass the more politically driven penal discourses identified by Nellis (2005) as the 'punitive-repressive' and 'surveillant-managerial', along with the more traditional probation ethos of the 'humanistic-rehabilitative' discourse. Nellis (2005) notes that these additional discourses inherently sideline the moral dimension of criminal justice; notions of 'good' relate to compliance from both staff and offenders, rather than any reference to moral or ethical 'good' in terms of the process of professional practice. There is no easy or comfortable 'fit' to allow these discourses to coexist within the probation service. As Canton (2007) points out, not only is there a degree of tension in the influence of these discourses on policy generally and in their impact on organisational values, in some cases there is complete incompatibility.

The creation of the National Probation Service in 2001 marked a conceptual shift in the interpretation of values away from concerns with moral concepts that would inform the way in which staff worked with supervisees, towards a greater focus on pragmatic organisational concerns and priorities (Nellis and Gelsthorpe, 2003; Canton, 2007), an approach criticised by Nellis and Gelsthorpe (2003) as lacking coherence. Public protection is undoubtedly a proper aim for the modern probation service; as a core value, however, it represents an instrumental goal for policy and practice rather than a value position. Arguably, values are those beliefs and concepts that underpin the policies and practices necessary to carry out this function and the perspectives taken about focus, priorities and how they are informed by penal discourses (Kemshall, 2008).

The replacement of the National Probation Service with the broader correctional agency NOMS led to little significant change. The NOMS values statement is expressed, if anything, in broader terms of decency, respect and equality, although how these concepts are defined and operationalised is not necessarily clarified. Primacy is given to the aim of public protection, influenced by broader political and cultural concerns about risk and victims, and more specifically prompted by responses to official inquiries into serious further offences (SFOs) committed by offenders on probation supervision, making it harder to argue for values based on human rights (HMIP, 2005, 2006a, 2006b; Kemshall, 2008; Nash and Williams, 2008; Hill, 2009; O'Malley, 2010; Fitzgibbon, 2011). The fear of public approbation and political pressure has led to a shift towards a more 'risk-averse' approach based on a public protection model of risk management, and promoted an organisational climate where the rights of 'offenders' were given much less regard (Gelsthorpe, 2007; Kemshall, 2008). The contemporary penal context poses further new challenges in its more ideologically punitive and commercially driven priorities, which will inevitably create further dissonance between the values of the political superordinates and research-informed organisations and professionals. Robinson (2011) asks if a common set of values is possible across agencies involved in offender management. It could be argued, however, that the more generic values statements become in order to encompass a vast range of organisational roles, the less scope there is for developing a deep understanding of the concepts and how they might influence and be influenced by practice (Canton, 2007).

Sides

In considering the debate about 'sides', it is perhaps worth taking the advice of Becker (1967) and Liebling (2001) at this juncture and stepping back to view the various perspectives. Probation Trusts, the smaller regional units of organisation, are in a position of both superordinate and subordinate: subordinate to pressure from policymakers and the national structure of NOMS, and superordinate to practitioners. It could be argued that this accommodation of the two positions and the imperative to provide a values statement that encompasses the priorities and functions of both contributes to the lack of in-depth articulation of the meanings and understandings of key concepts. To attempt to fully articulate these may expose inconsistencies, tensions and unintended consequences, particularly around enforcement and public protection (Canton, 2007).

The professional practitioner, as identified earlier, is also in the position of both superordinate and subordinate: subordinate to organisational policy and the wider community, while superordinate and in a position of significant power in respect of decision-making in relation to the individuals subject to statutory orders. In the midst of the current organisational unease about the future – uncertainty that will inevitably raise concerns among staff regarding employment stability and professional progression – it would be easy for practitioners to feel overwhelmed by their subordinate status, and possibly to risk losing sight of the power that they hold. It is professional values, the core of which require a commitment to respect, rights, decency, fairness, ADP and accountability for actions, which can remind the practitioner that, despite the inward-facing concerns and tensions that they are experiencing themselves as employees/subordinates, there is a professional responsibility to maintain professional integrity and uphold values in practice.

The academic researcher, discussed by Becker (1967) and Liebling (2001), can usefully play a role in teasing out the various points of view (be they subordinate or superordinate), including those of the supervised. The academic researcher can contribute to the body of knowledge that informs practice, the importance of which is evident in both developments in Risk Need and Responsivity (RNR) and the growing influence of the desistance literature (Chapman and Hough, 1998; Trotter, 1999; Burnett and Roberts, 2004; McNeill et al, 2010; Porporino, 2010). There are inherent tensions in this process because research findings may not present an easy 'fit' with either penal policy or the organisational structures and processes of supervision and expectations of results. Also, ideological pressures may cause superordinate policymakers to be less receptive to findings that may prove incongruent with their political agendas for reform (see Chapter Twenty-one, this volume). The academic can, however, undertake research and present findings that can contribute the often unheard perspectives of ex-offenders and subordinates, and give voice to their experience in making positive contributions to professional practice (*Road from crime*, 2012; Stevens, 2013).

There is a further role for the academic in relation to professional education. Currently, the Probation Qualifying Framework (PQF) is embedded in academic qualifications and delivered by universities in partnership with NOMS and Probation Trusts. A key change in professional education has been the shift away from the recruitment of trainees at the point of entry to the qualification. Recruitment is now from the existing probation workforce along with some graduate entrants. These changes pose a number of challenges: first, bringing new graduate entrants (for whom qualification is undertaken over an 18-month period) up to speed with the knowledge necessary to meaningfully engage in the values debate as an essential learning outcome of the qualification; and, second, facilitating a safe environment for those experienced in the service to critically explore and challenge their own existing practice wisdom, which may at times be incongruous with the ethical demands of OM practice, particularly in relation to working with risk (not only risk of serious harm and reoffending, but also issues of child protection and mental health). For many in the latter group already imbued in the more utility-based culture of learning (Millar and Burke, 2012) of the service, taking this next step in the learning journey to the critical evaluation of practice in relation to ethics and values in a more abstract domain is a significant but necessary learning challenge, and one best achieved within the safety of a learning environment.

The tension between the pragmatic needs and requirements of the organisation in terms of competent practitioners and the demands of an ethical academically informed approach to practice are many. At a theoretical level, this could be seen as the tension between the OM as professional and bureaucrat, manifesting itself in the debates about the merits of reflective professional practice and some of the difficulties and obstacles faced by academies in facilitating and teaching content on reflection and values (Goldhill, 2010). It is within the discourse on accountability and professional discretion that the academic can support the learner in developing the academic grounding and reflexive skills to enable them to develop the knowledge that will support the confident use of professional discretion (NOMS, 2011a, 2011b).

Following Becker, Liebling (2001) identifies the need for an understanding of the power dynamic of superordinates and its nature and extent. An understanding of both the power of the organisation and the power of OMs in relation to those they supervise is crucial to practice that is underpinned by respect and principles of ADP (Canton, 2011). It is perhaps possible for the academic to step back in a similar manner to the researcher to identify the complexities of the power held by learners who themselves often feel somewhat powerless, and to encourage them to examine how this informs their practice explicitly and to reflect on the hidden dynamics of power within the supervisory relationship. This would be essential to promote the approach suggested by McNeill and Farrall (Chapter Nine, this volume). Although this learning process would not alter the dynamics of organisational power, it may contribute to the exercise of professional power in an increasingly just, fair and informed manner and promote the understanding of the relevance of professional values.

Much of this discussion has focused on 'sides' in respect of the relations between criminal justice organisations, professionals and supervisees. This risks falling into the inward-looking trap of discussing values in relation to the organisation and professional, and of seeing supervisees in a individualistic manner as 'objects' of supervision rather than individuals in the context of their broader social world (Weaver, 2012). While the concept of 'sides' can be a useful heuristic tool for examining the importance of values, we should not lose sight of the principles underpinning the values for professional practice. The inclusion of ex-offenders in communities that can offer positive social relational contexts to support and promote change on a long-term basis (Weaver, 2012) should be encouraged. 'Sides' suggests more immoveable, inflexible positions; the exclusionary potential of 'them and us' thinking on the part of communities and practitioners has been discussed earlier. Supervisees can also become trapped in mindsets that may prove to be a barrier to change and that support offending behaviour (Hercules, 2013). Value-based practice within a reflexive professional framework can support and challenge practitioners to overcome their own 'them and us' thinking. Unless practitioners can truly move beyond this polarised thinking, it is unlikely that they can successfully or ethically expect those they supervise to develop more pro-social values that might support their own integration into communities as 'ex-offenders' rather than as the excluded 'other'. Of course, nothing is quite that simple and the broader role of professionals and those concerned with supporting the desistance process is also breaking down the polarised thinking in the wider community that can pose a roadblock to individual efforts to change; perhaps a more difficult process than that of promoting individual change. Ironically, we are currently witnessing a political policy that appears to promote 'sides' and the 'othering' of 'offenders' in exclusionary language and punitive policies, while at the same time attempting to harness the experience and expertise of ex-offenders to support their initiatives, for example, with the 'through the prison gate' mentoring policy (*The Telegraph*, 2012; MOJ, 2013).

Such inconsistencies are likely to multiply as the contracting out of 'probation services' impacts on the structure and delivery of offender management. The values and ethics of the commercial marketplace will be added to the already complex relationships between the organisation, practitioner and supervisee. The voluntary sector has a much longer history of involvement with the delivery of offender management (Dominey, 2013). However, if we look at the example of voluntary drug treatment services, it could be argued that the value base of the less powerful voluntary agencies has been gradually changed and made subordinate to the superordinate position of the statutory criminal justice organisation with the power over funding and contracting (Hunt and Stevens, 2004). At present, one must be necessarily circumspect about future values for offender management at an organisational level. Putting the majority share of offender management provision out to tender could possibly see the private sector become a major provider of services, holding the superordinate power that brings with it the power to influence values, with the voluntary and state sector positioned as commercial competitors. This opens up the provision of community supervision to the broader forces of globalisation and fragmentation, which, far from promoting the localised community responses to crime and offending suggested by the Big Society policy (Flinders and Moon, 2011), distances provision from local control and inclusion in ways that are consistent with the expansion of the global power of multinational companies (Bauman, 1998).

In the midst of major upheaval, it is imperative that values are considered in the shaping of future provision. Without professional values supported by the organisations responsible for delivery, it is possible that the more punitive measures suggested by the current Home Secretary (MOJ, 2013) could be implemented with limited regard for the core values necessary for the delivery of offender management in a decent and fair manner that properly respects rights and retains legitimacy (Robinson and Ugwudike, 2012). As we have seen earlier, fragmentation at an organisational level could make the promotion of a unifying set of values beyond vague statements lacking in conceptual definition even more difficult. It is perhaps here that the reaffirmation of professional values can serve as a unifying bond for offender management. The National Association of Probation Officers has recently published guidance for professional practice, within which there is a statement of values for professional practice (NAPO, 2012). There has also been recent consideration of an initiative to promote the development of professional registration (PCA, 2013), along the lines of the registration of social workers (BASW, 2012). If implemented, registration should be integrated with professional standards, which could and should, include a statement of professional ethics. Canton (2011) puts forward a compelling argument for the centrality of a human rights professional value base for practice as a way in which to make an understanding of probation values accessible to the wider criminal justice community and beyond and to provide a legal legitimacy to support the values of professional practice, not just with those on supervision, but with all of those to whom probation practitioners are accountable. The notion of professional values for offender management can – and could – transcend organisational boundaries and competition, and provide professional guidance for practitioners in carrying out the role of OM regardless of location. It would be naive not to recognise that this might be contested ground between the superordinate employers and subordinate groups of employees, but the legal legitimacy suggested by Canton (2011) would afford the necessary gravitas to professional concerns. Perhaps now more than ever, the probation service as we know it and the voluntary sector have a vested interest in promoting professional values and the importance of professionally trained practitioners. It may be that the threat to much that has long been held dear and valued about professional practice will galvanise all involved in offender management to reinforce and strengthen the case for the importance of professional values and ethics to guide and shape practice with individuals subject to statutory supervision.

Whitehead and Statham (2006) talk of the need to renew some sense of professional cultural identity to repair the 'cultural fragmentation' caused by bureaucracy. The challenge in the current penal climate will be to promote and maintain a professional cultural identity as the organisational identity is eroded and fragmented. It is perhaps time for those in the criminal justice sector to overcome the superordinate– subordinate divide between organisation and professionals that has grown as organisations have tried to bow to political superordinates

(Senior, 2007). The uniting force should be the shared sense of professional values. By galvanising the less tangible professional culture, the spirit and ethos of probation could be maintained in a way that transcends disappearing and changing organisational structures.

References

Bauman, Z. (1998) *Globalization: the human consequences*, Cambridge: Polity Press.

Becker, H. (1967) 'Whose side are we on?', *Social Problems*, vol 14, pp 239–47.

Bottoms, A. (2001) 'Compliance and community penalties', in A. Bottoms, L. Gelsthorpe and S. Rex (eds) *Community penalties: change and challenges*, Cullompton: Willan, pp 87–116.

Bottoms, A. (2007) 'Populist punitiveness', in R. Canton and D. Hancock (eds) *Dictionary of probation and offender management*, Cullompton: Willan.

Brayford, J., Cowe, F. and Deering, J. (eds) (2010) *What else works? Creative work with offenders*, Cullompton: Willan.

BASW (British Association of Social Workers) (2012) *The Code of Ethics for Social Work: statement of principles*, London: BASW.

Burnett, R. and Roberts, C. (eds) (2004) *What works in probation and youth justice: developing evidence-based practice*, Cullompton: Willan.

Canton, R. (2007) 'Probation and the tragedy of punishment', *The Howard Journal*, vol 46, no 3, pp 236–54.

Canton, R. (2011) *Probation: working with offenders*, Abingdon: Routledge.

Canton, R. and Eadie, T. (2008) 'Accountability, legitimacy and discretion: applying criminology in professional practice', in B. Stout, J. Yates and B. Williams (eds) *Applied criminology*, London: Sage, pp 86–102.

Chapman, T. and Hough, M. (1998) *Evidence based practice*, London: HMIP.

Cherry, S. (2010) *Transforming behaviour: pro-social modelling in practice. A handbook for practitioners and managers*, Cullompton: Willan.

Deering, J. (2010) 'Attitudes and beliefs of trainee probation officers: a "new breed"?', *Probation Journal*, vol 57, no 9, pp 9–26.

Dominey, J. (2013) 'A mixed market for probation services: can lessons from the recent past help shape the near future?', *Probation Journal*, vol 59, pp 339–54.

Faulkner, D. (2008) 'The new shape of probation in England and Wales: values and opportunities in a changing context', *Probation Journal*, vol 55, pp 71–83.

Faulkner, D. and Burnett, R. (2012) *Where next for criminal justice?*, Bristol: The Policy Press.

Fitzgibbon, W. (2011) *Probation and social work on trial: violent offenders and child abusers*, Basingstoke: Palgrave Macmillan.

Flinders, M. and Moon, D.S. (2011) 'The problem of letting go: the "Big Society", accountable governance and "the curse of the decentralizing minister"', *Local Economy*, vol 26, p 652.

Garland, D. (1990) *Punishment and modern society: a study in social theory*, Oxford: Clarendon Press.

Gelsthorpe, L. (2007) 'Probation values and human rights', in L. Gelsthorpe and R. Morgan (eds) *Handbook of probation*, Cullompton: Willan, pp 485–517.

Goldhill, R. (2010) 'Reflective practice and distance learning: problems and potentials for probation training', *Reflective Practice: International and Multidisciplinary Perspectives*, vol 11, no 1, pp 57–70.

Hercules, T. (2013) 'Understanding the "Social Deprivation Mindset": an ex-offender speaks', *British Journal of Community Justice*, vol 10, no 3, pp 7–21.

Hill, L. (2009) *Investigation into the issues arising from the Serious Further Offence Review: Dano Sonnex*, London: NOMS.

HMIP (Her Majesty's Inspectorate of Probation) (2005) *Inquiry into the supervision of Peter Williams by Nottingham City Youth Offending Team*, London: HMIP.

HMIP (2006a) *An independent review of a Serious Further Offence case: Damien Hanson & Elliot White*, London: Home Office.

HMIP (2006b) *An independent review of a Serious Further Offence case: Anthony Rice*, London: HMIP.

Hudson, B. and Bramhall, G. (2005) 'Assessing the "other": constructions of "Asianess" in risk assessments by probation officers', *British Journal of Criminology*, vol 45, pp 721–40.

Hunt, N. and Stevens, A. (2004) 'Whose harm? Harm reduction and the shift to coercion in UK drug policy', *Social Policy and Society*, vol 3, pp 333–42.

Kemshall, H. (1998) 'Defensible decisions for risk: or "It's the doers wot get the blame"', *Probation Journal*, vol 45, no 2, pp 67–72.

Kemshall, H. (2008) *Understanding the community management of high risk offenders*, Maidenhead: OUP.

Lancaster, E. (2008) 'Values talk in the criminal justice system', in S. Green, E. Lancaster and S. Feasey (eds) *Addressing offending behaviour: context, practice, and values*, Cullompton: Willan, pp 368–84.

Liebling, A. (2001) 'Whose side are we on? Theory, practice and allegiances in prisons research', *British Journal of Criminology*, vol 41, pp 472–84.

Mair, G. (ed) (2004) *What matters in probation?*, Cullompton: Willan.

Mair, G. and Burke, L. (2012) *Redemption, rehabilitation and risk management: a history of probation*, Abingdon: Routledge.

Maruna, S. (2001) *Making good: how ex-convicts reform and rebuild their lives*, Washington, DC: American Psychological Association.

McGuire, J. (2000) *Cognitive-behavioural approaches: an introduction to theory and research*, London: HMIP, HMS.

McNeill, F. and Weaver, B. (2010) *Changing lives? Desistance research and offender management Report 3/2010*, Glasgow: Scottish Centre for Crime and Justice Research.

McNeill, F., Raynor, P. and Trotter, C. (eds) (2010) *Offender supervision: new directions in theory, research and practice*, Cullompton: Willan.

Millar, M. and Burke, L. (2012) 'Thinking beyond "utility": some comments on probation practice and training', *The Howard Journal of Criminal Justice*, vol 51, no 3, p 317.

MOJ (Ministry of Justice) (2012a) *Punishment and reform: effective probation services. Consultation paper CP7/2012*, London: TSO.

MOJ (2012b) *Punishment and reform: effective community sentences. Consultation paper CP8/2012*, London: TSO.

MOJ (2013) *Transforming rehabilitation: a revolution in the way we manage offenders. Consultation paper CP1/2013*, London: TSO.

NAPO (2012) *2012 Professional Practice Book*, London: NAPO.

Nash, M. and Williams, A. (2008) *The anatomy of serious further offending*, Oxford: Oxford University Press.

Nellis, M. (2005) 'Dim prospects: humanistic values and the fate of community justice', in J. Winstone and F. Pakes (eds) *Community justice: issues for probation and criminal justice*, Cullompton: Willan, pp 33–51.

Nellis, M. and Gelsthorpe, L. (2003) 'Human rights and the probation values debate', in W.H. Chui and M. Nellis (eds) *Moving probation forward: evidence, arguments and practice*, Harlow: Pearson Longman, pp 227–44.

NOMS (National Offender Management Service) (2011a) *National standards for the supervision of offenders in England and Wales*, London: Ministry of Justice.

NOMS (2011b) 'Offender engagement programme news. Sep 2011'. Available at: http://www.essexprobationtrust.org.uk/doc/Offender_Engagement_Programme_News_Sept_11.pdf (accessed 11 February 2013).

O'Mally, P. (2010) *Crime and risk*, London: Sage.

Porporino, F.J. (2010) 'Bringing sense and sensitivity to corrections: from programmes to "fix" offenders to services to support desisters', in J. Brayford, F. Cowe and J. Deering (eds) *What else works? Creative work with offenders*, Cullompton: Willan, pp 61–85.

PCA (Probation Chiefs Association) (2013) website, http:// probationchiefs.org/?s=professional+registration&submit=Search

Raynor, P. (2012) 'Is probation still possible?', *The Howard Journal of Criminal Justice*, vol 51, no 2, pp 173–89.

Raynor, P., Ugwudike, P. and Vanstone, M. (2010) 'Skills and strategies in probation supervision: the Jersey study', in F. McNeill, P. Raynor and C. Trotter (eds) *Offender supervision: new directions in theory, research and practice*, Cullompton: Willan.

Road from Crime (2012) Film, Discovering Desistance Project, Institute for Research and Innovation in Social Services (IRISS). Available at: www.iriss.org.uk/resources/the-road-from-crime (last accessed 12 June 2013).

Robinson, A. (2011) *Foundations for offender management: theory, law and policy for contemporary practice*, Bristol: The Policy Press.

Robinson, G. and Ugwudike, P. (2012) 'Investing in "toughness": probation, enforcement and legitimacy', *The Howard Journal of Criminal Justice*, vol 51, no 3, pp 300–16.

Schön, D.A. (1983) *The reflective practitioner: how professionals think in action*, New York, NY: Basic Books.

Scott, D.M. (2010) 'Who's protecting who?', *Probation Journal*, vol 57, no 3, pp 291–5.

Senior, P. (1984) 'The probation order: vehicle of social work or social control?', *Probation Journal*, vol 31, no 64, pp 64–70.

Senior, P. (2007) 'Modernisation and the correctional service', in P. Senior, C. Crowther-Dowey and M. Long (eds) *Understanding modernisation in criminal justice*, Maidenhead: Open University Press.

Stevens, A. (2013) *Offender rehabilitation and therapeutic communities: enabling change the TC way*, International Series on Desistance and Rehabilitation, London: Routledge.

The Telegraph (2012) 'Chris Grayling proposes jail-gate mentors to help cut reoffending', 20 November. Available at: www.telegraph.co.uk/news/uknews/crime/9690272/Chris-Grayling-proposes-jail-gate-mentors-to-help-cut-reoffending.html (accessed 6 February 2013).

Thompson, N. (2012) *Anti-discriminatory practice* (5th edn), London: Sage.

Trotter, C. (1999) *A guide to working with involuntary clients*, London: Sage.

Vanstone, M. (2004) *Supervising offenders in the community: a history of probation, theory and practice*, Aldershot: Ashgate.

Ward, T. and Maruna, S. (2007) *Rehabilitation: beyond the risk paradigm*, London: Routledge.

Weaver, B. (2012) 'The relational context of desistance: some implications and opportunities for social policy', *Social Policy and Administration*, vol 46, no 4, pp 395–412.

Whitehead, P. and Statham, R. (2006) *The history of probation: politics, power and cultural change 1876–2005*, Crayford: Shaw & Sons.

Whyte, R. and Graham, H. (2010) *Working with offenders: a guide to concepts and practices*, Cullompton: Willan.

Young, J. (1999) *The exclusive society*, London: Sage.

Young, J. (2003) 'Merton with energy, Katz with structure: the sociology of vindictiveness and the criminology of transgression', *Theoretical Criminology*, vol 7, p 388.

Young, J. (2007) *The vertigo of late modernity*, London: Sage.

ELEVEN

Developments in police education in England and Wales: values, culture and 'common-sense' policing

Craig Paterson and Ed Pollock

Introduction

The dominant reform agenda of the police service in England and Wales for the last three decades has revolved around the re-emergence of community policing and a languorous cultural shift from 'rules' to 'values' (Clark, 2005). At the heart of this shift is conflict between a reflective emphasis on the underpinning 'values' of policing and a pragmatic emphasis on the common-sense 'craft' of police work. This presents challenges for training and education and, for police officers, raises the question, 'Whose side are we on?'. Attempts to inculcate more flexible thinking about values, bringing police officers closer to the communities they serve, has often met with resistance manifested through a myriad of police occupational cultures. Consequently, an implementation gap has appeared between the resurgence of a community policing philosophy, the training and development police officers receive to carry out this role, and the practice of street-level community policing.

A new model of police education and development has emerged in England and Wales, running from pre-entry recruitment, through career qualifications, to preparation for leadership and senior command (Flanagan, 2008; Neyroud, 2011; Sherman, 2011). A shift towards police education has long been advocated by international scholars as a mechanism for broader police reform (Bayley and Bittner, 1984; Chan, 1997; Roberg and Bonn, 2004), yet the community values that lie at the heart of this reform agenda have been met with sustained resistance by in-service police officers across a number of international jurisdictions and at all levels of the police hierarchy. This chapter identifies problems encountered when researching personal or professional values and outlines how changes to the provision of police training and education can address the cultural issues that have been subject to sustained public criticism. The chapter subsequently draws on evidence from training and education programmes in Europe and the US and puts forward an understanding of values that is able to envisage long-term change and reform within the police service.

Police education in England and Wales

The regionalised structure of the police in England and Wales makes it difficult to develop a coherent national strategy for police learning and development, resulting in fragmented training provision, little oversight of training delivery and the absence of a clear evidence base to support policy developments (Peace, 2006). Reform has also been inhibited by resistance from police officers to academic study in what is regarded as a practice-focused vocation. Put succinctly, educational programmes are not seen to fit within the 'socio-political context of police work' (Chan, 1996, p 110). Kratcoski (2004, pp 103–4) defines education as 'developing the ability to conceptualize and expand the theoretical and analytical learning process', whereas training involves 'gaining the skills needed to accomplish the immediate tasks and goals of police operations'. This definition is contested but, for the purposes of this chapter, means that any significant reform of police development programmes must be cognisant of cultural reactions to change and the symbolic meaning for police officers of a shift from training to education.

The roots of reform in police learning emerged out of the 2002 Her Majesty's Inspectorate of Constabulary (HMIC, 2002) report on police training that was instigated by the damning conclusions on police culture from the MacPherson Report (MacPherson, 1999), following the inquiry into the death of Stephen Lawrence. The findings and recommendations of the 2002 HMIC report led to the development of the Initial Police Learning and Development Programme (IPLDP) with the aim of delivering cultural change and an ethos of continued professional development within the police service. More recently, the Flanagan (2008) and Neyroud (2011) reviews provided renewed momentum for reform and the establishment of more explicit links with educational institutions. At the same time, the national roll-out of neighbourhood policing in England and Wales in 2008 further enhanced the need for community-oriented police training, foregrounding communication skills and conflict resolution (Feltes, 2002; Peace, 2006).

More recently, the police service has encouraged a greater educational focus on reasons, judgements and values (Lee, 2011). This has enabled police officers in England and Wales to take ownership of their decision-making and now incorporates partnerships with universities with experience of delivering the deeper learning required in these areas. This shift in educational focus reflects the sustained challenge faced by the police service in delivering cultural change and an emphasis on reflective practice. A long history of reflective practice exists in other professions, such as law, medicine, teaching and social work. However, this has been resisted by the police service until the introduction of IPLDP. IPLDP has been delivered pre- and post-employment, yet local implementation has resulted in significant variation in its delivery via experienced police trainers, former police officers and trained civilians. These delivery mechanisms are expected to diversify further, with strategic imperatives pointing towards flexible entry routes that either retain provision within forces or use external agencies from the higher education and private sectors (NPIA, 2011).

In 2011, the police service in England and Wales launched a new statement of mission and values, putting forward the purpose and objectives of the organisation and embracing the historical legacy of Peel's principles, previous values statements and the Human Rights Act 1998. The new statement clearly articulates values and acknowledges their impact on practice:

> We will act with integrity, compassion, courtesy and patience, showing neither fear nor favour in what we do. We will be sensitive to the needs and dignity of victims and demonstrate respect for the human rights of all. We will use discretion, professional judgement and common sense to guide us and will be accountable for our decisions and actions. (ACPO, 2011)

A common decision-making process was issued alongside the new statement of mission and values. The 'national decision making model aims to improve the delivery of policing in accordance with our values' and to enhance 'the use of discretion and professional judgement' (ACPO, 2011). This statement acknowledges the contested relationship between values at the policy level and values in practice once they have come into conflict with the 'common-sense' organisational assumptions that condition the policing environment. Within this context, a multitude of contested value systems emerge, both embracing and contesting official codes of standards, ethics and behaviour. This helps to explain the resistance to police education that becomes apparent among some experienced police officers (see Haynes, 2009) and allows us to envisage a growing cohort of police officers emerging from a reformed police education system who embrace the democratic values intrinsic to community policing philosophies. The next section highlights the methodological issues raised when researching values in policing and the consequences for police reform.

Researching subcultural values in policing

In research, studying those whose value systems are different from our own or that might be considered 'mainstream' can be difficult (see Chapter Twenty-one, this volume). For example, police subculture influences the construction of a value system that determines how police officers might perceive and think about those with whom they come into contact in the course of their work. This theoretical perspective also attempts to explain how these values are culturally transmitted in the course of a group's social interaction and then embedded in the minds of individuals. However, it is important to give a voice in research to those who hold different values and, at the same time, to strive to maintain our objectivity. As Ely (1993, p 218) states: 'striving to be faithful to another's viewpoint is striving to be ethical'. What we see and hear in research may run counter to our own experience, beliefs or moral principles, and because the police are meant to be an impartial and non-discriminatory public service, unethical and prejudicial views encountered in police research may be in conflict with both public opinion and the code of conduct to which the police service is bound. This raises questions for researchers about who we align ourselves with when conducting research and who owns or has access to the research findings. Criminological research has split into two schools of police research with *critical criminologists* questioning the role and function of the police within society and *police-friendly* researchers focusing on policy, strategy and performance (Paterson and Pollock, 2011). Both schools would claim to represent the *public* or *community*, yet their generation of knowledge and its subsequent use is also driven by the values within which they situate police work.

In a profession such as policing, value and moral judgements and discretionary decision-making is an essential part of operational practice. Under the provisions of the Police Act 2002, every newly appointed police officer must swear an *oath of office* in front of a magistrate promising that:

> I ... do solemnly and sincerely declare and affirm that I will well and truly serve the Queen in the office of constable, with fairness, integrity, diligence and impartiality, upholding fundamental human rights and according equal respect to all people; and that I will, to the best of my power, cause the peace to be kept and preserved and prevent all offences against people and property; and that while I continue to hold the said office I will to the best of my skill and knowledge discharge all the duties thereof faithfully according to law. (Police Act 2002)

A clear sense of police officer values can be found within this oath as well as an indication of the challenges presented in implementing these values in practice. Research into the methodological issues raised in researching people's professional values and perspectives has most prominently been connected with the disciplines of education and social work – professions where the welfare of an individual and responses to problems need a 'human' approach rather than an approach that is dictated by rules, regulation and law. The term 'values' implies the use of subjective judgements and attitudes towards others, while legal perspectives place an emphasis on 'rules', which can be seen to impart restrictions on discretionary decision-making. This can create a perception that legal rules are in conflict with values and individual perspectives given that, as Banks (2006, p 11) states, 'laws do not tell us what we ought to do but just what we can do'. This complexity led Lord Scarman, in the wake of the Brixton riots, to define discretion as 'the art of suiting action to a particular circumstance' (Scarman, 1981, p 63).

Research on policing has consistently demonstrated that operational police work is rarely guided solely by legal precepts, but also by the extensive discretion of police officers in how they enforce the law (Chan, 1997; Reiner, 2010). The impact of the values of individual police officers (regardless of whether, as Burgess [1954] contends, such values result from innate biologism or cultural transmission) is therefore experienced by the general public at the street level, where operational policing is practised.

Research on police values and culture has often focused on how employees are racially and sexually discriminatory towards the public as service users or towards fellow police service employees. Several studies have been conducted into racial discrimination towards service users since the 1981 riots in Brixton, London, and other parts of the UK. The riots were caused by social and economic problems affecting Britain's inner cities, racial disadvantage, and a loss of confidence and mistrust in the police among minority ethnic communities (Scarman, 1981). Similarly, the more recent riots in several UK cities in August 2011 were attributed, in part, to the 'widespread anger and frustration at people's treatment at the hands of the police' (*The Guardian* and LSE, 2011, p 4). Much of this resentment emanated from the ways the police used stop-and-search powers, which were perceived to be unfairly targeted at black and Asian people and conducted in an aggressive and discourteous manner.

The inquiry into the investigation of the murder of Stephen Lawrence further highlighted the impact of an institutionally racist police culture upon police employees and professional competence (MacPherson, 1999). The police service has subsequently tried to address discriminatory police culture by developing a more citizen-focused, proactive and community-oriented policing approach in order to improve relations between the police and the wider community. However, changing the prejudicial attitudes of individual police officers towards a group, or members of a group, is difficult to achieve given the often covert or hidden nature of individual prejudices. For example, any employee of the police service is prohibited from joining or promoting groups that endorse or support prejudice. However, although this might prevent overt prejudice, it does not prevent those working for the police service from expressing their prejudice in private or when among like-minded colleagues.

Racial discrimination directed towards police service employees has been highlighted by MacPherson (1999), and there is a wide body of similar research (see, eg, Fielding, 1994; Gregory and Lees, 1999) outlining the malign influence of hegemonic masculinity and misogyny upon female police service employees. Westmarland (2001) has found evidence of sexism in police officer contact with female service users, most prevalent in relation to offences seen as women-specific, such as domestic violence (see also IPCC, 2010) and sexual abuse (Laville, 2009). The police service has attempted to address this form of police culture by improving internal policies and procedures in the arenas of diversity awareness, complaints and the recruitment, selection, retention and promotion of a wider demographic of police officers, but while gradual change is evident, many of these initiatives still meet with cultural resistance at all levels of the police service (Holland, 2007; Stanko, 2007). This has led to much cynicism from liberal academics about the possibility of reform within the police service (for a recent example, see Loftus, 2009).

Conversely, other contemporary analyses of police culture emphasise its interpretive and creative aspects as well as the existence of a multitude of cultural layers, which can help us to envisage processes of organisational change. Most usefully, Manning (1993) has suggested that there are three subcultures of policing – senior command, middle management and the rank and file – which can be used to enable processes of police reform. Chan (1996, p 110) takes this further and suggests that police culture 'results from the interaction between the socio-political context of police work and various dimensions of police organisational knowledge'. This framework provides an acknowledgement of multiple police cultures that work both horizontally and vertically within the organisation as well as across time and space. Manning's conceptual separation of three subcultures of policing helps us to interpret the organisational emphasis that is placed upon values and ethics at different levels of the police hierarchy and explains police resistance to new initiatives that do not already exist within the framework of existing police (cultural) knowledge. Thus, rather than understanding police culture as static and monolithic, it is more helpful to emphasise the importance of the social, legal and political sites in which policing takes place. Reforming police culture and providing a meaningful position for values within policing demands change from all three subcultures of policing (Chan, 1996; Heslop, 2011). This perspective can be applied to current thinking on the shift from police training to police education.

Values and culture in police education

The historical roots of the police service – within the blue-collar traditions of working-class communities and the hierarchical organisational model of the military – produced a masculine and conservative occupational subculture that embraced homogeneity and hierarchy ahead of diversity. For the majority of police history, the public (and especially offenders) appeared at the bottom of this hierarchy – as those with least knowledge about crime problems. Community policing inverts this hierarchy and resituates communities as sources of knowledge for the police at all levels of the hierarchical structure. Police education represents a central shift in this reform process, with officers encouraged to question the established hierarchical order that generates police organisational knowledge and to seek answers from empowered communities. Whereas police training taught officers how to deliver policing *to* the public, police education seeks to encourage more flexible values thinking from officers who actively engage *with* diverse communities. The absence of a police education programme helps to explain the time lag identified by Cox between the official introduction of community policing and its actual appearance within street–level policing: 'Policing is socially constructed and thus is in a constant state of flux as to its meaning and value ... the three decade lag in getting police education to align with community policing is not easily explained' (Cox, 2011, pp 14–15).

Policing across democratic societies takes place within a political landscape that acknowledges the importance of social justice, social cohesion, fairness, equity and human rights. Bayley and Bittner (1984) argue that these values can be taught to police recruits. Roberg and Bonn (2004) take this further and argue that education (rather than training) is necessary for the development of these values and the effective use of discretion that maintains and enhances police performance, police accountability and police professionalism. Nevertheless, the conceptualisation and articulation of a values-based culture is a challenging task for police organisations, and measuring the extent to which it has been integrated into policing remains an insurmountable challenge (Cox, 2011, p 17). The history of police reform, particularly in the areas of training and education, has been littered with recurrent chronological themes of new ideas, policy implementation, cynicism and eventual institutional memory loss (Holland, 2007; Skogan, 2008).

The resistance presented by police culture to the integration of ethical values into a pragmatically focused police role has been highlighted in a number of Western countries (Chan, 1997; Skolnick, 2008; Reiner, 2010), although it can be difficult to articulate exactly why this resistance occurs. While law, ethics and policing are by no means seen as mutually exclusive, there is a body of evidence indicating that police personnel may view ethical and legal principles as obstacles to effective police practice (Neyroud and Beckley, 2001). This helps us to understand the delay between the rediscovery of community policing at the policy level and a suitable programme of police education to make it happen on the ground. Police resistance to the value of education has been identified in a number of international jurisdictions (Roberg and Bonn, 2004; Wimhurst and Ransley, 2007; Haynes, 2009) and encourages us to look elsewhere for guidance in the development of police education programmes.

The shift to community policing in Northern Europe has been accompanied by reforms in police education that focus on an improvement in the quality of policing. In the Netherlands, the police use a dual system of education and training in order to facilitate clear links between theory and practice (Peeters, 2010). This involves collaborative frameworks for police training and education, with police institutions articulating the occupational requirements of different policing functions, while educational institutions identify the curriculum and learning requirements that correspond to the occupational role. Similarly, Feltes' (2002) work in Germany emphasises the importance of communication and conflict resolution skills alongside the traditional focus on the law for community-oriented police. Both Feltes (2002) and Peace (2006), writing in the UK context, indicate that models of police education emphasising the values of community policing should contain: clear objectives; community-oriented curriculum content; and an appropriate method to facilitate the transition from a focus on law enforcement to a focus on community.

Jaschke (2010, p 303) points outs that policy developments in the EU have already led towards the establishment of a 'modern police science', an integrative academic discipline that draws from a range of knowledge bases from within and outside the police with the aim of enhancing police professionalism and the quality of service. The development of police studies in Germany was justified by the value it offered to the police and society to: increase professionalism; develop a research-based approach to crime reduction; develop a portfolio of police programmes for different levels; and encourage a comparative approach that makes the most of developments in other countries (Jaschke and Neidhart, 2007).

This evidence base highlights the importance of a clear concept of what police 'values' might be and the value of police education in enacting sustainable reforms. Criticism of the police often emerges when police officers do not demonstrate the values expected by members of the public, hence the emphasis in policy in England and Wales on civility and procedural justice. Hough et al (2010) identified a clear relationship between the way policing is carried out and experienced by the public (procedural justice) and levels of public trust and confidence in the police. The introduction of a professional body for policing provides the potential for an agreement about what the core police mission is, how this mission can be achieved and the values that the police service should embrace (Sherman, 2011). This agreement can be conveyed to police officers of all ranks across the country and to the wider public via the independent members of the police body. This presents a unique opportunity to enact radical reform in the arena of values and culture.

As Cox (2011) has acknowledged, reform in police education and training requires a clear conceptualisation of police 'values' that can be operationalised across all three strata of police subculture. Marenin's (2005, p 109) requirements of democratic policing (*professionalism, legitimacy* and *accountability*) provide a potential framework for understanding how a focus on police education can contribute to the learning and development of police officers at all levels of the police hierarchy and an appreciation of the practical use of 'values' as drivers of police reform. The final section uses this framework for understanding police values, and the related role of police education.

Marenin's framework for democratic policing

Professionalism

Across Western countries, values have been integrated into police training and education as part of the process of professionalisation and organisational reform. At the senior and middle management levels, this process of reform aims to enact a shift away from strong command and control systems, which emphasise the importance of hierarchy. At the officer level, Schein's (1996) work on organisational culture points to the importance of recruiting graduates who have the critical thinking skills to challenge managers and traditional modes of thinking, as outlined in the literature on police culture. This echoes the work of Lee and Punch (2004), who note that police education is emphasised in a range of policing and crime-focused undergraduate courses that aim to develop police officers' critical thinking skills or 'sense-making' (Cox, 2011) within the context of their police knowledge. At the street level, this deeper learning encourages the development of a more flexible value system while also generating transferable skills that help individuals to develop competence in a number of areas (Jaschke and Neidhardt, 2007). The success of these initiatives is demonstrated in practice through improvements in officer attitudes, the more effective use of discretion, reduced complaints and increased public support for the police. The evidence for these improvements is outlined in the following pages, although it is important to note that the evidence base for improved police performance remains unclear.

Both Conti and Nolan (2005) in the US and Peace (2006) in England and Wales argue that the focus within police training upon law enforcement conducted via isolated police training schools runs contrary to the acknowledged values set out in models of community policing. Thus, the current police structure (both the curriculum and the training school) acts as an inhibitor to organisational reform and is unlikely to counteract the emergence of authoritarian values that provoke crises surrounding police professionalism (Wimshurst and Ransley, 2007; Blakemore and Simpson, 2010). Birzer (2003) and Peace (2006) advocate a dual educational strategy with teacher-centred tuition for programmed instruction related to law and procedure, and humanistic, student-oriented strategies for the exploration of the affective issues related to values and community policing conducted in neutral environments. This strategic approach emphasises the importance of contextual police knowledge alongside the pragmatic emphasis on legal process (Chan, 1997) to envisage a change in police practice and to enhance police professionalism. Heslop (2011) posits a valuable warning here: the university environment also has the potential to reproduce negative facets of both academic and police culture and to generate unintended and unforeseen conflict as two different and distinct organisational cultures collide (see Wood and Tong, 2009).

Legitimacy

A key area of concern for all democratic countries involves the quality of the relationship that the police have with civil society. Police legitimacy (most commonly interpreted as 'public confidence' in England and Wales) can be enhanced through the accreditation of police training and education. The introduction of higher education certificates in Australia led to increased public support for the police. Similarly, in the US, Paoline and Terrill (2007) found that officers with higher levels of education received fewer complaints and worked in areas with higher citizen satisfaction. The accreditation of police knowledge in the form of academic qualifications in England and Wales emphasises the importance of a transparent evidence base that underpins policing strategies (Sherman, 2011) and can also be expected to improve police legitimacy with the general public, other state agencies and the police service itself (Heslop, 2011).

Ivkovic (2008) has demonstrated that public confidence in the police across jurisdictions is related to the quality of governance in each country as well as the contact individuals have with the police. Research from the US has shown that higher education leads to improvements in officer attitudes, behaviour (reduced complaints) and the use of discretion, which improves public perception of police fairness as well as police performance (Roberg and Bonn, 2004, p 474), particularly when it is combined with job experience (Paoline and Terrill, 2007). Studies in the US have emphasised that the educational process to engender long-term change should focus specifically on new recruits, rather than those who are already employed by the police service and are weighed down by practical cynicism (Roberg and Bonn, 2004). Ultimately, it is the consumer who defines the true nature of any organisation's values (Wasserman and Moore, 1988, p 2), and, within a policing context, improvements in public confidence in the police lead to enhanced police legitimacy. The value of procedural legitimacy and public confidence in the police further relates to levels of trust and engagement with the community and the value of effective public accountability mechanisms.

Accountability

Present accountability mechanisms have emerged over the past half-century from, for example, the implementation of legislation such as the Human Rights Act 1998 and Police Reform Act 2002, and the establishment of the Royal Commissions to review the constitutional position of the police in 1960 and criminal procedures in 1981. However, these modes of accountability do not provide an opportunity for the public to influence operational policing priorities, and the structures that do (eg police authorities) have been viewed by the public as largely ineffective (see Docking, 2003). Consequently, the Coalition government has created the posts of elected Police and Crime Commissioners (PCCs), who, from November 2012, have replaced Police Authorities in every constabulary in England and Wales. The government hopes that local PCCs will be more accessible and responsive to the public than Police Authorities and that their elected status will render police action more accountable to local citizens and the values held by local communities.

There is also a desire among senior police officers and politicians in the UK to improve accountability between the community and police service at street level, but the process of translating this commitment into practice is bound to encounter resistance from front-line officers inculcated in a myriad of different cultures, values and practices (Lipsky, 1980). Engendering community-focused policing strategies has lain at the heart of policing philosophy since the election of the New Labour government in 1997. Neighbourhood, citizen-focused and reassurance policing strategies and police Community Support Officers were all introduced to improve relations between the police and public via enhanced mutual engagement. Community-oriented policing aims to convince the public that they and the police are working on the same side and with mutual values (creating safe communities, reducing fear of crime, building and maintaining mutual trust, and improving the visibility of and access to policing agents). Hence, a community-oriented policing philosophy can only work to its maximum degree if the myriad of cultures, values and practices to which Lipsky (1980) refers secures the full appreciation of both the police and public.

The professional use of police officer discretion, understood as making appropriate situational judgements (Marenin, 2005, p 109), is a central factor in improving public perceptions of the police and their accountability to the public. Research by Docking (2003) has identified a gap between the public's expectation of policing and the service provided to them, as well as a perception that police officers subscribe to a separate set of values to other members of society. This explains why the outcomes of traditional police procedures in England and Wales have frequently been unsatisfactory for victims, offenders and the wider community (Bradford et al, 2009). The disjuncture in service delivery became evident through public surveys of police performance in England and Wales, which indicated a general decline in satisfaction with the police during the 1990s and specific rises in dissatisfaction whenever there was contact with an individual, even at a time when substantial and sustained reductions in crime were taking place (Bradford et al, 2009). Thus, public frustration emanated from day-to-day contact with the police caused by incivility and the poor use of discretion in earlier forms of community policing. The proliferation and democratisation of social media, as well as news reporting of police misconduct and incivility, mean that the street-level accountability of police officers and public scrutiny of their use of discretion will continue to increase.

Teaching officers how to operationalise their values and beliefs in a way that coexists with the different values and beliefs of other citizens is a formidably complex and momentous challenge for police training, particularly in an organisation that can resemble a paramilitary institution during times of social conflict (Waddington, 1998). International evidence indicates that giving priority to an educational focus on critical thinking over an emphasis on control can aid the development of more flexible value systems suited to the demands of community-oriented policing (for an overview, see Roberg and Bonn, 2004; Paterson, 2011). This can benefit public confidence and perceptions of police accountability. Research from the US during the 1970s demonstrated that university-educated police officers were less authoritarian than non-university-educated police officers and that the higher the level of education attained, the more flexible the officers' value systems became (Roberg and Bonn, 2004). In particular, this evidence points to improved attitudes towards minority groups as well as a more sensitive or humanistic approach being taken by police officers towards members of the public (Roberg and Bonn, 2004).

Conclusion

Becker's (1967) hierarchy of credibility can relate, first, to the function of police in defining what crime is and, second, to the function of police organisational culture in defining how policing should be delivered through a quasi-militaristic hierarchical structure. Thus, as the police perform a myriad of functions within society, the official aims of the police service can be diluted via the cultural values of the management suite, the station canteen and the classroom, and the style of policing this encourages. The style of policing provided by a police officer or organisation is influenced by the side they have chosen to take and the values they exhibit. These policing values can be understood in terms of the groups with which police officers align themselves (their peers, their managers, the public, victims, offenders). Community policing philosophies encourage a shift beyond traditional alignments towards a flexible value system that is informed by social context. This approach challenges the cultural assumptions that underpin much police policy and practice and requires education to facilitate the critical thinking that questions and develops police organisational knowledge.

In 2006, Peace noted the gap between the community policing philosophy espoused by senior police officers and the methodology employed in police training (although more recent anecdotal evidence indicates that this gap is shrinking[1]). The late-modern emphasis on community values, engagement and interaction remains a challenge for a police institution founded on modernity's conception of an all-powerful state that provides security and order across society. This raises two conceptual questions for the promulgation of police education and community policing. Does the hierarchical structure of the police service censure the creative thinking that police education seeks to encourage? Do broader social structures and the symbolic meanings of crime and policing mean that community policing values cannot be embedded into either police culture or communities? It is unsurprising that policy implementation gaps have emerged across jurisdictions as the incomplete late-modern shift to democratic, community-focused policing values comes into conflict with the existing structure and culture of police institutions. This chapter has laid out a conceptual framework that provides a potential way forward for police learning and development and places equal weight upon pre-existing and idealised values and the cultural systems that they inhabit.

Note

[1.] The authors' conversations with police trainers have revealed frustration about what is considered to be out-of-date academic knowledge on the community policing training gap. These comments remain difficult to corroborate as, despite significant advances in police–academic collaborative relationships, some areas of policing remain difficult to access and/or do not allow outsiders to infiltrate their social world (Pollock, 2010). The dearth of recent independent and meaningful research on police officer values in England and Wales is a product of this ethical paradox.

References

ACPO (Association of Chief Police Officers) (2011) 'ACPO professional ethics'. Available at: http://acpoprofessionalethics.org/default.aspx?page=ndm

Banks, S. (2006) *Ethics and values in social work* (3rd edn), Basingstoke: Palgrave Macmillan.

Bayley, D. and Bittner, E. (1984) 'Learning the skills of policing', *Law and Contemporary Problems*, vol 47, no 4, pp 35–59.

Becker, H. (1967) 'Whose side are we on?', *Social Problems*, vol 14, no 3, pp 239–47.

Birzer, M. (2003) 'The theory of andragogy applied to police training', *Policing: An International Journal of Police Strategies and Management*, vol 26, no 1, pp 29–42.

Blakemore, B. and Simpson, K. (2010) 'A comparison of the effectiveness of pre- and post- employment modes of higher education for student police officers', *The Police Journal*, vol 83, pp 29–41.

Bradford, B., Jackson, J. and Stanko, E. (2009) 'Contact and confidence: revisiting the impact of public encounters with the police', *Policing and Society: An International Journal of Research and Police*, vol 19, no 1, pp 20–46.

Burgess, E. (1954) 'Values and sociological research', *Social Problems*, vol 2, no 1 pp 16–20.

Chan, J. (1996) 'Changing police culture', *British Journal of Criminology*, vol 36, no 1, pp 109–34.

Chan, J. (1997) *Changing police culture: policing in a multi-cultural society*, Cambridge: Cambridge University Press.

Clark, M. (2005) 'The importance of a new philosophy to the post modern policing environment', *Policing: An International Journal of Police Strategies and Management*, vol 28, no 4, pp 642–53.

Conti, N. and Nolan, J. (2005) 'Policing the platonic cave: ethics and efficacy in police training', *Policing and Society*, vol 15, no 2, pp 166–86.

Cox, D. (2011) 'Educating police for uncertain times: the Australian experience and the case for a "normative" approach', *Journal of Policing, Intelligence and Counter Terrorism*, vol 6, no 1, pp 3–22.

Docking, M. (2003) *Public perceptions of police accountability and decision making*, Home Office Online Report 38/03, London: Home Office. Available at: http://collection.europarchive.org/tna/20080305164517/homeoffice.gov.uk/rds/pdfs2/rdsolr3803.pdf

Ely, M. (1993) *Doing qualitative research: circles within circles*, London: The Falmer Press.

Feltes, T. (2002) 'Community-oriented policing in Germany', *Policing: An International Journal of Police Strategies and Management*, vol 25, no 1, pp 48–59.

Fielding, N. (1994) 'Cop canteen culture', in T. Newburn and E.A. Stanko (eds) *Just boys doing business? Men, masculinities and crime*, London: Routledge.

Flanagan, R. (2008) *The review of policing*, London: HMSO.

Gregory, J. and Lees, S. (1999) *Policing sexual assault*, London: Routledge.

Haynes, C. (2009) 'Boffin bobbies and cop degree is intellectual snobbery', *Police Review*, no 6, March.

Heslop, R. (2011) 'Reproducing police culture in a British university: findings from an exploratory case study of police foundation degrees', *Police Practice and Research*, vol 12, no 4, pp 298–312.

HMIC (Her Majesty's Inspectorate of Constabulary) (2002) *Training matters*, London: HMIC.

Holland, B. (2007) 'View from within: the realities of promoting race and diversity inside the police service', in M. Rowe (ed) *Policing beyond MacPherson*, Cullompton: Willan.

Hough, M., Jackson, J., Bradford, B., Myhill, A. and Quinton, P. (2010) 'Procedural justice, trust and institutional legitimacy', *Policing: A Journal of Policy and Practice*, vol 4, no 3, pp 203–10.

IPCC (Independent Police Complaints Commission) (2010) *IPCC independent investigation: Greater Manchester Police contact with Clare Wood prior to her death*, London: IPCC.

Ivkovic, S. (2008) 'A comparative study of public support for the police', *International Criminal Justice Review*, vol 18, no 4, pp 406–43.

Jaschke, H. (2010) 'Knowledge-led policing and security', *Policing: A Journal of Policy and Practice*, vol 4, no 3, pp 302–9.

Jaschke, H. and Neidhart, K. (2007) 'A modern police science as an integrated academic discipline', *Policing and Society*, vol 17, no 4, pp 303–20.

Kratcoski, P. (2004) 'Police education and training in a global society: a guest editor's introduction', *Police Practice and Research: An International Journal*, vol 5, no 2, pp 103–5.

Laville, S. (2009) 'Metropolitan police accused of institutional sexism over serial sex attacker cases', *The Guardian*, 26 March. Available at: www.guardian.co.uk/uk/2009/mar/26/metropolitan-police-sexism-rape

Lee, A. (2011) 'Police learning: professionalisation and partnerships', paper presented at the Higher Education Forum for Police Education Conference, University of Northampton.

Lee, M. and Punch, M. (2004) 'Policing by degrees: police officers' experience of university education', *Policing & Society*, vol 14, no 3, pp 233–49.

Lipsky, M. (1980) *Street-level bureaucracy: dilemma of the individual in public service*, New York, NY: Russell Sage Foundation.

Loftus, B. (2009) *Police culture in a changing world*, Oxford: Oxford University Press.

MacPherson, Sir W. (1999) *The Stephen Lawrence inquiry*, London: HMSO.

Manning, P. (1993) 'Toward a theory of police organization: polarities and change', paper presented at the International Conference on Social Change in Policing, 3–5 August, Taipei.

Marenin, O. (2005) 'Building a global police studies community', *Police Quarterly*, vol 8, pp 99–136.

Neyroud, P. (2011) *Review of police leadership and training* (vol 1), London: HMSO.

Neyroud, P. and Beckley, A. (2001) *Policing, ethics and human rights*, Cullompton: Willan.

NPIA (National Police Improvement Agency) (2011) *Professional entry to policing: pre-join strategy and guidance*, London: NPIA.

Paoline, E. and Terrill, W. (2007) 'Police education, experience and the use of force', *Criminal Justice and Behavior*, vol 34, pp 179–96.

Paterson, C. (2011) 'Adding value? A review of the international literature on the role of higher education in police training and education', *Police Practice and Research: An International Journal*, vol 12, no 4, pp 286–97.

Paterson, C. and Pollock, E. (2011) *Policing and criminology*, Exeter: Learning Matters.

Peace, R. (2006) 'Probationer training for neighborhood policing in England and Wales: fit for purpose?', *Policing: An International Journal of Police Strategies and Management*, vol 29, no 2, pp 335–46.

Peeters, H. (2010) *Constructing comparative competency profiles*, Paper presented at the Inaugural Conference of the Higher Education Forum for Learning and Development in Policing, Preston, England.

Pollock, E. (2010) 'Researching white supremacists online: methodological concerns of researching "speech"', *Internet Journal of Criminology*. Available at: www.internetjournalofcriminology.com/ Pollock_Researching_White_Supremacists_Online.pdf

Reiner, R. (2010) *The politics of the police*, Oxford: Oxford University Press.

Roberg, R. and Bonn, S. (2004) 'Higher education and policing: where are we now?', *An International Journal of Police Strategies and Management*, vol 27, no 4, pp 469–86.

Scarman, Lord L. (1981) *Report into the inquiry of the Brixton disorders 10–12 April 1981*, London: HMSO.

Schein, E. (1996) 'Culture: the missing concept in organization studies', *Administrative Science Quarterly*, vol 41, no 2, pp 229–40.

Sherman, L. (2011) 'Professional policing and liberal democracy', the 2011 Benjamin Franklin Medal Lecture, paper presented to the Royal Society for the Encouragement of Arts, Manufactures and Commerce, London. Available at: www.crim.cam.ac.uk/research/experiments/ franklinfinal2011.pdf

Skogan, W. (2008) 'Why reforms fail', *Policing and Society*, vol 18, no 1, pp 23–34.

Skolnick, J.H. (2008) 'Enduring issues of police culture and demographics', *Policing and Society*, vol 18, no 1, pp 35–45.

Stanko, E. (2007) 'Managing performance in the policing of domestic violence', *Policing: A Journal of Policy and Practice*, vol 2, no 3, pp 294–302.

The Guardian and LSE (London School of Economics) (2011) 'Reading the riots: investigating England's summer of disorder', *The Guardian*, in partnership with the LSE, supported by the Joseph Rowntree Foundation and the Open Society Foundation. Available at: https:// www.guardian.co.uk/interactive/dec/14/ Reading the Riots: Investigating England's Summer of Disorder-full-report

Waddington, P.A.J. (1998) *Policing citizens*, London: UCL Press.

Wasserman, R. and Moore, M.H. (1988) *Values in policing*, Washington, DC: National Institute of Justice.

Westmarland, L. (2001) *Gender and policing: sex, power and police culture*, Cullompton: Willan.

Wimhust, K. and Ransley, J. (2007) 'Police education and the university sector: contrasting models from the Australian experience', *Journal of Criminal Justice Education*, vol 18, no 1, pp 106–22.

Wood, D. and Tong, S. (2009) 'The future of initial police training: a university perspective', *International Journal of Police Science and Management*, vol 11, no 3, pp 294–305.

TWELVE

Race, religion and human rights: valuable lessons from prison

Muzammil Quraishi

Introduction

This chapter charts the complex ways in which counter-racism and multi-faith policies have addressed (or rather managed) the discrimination perceived and experienced by Muslim prisoners. In the area of interpreting and articulating religious rights, the example of Muslim prisoners allows discussion of the significance of Islamic Law (*shar'iah*) for secular societies with established Muslim populations. This discussion is particularly pertinent in the UK following the recent establishment of civil *shar'iah* courts in a number of British cities by the Muslim Arbitration Tribunal organisation based upon powers under the Arbitration Act 1996.

The relatively recent rise in the number of Muslim male prisoners has presented various challenges to HM Prison Service, including the provision of a *halal* diet, congregational prayers and access to *imams* as well as security concerns regarding potential radicalisation and extremism. These concerns have led to the creation of the role of the Muslim Advisor, who is responsible for all matters concerning the religious provision for Muslim prisoners. Symbolising the multi-faith agenda in HM Prison Service, the creation of the Muslim Advisor and full-time salaried Muslim chaplains may be understood as representing a politicised situation in which they, to borrow Becker's term, become 'spokesmen to attempt to change existing hierarchical relationships' (Becker, 1967, p 243). Therefore, the chapter identifies inherent tensions between the role of the prisons and the officials within them to incarcerate, punish and rehabilitate in light of prisoners' values, rights and experiences. Academic research in this area tends to side with the 'subordinates' (Muslim prisoners), but does not, in many cases, exclude the opportunities for 'superordinates' (prison officers and managers) to relate their experiences of interaction with Muslim prisoners (Beckford et al, 2005; Quraishi, 2008a).

The chapter also evaluates the history and impact of the multi-faith and anti-racism agendas against the background of research that demonstrates significant levels of discrimination experienced by minority ethnic groups and Muslims in British prisons. The discussion of faith-based provision in prison is set against broader debates about the rehabilitative potential and limits of religion for the resettlement of offenders. Prominent criminological research regarding the role of religion in the lives of prisoners, known as the 'Hellfire thesis' – which examines the degree to which a belief in divine judgement deters offending (Hirschi and Stark, 1969) – has provided only limited evidence about the impact of faith upon recidivism. A more meaningful criminological engagement emerges when religious adherence is viewed as another facet of identity influencing prisoners as part of their life course. This provides an important lens through which we can apply Howard Becker's (1967) arguments about the values represented by sociologists and criminologists in their work on 'subordinates' and 'superordinates' in the 'hierarchy of credibility' within prison contexts.

In sum, this chapter uses the example of Muslim male prisoners to illustrate that prison has become an important arena for debates about religious and racial discrimination and religious freedoms granted to minority faiths. These debates are of importance not only for the incarcerated, but also for wider British society.

The legal framework within prisons in England and Wales

In order to fully appreciate the debate around religious rights in prison, the broader legal obligations of the state and civil rights of prisoners as a group need to be outlined. Legal relationships can be understood in terms of civil and criminal liabilities, the former relates to disputes between two or more private individuals or organisations, whereas matters of crime involve the application of legal punishment(s) between the state and an individual or group of individuals. In relation to prisons, the civil law relates to disputes between public (eg HM Prison Service) and private parties (eg prisoners) and includes contractual law, the law of torts (eg personal injury) and human rights legislation. The criminal law also applies in prison to matters arising between staff and prisoners, between staff and among prisoners (Loucks, 2000). In other words, although the closed nature of prison means that the general public may not be privy to the extent of infractions of the law in the prison estate, all prisoners and staff are still subject to the criminal and civil laws of the land. In fact, we may go a step further and observe that by virtue of a second raft of legal and procedural rules applicable only to the incarcerated, prison provides an extra dose of legal obligations for all contained within and for those who try to ensure their containment.

The Prison Rules 1999 (PR 1999) and Young Offender Institution Rules 2000 [consolidated] are examples of secondary legislation, and rules 13–19 of PR 1999 contain regulations dealing with religious provision. Such secondary legislation allows senior ministers (eg the Minister for Justice) the flexibility to draft rules for the regulation and management of prisons, in turn acknowledging that often rather rapid directives, circulars and guidance are required in the management of the prison population.

These Rules are actually rather basic, so they have been supplemented by Prison Service Orders (PSOs), Advice and Instruction (PSIs), and Advices and Instructions to Governors (AG/IG) relating to all aspects of prison life. Technically, these instructions and orders possess no force of law in themselves, but there is some ambiguity about this position. For example, when discussing Prison Rule 44(1), the Prison Officer Training Manual states: 'these rules are statutory rules and accordingly have the force of the law' (Loucks, 2000, p 15). The application of the advice and orders in the prison context, therefore, does represent a form of legal system in operation and, more importantly, with regard to the management of religious practices laid out in the PSO 4550 Religion Manual, provides an avenue for theological and jurisprudential interpretation.

The Prison (Amendment) (No 2) Rules 2000 cover a range of what may be termed 'welfare' or 'human rights' provisions relating to matters such as the use of force by staff, searches of prisoners and prison discipline. The European Convention on Human Rights (ECHR) was only incorporated into domestic law with the passing of the Human Rights Act 1998, which came into force in October 2000. The ECHR confers general minimum standards for the protection of human rights for all citizens. It is worth noting, however, that prisoners were not a group specifically in mind when the law was enacted. Prisoners have to infer that specific rights have been transgressed from the general prohibitions contained in the articles, such as Article 3, which prohibits 'torture or inhuman or degrading treatment', or Article 5, which deals with 'the right to liberty' (Livingstone and Owen, 1999).

Even prior to the Human Rights Act 1998, there had been an established principle via the case of *Raymond v Honey* (1982) AC 1 that prisoners retain all civil rights that are not expressly taken away by an Act of Parliament, such as the right to vote, or which are inconsistent with the very nature of imprisonment. For example, it would be absurd in most cases for a prisoner to argue that his right to freedom of movement was being violated by virtue of his incarceration. Furthermore, breach of Prison Rules alone would not constitute grounds for legal redress (see *R v Deputy Governor of Parkhurst ex parte Hague* (1992) AC 58); prisoners must prove that they have suffered some form of injury or loss in addition to and as a direct result of the breach of the Rules. Furthermore, since 1973, the Council of Europe has acknowledged the importance of this area via the Standard Minimum Rules for the Treatment of Prisoners (European Prison Rules), reformulated in 1987 and updated in January 2006. Although the European Prison Rules are not binding on member states, they do acknowledge the importance of a rights-based approach to incarceration in Europe. Rule 29 of the European Prison Rules specifically seeks to protect freedom of thought, conscience and religion and places an onus upon prison authorities to allow prisoners to practise their faith so far as is practicable (Council of Europe, 2006).

By taking stock of the preceding, we can conclude that prisoners, in theory at least, have a fair range of legal remedies at their disposal, notwithstanding their subordinate position in class or structural hierarchies. In practice, there are a number of obstacles preventing prisoners (either as individual plaintiffs or as part of a class action) from seeking successful redress (Easton, 2011). The key factors include the confusing and complex nature of legal terminology as perceived by prisoners and the worry that appeals and challenges may negatively impact on the day-to-day lifestyles and quality of life of complainants. Furthermore, an important factor for prisoners is how to access appropriate legal advice and then how to fund a case (Wilson, 2001). A more fundamental point to observe is that prison researchers have consistently concluded that, despite formal rules and regulations, the way that prisoners are dealt with in practice is subject to the discretion of officials. Alison Leibling, for example, has argued that prison officers often use 'authority' rather than 'rules' and tend to adopt 'informal rules' following a 'negotiation model' dependent upon individual discretion (Liebling, 2000, p 333). International evaluations similarly assess the ways in which human rights are adapted, co-opted and changed by individual state officials within their highly localised social settings (Jefferson and Jensen, 2009).

Therefore, legal challenges against the UK from prisoners in the European Court of Human Rights at Strasbourg have not been numerous, while the few that have been heard have not concerned religious rights. Nevertheless, HM Prison Service, through the development of the PSO 4550 Religion Manual and the policies and practices that preceded it, has firmly acknowledged the potential for challenges against religious discrimination from staff perceived by prisoners. Therefore, the pre-empting and facilitation of religious rights by HM Prison Service may be motivated by the smooth running of the prison estate and compliance with national diversity strategies and laws rather than any perceived threat of human rights litigation in the European Court.

Counter-racism policies in HM Prison Service and their impact

The Prison Service was one of the first criminal justice institutions to acknowledge a need to counter racial discrimination as well as to consider the intersection between faith identities and race. The need for a policy was reflected in the Prison Service Circular of 1981 (CI/28/1981), which set out firm principles for good community relations, equal treatment and a curb on exploiting racial differences. The Prison Service also established the role of the Race Relations Liaison Officer (RRLO) in prisons where there was a significant minority ethnic prisoner population. The RRLO was tasked with being a source of information for prisoners and staff about relevant legislation, developing links with outside community groups, assisting in training and informing the governor of potential or actual problems and solutions for them (C127/1982).

By 1986, the Prison Service had established the need for an internal Race Relations Management Team in each prison and, in turn, produced a statement prohibiting racial discrimination. In 1991, a specific Race Relations Manual had been produced by the Prison Service and, in 1997, Prison Service Order 2800 was produced, coupled with a revised statement following consultation with the now-defunct Commission for Racial Equality (CRE). Interestingly, the revised statement included discrimination based on religion alongside race; the general British public, particularly non-Christians, would have to wait almost a decade for similar prohibitions in the guise of the Racial and Religious Hatred Act 2006. What the policy acknowledged was that many religious minorities also belong to a minority ethnic group. Furthermore, it illustrated the way in which faith identities intersect with those of race and ethnicity. In 1999, the Prison Service developed a standard for curbing racial discrimination against which each institution would be audited. Following the Macpherson Inquiry, the Prison Service produced five main anti-racist strategies under the collective banner of Racial Equality for Staff and Prisoners (RESPOND). The Race Relations (Amendment) Act 2000 broadened the scope of previous legislation, compelling specified public authorities to have due regard to the need to eliminate unlawful discrimination and to promote equality of opportunity and good relations between persons of different racial groups in carrying out their functions. The 2000 Act introduced Section 19B which prohibits race discrimination in all public sector functions, including the core functions of the Prison Service, for example, prison allocation, discipline, punishment and the searching of visitors.

Despite the policy inroads just outlined, a large body of academic and government data has consistently found significant levels of racial and religious discrimination within the prison estate (see NACRO, 2000, 2003, 2004; Spalek and Wilson, 2001; Cheliotis and Liebling, 2006; Bhui, 2009). One of the first academic evaluations of this topic was conducted by Genders and Player in 1989. Their study was commissioned and funded by the Home Office Research and Planning Unit and their methodology included analysing prison records, interviewing staff and prisoners, and observing the day-to-day routine of prison life. They concluded that although race relations were not viewed as problematic by staff, rank-and-file officers commonly used racial stereotypes, such as black prisoners being viewed as lazy and Asian prisoners being model prisoners yet also devious and prone to lying (Genders and Player, 1989). Black prisoners were also viewed as problematic for management in terms of being viewed as anti-authoritarian. Furthermore, there was evidence of higher rates of adjudication and discipline of black prisoners compared to their white or Asian peers and they were also less likely to be employed in the more desirable jobs in prison. Kathleen McDermott's (1990) study of five male prisons highlighted a backlash against policy among black and Asian prisoners and evidence of individual and cultural racism among staff and prisoners. Burnett and Farrell's (1994) study of racial victimisation in the Prison Service demonstrated high levels of repeat victimisation of black and Asian prisoners, which they chose not to report due to their perception that no action would be taken. The same study also concluded that RRLOs and other prison officers would often not report racial incidents, preferring to resolve the matters internally.

In March 2000, an Asian Muslim young man named Zahid Mubarek was murdered by his racist cellmate in Her Majesty's Young Offender Institution (HM YOI) Feltham the night before he was due to be released. The murder prompted an investigation by the CRE (2003) and a public inquiry ordered by the Home Secretary. The public inquiry concluded that the Prison Service had failed to deliver equivalent protection to all prisoners in its care and to deliver race equality in the way it employed staff or treated prisoners (Keith, 2006). The CRE (2003) report highlighted that racism was still a persistent feature of prison life, with staff operating in a discriminatory way, ignoring race relations training and tolerating racist attitudes and behaviour. The CRE report prompted HM Prison Service to establish a dedicated Race Equality Action Group (REAG), which, inter alia, includes race equality reviews of all establishments and the redrafting of a new PSO on race. HM Inspectorate of Prisons (HMIP, 2005) also conducted a thematic review of race relations in prisons, which concluded that there was no shared understanding of race relations within prison. Instead, a series of parallel worlds exist occupied by different groups of staff and visitors and reflecting widely divergent views and experiences in relation to racism in prison. Governors and white RRLOs expressed the most optimistic managerial view, generally believing that the regime was operating fairly while recognising that more needed to be done to prevent racism. Black and minority ethnic staff found it difficult to influence change and although few talked of experiencing overt racism, many complained about subtle forms of racial discrimination. Safety was a prominent concern for Asian prisoners, whereas black prisoners were more likely to complain about a lack of respect from staff (HMIP, 2005).

Muslims in prison: differing perspectives

As previously indicated, there is an intersection between race and faith with regards to Muslim prisoners, requiring discussions to be evaluated against the related debates on Islamophobia and counter-terrorism (HMIP, 2010; Sayyid and Abdoolkarim, 2010; Morgan and Poynting, 2012). The difficulty of engaging with the connections between offending, faith and ethnicity is to balance between deconstructing the debate while not reinforcing or reifying distorted associations being asserted by the Far Right, parts of the media or sections of the government (Moore et al, 2008; Fekete, 2009; Morey and Amina, 2011).

Many of the studies mentioned in the preceding section included Muslim prisoners, but individual respondents were likely to be classified according to their ethnicity rather than faith (see Quraishi, 2005). However, the distinct focus upon Muslim prisoners in the UK has a relatively recent history. The Muslim prison population has experienced significant expansion over the last decade and currently accounts for approximately 11% of the prison population of England and Wales, forming the second-largest religious group after Christians (NOMS, 2011, p 32). Asian males account for 42% of Muslim prisoners, with 34% having a black ethnicity (Guessous et al, 2001). The ethnic composition of the male Muslim prisoner population does not reflect the population density by ethnicity of the Muslim UK population as a whole; part of the reason for this difference lies in the practice of conversion to Islam by black prisoners (Quraishi, 2005).

The rise in the Muslim prisoner population – and specifically those detained for alleged and proven terrorist crimes – has led to media- and government-driven rhetoric about the potential for prisons to become sites of Islamic extremism and radicalisation (Quraishi, 2010). However, the minimal amount of qualitative academic research to date does not provide evidence of Islamic radicalisation and extremism in British prisons. The first substantial study by Beckford, Joly and Khosrokhavar (2005) compared the experiences of Muslim prisoners in the UK and France. Their investigation into the nature and substance of religious instruction delivered by *imams* as well as the experiences of Muslim prisoners in three UK prisons concentrated on discrimination, racism and access to religious support. They also analysed how prison staff, including chaplains, interpreted the rise in Muslim prisoners and whether this presented the prison estate with particular challenges. The main conclusions of this study highlighted significant experiences of discrimination as perceived by Muslim prisoners and *imams* as well as an assertion that Islam was being institutionalised effectively in prisons through the creation of the Office of the Muslim Advisor in the Prison Service and the appointment of full-time Muslim chaplains (Beckford et al, 2005). However, the overall study is important for three key findings. First, Muslim prisoners were able to negotiate access to a package of religious rights prompted by the emergence of a multi-faith agenda within HM Prison Service. Second, the employment of fully contracted Muslim chaplains (*imams*) with specified job descriptions demonstrates an example of the institutionalisation of Islam by the UK government. Third, the creation of the role of Muslim Advisor in HM Prison Service has, in turn, enabled the interpretation and application of *shari'ah* to the prison 'legal' system in so far as prison rules are being evaluated against compliance with Islamic religious norms, customs and laws.

While radicalisation was not the specific focus of Beckford et al's study, the events of 11 September 2001 took place during their period of research fieldwork. The findings did not reveal any significant levels of radicalisation or extremism among Muslim prisoners in the UK or in the preaching or approach taken by full- or part-time *imams* over the course of the research (Beckford et al, 2005). However, since France had experienced politicised extremism during the 1990s from activists such as the Algerian Groupe Islamique Armé (GIA), it had developed counter-terrorism policies and interventions ahead of other European states. Therefore, by 1995, there were more than 200 people imprisoned for terrorism in French prisons and the researchers were able to interview 15 prisoners held on terrorism offences. Despite French prison *imams* perceiving radicalised prisoners as threats to their role, prison authorities often utilised the very same people as arbiters in disputes. By way of reciprocation, the radicals were occasionally granted concessions, such as being permitted to perform collective worship. Furthermore, there was potential, at least in the French system, for such radicals to earn the esteem of fellow Muslim prisoners, although the general attitude towards them could most accurately be summarised as ambivalent (Beckford et al, 2005).

Radicalisation has, however, been the focus of other studies. Spalek and El-Hassan (2007) examined the experiences of Muslim converts in two English prisons, explicitly challenging the populist assertion that converts to Islam in a prison setting are vulnerable to extremist ideology. Rather, the study claimed that converts utilise Islamic teachings not only to cope more easily with the conditions of incarceration, but also for the provision of a moral framework in preparation for their life post-incarceration. Gabriele Marranci, who spent four years (2003–07) interviewing over 170 Muslim prisoners and ex-prisoners from Scotland, England and Wales (Marranci, 2009a), argues that the potential for prison *imams* to radicalise prisoners has been exaggerated. He found no evidence to suggest that prison *imams* were facilitating radicalisation; instead, his work emphasises the positive role prison *imams* play in countering extremism in prison. Marranci also highlighted the complexity facing the prison authorities in formulating coherent and practical guidelines to identify behaviour among Muslim prisoners that signals 'radicalisation'. Despite rejecting radicalisation among prison *imams*, Marranci concludes that some disassembled militant organisations do try to 'talent scout' young former Muslim prisoners, expressing extreme concern that some of his respondents had 'formed an Islamic gang' upon having converted their group to Islam (Marranci, 2009a). Importantly, Marranci's study claims that prison authorities, by overemphasising extremism, have neglected the more pressing problem of the challenge of reintegrating Muslim ex-offenders into society.

In contrast to the academic picture, the British media has produced many articles raising concerns about potential radicalisation among

Muslim prisoners and problems prompted by a rising Muslim prison population (Doward, 2008; Ford, 2008; Pidd, 2008; Travis, 2008a, 2008b). The articles are, in part, reactions to the release of official reports and observations from prison-related organisations and watchdogs, including the Prison Officers Association, Independent Board of Monitors and HMIP. The concerns raised centre upon the perceived vulnerability of prisoners to radical influences from extremist inmates (including those detained pursuant to terrorist offences) and, in some rare cases, from prison *imams*. It is worth emphasising that the reports tend to focus on maximum security prisons or those where the Muslim prison population is particularly large, and say less about the prison estate as a whole. HMP Belmarsh has figured prominently in the media on account of some of its high-profile inmates, whereas HMP Wandsworth has attracted attention over allegations of rival Muslim factions and disagreements between Muslim prisoners and an *imam*. The government perceives the problem of radicalisation as a genuine and escalating issue, with the Ministry of Justice predicting a tenfold rise in the number of terrorist suspects held in prisons in England and Wales over the next 10 years (Travis, 2007). Policy has been extended by the Home Office to provide a nationwide 'deradicalisation' programme and the deployment of £12.5 million for counter-terrorism measures, including tackling radicalisation in prisons (Home Office, 2008; Travis, 2008b). Furthermore, the Metropolitan Police Authority (2007) has acknowledged the operation of discreet 'deradicalisation' teams headed by Islamic scholars to theologically deprogramme extremist prisoners in some UK prisons. The establishment of such teams has been criticised by some scholars as representing the conflation of threats from *al-Qaida* with the political and religious views of peaceful adherents to *Salafism* in the UK (Spalek and Lambert, 2007).

The anomaly between media and government perspectives about Muslim radicalisation in prisons and the contributions from studies can be interpreted in different ways. It could be the case that the researchers have not been privy to government intelligence about the extent of the problem, or that the fieldwork was not primarily in maximum security prisons housing terrorist prisoners. The qualitative nature of the studies enabled them to reflect upon often mundane pastoral issues coupled with experiences of discrimination, which are the central concerns for many Muslim prisoners. Muslim chaplains are not viewed as the agents of radicalisation, but, more accurately, as intermediaries in checking extremism. The picture is undoubtedly complex but a moral panic over radicalisation only reduces such complexity and acts as a distraction from engagement with the pressing issues of faith-based initiatives in rehabilitation and resettlement for a predominantly non-radical Muslim prison population.

Criminology and religion

Traditionally, the confluence of religion and crime tended to occupy the realm of social control theory. More specifically, it was the work of Hirschi and Stark and their 'Hellfire' thesis that attracted significant interest in criminology and penology (Hirschi and Stark, 1969). The Hellfire thesis examines the extent to which having a religious conviction can inhibit the propensity for crime. Studies examining this thesis among prisoners have tended to evaluate adherents to Christianity in the US (Fernander et al, 2005). A meta-analysis of 60 studies in this field by Baier and Wright (2001) concluded that religion provided a moderate deterrent effect in terms of delinquency. Furthermore, there are a number of studies that question the deterrent effect of religion upon crime (Jensen and Erickson, 1979; Evans et al, 1995; Benda and Corwyn, 1997; Cretacci, 2003). The principal points of contention are how to measure 'religiosity' and the types of crime being evaluated. Nevertheless, turning to the case of Muslim prisoners, contemporary British criminological research tends not to examine the deterrent impact of the faith. Instead, scholars have sought to provide a more meaningful counter-literature to highlight and reverse the demonisation and criminalisation of Muslim populations prompted by discriminatory policing and surveillance strategies under the guise of the 'war on terror' mantra (see Kundnani, 2007; Spalek and Lambert, 2007; Quraishi, 2008a; Fekete, 2009; Marranci, 2009b; Patel and Tyrer, 2011). Furthermore, British scholars have been less interested in the Hellfire thesis and more in the role religion plays in social identity and how this intersects with dimensions of gender, class and ethnicity. In particular, some scholars have challenged the largely secularist intellectual tradition within British social sciences for ignoring the role religion plays as a marker of identity, not only in terms of what it means for social actors, but also as integral to coherent research methodologies (Spalek and Imtoul, 2008; Quraishi, 2008b).

Returning to the issue of values, the discussion illustrates the motivations that have prompted scholars to undertake research in this field. There is a sense that the researchers are driven by a series of perceived injustices, such as the way in which Muslim prison populations have been falsely represented in the media as promoters of radicalisation, or where they face discrimination in a closed institution as a result of their ethnic or religious identities (Quraishi, 2008a).

Importantly, a distinction should be made between the subjective factors that influence an individual researcher or team of researchers to engage with a perceived injustice, and an assessment of the academic rigour of their final output. Although it can be said that all research has subjective drivers, the adoption of qualitative methodological protocols enables such scholarship to provide meaningful and valid findings about the populations studied. The research outlined in the preceding discussion clearly follows an ethos of providing a voice for the marginalised and utilises biographical and standpoint methodologies (Quraishi, 2008a). It represents an attempt to enable less powerful, disadvantaged and silenced populations to articulate their experiences, which has been the mandate of critical researchers of race for many decades (Delgado and Stefancic, 2001). In this respect, it is value-laden and is 'on the side' of the subordinates (Muslim prisoners). However, since qualitative methodological protocols inform such research, it would be a misunderstanding to assert that it is somehow non-academic or without validity. Furthermore, some of the research discussed in this chapter also engages with the 'superordinates' (prison officers and managers) within the 'hierarchy of credibility' in an attempt to counter allegations of bias and, more importantly, to allow an examination of how religious human rights are protected, negotiated and curtailed within an institution.

Conclusion

The key studies evaluated in this chapter indicate differing perspectives on racial and religious discrimination as experienced by Muslim prisoners in the UK. The prevalence of such discrimination, despite official policy changes, harks back to Becker's (1967) claim that institutions such as prisons are essentially refractory and so develop ways by which to deny their failures. The study of Muslim prisoners has yielded significant intellectual fruit, which has ramifications for a wide range of academic disciplines. Studies illustrate the complex overlap or intersection of race and faith identities within an institutional setting. HM Prison Service acknowledged, ahead of mainstream society, the need to treat issues of religious discrimination on a par with those of racism. The prison also represents the first arena in which a multi-faith agenda could find purchase, as demonstrated by the concessions and securities offered to Muslim chaplains and Muslim prisoners. Furthermore, the research demonstrates the facilitation and interpretation of international and European human rights standards and laws for the humane treatment of prisoners, wherein religious rights are in principle protected. Turning to the issue of radicalisation among Muslim prisoners, the research clearly illustrates a discord between the media and government rhetoric and the academic picture. Where the media and government have depicted Muslim prisoners as potential terrorists, in contrast, the academic studies depict a more complex social reality. For the academics, Muslim prisoner populations constitute marginalised and discriminated against populations who are more preoccupied with the mundane challenges affecting their daily incarceration than with the articulation of a politicised violent *jihad*. In this sense, the value of academic contributions here serves as a useful counter-literature against the emotive and provocative rhetoric of the media and government alike.

The emergence of the specific role of the Muslim Advisor in the Prison Service demonstrates a number of key developments in the position of Islam and Muslims in the UK. The appointment permits a high-ranking civil servant effectively to consult Islamic scholarship and scholars to determine, interpret and apply aspects of *shari'ah* to the prison estate, which represents a sub-legal system. Given the legitimacy of *shari'ah* councils afforded by the Arbitration Act 1996, the previous statement may not be so remarkable. However, whereas litigants in the various *shari'ah* councils empowered by the 1996 Act operate in a voluntary capacity, prisoners are bound unilaterally by the Prison Rules by virtue of their incarceration. Furthermore, the pluralism of Islam as evident in British society is not immediately reflected in the institutionalised version available to prisoners. The example illustrates an area of politicisation whereby the Muslim Advisor and particularly the Muslim chaplains become spokespersons pushing for organisational change within an institution (Becker, 1967).

References

Baier, C.J. and Wright, B.R.E. (2001) 'If you love me keep my commandments: a meta-analysis of the effect of religion on crime', *Journal of Research in Crime and Delinquency*, vol 38, no 1, pp 3–21.

Becker, H.S. (1967) 'Whose side are we on?', *Social Problems*, vol 14, no 3, pp 239–47.

Beckford, J.A., Joly, D. and Khosrokhavar, F. (2005) *Muslims in prison: challenge and change in Britain and France*, Hampshire: Palgrave Macmillan.

Benda, B. and Corwyn, R. (1997) 'Religion and delinquency', *Journal for the Scientific Study of Religion*, vol 36, no 1, pp 81–92.

Bhui, H.S. (2009) 'Prisons and race equality', in H.S. Bhui (ed) (2006) *Race and criminal justice*, London and Thousand Oaks, CA: Sage, pp 83–101.

Burnett, R. and Farrell, G. (1994) *Reported and unreported racial incidents in prisons*, Occasional Paper No14, Oxford: University of Oxford Centre for Criminological Research.

Cheliotis, L.K. and Liebling, A. (2006) 'Race matters in British prisons: towards a research agenda', *British Journal of Criminology*, vol 46, no 2, pp 286–317.

Council of Europe (2006) *The European Prison Rules 2006*, Strasbourg: The Council of Europe Publishing.

CRE (Commission for Racial Equality) (2003) *Race equality in prisons: a formal investigation by the Commission for Racial Equality in HM Prison Service of England and Wales, Part 1, July, 2003, Part 2 December 2003*, London: CRE.

Cretacci, M. (2003) 'Religion and social control: an application of a modified social bond on violence', *Criminal Justice Review*, vol 28, no 2, pp 254–77.

Delgado, R. and Stefancic, J. (2001) *Critical race theory: an introduction*, New York, NY, and London: New York University Press.

Doward, J. (2008) 'Muslim gangs "are taking control of prison"', *The Guardian*, 25 May.

Easton, S. (2011) *Prisoners' rights: principles & practice*, Abingdon: Routledge.

Evans, T.D., Cullen, F.T., Dunaway, R.G. and Burton, V.S., Jr (1995) 'Religion and crime re-examined: the impact of religion, secular controls and social ecology on adult criminality', *Criminology*, vol 33, no 2, pp 195–217.

Fekete, L. (2009) *A suitable enemy: racism, migration and Islamophobia in Europe*, London: Pluto Press.

Fernander, A., Wilson, J.F., Staton, M. and Leukefeld, C. (2005) 'Exploring the type-of-crime hypothesis, religiosity, and spirituality in an adult male prison population', *International Journal of Offender Therapy and Comparative Criminology*, vol 49, no 6, pp 682–95.

Ford, R. (2008) 'Prisons watchdog says Belmarsh risks making Muslims more extreme', *The Times*, 15 April.

Genders, E. and Player, E. (1989) *Race relations in prison*, Oxford: Clarendon Press.

Guessous, F., Hooper, N. and Moorthy, U. (2001) 'Religion in prison 1999 and 2000 England and Wales. Bulletin 15/01', Home Office National Statistics, London, Crown. Available at: http://webarchive. nationalarchives.gov.uk/20110220105210/rds.homeoffice.gov.uk/rds/pdfs/hosb1501.pdf

Hirschi, T. and Stark, R. (1969) 'Hellfire and delinquency', *Social Problems*, vol 17, pp 202–13.

HMIP (HM Inspectorate of Prisons) (2005) *Parallel worlds: a thematic review of race relations in prisons*, London: HMIP.

HMIP (2010) *Muslim prisoners' experiences: a thematic review*, London: HMIP.

Jefferson, A.M. and Jensen, S. (eds) (2009) *State violence and human rights: state officials in the South*, Abingdon and New York, NY: Routledge & Cavendish.

Jensen, G. and Erickson, M. (1979) 'The religious factor and delinquency: another look at the Hellfire hypothesis', in R. Withnow (ed) *The religious dimension*, New York, NY: Academic Press, pp 157–77.

Keith, L.J. (2006) *Report of the Zahid Mubarek inquiry*, London: The Stationery Office.

Kundnani, A. (2007) *The end of tolerance: racism in 21st century Britain*, London: Pluto Press.

Leibling, A. (2000) 'Prison officers: policing and the use of discretion', *Theoretical Criminology*, vol 4, no 3, pp 333–57.

Livingstone, S. and Owen, T. (1999) *Prison law* (2nd edn), Oxford: Oxford University Press.

Loucks, N. (2000) *Prison rules: a working guide*, London: Prison Reform Trust.

Marranci, G. (2009a) *Faith, ideology and fear: Muslim identities within and beyond prisons*, London and New York, NY: Continuum.

Marranci, G. (2009b) *Understanding Muslim identity: rethinking fundamentalism*, Basingstoke and New York, NY: Palgrave/Macmillan.

McDermott, K. (1990) 'We have no problem: the experience of racism in prison', *New Community*, vol 16, no 2, pp 213–28.

Metropolitan Police Authority (2007) *Counter terrorism: the London debate*, London: MPA.

Moore, K., Mason, P. and Lewis, J. (2008) *Images of Islam in the UK: the representation of British Muslims in the national print news media 2000-2008*, Cardiff: Cardiff School of Journalism, University of Cardiff.

Morey, P. and Amina, Y. (2011) *Framing Muslims: stereotyping and representations after 9/11*, Cambridge, MA, and London: Harvard University Press.

Morgan, G. and Poynting, S. (eds) (2012) *Global Islamophobia: Muslims and moral panic in the West*, Farnham and Burlington, VT: Ashgate.

NACRO (2000) *Race and prisons: a snapshot survey*, London: NACRO.

NACRO (2003) *Race and prisons: where are we now?*, London: NACRO.

NACRO (2004) *Barriers to equality: challenges in tracking black and minority ethnic people through the criminal justice system*, London: NACRO.

NOMS (National Offender Management Service) (2011) *Equalities annual report, 2010/11*, London: Ministry of Justice.

Patel, T.G. and Tyrer, D. (2011) *Race, crime and resistance*, London: Sage.

Pidd, H. (2008) 'Staff unable to handle prison's Muslim gangs says report', *The Guardian*, 26 May.

Quraishi, M. (2005) *Muslims and crime: a comparative study*, Aldershot: Ashgate.

Quraishi, M. (2008a) 'Researching Muslim prisoners', *International Journal of Social Research Methodology*, vol 11, no 5, pp 453–67.

Quraishi, M. (2008b) 'Religion, spirituality and social science: researching Muslims and crime' in B. Spalek and A. Imtoual (eds) *Religion, spirituality and the social sciences: challenging marginalisation*, Bristol: The Policy Press, pp 177–89.

Quraishi, M. (2010) *Researching Muslim ex-offenders*, Markfield: The Islamic Foundation.

Sayyid, B. and AbdoolKarim, V. (2010) *Thinking through Islamophobia: global perspectives*, London: Hurst.

Spalek, B. and El-Hassan, S. (2007) 'Muslim converts in prison', *The Howard Journal of Criminal Justice*, vol 46, no 2, pp 99–114.

Spalek, B. and Imtoual, A. (eds) (2008) *Religion, spirituality and the social sciences: challenging marginalisation*, Bristol: The Policy Press.

Spalek, B. and Lambert, R. (2007) 'Terrorism, counter-terrorism and Muslim community engagement post 9/11', in R. Roberts and W. McMahon (eds) *Social justice and criminal justice*, London: Centre for Crime and Criminal Justice Studies, pp 202–15.

Spalek, B. and Wilson, D. (2001) 'Not just "visitors" to prison: the experiences of imams who work inside the penal system', *Howard Journal of Criminal Justice*, vol 40, no 1, pp 3–13.

Travis, A. (2007) 'Tenfold rise in terrorism prisoners forecast', *The Guardian*, 8 November.

Travis, A. (2008a) 'Jail staff failing to counter extremism warns inspector', *The Guardian*, 15 April.

Travis, A. (2008b) 'New plan to tackle violent extremism', *The Guardian*, 3 June.

Wilson, C. (2001) 'The European Convention on Human Rights: bringing rights home', in M. Leech and D. Cheney (eds) *The prisons handbook*, Winchester: Waterside Press, pp 523–32.

THIRTEEN

The public–private divide: which side is criminal justice on?

Stephen Riley

Introduction

The division between 'public' and 'private' is fundamental to criminal law and a focus of criminal justice policy debate. This chapter argues that the division should be understood as an ongoing social process to which criminal justice contributes, rather than as something demarking defined spaces or static roles. Criminal justice plays a critical role in this process, a process of drawing proper limits to the power of the state, including the state's ability to intrude into the personal sphere. It will be argued that maintaining a division between public and private should be seen as an intrinsically valuable project, one that cannot be pursued without affording considerable power to criminal justice agencies and placing considerable constraints upon them.

The social process of creating, drawing and redrawing the divide between public and private is nothing less than the ongoing project of maintaining the rights of the individual and limiting the power of public actors. It is, more precisely, a project of excluding arbitrary interests and preferences from public life and, conversely, limiting certain kinds of public intervention into conscience, preference or personality. This allows two different groups of values to exist. Without such limitations and exclusions, there could be no *personal autonomy*: the state would dictate the standards of legitimate behaviour in every aspect of our lives, leaving no room for individual conceptions of a good life (Mill, 2008). Equally, without identifying standards and practices proper to public life, there could be no *impartial administration of justice* because individuals would be judged by their character, rather than by general standards appropriate to those adopting public roles (Fuller, 1969).

This complex relationship between values and the public–private divide has consequences for the regulation of, and the division of labour between, public and private actors in the delivery of criminal justice.

Criminal justice actors must be sufficiently powerful to constrain the state itself from undue interference in our lives, but also sufficiently accountable to prevent such power becoming oppressive. Not only is it uncertain whether private actors are sufficiently accountable for this role, but the authority of criminal justice agencies flows from the exclusion of private interest, an exclusion which is difficult or impossible for entities owing their existence to private interest (Loader, 2006).

More generally, because it is a project, as opposed to a single set of social facts – a project constituted by social practices, discourse, agency and social structures – the public–private division is susceptible to various forms of scepticism. Conceptually, there is no logical necessity for the public–private division, it is always dynamic and local; pragmatically, the public benefits from intrusions into the private sphere and the public sphere benefits from private virtues; and morally, the public has a responsibility to limit the freedoms of the private sphere (Kennedy, 1982; Grear, 2003). The existence of a divide is easily cast into doubt by the encroachment of law into the private sphere for crime control purposes, and by the uncertain boundaries between public and private actors and actions (Palmer, 2007; Almandras, 2010). Private ethical commitments, and public responsibilities, can be found – blurred or mutually reinforced – in the activities of private companies providing public service (Kempa and Singh, 2008); in the exercise of our civil liberties, where private commitments are made public (Brettschneider, 2007); and in the norms of criminal law, where private conduct is criminalised (Lacey, 2011). Nonetheless, despite such scepticism, criminal justice needs the divide and the divide needs criminal justice.

First, criminal justice needs the public–private divide in order to function within reasonable limits. The public and the private are both policed, but are policed differently, by criminal justice agencies. The legal demarcation of different practices for different spheres ensures that the powers at the disposal of criminal justice agents for the purposes of maintaining public order are tempered or revoked when policing our homes or personal lives (Fuller, 1969; Mill, 2008). To investigate the private, be it the body or the home, requires additional justification and authorisation; the policing of public spaces involves deployments of violence and displays of power that are inappropriate in the private sphere (Thornton, 1991).

Second, the public–private divide needs criminal justice because criminal law draws boundaries between permissible and impermissible, including what is permissible or impermissible for the state itself.

Without identifying impermissible intrusions into the private sphere by regulating its investigatory and disciplinary powers, the state would lose any claim to liberalism, that is, the granting of the maximum possible freedom for private choices and the exercise of private virtues (Rawls, 1999; Mill, 2008). Accordingly, any state seeking to place limits on its powers, and certainly any state claiming liberal foundations, must have a criminal justice system that both polices, and is policed by, different sets of public and private responsibilities (Wakefield, 2003). In liberal states, there is a constructive relationship, but also an irreconcilable difference, between the private and the public.

In order to understand the links between the public–private division, values and criminal justice, we initially consider the classic articulation of the divide as it has been received by the modern liberal political tradition. This involves the familiar division between public and private 'spheres', and requires us to posit a dual relationship between the divide and values: that the divide is valuable, and that the divide supports other kinds of values. This prefaces discussion of some contemporary tensions and trends associated with the division. The chapter concludes with a defence of the public–private division as a necessary, and not just contingent, part of our criminal justice landscape.

Spheres and values

Any opposition between the public and the private is beset by terminological pitfalls: metaphors, changes of meaning and competing meanings in different contexts. The distinction can be used to analyse space, responsibility, services, status or identity. Accordingly, we cannot ask *where* this divide exists. We also have to ask *if* and *how* it exists. In the first instance, the existence of the divide can be explained in regulatory and in interpersonal terms.

The division exists through a set of legal, political, social and economic processes encompassing a range of actors. These processes can be said to have a common denominator in their requiring decisions about regulation: what to regulate and how to regulate. Practices of regulation variously justify, prohibit or mandate, but those practices drawing a division between public and private can be said to be maintaining two values: autonomy in the private sphere and consistency in the public sphere (see Fuller, 1969; Arendt, 1998; Grear, 2003). Autonomy – choice, self-creation and self-realisation – are permitted and encouraged in the private sphere, while the public sphere is characterised by the consistency provided by rights and legislation. In this sense, the two spheres are mutually regulating. Encouraging private autonomy demands limiting the power of the state and of public bodies. Prioritising consistency in the public sphere demands the exclusion of private interest.

Another way to understand the divide, reflecting its personal and interpersonal significance, is to contrast the private, understood as *personal* and *particular*, with the public, understood as *impersonal* or *general*. Our personality determines our private roles and choices; adopting public, professional or political roles is a partial negation of that personality. Conversely, public virtues like impersonality or formal equality are often inappropriate in private life. This difference between public and private behaviours is the, often unspoken, precondition of discourses of identity and duty (Goffman, 1971).

Together, the regulatory and interpersonal aspects of the divide give rise to the persistent metaphor of the 'sphere'. A distinction between public duties and private virtues was a preoccupation of Ancient Greek and Roman thought, but a stricter division into spheres – where one is protected from the other – is characteristic of modernity (Habermas, 1992). This can be said to have been driven by a number of ideological trends in Revolutionary and Enlightenment political thought, and by the material changes of industrialisation and urbanisation. Modernity sharpened distinctions between public and private property, between public and private work, and between private conscience and public opinion:

> Two quite different traditions of political thought are at work in the public/private distinction: classical and modern. In the first, the ancients distinguished between *oikos* [home] and *polis* [state]; in the second, liberals distinguish between the freedom, autonomy, and rights of private individuals and/or families and the legitimate or unwarranted power of society or state. (Coole, 2000, p 339)

The idea of public and private spheres has among its principal manifestations the division between the private home and those public spaces where individuals encounter one another, not as friends or family, but as citizens. The home as 'castle' and the public space as 'marketplace' are ideological constructions with continuing currency (Sunstein, 2001). Such constructions undoubtedly over-idealise de facto divisions in space. For example, the public sphere is fragmented along lines of class, gender and race (Blomley, 2005). The legal system has been shaped by the interests of property-owning classes, for whom a fully private sphere, from which the public can be effectively excluded, is meaningful (Rose, 1987). The existence of physical spheres is also problematised by the ability to render public places private (through private security or 'gentrification') and private places public (through the extension of administrative, criminal and family law) (Binnie and Skeggs, 2004).

The regulatory and interpersonal dimensions of the divide become entwined where certain norms are correlated with the spheres, norms that can take on the appearance of necessity:

> The distinction serves or seeks to maintain the belief that social and economic life – business, education, community, family – are outside government and law, simultaneously denying the role of political processes in constituting and maintaining them, and legitimating these arrangements by implying that they have arisen from decisions and choices freely made by individuals. This protects existing hierarchies yet delegitimises alternative forms of group solidarity – unions, universities, communities – which cannot fit within the public/private divide. (Rose, 1987, p 63)

The ideology of spheres has allowed, for instance, attributing labour responsibilities to women in a de facto division of labour between the sexes, along with the attendant norm that women have only a conditional right to audience in the public sphere (Thornton, 1991). Heightened policing of certain zones, for example, the creation of 'walled communities', adds further complexities where a community's norms are enforced in what would otherwise be a public space governed by the general rules of public law (Wakefield, 2003; Kempa and Singh, 2008).

The idea of a division bisecting spaces and identities is also challenged by communication technologies. Through new media, the private can be made instantly public and the public sphere channelled directly into the private (Sunstein, 2001). The internet, in particular, has demanded a redrawing of our conceptions of public–private boundaries given the willingness of internet users to publicise what would once have been considered private (Liu, 2004) and recent legislative measures criminalising certain instances of private possession and consumption (Walden and Wasik, 2011). The UK's patchwork of privacy laws – an uneasy mixture of data protection, human rights and common law – have been pushed to their limits as private lives are exposed, willingly and unwillingly, in cyberspace (O'Floinn and Ormerod, 2012).

Despite an over-idealisation of distinct spheres, be they physical or personal, the negative prohibition against unnecessary intrusion into the private sphere is essential to the liberal 'priority of right' (Rawls, 1988, 1999). The calculation, and compulsion, exercised in the governance of the state and political economy should not, it is held, intrude as far as the private conscience of the individual. By the same token, the private ends, and private conscience, of the individual should be excluded from the public sphere. The good – associated with the fulfilment and flourishing of the individual – is relegated to a sphere of activity where it cannot determine the shape of social and political life (Fuller, 1969). To allow private conceptions of the good to dominate public life would be to endorse the project of 'making people good'; a project that is paternalistic, authoritarian or eugenic, not liberal (Mill, 2008).

Consequently, from the point of view of states committed to liberal principles (most fundamentally, the deliberate minimisation of state intrusion into the private sphere), the public–private division both informs our values and is valuable. It is (morally and politically) defensible to insulate a sphere of private activity and private interests from public intrusions. To this extent, it can be said to be *intrinsically valuable*. The drawing of limits between the personal and the public is an end in itself and maintaining a difference between two spheres requires no further justification. It is also the case that the different spheres are generative of different obligations: the categories public and private are *instrumental* in the creation of values. For example, to denote the provision of certain services as public is to demand that their delivery be judged by public systems of accountability; to designate conflicts as private matters is to exclude them from public systems of adjudication. To designate action as private or public is a means to an end: to decide where public resources will be spent, where publicity is appropriate and whether regulation should take place through public or private law (see Palmer, 2007).

It is worth noting that because different intrinsic and instrumental values are associated with the divide, some critical analyses run the risk of conflating inadequate acknowledgement of certain values with judgements about the divide itself being unsustainable (see Kennedy, 1982). For example, sexual offences have been inadequately regulated, or ignored, when they have taken place in the private sphere (Moran and Skeggs, 2004; Temkin and Krahé, 2008). This calls into question why lawmakers have failed to engage adequately with crime in the private sphere, that is, why the divide has been used instrumentally to render certain kinds of crime invisible. The value *of* the divide, nonetheless, remains unchallenged. We are not obliged to demonstrate all private virtues in public, or public virtues in private.

Conversely, it is also misleading to assume that, despite theoretical complexities, there must be formal legal means to distinguish public from private actors. In fact, there are no stable principles allowing the state, or the courts, to predetermine public or private status. Differences between private law and public law, between contractual and statutory regulation, mean that legal persons can exist within a number of competing regulatory regimes. The expansion of judicial review, alongside the embedding of human rights law in English jurisprudence, has only made such determinations more frequent and more problematic (Prosser, 2000; Palmer, 2007). The divide is ultimately a process: one regulated, but not constituted, by law.

Tensions and trends

It should be clear that while we cannot find the physical boundary between public and private, we can certainly see the boundary at work in political and social discussion. The divide is assumed in any debate where a liberal state seeks greater criminal justice powers, be they investigative or punitive. These are classic 'threats to our liberties': threats to our personal choices, and the threat of being judged publicly for our private actions or commitments. Any public debate concerning the intrusion of private interest into public services, or the intrusion of public services into private affairs, represent the ongoing process of maintaining and reconsidering what we expect of private conduct and public responsibility. We will turn to two, contemporary, areas where the divide is being both maintained and reconsidered: privatisation of criminal justice services, and admission of 'evidence of bad character' in criminal trials.

The movement of public funds into private hands, the policing of public activities by private actors or the imposition of market disciplines on the delivery of public services show that the public—private divide exists, but is changing. Private provision of criminal justice services encompasses a range of practices: 'security' in public spaces and in detention facilities; monitoring of offenders in the community; immigration and translation services; and 'backroom services', including the processing and storage of forensic evidence (eg Bluelight Tendering, 2012; G4S, 2012; Scenesafe, 2012). Such partnership or outsourcing processes are justified on the basis of 'best value' in public spending (HM Treasury, 2004), and of professionalisation of services (Ministry of Justice, 2012). These services, and the tendering processes through which they are contracted, are regulated both by contract and by statute (Arrowsmith, 1994).

'Outsourcing' and 'privatisation' turn what is in the first instance a public right or duty into, respectively, something partially or wholly private (Joh, 2004; Ministry of Justice, 2011). In such transfers of power, the appropriate form of legal regulation can become uncertain:

> It is clear that there is, under the impetus of privatisation, a movement of 'public' functions into the private sphere – through, for example, outsourcing.… It is also clear that the state regulates the private sector in the public interest, thus sometimes effecting the movement of a matter from the private sphere into the public sphere.… Functional overlap, taken together with the dynamism of changing roles and realities in the balance of public and private sector power, means that it is very difficult to separate public law and private law in practice, particularly in borderline cases of public or private power. (Grear, 2003, p 179)

The lines of accountability governing private actors may not be so rigorous, or so determinate, as they are for public bodies. With only indirect executive accountability, private bodies are at liberty to alter or rescind their contractual responsibilities (eg CPS, 2012; Reuters, 2012). However, whether or not contractual regulation of private bodies can be given the same force as direct executive accountability, private provision creates tensions related to the two distinctive forms of value maintained by the public–private divide.

These 'private actors' do not exhibit quite those characteristics associated with private citizens. They cannot exhibit or pursue *personal autonomy*; they do not have aspirations to cultivate integrity, care or self-improvement in the same way as the private individual does. Certainly, such legal persons have many of the protections afforded to the private citizen. However, lacking complex interpersonal interests to protect, and lacking direct or indirect democratic foundations, private service providers are formal legal persons who cannot be said to be either citizens or citizens' representatives. More strongly, companies may have mission statements, but they cannot possess the, distinctively human, interest in living a just and fulfilling life with others (Finnis, 2011).

This complex mixture of the regulatory and the personal is crucial to understanding why discussion of the 'public' and the 'private' in criminal justice veers between hard-headed economic analyses on the one hand, and sometimes opaque appeals to public service and accountability on the other:

> Policing provision can never be entirely depoliticized and transferred to the market, first, because it possesses elements of compulsion from which it is impossible to 'contract out' and which necessarily raise problems of authority and its need for legitimation (a fact that is curiously effaced in libertarian writing on this subject, where benign phrases such as 'policing services' are often preferred ...); and, secondly, because the impact (for better and worse) that policing has upon the quality of people's lives means that all citizens ... have a stake in how it is performed and who by. (Loader, 1997, p 382)

In other words, the concerns associated with the private provision of criminal justice services point to two problems that have to be conceptualised in normative terms. First, the power and authority of criminal justice flows from the state and must therefore partake of whatever normative justification the state has for using coercive means. The state's justification for exercising criminal justice powers – its monopoly on the legitimate use of violence premised on democratic will – is conditional on its representing, and protecting, the welfare and basic rights of citizens. Private actors are the beneficiaries of, but not parties to, this social contract. Second, without the full panoply of private interests we associate with the natural human person, the demand for public virtues on the part of private entities becomes paradoxical. Public virtue demands the effacement or negation of private interest. However, where private interest is the sole rationale for existence, such a negation becomes impossible. To engage in public activity and exercise public virtue involves exercising *self-constraint* in pursuit of *collective goods*, a constraint that is neither intelligible nor desirable for private companies.

'Bad character' evidence represents a movement in the opposition direction: to make the private public, and visit judgement on private action. Such evidence, authorised by Part 11 of the Criminal Justice Act 2003, is typically evidence of a pattern of action intended to demonstrate a behavioural or psychological 'propensity' (section 103). This judicially regulated (s 101(3)) evidence is particularly important in the prosecution of crimes that have taken place in the private sphere. Evidence offered by a complainant may be impossible to corroborate. However, evidence of bad character admits personal and behavioural facts, constituting 'important explanatory evidence' with 'probative value' (s 101), in order to compensate for the prosecution's dependency on the testimony of a single witness.

This form of evidence is neither novel nor unique. It is a partial return to forms of evidence common to English criminal law prior to the 20th century (Lacey, 2011), and widely admissible in civil law jurisdictions (Cooper, 1991). The generally exclusionary nature of English evidentiary rules have, over the last century, sought to ensure that guilt could only be established through careful disclosure and contestation of material evidence, excluding any kind of holistic assessment of the defendant (see Alldridge and Brants, 2001). Admission of expert testimony may include conjectures on the defendant's state of mind during the criminal act at issue, and general appeals to the character of the defendant have long been admissible at the sentencing stage. Nonetheless, under the prevailing trends in English criminal trials, the jury attributes guilt on the basis that a specified act, and the intention to engage in that act, have been proven beyond reasonable doubt. In contrast, evidence of bad character provides an aperture through which the defendant's life and lifestyle can become material to their prosecution.

Recall the two groups of values associated with the divide. Personal autonomy requires that the state should, wherever possible, avoid dictating standards of personal behaviour. Furthermore, without identifying standards and practices proper to public life, there can be no impartial administration of justice because individuals would be judged by their character, rather than by general standards appropriate to those in the public sphere. Evidence of bad character generates problems on both grounds.

With regards to personal autonomy, there is a danger – only partly assuaged by the demand that it relate to propensity – that evidence of bad character can make a criminal trial a trial of character rather than action. This is a general issue of justice concerning the standard and burden of proof in prosecutions. Juries should be asked whether culpability for a criminal action has been proven beyond reasonable doubt, not invited to make a more general 'assessment of a defendant's guilt'. More specifically, such evidence allows a defendant's life as a whole into court, their behavioural tendencies, their lifestyle and their choices. Although such holistic assessments can lead to 'better judgement' on the part of the jury in the sense of having a greater quantity of information at their disposal, public judgement on private lifestyles is precisely what the public–private divide seeks to prevent.

In public, we should be judged by the formal justice of public laws, not whether 'life choices' amount to the likelihood of guilt.

That norms, and not just actions, are at issue here bespeaks the interpenetration between the regulatory and interpersonal bases of the public–private divide. In the French criminal context, where a shared, normative conception of citizenship is assumed (Field, 2006), there is no hesitation in accepting that a jury's decision is a decision based, at least in part, on the character of the defendant and not simply guilt for a narrowly specified charge (Cooper, 1991). The implicit introduction of this into English law – where 'citizen' is replaced with the far less prescriptive notion of 'subject' – means that social norms can come into play, albeit without implicit consensus on what would constitute a 'bad character'. Such free-floating judgement of character and personality may allow empathy and leniency; it may be an opportunity for gender, class or racial assumptions to come into play. The encompassing of an individual's character within judgements of criminal responsibility comes close to blurring criminal and moral guilt, and loses sight of the narrower idea of culpability, that is, guilt for one particular crime. In sum, when character is the determinant of guilt, the likelihood of criminal justice becoming a tool of normalisation becomes greater (Foucault, 1977).

Conclusion

Criticisms of liberalism, particularly from 'communitarian' commentators, provide objections to the conclusions drawn in the foregoing analyses, particularly where they depend upon a conception of the individual and their identities. For communitarians, both identity and virtue depend upon structures of social existence, structures that are far more decisive than liberalism allows (Taylor, 1992). The idea of creating or cultivating our identity exclusively in the private sphere is senseless: a linguistic and cultural community is a necessary condition of personhood (MacIntyre, 1981; Taylor, 1992). Moreover, virtues, as the fulfilment of aspirations that transcend the merely lawful and represent truly *private* obligations like self-realisation or affective commitment to friends and family, depend upon complex familial and cultural structures that are not only obscured by liberal political philosophy, but also harmed by them. Morality and virtue are not a set of autonomous choices or preferences, and to treat them as such is the route to a corrosive individualism. In fact, the individual is irreducibly 'situated' in time and space, and their obligations are determined by such situations. Accordingly, private virtues cannot be understood without acknowledging the public context on which they depend, and social bodies must pursue substantive moral projects far beyond 'consistency' and 'accountability' if they are to maintain society and personhood in the way hoped for by liberalism.

Such criticisms encourage us to sharpen our understanding of the relationship between liberalism and the public–private divide. They point to two different conclusions that underline the complex relationship between regulation and personhood in constituting the divide. On the one hand, 'virtue' and 'virtues' have served as a common denominator between what can be demanded either publicly or privately. Different virtues exist, but whether they are positive virtues of self-improvement or negative virtues of self-constraint, any virtue is an instance of *self*-regulation. The kinds of systematic self-regulation realised through criminal justice – the *self-imposed* constraint on citizens' actions arising from the democratic authority of laws and lawmakers – will always have a temporary and conditional appearance precisely because they are self-imposed. In this sense, the temporary, conditional and self-interested provision of criminal justice services by private entities only sharpens an existing tension between appearance and reality: criminal justice seeks an appearance of timeless necessity, but it is a dynamic process of self-regulation realised by self-regulating actors.

On the other hand, even communitarianism's disruption of the divide between public and private must continue to presume the divide or risk becoming a defence of authoritarianism. Communities and individuals may well be able to police their own persons and property, but unless such practices have been given explicit or implicit democratic assent, self-policing represents the dissolution of the state (defined by its monopoly of the authorisation of violence) and dissolution of society (defined by the assumption of bonds and obligations beyond our immediate community). Equally, the communitarian picture of the imposition of values on the individual by their social situation ignores a division between fact and value maintained in liberal political philosophy: the fact that those around us make demands upon us does not entail that such obligations should be honoured. In contrast, public statutory law, and private contractual arrangements, are distinct sets of obligations that *are* enforceable precisely because they assume, respectively, duties distinct to the *public* realm and *freely chosen private obligations*. Statute and contract provide varying degrees of control over private entities, but the existence of the two regulatory regimes reflects the coexistence of public obligations and private commitments necessary in any democratic, and autonomy-respecting, state.

For these reasons, the public–private division can be said to withstand both external criticisms from communitarians and internal criticisms generated by the privatisation of public services. The division, like criminal justice itself, is a process of self-regulation forming part of an overall process of society subjecting itself to the self-discipline of lawfulness. Lawfulness, if it is to be democratic lawfulness and not simply rule by publicised fiat, must allow the coexistence of public laws and private interests. The fact that the latter can intrude into criminal justice – through privatisation or evidence of bad character – is evidence that the division between public and private is changing. It is also evidence that a space for autonomy, choice and 'self-regarding action' (Mill, 2008, pp 85–7) continues to be carved out of the public realm through self-limitation on the part of the state.

References

Alldridge, P. and Brants, C. (eds) (2001) *Personal autonomy, the private sphere and the criminal law: a comparative study*, Oxford: Hart.

Almandras, S. (2010) 'Use of force against intruders', House of Commons Research Library. Available at: www.parliament.uk/documents/commons/lib/research/key_issues/Key%20Issues%20Use%20of%20force%20against%20intruders.pdf

Arendt, H. (1998) *The human condition* (2nd edn), Chicago, IL: University of Chicago Press.

Arrowsmith, S. (1994) 'Developments in compulsory competitive tendering', *Public Procurement Law Review*, pp 153–72.

Binnie, J. and Skeggs, B. (2004) 'Cosmopolitan knowledge and the production and consumption of sexualized space: Manchester's gay village', *The Sociological Review*, vol 52, no 1, pp 39–61.

Blomley, N. (2005) 'Flowers in the bathtub: boundary crossings at the public–private divide', *Geoforum*, vol 36, no 3, pp 281–96.

Bluelight Tendering (2012) 'Homepage'. Available at: https://www.bluelight.gov.uk/

Brettschneider, C. (2007) 'The politics of the personal: a liberal approach', *The American Political Science Review*, vol 101, no 1, pp 19–31.

Coole, D. (2000) 'Cartographic convulsions: public and private reconsidered', *Political Theory*, vol 28, no 3, pp 337–54.

Cooper, J. (1991) 'Criminal investigations in France', *New Law Journal*, vol 141, no 6496, pp 381–9.

CPS (Crown Prosecution Service) (2012) 'CPS decision on death of Jimmy Mubenga (17/07/12)'. Available at: www.cps.gov.uk/news/press_statements/cps_decision_on_death_of_jimmy_mubenga/index.html

Field, S. (2006) 'State, citizen and character in French criminal process', *Journal of Law and Society*, vol 33, no 4, pp 522–46.

Finnis, J. (2011) *Natural law and natural rights* (2nd edn), Oxford: Oxford University Press.

Foucault, M. (1977) *Discipline and punish: the birth of the prison*, Harmondsworth: Penguin Books.

Fuller, L.L. (1969) *The morality of law* (rev edn), New Haven, CT: Yale University Press.

G4S (2012) 'Homepage'. Available at: www.g4s.com/

Goffman, E. (1971) *The presentation of self in everyday life*, Harmondsworth: Penguin Books.

Grear, A. (2003) 'Theorising the rainbow? The puzzle of the public–private divide', *Res Publica*, vol 9, no 2, pp 169–94.

Habermas, J. (1992) *The structural transformation of the public sphere: inquiry into a category of bourgeois society*, Cambridge: Polity Press.

HM Treasury (2004) 'Releasing resources for the frontline: independent review of public sector efficiency'. Available at: http://webarchive. nationalarchives.gov.uk/+/http://www.hm-treasury.gov.uk/ spending_sr04_efficiency.htm

Joh, E.E. (2004) 'The paradox of private policing', *The Journal of Criminal Law and Criminology*, vol 95, no 1, pp 49–132.

Kempa, M. and Singh, A.-M. (2008) 'Private security, political economy and the policing of race: probing global hypotheses through the case of South Africa', *Theoretical Criminology*, vol 12, no 3, pp 333–54.

Kennedy, D. (1982) 'The stages of the decline of the public/private distinction', *University of Pennsylvania Law Review*, vol 130, no 6, pp 1349–57.

Lacey, N. (2011) 'The resurgence of character: criminal responsibility in the context of criminalisation', in A. Duff and S. Green (eds) *Philosophical foundations of criminal law*, Oxford: Oxford University Press, pp 151–78.

Liu, C. (2004) 'A brief genealogy of privacy: rhetorics of surveillance from Bentham to Big Brother', *Grey Room*, no 15, pp 102–18.

Loader, I. (1997) 'Thinking normatively about private security', *Journal of Law and Society*, vol 24, no 3, pp 377–94.

Loader, I. (2006) 'Policing, recognition, and belonging', *Annals of the American Academy of Political and Social Science*, vol 605, no 1, pp 202–21.

MacIntyre, A. (1981) *After virtue: a study in moral theory*, London: Duckworth.

Mill, J.S. (2008) *On liberty and other essays*, Oxford: Oxford University Press.

Ministry of Justice (2011) 'Offender management reform and payment by results', 17 March. Available at: www.justice.gov.uk/offenders/payment-by-results

Ministry of Justice (2012) 'Swift and sure justice', 13 July. Available at: www.justice.gov.uk/news/speeches/nick-herbert/speech-swift-and-sure-justice

Moran, L. and Skeggs, B. (2004) *Sexuality and the politics of violence and safety*, London: Routledge.

O'Floinn, M. and Ormerod, D. (2012) 'Social networking material as criminal evidence', *Criminal Law Review*, vol 7, pp 486–512.

Palmer, S. (2007) 'Public, private and the Human Rights Act 1998: an ideological divide', *Cambridge Law Journal*, vol 66, no 3, pp 559–73.

Prosser, T. (2000) 'Common values and the public–private divide', *Public Law*, Summer, pp 337–9.

Rawls, J. (1988) 'The priority of right and ideas of the good', *Philosophy & Public Affairs*, vol 17, no 4, pp 251–76.

Rawls, J. (1999) *A theory of justice* (rev edn), Cambridge, MA: Belknap.

Reuters (2012) 'Wheels could wobble on Britain's outsourcing drive', 25 June. Available at: http://uk.reuters.com/article/2012/07/25/uk-britain-outsourcing-idUKBRE86O0WK20120725

Rose, N. (1987) 'Beyond the public/private division: law, power and the family', *Journal of Law and Society*, vol 14, no 1, pp 61–76.

Scenesafe (2012) 'Homeapage'. Available at: https://www.scenesafe.co.uk/

Sunstein, C.R. (2001) *Republic.com*, Princeton, NJ: Princeton University Press.

Taylor, C. (1992) *Sources of the self: the making of the modern identity*, Cambridge: Cambridge University Press.

Temkin, J. and Krahé, B. (2008) *Sexual assault and the justice gap: a question of attitude*, Oxford: Hart.

Thornton, M. (1991) 'The public/private dichotomy: gendered and discriminatory', *Journal of Law and Society*, vol 18, no 4, pp 448–63.

Wakefield, A. (2003) *Selling security: the private policing of public space*, Cullompton: Willan.

Walden, I., and Wasik, M. (2011) 'The internet: access denied controlled!', *Criminal Law Review*, no 5, pp 377–87.

FOURTEEN

Working with victims: values and validations

Marian Duggan

Introduction

Notions of victimisation in the UK have transformed in the past two decades. Once largely overlooked, the victim is now a far more strategic stakeholder in the British criminal justice system (CJS), inspiring a host of academic research, government policies and reports into best practice and victim satisfaction (Rock, 2002; Goodey, 2004). Myriad forms of victimisation have been officially recognised through new laws, particularly with regards to identity prejudice. The socially constructed nature of identity and its corresponding impact on legal engagement with victims and offenders provides an ample site for investigation to assess how value and validation shape the CJS's response to specific types of victimisation.

Addressing identity prejudice is the focus of both 'hate crime' legislation and the Equality Act 2010. 'Hate crime' refers to acts motivated by racial, religious, sexual orientation, disability and transgender prejudice, addressing this in the offence/sentencing process (see Chakraborti and Garland, 2009). The Equality Act consolidates and/or replaces pre-existing equality and anti-discrimination laws pertaining to seven 'protected characteristics': race, religion, sexual orientation, disability, gender identity, gender and age. The Act also extends protections afforded to persons discriminated against because of their perceived or actual *affiliation* to someone with a protected characteristic. Carers of disabled people or partners/relatives of transsexual people are protected. Symbolically, addressing inequality or prejudice through such legislation promotes a broader message of intolerance to identity discrimination. However, while such measures appear progressive in theory, how applicable they are in practice may be impeded by social prejudices held towards historically marginalised groups.

The notion of 'vulnerability' is central to understanding these legal developments. In 2001, Betsy Stanko (2001, p 318) wrote of a need for the CJS to address 'targeted victimisation' through a conceptual lens of *vulnerability*, rather than creating new 'hate crimes' based on vaguely defined concepts of identity prejudice: 'The social context of targeted violence recognises the special vulnerability of individuals because they are in some relational "disadvantage" to the perpetrator without bracketing the kind of vulnerability into a category'. Nonetheless, the legal incarnations that emerged firmly entrenched specified identity categories, diverting ensuing debates away from theorising vulnerability in favour of ascertaining the pros and cons of 'hate crime'.

This chapter focuses on vulnerability, suggesting that factors exist that render certain victims more vulnerable to victimisation, but simultaneously impede them from accessing 'justice' or recognition. It examines the experiences of, and responses to, victimisation encountered by two identifiable groups commonly perceived as vulnerable to victimisation: Romany Gypsies and Irish Travellers (hereafter, 'Gypsies and Travellers') and street-sleeping homeless people. The former constitute a legally recognised category, the latter do not. Gypsies and Travellers and street-sleeping homeless people may incur prejudice related to their use of space and how this is factored into the construction of their identities. For Gypsies and Travellers who live in mobile homes in communities formed upon large expanses of land, there is a visibility and vulnerability issue in that they are set apart from the domiciled norm; this may form a basis for their victimisation (James, 2007). For street-sleeping homeless people, the occupation of public spaces provides an exposure that, coupled with a generally negative social construction, may serve to heighten their vulnerability to victimisation (Fitzpatrick and Kennedy, 2000).

The chapter explores the victimisation incurred by these groups that reinforces the undervalued position they occupy in both society and political discourses. It illustrates how, rather than being seen as *more* vulnerable and in need of protection, their identities have been devalued (Gypsies and Travellers) or deemed invalid (street-sleeping homeless people). Prioritised minority groups have achieved recognition through capitalisation on high-profile cases and/or grass-roots activism; for those where no cause célèbre or pressure group exists, their marginalised status quo remains (Strolovitch, 2006). Therefore, the chapter concludes by suggesting the adoption of Stanko's (2001) 'targeted victimisation' framework to marginalised and vulnerable groups in order to focus on enhanced levels of vulnerability rather than socially constructed identity when validating victims' experiences.

Socially constructed frameworks of 'valid' victim identities

Developments in victimology have progressed notions of victimisation from an early 20th-century positivistic domain seeking to account for victim precipitation or culpability to a broader understanding of needs and wants following hostility and prejudice in light of an increasingly diverse society (Spalek, 2006). A significant proportion of these developments arose as a result of feminist interventions into the construction of, and response to, female victims of domestic and sexual assault (Rock, 2002). These investigations into the previously 'gender-blind' (Walklate, 2004) nature of criminology spawned a related victim-centred approach to understanding crime and victimisation (Goodey, 2004; Walklate, 2007). As a result, much victimological research has been conducted into the persecution of the traditionally powerless in society, taking, as Becker (1967) suggested, the 'side' of those less able to represent themselves.

The growth in a victim focus has aided the development of theorising and policy initiatives targeted at specific forms of victimisation or the persecution of certain groups of people. Within some Western societies, 'hate crime' research has become a distinct academic discipline, addressing laws that recognise an offender's motivation for a crime as being based on the victim's inferred or actual identity affiliation (Hall, 2005; Chakraborti and Garland, 2009). Some contention surrounds what a 'hate crime' is, or who can be affected by it. For most scholars, an adoption of Barbara Perry's definition has been the starting point for both academic writing and policy reports in this area. Perry (2001, p 10) outlines hate crime as involving 'Acts of violence and intimidation, usually directed towards already stigmatized and marginalized groups. As such, it is a mechanism of power and oppression, intended to reaffirm the precarious hierarchies that characterize a given social order'.

Similarly, Mason (1993) suggests that hate crime is victimisation directed towards a class of people, rather than a specific individual; thus, it can be considered a 'message' regarding the perpetrator's feelings towards the targeted identity. Such acts are symbolic of inferred value; it simultaneously reflects the difference afforded to the persecuting and persecuted groups in line with a valued–devalued binary. Thus, 'hate crime' may be less based on hatred and more representative of power dynamics between groups.

The wider adoption of *prejudice* rather than *hatred* is reflected in UK policy guidance, compiled by the Association of Chief Police Officers (ACPO) in 2000 and revised in 2005 and 2010. The approach taken by ACPO indicates a commitment to encompassing as many types of hate-motivated events as possible. They distinguish between hate incidents and hate crimes; this is an important measure as many interactions between people involve what are commonly termed 'low-level incidents' that may cause upset or distress but may not technically be a crime in the UK. (The case of Fiona Pilkington, who killed herself and her mentally disabled daughter, Francecca, indicated the need to recognise the severe mental trauma that can arise after prolonged exposure to so-called 'low-level' hate incidents.) ACPO's inclusionary approach in the field of hate crime can be seen as an effort to record as diverse a range of incidents and crimes as possible, perhaps to provide an indication of the current nature and prevalence of such occurrences in the UK. A more pessimistic reading of this wide-ranging approach might suggest that in the wake of the Macpherson Report (Macpherson, 1999), there is a need to regain the public's trust, particularly among communities disproportionately affected by interpersonal victimisation.

Racial victimisation has been recognised in law since the 1960s; victimisation on the basis of religion/faith, sexual identity, disability and gender identity are more recent additions. A person can be convicted for a racially or religiously aggravated crime. In the case of a crime motivated by a prejudice against the victim's sexual orientation or disability, the conviction is for an existing crime only (ie assault or criminal damage), with a potential sentence enhancement enacted to reflect the prejudicial factor. In cases where there is no evidence of provocation or previous interactions/altercations between the victim and the perpetrator, and no other rationale for the violence used, the implication that the victim has been selected for the identity he or she is seen to represent is a fundamental starting point for understanding how hierarchies of power are being symbolised through this violence.

Iganski (2008) illustrates how hate crimes can 'hurt' victims and communities more than other crimes as a result of this targeted element. Garland and Chakraborti (2004) demonstrate the increased negative experiences of immigrant communities in rural as opposed to urban environments, where they may be experiencing even greater marginalisation. Spalek (2006) depicts the resultant impact of 9/11 on 'Islamophobia' and hostility directed towards Muslim communities, particularly Muslim women. Finally, Duggan (2012) highlights the cultural specifics relevant to addressing hate crime in post-conflict societies such as Northern Ireland. The importance of recognising these elements of power therefore render the need to prove or determine actual 'hatred' redundant. Perry (2001) indicates that these power dynamics retain the dominant and subordinated positions of social groups and the identities of the individuals involved. As a result, acts that are defined as hate crimes can be read within the wider socio-political context in which they occur as a means of conveying a message to both the victimised group and the wider community.

Although this is still a nascent area of study, particularly in the UK, several hate crime scholars (Jacobs and Potter, 1998; Perry, 2001, 2003) have motivated academics to investigate the divisions between crimes seemingly motivated by identity politics such as race, ethnicity, faith and religion (Iganski, 2008, 2011; Chakraborti and Garland, 2009), sexual orientation (Stanko, 1997; Duggan, 2012), disability (Roulstone and Mason-Bish, 2012) and transgender groups (Turner et al, 2009). Similarly, the deaths of Stephen Lawrence and, later, Anthony Gardener (racially motivated), Jody Dubrowski (homophobically motivated), and Brent Martin (disability motivated) are cases in point that are often alluded to by special interest groups eager to highlight the necessity for such legislation. In each of these cases, the police and special-interest community pressure groups highlighted the need to take targeted forms of victimisation seriously. For groups where advocates are less established, enacting justice may be a more complex process.

Devalued victimisation? Prejudice against Gypsies and Travellers

Gypsies and Travellers may be distinct ethnic groups, but share a long-contested history in the UK. Discourses pertaining to Gypsy and Traveller groups often focus on the social control of these communities, which understandably strains relations between them and criminal justice agents (James and Richardson, 2006, 2007). The social construction of these communities' identities as deviant puts them at a disadvantage, as they are often seen as a legitimate target of victimisation or as precipitating incidents in some way (Scraton, 2007).

Gypsy and Traveller communities encounter some of the most intense and persistent victimisation in the UK, as well as wider Europe (Iganski, 2011). Examples of systematic discrimination outlined by Donnelly (2002) include exclusion from health care interventions, Traveller children being bullied at school, non-admittance into restaurants and public houses, and ill-treatment while in police custody. Cemlyn et al (2009, p v) suggest that:

> Racism towards most ethnic minority groups is now hidden, less frequently expressed in public, and widely seen as

unacceptable. However, that towards Gypsies and Travellers is still common, frequently overt and seen as justified. Abusive media coverage and overtly racist statements from local and national politicians add to the ignorance and prejudice of many members of the settled population, while those in authority frequently fail to challenge them.

In 2003, two teenagers were imprisoned for the manslaughter of 15-year-old Irish Traveller Johnny Delaney after repeatedly kicking him in the head (BBC, 2003). One of the defendants had stamped on Johnny's head with both feet, saying he deserved it because "he was only a fucking Gypsy". The Race Relations Act 1976 (amended by the Race Relations Act 2000) included Gypsies and Travellers as recognised minority ethnic groups who may be subject to racial discrimination. The judge in this case, however, decided that the attack was not racially motivated and so did not treat it as such. The chair of the Commission for Racial Equality (CRE) at the time queried this decision, stating: 'it is extremely hard to see how this particular killing wasn't motivated in some way by racial prejudice' (Greenfields, 2006, p 158, cited in Cemlyn et al, 2009, p 149). The repercussions of this attack were felt among the wider Traveller community, who considered such attacks against them to be rooted in deeper prejudices that often stifle their everyday activities (Gillan, 2003).

Much of this prejudice and discrimination comes as a result of misconceptions about otherwise unconventional, nomadic lifestyles (Scraton, 2007; Iganski, 2011). Despite numerous legislative shifts to address the legality of Travellers' sites (Donnelly, 2002), in 2011, Essex Council's decision to evict a large proportion of Traveller families from the Dale Farm campsite was notable for the significant proportion of negative media coverage based around the contested legality of the site and, by default, those occupying it. Members of Roma communities have also cited the frequency of hostility they incur from the public with regards to being seen as unwelcome (Iganski, 2011). In 2009, up to 100 Roma Gypsy people fled Northern Ireland after encountering hostility (Council of Europe, 2012). Many had been begging or selling copies of *The Big Issue* (a magazine sold by the homeless to give them a form of income) in and around Belfast city centre as they were not allowed to claim benefits and were only allowed to work if they had secured employment prior to arriving in Northern Ireland. Within the space of a few days, many had been targeted, with crowds gathering outside some of the families' homes shouting racist remarks and causing criminal damage (McDonald, 2009a, 2009b). Fearing for their safety, many Roma were forced to take refuge elsewhere. Temporary accommodation was initially sourced for the targeted families, first in the City church and later in the halls of local sports venues. After a week of persistent harassment, many families chose to return to Romania instead (BBC, 2009; Amnesty International, 2009). Iganski (2011) has described this turn of events as a form of social or ethnic cleansing; in order to remove the problem, it is deemed easier to remove those being victimised.

Gypsies and Travellers rarely report the victimisation they experience, racially motivated or otherwise, creating a dearth in official statistics regarding their victimisation and a gulf between them and the CJS (Morris and Clements, 1999; Donnelly, 2002; Power, 2004). Research by James (2007) and Greenfields (2006) has indicated the under-reporting of crime experienced by Gypsies and Travellers compared to normal crime victimisation trends, and also racially motivated crimes. Cemlyn et al (2009, p 8) identified a 'cultural trauma' among Gypsy and Traveller communities, which resulted in 'high rates of anxiety, depression and at times self-destructive behaviour (for example, suicide and/or substance abuse)'. This, they suggested, was heightened through the 'failure [of public bodies] to engage in an equitable manner with members of the communities' (Cemlyn et al, 2009, p 9).

There may also be a form of indirect discrimination precluding their victimisation from being addressed as a hate crime. As a link with ethnicity must be established for the police to record incidents or crimes as motivated by hate, if this is not perceived or evident, then there is no such record made. The social development and integration of Gypsy and Traveller communities may mean that there is, at first, no ready means of connecting a person to a travelling community. For those born in England, there may also be a less immediately discernible Gypsy or Traveller identity, particularly if community members live in traditional houses due to a lack of available sites to pitch on. Some may even have been pressurised into such moves through the provisions outlined in the Criminal Justice and Public Order Act 1994, which reduced access to established social and family support structures and alienated younger members of Gypsy and Traveller communities (Power, 2004).

In the sense that hate crimes are often seen as 'message crimes' (Iganski, 2008), victimising a member of a community that is characterised through close relationships and geographical proximity, such as Gypsies and Travellers, effectively ripples out towards indirect victims. The failure to categorise the death of Johnny Delaney as a hate crime, despite the clear and disparaging inferences made towards his race by his killers, coupled with the events surrounding the victimisation and intimidation of Romany Gypsies living in Northern Ireland in 2009, demonstrates the hostility faced by some members of these communities and the struggle they face to have victimisation taken seriously in law. Unlike some other recognised hate crime groups, Gypsies and Travellers are unlikely to have the same 'bargaining power' in society with regard to special-interest or community groups advocating for them. Becker (1967) outlined the importance of this when discussing the taking of 'sides' in sociological research. In discussing the political significance of having 'spokesmen', Becker (1967, p 243) outlined how the subordinated group 'engages in political activity designed to change existing hierarchical relationships and the credibility of its spokesmen directly affects its political fortunes'. Recognition of this is important: the lifestyles adopted by many Gypsies and Travellers means that many withdraw from mainstream education at an early age. This may have a subsequent effect on their ability to achieve a level of status or capital from which to shape or instigate theory, policy or legal practice from an 'insider' perspective in the way that many other marginalised groups currently do. Similarly, although academic research into racism has a long history, specific focus on the victimisation of Gypsy and Traveller people is less developed in comparison.

Invalid victimisation? The persecution of street-sleeping homeless people

Crimes against the homeless, in particular, street-sleepers or those who have no fixed place of residence, have become more widely recognised as a serious problem over the past decade (BBC, 1999; Fitzpatrick and Kennedy, 2000; Whitbeck et al, 2001; The Big Issue in the North, 2010; Garland, 2012). Ballintyne's (1999) research indicated that two thirds (63%) of his sample were physically attacked by members of the public. Homeless people experience dehumanisation (such as being spat at/ urinated upon), are 13 times more likely to be a victim of a violent crime and are 47 times more likely to be a victim of theft (Newburn and Rock, 2005). Women are particularly vulnerable to manipulation and sexual violence (McCoy et al, 2001), while young people are also at risk, more so if they have alcohol or drug dependencies; a factor that might add to their reluctance to engage with criminal justice agents for fear of prosecution (Whitbeck et al, 2001). Additional reasons for not reporting echo those of hate crime victims: fear of disbelief, not being taken seriously or of incurring further victimisation. A level of fatalism or expectancy of victimisation, or the internalising of negative stereotypes that thereby negate a legitimate victim status, may also be a factor (Wardhaugh, 2000). All of these factors are exacerbated if the homeless person is also sleeping rough (on the streets).

The significant levels of violence involved in attacks on street-sleeping homeless people mirror those cited in the worst cases of hate crimes. The murder of George Akers, who 'was subjected to a sustained and brutal assault, and died in the spot where he had slept for the previous few weeks' (Westcott, 2010), indicated the level of viciousness involved in crimes against the homeless. Similar cases have been identified in the US by the National Coalition for the Homeless (NCH), who show that the abuse experienced by homeless people mirrors that of recognised hate crime groups. This included people being set on fire, raped, sexually abused, physically attacked, assaulted with a weapon and murdered (NCH, 2010). They estimate that in the decade preceding 2010, nearly 300 homeless people were killed in the US (NCH, 2010, p 10). Many of these crimes were committed by multiple perpetrators, often young males under the age of 30, and they appeared to constitute some form of peer-bonding exercise (Fitzpatrick and Kennedy, 2000; NCH, 2010).

Advances in social networking can also be seen as having impacted on the targeting of street-sleeping homeless people. The social phenomenon of 'bum fights' – where homeless people, usually men, are filmed fighting each other or hurting themselves on command of the person operating the recording equipment – illustrates a worrying growth in popularity. Walshe (2010) suggests that more than 5,000 such videos were available on media-sharing website *YouTube*. At the time of writing, my search of this same website yielded over 29,900 'hits', or related video clips. In the UK, as in Canada and New Zealand, the sale of such videos is illegal, yet clips from them are still available for viewing on media-sharing websites. This form of class, economic and age exploitation (as those filming are usually younger than those being filmed) is rarely addressed, as those being exploited may be unaware of the situation or disbelieved/not taken seriously should they inform criminal justice authorities of such victimisation.

Fooks and Pantazis (1999) suggest that homeless people are conceptualised as at risk *to* rather than *from* society. They state that the homeless person's identity 'tends to disappear and instead the emphasis is placed on the risk to the "respectable" public of criminal victimisation from the homeless' (Fooks and Pantazis, 1999, p 124). This was the stance adopted by John Major, speaking as Prime Minister in 1994, who suggested that the situations of homeless people were entirely unnecessary and the result of their lifestyle choices. In stating that beggars were an 'eyesore', Mr Major also worried about their adverse impact on the economy as he believed that they could 'drive tourists and shoppers away from cities' (Watson, 1994, cited in Fooks and Pantazis, 1999, p 126). These sentiments were echoed by Tony Blair in 1998 as part of a speech on social exclusion soon after he became Prime Minister. Although less vindictive than his predecessor, Blair still situated homelessness within the context of posing risk to 'normal' society. Unsurprisingly, as part of his 'zero tolerance' drive towards, first, defining and, then, combating anti-social behaviour, eradicating visible homelessness was high on New Labour's agenda. This attitude may have been influenced by previous events in the US, where, as part of the 'zero tolerance' approach to cleaning up New York's streets, Mayor Rudy Guiliani ensured that all public 'nuisances' were targeted by the police. The removal of large areas of cardboard cities occupied by the urban homeless populations effectively criminalised the occupants (Fooks and Pantazis, 1999).

The victimisation of street-sleeping homeless people raises uncomfortable questions about morality and socio-political attitudes towards vulnerability. The construction of homeless people as criminals rather than victims may be informing prejudice against them. Stereotypes that infer substance misuse, work-shy attitudes and a lack of responsibility may arise as a result of conflating homelessness with begging; a practice predicated upon negative imagery (Chambliss, 1969). Such misconceptions surrounding homeless people may portray them as perpetrators of crimes or as deserving of their victimisation. Being vulnerable, visible and vilified may mean that homeless people face persecution on a more regular basis than some other, recognised minority groups, yet they are not considered eligible as a hate crime group (Mason-Bish, 2010). Scurfied et al (2009) reported that harassment was a daily occurrence for some in their study, with verbal abuse being the most common form of victimisation experienced by homeless sellers of *The Big Issue*. Selling *The Big Issue* may identify the person as homeless, but this was conflated with the assumption that the person was also abusing drugs and/or alcohol. While not all homeless people are battling against addictions, for those who are, this could be seen as increasing their vulnerability. Instead, such dependencies were often construed by their persecutor as enhancing their criminality (Scurfield et al, 2009).

Conclusion: valuing *vulnerability*

The discussion regarding victimisation in this chapter has demonstrated that for some identity groups, social or cultural barriers exist that prevent them availing themselves of, or being recognised by, hate crime prevention policies as a result of the value placed on the identity in question. The association of deviance with Gypsies and Travellers and street-sleeping homeless people is strongly rooted in society as a result of historic practices. McLaughlin (2008, p 41) suggests that the construction of nomadic groups as 'vagrants' was an effective and powerful weapon 'used by settled communities to more clearly, and literally, define their positions in European society. It was literally also used for keeping Gypsies at a distance, and for keeping them in their place'. Thus, the stigmatisation and exclusion of Gypsies as 'homeless' people (and, by default, homeless people themselves) put this group 'beyond the pale of civilisation' through the inferior status afforded to them by those in positions of power (McLaughlin, 2008, pp 41–2). Contemporary incarnations of hate crime and equality legislation could be seen as part of political attempts to redress this imbalance and offer reparation for historical persecution. However, current legislation and policies are designed to recognise, protect and value particular *identities*; a better way might be to address enhanced *vulnerability* to victimisation and the reasons behind this.

At present, vulnerability is considered in some statutes that recognise the enhanced level of violence used against particular victims; for example, in cases of sexual violence where additional harms may be caused by the victim being very young, very old or in a position of defencelessness. In essence, this approach feeds into the hierarchy that epitomises victimisation, alluded to by Christie (1986) as constructing an 'ideal victim' framework. He demarcated the popular stereotypes that characterised attributes affiliated to an 'ideal victim' identity. The victim would be: weak (in relation to the offender); virtuous; blameless; a stranger (to the offender); victimised by a big, bad offender; and able to elicit sympathy for their plight. As such, certain groups or identities may be omitted from this ideal, particularly if they are constructed in a negative way (such as prisoners). Viewing victimisation through a framework of deservedness illustrates how far removed Gypsies and Travellers and street-sleeping homeless people are from the socially constructed, and politically valued, ideal. Instead, such people are often reconceptualised as aggressive, provocative and dangerous. This then facilitates their marginalisation from society in a manner that may function to suggest that they are the victimisers, rather than the victimised.

Stanko's (2001) suggestion of reconceptualising persecution through a framework of vulnerability rather than identity allows for a broadening out of what 'targeted victimisation' may look like. Vulnerable victims, Stanko argues, are rendered as such through social constructions that cast them as legitimate targets of violence. Therefore, rather than focusing on group dynamics and perceived membership, she suggests that vulnerability should be conceptualised through 'the multiple of vulnerabilities/advantages victims and perpetrators have in relation to *each other*', thus recognising 'the significance of the assailant's *choice of victim* because of a perceived disadvantage' (Stanko, 2001, p 319, original emphasis). Such a broadening out of the analysis may facilitate a closer look at how ideologies concerning victims at the lower end of hierarchies have been informed and sustained, and what this might mean for those seeking protection from, or justice following, victimisation. However, recent developments in hate crime theorising have considered increasing hate crime legislation to include gender (McPhail, 2002; Mason-Bish, 2012), cultural identities such as 'Goths' (Garland, 2010) and the elderly (Garland, 2012). This recognition that current policies are too limiting does not necessarily warrant a move to expansion; this may not prove as effective as dismantling those already in place.

Although enhanced criminalisation may not be the most ideal way of preventing victimisation from occurring, such measures are prioritised by the current criminal justice system. If victimisation on the basis of identity really is about sending a message of presumed inferiority or deviance, then we must engage with this value base in order to address the harmful or negative stereotypes informing such perspectives. A tokenistic or selective application of laws designed to combat prejudice may instead reinforce, not repeal, these very stereotypes.

References

Amnesty International (2009) 'Belfast Roma attacks highlight European racism issue', Amnesty International, 17 June. Available at: www.amnesty.org/en/news-and-updates/news/belfast-roma-attacks-highlight-european-racism-issue-20090617 (accessed 10 January 2012).

Ballintyne, S. (1999) *Unsafe streets: street homelessness and crime*, London: Institute for Public Policy Research.

BBC (British Broadcasting Corporation) (1999) 'Homeless "abused by public"', BBC News, 13 December. Available at: http://news.bbc. co.uk/1/hi/uk/562151.stm (accessed 5 December 2011).

BBC (2003) 'Boys guilty of killing "Gypsy"', BBC News, 28 November. Available at: http://news.bbc.co.uk/1/hi/england/ merseyside/3246518.stm (accessed 5 December 2011).

BBC (2009) 'Romanians leave NI after attacks', BBC News, 23 June. Available at: http://news.bbc.co.uk/1/hi/8114234.stm (accessed 5 December 2011).

Becker, H. (1967) 'Whose side are we on?', *Social Problems*, vol 14, no 3, pp 239–47.

Cemlyn, S., Greenfields, M., Burnett, S., Matthews, Z. and Whitwell, C. (2009) 'Inequalities experienced by Gypsy and Traveller communities: a review', Research Report 12, Equalities and Human Rights Commission.

Chakraborti, N. and Garland, J. (2009) *Hate crime: impacts, causes and consequences*, London: Sage.

Chambliss, W. (1969) *Crime and the legal process*, London: McGraw-Hill.

Christie, N. (1986) 'The ideal victim', in E. Fattah (ed) *From crime policy to victim policy*, Basingstoke: Macmillan.

Council of Europe (2012) *Human rights of Roma and Travellers in Europe*, Strasbourg: Council of Europe Publishing.

Donnelly, E. (2002) 'Hate crimes against Travellers', *Criminal Justice Matters*, vol 48, no 1, pp 24–5.

Duggan, M. (2012) *Queering conflict: examining lesbian and gay experiences of homophobia in Northern Ireland*, Farnham: Ashgate.

Fitzpatrick, S. and Kennedy, C. (2000) *Getting by: begging, rough sleeping and The Big Issue in Glasgow and Edinburgh*, Bristol: The Policy Press.

Fooks, G. and Pantazis, C. (1999) 'The criminalisation of homelessness, begging and street living', in P. Kennett and A. Marsh (eds) *Homelessness: exploring the new terrain*, Bristol: The Policy Press.

Garland, J. (2010) 'The victimisation of Goths and the boundaries of hate crime', in N. Chakraborti (ed) *Hate crime: concepts, policy, future directions*, Cullompton: Willan.

Garland, J. (2012) 'Difficulties in defining hate crime victimisation', *International Review of Victimology*, vol 18, no 1, pp 25–37.

Garland, J. and Chakraborti, N. (2004) 'Another country? Community, belonging and exclusion in rural England', in N. Chakraborti and J. Garland (eds) *Rural racism*, Cullompton: Willan.

Gillan, A. (2003) 'Brutal death of a travelling child', *The Guardian*, 10 June. Available at: www.guardian.co.uk/uk/2003/jun/10/ukcrime. childprotection

Goodey, J. (2004) *Victims and victimology: research, policy and practice*, London: Longman.

Greenfields, M. (2006) 'Gypsies, Travellers and legal matters', in C. Clark and M. Greenfields (eds) *Here to stay: the Gypsies and Travellers of Britain*. Hatfield: University of Hertfordshire Press, pp 133–81.

Hall, N. (2005) *Hate crime*, Cullompton: Willan.

Iganski, P. (2008) *'Hate crime' in the city*, Bristol: The Policy Press.

Iganski, P. (2011) 'Racist violence in Europe', European Network Against Racism/Open Society Foundation, Brussels. Available at: http://cms.horus.be/files/99935/MediaArchive/publications/Comparative%20report%20-%20EN%20Final.pdf

Jacobs, J. and Potter, K. (1998) *Hate crimes*, Oxford: Oxford University Press.

James, Z. (2007) 'Policing marginal spaces: controlling Gypsies and Travellers', *Criminology and Criminal Justice*, vol 7, no 4, pp 367–89.

James, Z. and Richardson, J. (2006) 'Controlling accommodation: policing Gypsies and Travellers', in A. Dearling, T. Newburn and P. Somerville (eds) *Supporting safer communities – housing, crime and neighbourhoods*, Coventry: Chartered Institute of Housing.

Macpherson, W. (1999) *The Stephen Lawrence inquiry. Report of an inquiry by Sir William Macpherson of Cluny* (Cm 4262), London: The Stationery Office.

Mason, G. (1993) *Violence against lesbians and gay men*, Crime Prevention Today No 2, Canberra: Australian Institute of Criminology.

Mason-Bish, H. (2010) 'Future challenges for hate crime policy: lessons from the past', in N. Chakraborti (ed) *Hate crime: concepts, policy, future directions*, Cullompton: Willan.

McCoy, H.V., Messiah, S.E. and Yu, Z. (2001) 'Perpetrators, victims and observers of violence: chronic and non-chronic drug users', *Journal of Interpersonal Violence*, vol 16, no 9, pp 890–909.

McDonald, H. (2009a) 'Racist attacks on Belfast Roma: it doesn't happen in Republican areas, only Loyalist areas', *The Guardian*, 18 June. Available at: www.guardian.co.uk/uk/audio/2009/jun/18/roma-belfast-race-attack (accessed 10 January 2012).

McDonald, H. (2009b) 'Romanian gypsies beware beware. Loyalist C18 are coming to beat you like a baiting bear' *The Guardian*, 21 June. Available at: www.guardian.co.uk/world/2009/jun/21/race-northern-ireland-romanian-gypsies (accessed 5 December 2011).

McLaughlin, J. (2008) 'Gypsies as "other" in European society: towards a political geography of hate', *The European Legacy: Toward New Paradigms*, vol 4, no 3, pp 35–49.

McPhail, B. (2002) 'Gender-bias hate crimes: a review', *Trauma Violence Abuse*, vol 3, pp 125–43.

Morris, R. and Clements, L. (1999) *Gaining ground: law reform for Gypsies and Travellers*, Herts: University of Hertfordshire Press.

NCH (National Coalition for the Homeless) (2010) 'Hate crimes against the homeless: violence hidden in plain view'. Available at: www.nationalhomeless.org/publications/hatecrimes/hatecrimes2010.pdf

Newburn, T. and Rock, P. (2005) *Living in fear: violence and victimisation in the lives of single homeless people*, London: Crisis.

Perry, B. (2001) *In the name of hate: understanding hate crimes*, London: Routledge.

Perry, B. (2003) 'Where do we go from here? Researching hate crime', *Internet Journal of Criminology*. Available at: www.internetjournalofcriminology.com/Where%20Do%20We%20Go%20From%20Here.%20Researching%20Hate%20Crime.pdf

Power, C. (2004) *Room to roam: England's Irish Travellers*, London: Action Group for Irish Youth.

Rock, P. (2002) 'On becoming a victim', in C. Hoyle and R. Wilson (eds) *New visions of crime victims*, Oxford: Hart Publishing.

Roulstone, A. and Mason-Bish, H. (2012) *Disability, hate crime and violence*, Abingdon: Routledge.

Scraton, P. (2007) *Power, conflict and criminalisation*, London: Taylor and Francis.

Scurfield, J., Rees, P. and Norman, P. (2009) 'Criminal victimisation of the homeless: an investigation of Big Issue vendors in Leeds', *Radical Statistics*, no 99. Available at: www.radstats.org.uk/no099/index.htm (accessed 5 December 2011).

Spalek, B (2006) *Crime victims: theory, policy and practice*, Hampshire: Palgrave Macmillan.

Stanko, B. (1997) 'Homophobic violence and the self "at risk": interrogating the boundaries', *Social and Legal Studies*, vol 6, no 4, pp 513–32.

Stanko, B. (2001) 'Re-conceptualising the policing of hatred: confessions and worrying dilemmas of a consultant', *Law and Critique*, vol 12, pp 309–29.

Strolovitch, D. (2006) 'Do interest groups represent the disadvantaged? Advocacy at the intersections of race, class, and gender', *The Journal of Politics*, vol 68, no 4, pp 894–910.

The Big Issue in the North (2010) 'Minority report', 24 October. Available at: www.bigissueinthenorth.com/2010/10/minority-report/ (accessed 10 January 2012).

Turner, L., Whittle, S. and Combs, R. (2009) *Transphobic hate crime in the European Union*, Brussels: ILGA–Europe/Press For Change.

Walklate, S. (ed) (2004) *Handbook of victims and victimology*, Cullompton: Willan Publishing.

Walklate, S. (2007) *Imagining the victim of crime*, Maidenhead: Open University Press.

Walshe, S. (2010) 'Hate crimes against the homeless', *The Guardian*, 20 August. Available at: www.guardian.co.uk/commentisfree/cifamerica/2010/aug/20/homeless-bum-fight-hate-crime (accessed 5 December 2011).

Wardhaugh, J. (2000) *Sub city: young people, homelessness and crime*, Aldershot: Ashgate.

Westcott, M. (2010) 'Homeless Darlington man dies after "sustained, unprovoked attack"', *The Northern Echo*, 24 June. Available at: www.thenorthernecho.co.uk/news/8236978.Homeless_Darlington_man_died_after__sustained__unprovoked_attack_/ (accessed 10 January 2012).

Whitbeck, L., Hoyt, D., Yoder, K., Cauce, A. and Paradise, M. (2001) 'Deviant behaviour and victimization among homeless and runaway adolescents', *Journal of Interpersonal Violence*, vol 16, no 11, pp 1175–204.

FIFTEEN

Money as the measure of man: values and value in the politics of reparation*

Claire Moon

Introduction

This chapter addresses both 'values' and 'value' in reconciliatory political practices and looks in particular at the significance and meaning of reparative justice values and practices. These are often claimed to service the aims of political reconciliation, where reckoning with past state crimes is made central to transitions from authoritarianism to more democratic political orders, such as in Argentina, Chile and South Africa. This chapter pays particular attention to the practice of granting compensation to victims of atrocities in order to investigate and critique both 'values' – that is, some of the normative dimensions of reconciliation – and the idea of 'value' (as compensation) in repairing the crimes of the past regime. In order to do this, the chapter takes a primarily empirical approach to Becker's (1967) question of 'taking sides' by engaging with the ways in which some victim groups have contested, and even refused, reparatory attempts. By analysing the *reception* of reparations by victims, this chapter consequently helps us to rethink in a more nuanced way the normative terrain and, by implication, the practices of power upon which human rights and reconciliatory politics are predicated and executed. In so doing, it attends to what these contestations tell us about the social and political

---

* This chapter reproduces (with permission) some arguments and empirical material previously published in Claire Moon (2008) *Narrating political reconciliation: South Africa's Truth and Reconciliation Commission* (Lanham, MD: Lexington Books/Rowman and Littlefield), 'Conclusions', and in Claire Moon (2012) '"Who'll pay reparations on my soul?" Compensation, social control and social suffering', *Social and Legal Studies*, vol 21, no 2, pp 187–99.

power that humanitarian values – in this case, reparatory ones – accrue at particular historical junctures.

The departure point for this discussion concerns current debate about the imperative to repair past wrongs. This is grounded in the idea that state reparation benefits the victims of atrocity by acknowledging wrongful acts, recognising harms and ameliorating victim suffering. As a consequence of this assumption, much theoretical and practical work has concurred to establish state reparation to victims of state crimes as a cornerstone of human rights. Most recently, reparation has been cast as a 'right' in itself: in 2005, the UN General Assembly adopted *The Basic Principles and Guidelines on the Right to a Remedy and Reparation for Victims of Gross Violations of International Human Rights Law and Serious Violations of International Humanitarian Law*. The legalisation of reparation is testimony to the moral certainty that characterises the contemporary debate and practice around reparations.

However, this chapter argues that such reparation can *also* function to placate victim demands for criminal justice and regulate the range of political and historical meanings with which the crimes of the past are endowed, and through which they are interpreted and acted upon. This is most evidently the case in transitional contexts, in which gestures of state reparation are often conditioned by the inauguration of new political orders in which formal statements about past atrocity – what happened, who is responsible and whether and how the book should be closed – are the subject of a precarious politics, of balancing the political demands of an outgoing authoritarian order against the moral demands placed on the nascent political regime: demands for truth, accountability, justice and reparation.

This chapter argues that in such contexts, reparation can work to administer and control social suffering and can sometimes intensify rather than ameliorate it. This empirically develops Kleinman et al's (1997, p ix) assertion that social suffering not only 'results from what political, economic and institutional power does to people', but also emerges 'from how these forms of power themselves influence responses to social problems'. In order to advance this claim, the chapter investigates both the contestation and the refusal of reparations by the very victims towards whom it is addressed. Two cases are significant and are investigated here: first, the refusal of reparation by the *Madres de Plaza de Mayo*, Argentina's 'mothers of the disappeared'; and, second, the South Africa Khulumani Support Group, who, dissatisfied with the Truth and Reconciliation Commission's (hereafter, TRC) reparations programme, pursued a case for reparations from multinational corporations outside the state. These victim contestations of state reparation are not a refusal of the gesture of repair per se, but constitute a rejection of the range of political and historical meanings and their coercive potential to which state reparation is attached in transitional politics. Reparations are symbolically freighted due to a central challenge of transitional states that is concerned with asserting 'control by opening and control by closing' the past (Cohen, 1995, p 47), by simultaneously recovering certain memories and eradicating others in the maintenance of public order. It is precisely at the site of victim contestation of reparation that the range of meanings and memories to which it is attached, and hence its public order function, become visible.

Reparative values

Reparation has come to be a touchstone of reconciliatory politics. The term itself denotes a complex and dynamic combination of elements, but is grounded in 'the simple fairness of replacing what one has taken or destroyed' (Sharpe, 2007, p 24). This principle has come to engage a cluster of related ideas with their origins in different aspects of social life, such as religion (confession, atonement, forgiveness), justice (correction, remedy, restitution), the emotions (guilt, shame, remorse, apology) and the economy (compensation, damages). The etymology of the word gives us clues as to its social function: it is derived from 'repair', meaning to mend, fix or restore. Reparation aims to reduce inequity arising from the original injustice and, in the process, decrease the suffering of the offended. Both *replacement* and *repair* are its conditioning qualities.

Both human rights and transitional justice debates and practice have secured for reparation a new normative status and power and, along with it, a set of categorical claims and assumptions about what reparation, broadly conceived, can achieve. In two of the most influential works in the field, Minow and Hayner highlight its alleged therapeutic benefits: 'unlike retributive practices which may reinforce anger and a sense of victimhood, reparative approaches instead aim to help victims move beyond anger and a sense of powerlessness' (Minow, 1998, p 92); reparations 'can serve an important psychological role of acknowledging wrongs' (Hayner, 2001, p 171).

'Acknowledgement', 'healing' and 'closure' are powerful tropes animating the contemporary assumption about the relationship of reparation to mental health. According to Zehr (2003, p 75), a further function is that reparation makes a 'moral statement to the community that they [the victims] were right'. This is crucial, since state crime is routinely accompanied by state denial and any process of reparation must involve 'setting the record straight'. Further, in declaring that victims were 'right', a wrong is affirmed and some measure of responsibility might be established in fulfilment of the obligation to repair the harm (Zehr, 2003, p 79). The accepted wisdom about reparation can be summarised as follows: (i) it repairs harm (psychological, physical or economic); (ii) it vindicates victims; and (iii) it determines responsibility. These assertions are a window onto the ways in which the central tropes of reconciliatory politics – truth, justice, forgiveness, healing – flow through and are conjoined by reparative practices.

In the context of transitional justice debates, two practical and analytical schisms have become compelling. The first of these hives reparation off from, and sets it up in opposition to, retributive justice. This is an effect of the way in which political debate about justice in transition, such as in South Africa, has frequently been cast as a trade-off between retributive and restorative justice, where criminal trials of members of the former regime are practically impossible due to their persistent power, and reparation to victims serve as 'compensation' for the absence of criminal justice. In order to legitimise such justice 'choices', democratising states often characterise retributive justice as being akin to vengeance, a barbaric relic that serves to increase anger and perpetuate cycles of violence (Moon, 2009). In contrast, restorative approaches have been promoted as best serving reconciliatory politics because they help to 'heal' past wounds and close the door on the past. As such, the two styles of retributive and restorative justice have come, in some transitional contexts, to be cast as distinct and separable, one from the other. This schism, however, is not 'natural', but historically and politically contingent on the specific political conditions in which it has arisen.

The second schism is constituted by the popular practical and analytical distinction between 'material' and 'symbolic' reparations. De Grieff's (2006, p 10) touchstone text documents 'complex' reparations programmes that include 'symbolic as well as material reparations'; Minow (1998, p 91) writes of 'economic and symbolic acts of reparation'; and Sharpe (2007, p 27) of reparations as 'either material or symbolic'. This separation is widely constituted, maintained and naturalised in law, policy and analysis. 'Material' usually designates monetary reparation, while 'symbolic' refers to apologies, exhumations, memorial practices or 'communicative history' (Torpey, 2003, p 6) that shape public discourses about the past. The material–symbolic binary currently defines the field of reparations and is instrumental to how reparations are thought, planned and administered. However, this distinction, symptomatic of the enduring dualisms grounded in Enlightenment thought, is rendered immediately nonsensical at the moment of *reception* of reparation, at which point the symbolic freight of the material gesture is rendered immediately visible. This connection between the material and symbolic is, as Raymond Williams (1977, p 80) (following Marx) has argued, 'indissoluble'.

This dualism in the thought and practice of reparation has been sustainable in part due to the lack of proper attention to the ways in which victim groups contest reparation, and a general neglect of the *meanings with which the intended recipients* endow the practice of state reparation, as the following sections of this chapter show. The distinction between 'material' and 'symbolic' is questionable precisely because the refusals of material reparation are a refusal of the *meanings* – historical, social and political – to which they are attached. As such, the taxonomical and oppositional qualifications of 'material' and 'symbolic' regularly attendant upon the practice of reparation ought to be discarded so that we might properly analyse the social performance of reparations as a 'whole and connected social material process' by which we produce and reproduce social relations (Williams, 1977, p 140). This chimes with the spirit of immanent critique in which contradictions within the analytical architecture are revealed in the moment of its *practical application*, demonstrating internal inconsistencies within the theoretical and professional discourses on reparation that make it amenable to challenge.

An examination of the two case studies – Argentina and South Africa – is instructive. The case of the *Madres* and their refusal of reparation, both 'material' (in the form of financial compensation) and 'symbolic' (in the form of exhumations and memorial practices), reveals the indivisibility of these categories *and* makes visible the regulatory and coercive – or social control – dimensions of reparation. South Africa's Khulumani case illustrates something different that is only really revealed, again, by engaging with victim action around reparations. This case demonstrates the social control dimensions of a state reconciliation narrative that was interested primarily in attempting to identify and reconcile the perpetrators and the victims of party-political violence. This, of course, is only one part of the apartheid story and the Khulumani contestation of state reparations challenges the dominant reconciliatory narrative by bringing into view a different set of agents of state crimes: the multinational economic *beneficiaries* of the apartheid. Thus, this contestation requires that both the subjects *and* the optic of reconciliation shift because the case also shows how reconciliation cannot simply be something that is orchestrated within the boundaries of the state because responsibility for state crimes lies both within *and* outside the state.

Argentina: contesting reparations

The *Madres de Plaza de Mayo* played a significant part in Argentina's struggle over justice, reparation and the politics of the past (Moon, 2012). By 1983, the beginning of Alfonsín's transitional regime, they had secured for themselves a conspicuous presence in Argentina's political landscape. Since their first public demonstration in the *Plaza de Mayo* in April 1977, the *Madres*, led by Hebe de Bonafini, had persistently petitioned successive political regimes for information about the fate of their children and for the prosecution of those responsible for their disappearance. One branch of the original *Madres* group greeted the new government with a refusal of its offer of financial and memorial reparation, which, they argued, aimed to buy their silence, arrest the truth recovery process and avoid bringing perpetrators to trial. Truth, official acknowledgement, retributive justice and the reappearance of those disappeared not properly accounted for were the only acceptable forms of repair, the *Madres* claimed. It is in their refusal of financial and memorial reparation that their performance as instruments of social control – of the past, and of calls for justice – becomes most evident. In addition, the substance of their refusal reveals as problematic the theoretical and practical distinction between 'material' and 'symbolic' reparation.

The essence of the *Madres*' refusal is captured by the various slogans of their long campaign – 'judgment and punishment of all culprits'; 'no exhumations, no posthumous homage, and no economic reparation'; 'bring them back alive'; 'put those who committed genocide behind bars' (Guzman Bouvard, 1994) – and can be summarised as follows.

The *Madres* rejected Alfonsín's offer of monetary compensation because it was predicated on presumption of the death of the victim. Yet, many deaths had not been confirmed and families had not given up on finding them alive. Accepting compensation meant relinquishing hopes for the reappearance of the disappeared, and, crucially, accepting that a full and proper accounting of each and every disappearance would not take place. 'Bring them back alive' radically contested the state's attempt to get the *Madres* to accept the presumption of death and to close down their appeal for truth. The *Madres* also categorically refused 'symbolic' reparations in the form of official exhumations and memorials, provision for which was made by Alfonsín at the time that he instituted the Full Stop Law, which was designed to limit prosecutions. The two seemed inextricably linked. The *Madres* responded, 'we are not going to allow ... that they should make a monument ... brick by brick the mothers will tear it apart, since our children do not want monuments' (cited in Roniger and Sznaider, 1999, p 199). The refusal of exhumation and memorialisation seemed to be a refusal of their children's deaths. However, De Bonafini (1990, p 42) argued:

> we don't accept them as dead. We demand their re-appearance as living entities, which does not mean that we think they are alive. Our demand questions the system, and we will not accept their deaths until someone is made responsible.

For the *Madres*, memorial reparation was akin to monetary reparation in that it also worked to 'presume death', yet the circumstances of disappearance had not been established, nor the bodies recovered, nor responsibility for the deaths investigated. Memorials, then, operated as a technique of the social control of the past, of both opening it (acknowledging and honouring the dead) and simultaneously closing it (by presuming death without full and proper investigation of the circumstances of death and without bringing those responsible to trial).

There is a biopolitical aspect to the mothers' refusal. The *Madres* deliberately sustained the liminal ('between life and death') status of the disappeared in the face of the government's attempt to confirm them as dead. The *Madres*' objection was a refusal of the government's reordering of the past. For the mothers, the disappeared could only properly be returned to the social order through a full explanation of the circumstances surrounding their disappearance, acknowledgement of responsibility and punishment of those responsible. Their protest contested the power of the state to take life away with impunity and subsequently to control, politically, the memory of the dead by placing them within the new official narrative about the past and settle claims to justice by finding and acknowledging the dead (through exhumations and lists of the *junta*'s victims), and attempt repair through memorialisation and public mourning. Both exhumations and monetary compensation carried a condition. When the government started to exhume mass graves in 1984, a number of the *Madres* received telegrams asking them to collect their children's remains along with an indemnity payment, and were asked to sign a certificate stating that 'the child had fought with the police and was killed as a consequence' (Guzman Bouvard, 1994, p 140). This injury was compounded when it was discovered that some of the human remains had been erroneously identified. The *Madres* responded by demonstrating at the site of exhumations to bring the proceedings to a halt. On her arrest and appearance in court after one such demonstration, De Bonafini asked the judge, 'why are you ordering the exhumation of remains to find out to whom they belonged instead of finding out who ordered their burial?' (Guzman Bouvard, 1994, pp 149–50). Her question sheds light on the state's privileging of *certain types* of truth (who died, how many and how), which displaced, for the mothers, the most important truth: who killed them?

The *Madres* opposed state reparation because it entailed an acceptance of Alfonsín's narrative about the past – the theory of the 'two devils' – which conferred moral equality on state and guerrilla terror, and which underpinned the trial process by which both state security agents *and* opponents were to be held accountable for atrocities. This narrative emerged out of Alfonsín's attempt to balance the continued power of the military against popular calls for justice and was part of the new regime's attempt to enforce a sense of continuity over time – embedded in the narrative that diverse parties were culpable and that Argentineans had to find a way of living together now – and maintain public order. The *Madres* were suspicious of the 'two devils' argument since it provided justification for the *junta*'s Dirty War and simultaneously implied the guilt of their missing children. If they accepted financial reparation, they would, by implication, be accepting this official version of the past. The *Madres* sought to undermine the 'two devils' story by seeking recourse to the legal norms that had been endorsed by Alfonsín's recognition of the key human rights instruments on his entry into power, which, after all, underwrote the legitimacy of his regime:

> we don't judge our *detained-disappeared* children, nor do we ask for their freedom. We want to be told where they are, what they are accused of, and ask that they be judged according to legal norms with the legitimate right of self-defense if they have committed any crimes. (Guzman Bouvard, 1994, pp 94–5)

The *Madres* persisted instead in drawing attention to the *junta*'s crimes – articulated in one of their campaign slogans, 'put those who committed genocide behind bars' – and unmasking what they saw as the true intent of the new government: reconciliation as pacification of the military.

The *Madres* saw financial reparation as a means by which the state attempted to buy their silence and end their campaign for trials: 'we reject any force that wants to bribe us … we insist that the murderers must be put in prison. This is our principal aim' (De Bonafini, 1990, p 42). Their refusal here highlights the political deployment of reparations laws, which tended, strategically, to accompany amnesties and military pardons, thus seeming to pacify calls for trials. For example, Alfonsín's Full Stop Law was accompanied by memorial reparatory measures, and Menem's lauded reparations laws were inaugurated simultaneously with his pardon of military elites and the release from prison of some serving sentences for atrocities.

The *Madres* also rejected financial reparations because they saw them as a wholly inadequate response to terror: 'there is no money that can pay for torture, for death, for the forced disappearance ... for the kidnapping of children ... for state terrorism' (Roniger and Sznaider, 1999, p 199). This instinct is reflected in Simmel's claim that because financial reparation sets up a system of equivalent exchange that transfers different lexicons of value, from pecuniary to human, it results in 'the tendency to reduce the value of man to a monetary expression', which 'not only makes money the measure of man, but it also makes man the measure of the value of money' (Simmel, 2004, p 356). In powerful illustration of this claim, De Bonafini protested, 'would you be able to bring a morsel to your mouth knowing that you bought it with the money they gave you because they killed your child ... the life of our children has no price' (cited in Guzman Bouvard, 1994, p 142). De Bonafini's comment reveals something both alchemical and contaminating in financial reparation, suggesting that it performs a strange transubstantiation in which money granted in recompense for the dead makes their bodies exchangeable for, or 'turns them into', other commodities such as food, constituting an especially strong defilement. The mothers also saw monetary compensation as an insult to human dignity and an abuse of poverty since it was an inevitable temptation to those who needed the money. For the *Madres*, dignity was asserted not in the granting and grateful receipt of financial reparation, but only in its refusal, thus challenging the received wisdom in the field which asserts that human dignity is recognised and affirmed through the granting of reparation.

Finally, and crucially, the *Madres* saw the offer of monetary compensation as an extension of the crimes of the *junta*. This is due to the fact that *the very first reparations laws were drawn up by the junta itself*. Two laws on 'presumption of death' were instituted in 1979 in response to the *Madres'* persistent demonstrations against facilitating the payment of pensions to relatives of persons who had been disappeared for one year, and which accompanied another law stating that someone was to be legally determined as dead if they did not reappear within a 90-day period after being reported missing. These laws constituted a redescription of the disappeared as 'presumed dead', making them institutionally 'controllable', attempting to prevent relatives from persisting in their claims for information about their whereabouts. The *junta* provided financial incentives for them to give up their search. Accepting compensation was intrinsically bound up with accepting the *junta*'s narrative that a relative who had been disappeared was engaged in terrorist activities and had been killed ('legitimately') as a consequence. These two laws were a clear attempt by the government to silence the voices of protest and to lay the issue of the disappeared to rest (Arditti, 1999, p 40). For this reason, reparatory gestures made by subsequent regimes presented, to the *Madres*, *continuity* with the *junta*, rather than a radical departure from it. It is striking that these laws are conspicuously absent from the influential debates on reparation in transitional justice, which always narrate the start of Argentina's reparations story with Alfonsín's measures (Hayner, 2001; De Grieff, 2006). This has the effect of excluding consideration of the political uses of reparations and reinforces the regular moral claims that underpin reparations by associating them solely with the civilian, human rights-respecting, regime.

South Africa: compensating apartheid

When South Africa embarked upon its reconciliatory project in 1995, one might have predicted that the amnesty provision that both preceded and precipitated the TRC's work would eventually prove reconciliation's undoing (Moon, 2008, ch 5). However, it was not amnesty, but reparations to victims, that came, at least in the immediate aftermath of the TRC, to represent the critical site of contestation of reconciliation. This is because the TRC privileged what it called symbolic reparations, embedded in the discourses of therapy and theology, healing and forgiveness, over material reparations in such a way as to leave severe material inequalities – an enduring consequence of apartheid governance – unaddressed. In response, the Khulumani Support Group pursued a compensation case against multinational corporations – who were complicit in, and had benefited from, apartheid governance – through courts in the US, questioning the centrality of the narrative about past *political* violence to reconciliation by shifting the story away from the perpetrators and victims of political violence and towards the economic *beneficiaries* of apartheid.

The case queried, implicitly, a key tenet of reconciliation: the centrality of the victim to the new moral order. This tenet was expressed through the main discourses of the TRC, which constructed victims as the new constitutive pillar of society (Moon, 2008). However, it is arguable that, instead, amnesty privileged perpetrators because it was granted with immediate effect, whereas victims had to wait years for decisions on reparations. In addition, many victims themselves placed a greater premium on *financial* compensation, counter to the TRC's broader discourse that emphasised symbolic or therapeutic reparations (restoring dignity and enacting healing through public truth-telling and official acknowledgement of victim experiences). While victims were also promised material compensation, the final financial settlement on reparations was made *over seven years after* the TRC began its work and more than four years after the TRC submitted its initial reparations recommendations to the government. In April 2003, Thabo Mbeki announced that victims who had testified before the TRC would be eligible for a single one-off payment of R30,000 (US$4,500), and that a total of US$85 million would be paid to just over 19,000 victims. The total amount allocated was much less than that initially recommended by the TRC, which stated that the government should pay the equivalent of US$474 million in reparations to all who testified. As Humphrey (2003, p 184) has argued, victimhood was arguably 'short-changed' by symbolic reparations. In response, victim support groups in South Africa, dissatisfied with state reparations, started the process of claiming financial compensation from multinationals for apartheid crimes. This claim was predicated upon an alternative story about South Africa's apartheid past that had been subordinated to the TRC's party-political violence narrative.

In *Khulumani et al v Barclays et al*, filed in November 2002 in New York, Khulumani ('Speak Out') represented some 33,000 South African victims and brought the case for reparations against a number of US, UK, German, Swiss and Dutch multinationals from the oil, armament, banking, transportation and information technology industries – including British Petroleum, Shell Oil, Barclays, Credit Suisse, Deutsche Bank, Ford Motors, IBM and Rio Tinto – all alleged to have profited from their business associations with South Africa (*Khulumani et al v Barclays National Bank et al*, 2002). The Khulumani group has a special relationship with the TRC because it was established by survivors of political violence in order to provide support for victims testifying to the TRC, helping the victims to register their testimonies and fill out applications for reparations and appeals, and providing individual and group counselling throughout the process. Khulumani also organised meetings with TRC officials and represented victim interests to the government, helping to give victims an active voice throughout the work of the TRC.

However, since 2001, Khulumani concentrated on addressing the 'unfinished business' of the TRC and stated that the TRC had underestimated the importance of financial compensation to reconciliation. In addition, Khulumani argued that the majority of victims of apartheid were excluded by the TRC's mandate as they were victims not of party-political violence, but of the systemic effects of apartheid, such as the pass laws, labour laws and forced migration, in which a number of multinationals were alleged by the group to be complicit. Khulumani argued that nothing in the Promotion of National Unity and Reconciliation Act that established the TRC prevented individual business personnel from making disclosures about complicity with the apartheid regime, and yet not one multinational approached the TRC to apply for amnesty.

Khulumani et al v Barclays et al called for compensation to be granted on an individual basis to provide redress for experiences of racially structured violence. This included specific acts of violence but referred more broadly to the lived experience of apartheid that subjected many to the pass laws, forced removals, job and housing restrictions, poor living conditions and education provision, and other direct forms of repression, in all of which the defendants were claimed to be complicit. The case argued that accountability for corporate violations should be established and referred to a host of international rulings on crimes against humanity, genocide, extrajudicial killings, torture, unlawful detention and cruel, inhumane and degrading treatment. It argued that apartheid was a *jus cogens* violation of international law equivalent to slavery by drawing upon Article I of the International Convention on the Suppression and Punishment of the Crime of Apartheid and the Rome Statute of the International Criminal Court. Both classify apartheid as a 'crime against humanity'. In addition, the case invoked the third-party liability precedent set by Nuremberg, which had held the bankers financing the Third Reich liable for crimes against humanity.

The lawsuit sought to prove two types of liability: third-party liability for 'aiding and abetting' the apartheid regime, and criminal enterprise liability (imposed by customary international law and domestic law). The case put it that 'during the relevant period, global industrialists and financiers knew or should have known of the danger to the black South African population' as the UN had 'put the world on notice' during the 1970s and an international boycott that included embargoes on arms, oil and technology was well under way by the 1980s. In spite of this, the defendants 'acted in conscious disregard of or with deliberate indifference to these dangers by providing substantial assistance or encouragement to the apartheid regime', with some corporations continuing to assist the regime throughout this period and, sometimes, concealing fraudulently their cooperation by establishing offshore trusts to obscure their transactions (*Khulumani et al v Barclays et al*, 2002, p 165). The lawsuit argued that the defendants were 'active participants and initiators in constructing a political and economic system that, in the end, was classified in international law as a crime against humanity', adding that, in fact, 'the period of extreme repression, from 1960 onwards, was intended to save the system that protected privilege based on race, thereby continuing to guarantee business its exclusive place in the South African economy and society' (*Khulumani et al v Barclays et al*, 2002, pp 75–80).

The lawsuit cited numerous examples of companies aiding and abetting apartheid, including IBM and Fujitsu ICL, who provided the computers that enabled South Africa to create the passbook system that facilitated control of the black population, and argued that passbooks made possible organised forced labour and gross violations of human rights such as murder, torture and massacre. Car manufacturers provided armoured vehicles used to patrol the townships, oil companies and arms manufacturers violated embargoes on sales to South Africa, and banks funded the expansion of the police and security apparatus. Some of the companies were charged with defrauding (mainly) black employees who deposited their money into pension, health, life, unemployment and retirement funds but received nothing in return.

Importantly for the analysis here, the lawsuit shifted the TRC's symbolic reparations – based on therapy and theology – into the realm of legal disputation, and is notable for two reasons. First, it was consistent with increasing pursuits of financial reparations for past injustices that have become a conspicuous and contentious feature of contemporary human rights claims, and the case looked, at the time, to be an important moment in its reinforcement. And, second, it rearticulated therapeutic reparations as financial compensation, communicating differently from the TRC the subjects, objects and practices central to reconciliation in South Africa. In contrast to the TRC's therapeutic regime, the lawsuit considered victims of *structural* rather than party-political violence, and enquired into the *beneficiaries* of apartheid. It considered the 'everyday violence' of apartheid that shaped and constrained the lives of those who were subject to its insidious regulatory architecture. Further, it sought financial compensation *in furtherance of reconciliation* from the corporations who benefited from apartheid, speaking of the need to 'broaden the victim's personal reconciliation processes beyond the scope of the TRC' (*Khulumani et al v Barclays et al*, 2002, p 8).

The reparations lawsuit shifted the focus from individual perpetrators to an analysis of violations as *systemic*, and made a strong case for charging the beneficiaries of the system with moral responsibility for apartheid, thus providing an alternative account to that narrated by the TRC of South Africa's political past. The lawsuit did, however, draw heavily upon evidence produced by the TRC's own enquiry into the role of the business community in sustaining the regime, thus generating a subordinate, and potentially destabilising, narrative strand about the economic underpinnings of apartheid. The lawsuit took up and foregrounded this story in a way that threatened to displace the morality tale about party-political violence and individual gross violations of human rights emanating from it, which was central to the TRC.

The lawsuit also played into long-standing debates in South Africa about the relationship between apartheid and capital, an argument that has a critical bearing on the question of corporate accountability for apartheid violence. This debate is usually pitched as one between 'liberals' and 'radicals', along with all the normative assumptions that those terms imply, and it shaped the business submissions to the TRC and responses to them. Briefly, liberal arguments claimed that apartheid was in conflict with free market capitalism since it entailed far-reaching state intervention into the labour market and other sectors of the economy, which affected profit negatively by undermining productivity growth (Moll, 1991). In contrast, radical perspectives claimed that apartheid was a system of racial capitalism in which segregation worked to minimise the cost of black labour in order to maximise white corporate profit (Lipton, 1985). The latter radical position provided the concordant basis for the claim to financial reparations since it recognised the enduring effects of apartheid ideology and practice on the economy, and upon the sector of the population subject to its deleterious material effects.

Conclusion

In attending to these refusals of reparation, this analysis chimes with Becker's (1967, p 240) call to distinguish between certain truth claims – that is, that reparations are unquestionably right and necessary – and 'an assessment of the circumstances' under which certain truth claims accumulate power and significance. That is to say, this chapter calls attention to the politics of normative claims, properly situating them in place and time, as products of particular places and times, and highlights the unintended consequences and multiple significations that reparations practices carry as a consequence of location. It elucidates the ways in which certain humanitarian values carry coercive as well as liberatory potential, with consequences that bear serious examination. This kind of critical engagement with reparation, and, by implication, with the humanitarian principles that underpin it, is particularly important because many of the claims of the field of reparations, its knowledge and its practice, seem self-evidently 'right'. As Derrida asks, who could 'decently dare to object to the imperative of reconciliation', which reparation aims to further, since, surely, 'it is better to put an end to the crimes and discords?' (Derrida, 2001, p 50).

This examination of victim contestations of reparations illuminates some of the issues (and the politics) that are at stake in the attempt to repair harm, including the particular *forms* that reparative gestures take, and the range of meanings that are attached to them. In the case of the *Madres*, their refusal is a rejection of the form of reparation, and their case demands that retributive responses to past crimes be reinterpreted as also, and potentially, restorative, something that the contemporary schism between restorative and retributive in transitional justice thinking does not readily allow. In both the Argentinean and South African cases, victim contestations repudiate the dominant state narratives about past violence. In the Argentinean case, this seemed to distribute blame equally to state agents *and* those contesting the authority of the state. In the South African case, victim contestation shifts the optic of the dominant narrative away from that deemed central to political reconciliation (party-political violence) and concentrates attention instead on a different set of apartheid agents – its beneficiaries – and the victims not of political violence, but of the quotidian, profound and enduring consequences of structured, institutionalised violence.

The act of 'taking sides', here, requires us to be alert to the possibility that gestures of reparation, while attempting to acknowledge and repair harm, can *also* perform a social control function that attempts to limit the range of meanings attached to past violence, and to close down the past in the name of reconciliation. These cases also demonstrate that it is not sufficient to perpetuate the normative assumptions that regularly cluster around reparation as idea and practice. What is revealed in these empirical accounts allows us to scrutinise with acuity the assumptions that underpin reparations thought and practice: that reparation assuages psychological and emotional harm, that it vindicates and dignifies victims, and that it assists in determining responsibility for past crimes. These examples require that greater attention is paid to the *reception* of reparation by those towards whom it is addressed – to write the victims back into the story – because this tells us something valuable, and largely ignored, about the coercive potential of reparative attempts. These examples also draw attention to both 'values' and 'value' in reconciliation, revealing internal inconsistencies within the analytical architecture of the scholarly and professional discourse – particularly the key distinction between 'material' and 'symbolic' reparations – and require us to attend to the political, rather than just the palliative, performance of reparation.

References

Arditti, R. (1999) *Searching for life: the grandmothers of the Plaza de Mayo and the disappeared children of Argentina*, Berkeley, CA: University of California Press.

Becker, H. (1967) 'Whose side are we on?', *Social Problems*, vol 14, no 3, pp 239–47.

Cohen, S. (1995) 'State crimes of previous regimes: knowledge, accountability, and the policing of the past', *Law and Social Inquiry*, vol 20, no 1, pp 7–50.

De Bonafini, H. (1990) 'The Madres de Plaza de Mayo (Argentina)', *Index on Censorship*, vol 19, no 9, p 42.

De Grieff, P. (2006) *The handbook of reparations*, Oxford: Oxford University Press.

Derrida, J. (2001) *On cosmopolitanism and forgiveness*, London: Routledge.

Guzman Bouvard, M. (1994) *Revolutionizing motherhood: the Mothers of the Plaza de Mayo*, Wilmington, DE: Scholarly Resources Inc.

Hayner, P. (2001) *Unspeakable truths: confronting state terror and atrocity*, London and New York, NY: Routledge.

Humphrey, M. (2003) 'From victim to victimhood: truth commissions and trials as rituals of political transition and individual healing', *The Australian Journal of Anthropology*, vol 14, no 2, pp 171–87.

Kleinman, A., Das, V. and Lock, M. (eds) (1997) *Social suffering*, Berkeley, CA: University of California Press.

Khulumani et al v Barclays National Bank et al (2002) Case No 02-CV5952 (S.D.N.Y. 2002).

Lipton, M. (1985) *Capitalism and apartheid*, Hounslow: Maurice Temple Smith.

Minow, M. (1998) *Between vengeance and forgiveness: facing history after genocide and mass violence*, Boston, MA: Beacon Press.

Moll, T. (1991) 'Did the apartheid economy fail?', *Journal of Southern African Studies*, vol 17, no 2, pp 271–91.

Moon, C. (2008) *Narrating political reconciliation: South Africa's Truth and Reconciliation Commission*, Lanham, MD: Lexington Books.

Moon, C. (2009) 'Healing past violence: traumatic assumptions and therapeutic interventions in war and reconciliation', *Journal of Human Rights*, vol 8, no 1, pp 71–91.

Moon, C. (2012) 'Who'll pay reparations on my soul? Compensation, social control and social suffering', *Social and Legal Studies*, vol 21, no 2, pp 187–99.

Roniger, L. and Sznajder, M. (1999) *The legacy of human rights violations in the southern cone: Argentina, Chile and Uruguay*, Oxford: Oxford University Press.

Sharpe, S. (2007) 'The idea of reparation', in G. Johnstone and D.W. Van Ness (eds) *Handbook of restorative justice*, Cullompton: Willan Publishing, pp 24–40.

Simmel, G. (2004) *The philosophy of money* (3rd enlarged edn), London and New York, NY: Routledge.

Torpey, J. (2003) *Politics and the past: on repairing historical injustices*, Lanham, MD: Rowman and Littlefield.

Williams, R. (1977) *Marxism and literature*, Oxford: Oxford University Press.

Zehr, H. (2003) 'Retributive justice, restorative justice', in G. Johnstone (ed) *A restorative justice reader: texts, sources, context*, Cullompton: Willan Publishing, pp 69–82.

Values in research, policy and practice

This final section responds to issues of values, the hierarchy of credibility and the structural positioning of superordinates and subordinates (Becker, 1967) in producing ethically defensible research, policy and practice. Any attempt to produce evidence-based policy and practice is bounded by disputes that occur at all levels of engagement. The selection of research method, the foregrounding of particular policy priorities, subject often to the whim of changing government ministers, and the appropriateness of engagement bounded by ethical probity must all be explored in explicating the direction of travel.

In Chapter Sixteen Kevin Wong explores the implications for policy and practice in the voluntary and community sector (VCS) of a 'sound bite' commitment by the incoming Coalition government to the concept of the 'Big Society'. He explores the way which the VCS has often been privileged in its structural positioning in relation to the service delivery of offender management services previously undertaken by the public sector. He points to a relative lack of scrutiny of its provision in comparison to the regular auditing and inspection of public services. He also explores the relative ineffectiveness of attempts to provide infrastructural support to the VCS through initiatives such as ChangeUp, Futurebuilders and others as the VCS seeks to engage more centrally in the delivery of public services.

Anne Robinson, in Chapter Seventeen, focuses on the impact of changing policy priorities in the provision of youth justice services since the inception of the New Labour government in 1997. She points to the overarching changes in policy direction that have served to challenge the innovative potential of the multi-agency youth offending teams created in that year. A commitment to evidence-based practice has produced somewhat stultified and prescriptive enforcement-led interventions, which have only been loosened in recent years. The creation of a separate professional identity of the 'youth justice worker' and the implications for multi-agency work are also examined. She points out that policy and practice is now constrained by the climate of austerity and the attendant public service cuts, which have hampered positive change in the initial years of the new Coalition government.

Chapter Eighteen, by Kevin Albertson, Katherine Albertson, Chris Fox and Dan Ellingworth, explores the role of economics in supporting evidence-based policy and practice. This chapter challenges the assumption that economics can provide a value-neutral mechanism for evaluating different criminal justice interventions. Rather, they point out that a range of value judgements need to be made before considering how the tools of economic analysis can help in determining the most appropriate and cost-effective interventions. That conclusion points to a range of ideological assumptions that are made before a cost–benefit analysis is undertaken and any research must ensure that this is understood and delineated explicitly before assessing the usefulness and salience of the subsequent analysis.

Paula Hamilton and Katherine Albertson, in Chapter Nineteen, explore narrative interviewing in the context of two studies on desistance. This chapter enables a thorough analysis of the potential, in Becker's terms, of how the subordinate can be foregrounded by the use of this particular research methodology. This presents challenges and difficulties for the researcher, and the chapter explores some of the techniques and ethical requirements that can ensure that the subject's interpretations are paramount in the research outcomes.

Chapter Twenty, written by Malcolm Cowburn, Marian Duggan and Ed Pollock, continues the themes developed in the previous chapter, although in circumstances, in two out of the three case studies, of racist hate crime and sexual offending, where the subordinate may be articulating views and behaviour that the researcher will find abhorrent and/or uncomfortable to hear. Using a common analytical framework, the three studies focus on the preparation and processes of research engagement needed both to protect the researcher and to ensure that useable and authentic data are still presented. This is articulated in the third area of study, by demonstrating how the research subjects could articulate homophobic life experiences by being encouraged to revisit their perceptions of their upbringing, helped by the reflective lens provided by the researcher.

Finally, Chapter Twenty-one, by Paul Senior, enters the 'murky' area of contract research. Accepting that critical criminological thinking regards such research as constructed and shaped by the positional power of the superordinates, such as government policy analysts, project site leads and the project staff themselves, the author articulates some of the practical tensions that the researcher faces in producing authentic and ethically defensible research outcomes. In focusing on five key themes, the chapter helps the reader steer through some of the pitfalls of this type of work. The chapter concludes with some practice guidelines that can protect the researcher from some of the worst excesses of this type of research engagement and find ways to articulate the voice of the subordinate in the process.

Reference

Becker, H. (1967) 'Whose side are we on?', *Social Problems*, vol 14, no 3, pp 239–47.

SIXTEEN

The Emperor's new clothes: can Big Society deliver criminal justice?

Kevin Wong

Introduction

> You can call it liberalism. You can call it empowerment.
> You can call it freedom. You can call it responsibility. I call
> it the 'Big Society'. (David Cameron, 2010)

It is reported that David Cameron first used the term 'Big Society'[1] on the eve of the launch of the Conservative Party manifesto in 2010. This was before the general election that saw the establishment of the first Coalition government (in this case, between Conservatives and Liberal Democrats) since the Second World War.

While there are conflicting views on what Big Society is, the one point on which commentators, politicians (exemplified by Cameron's previous remark), the media and think tanks appear to agree is that Big Society is difficult to define. A project funded by the Arts and Humanities Research Council (AHRC) Connecting Communities Programme and undertaken by the Centre for Research on Environment, Society and Health[2] has sought to provide a 'working definition' of Big Society in order to develop ways of measuring it, namely, that Big Society is 'a shift in the philosophy, power and practice of public service delivery'.

Their paper suggests that this involves: strengthening society and making public services serve the people who use them; decentralising power from central and local government to the community and the public; and passing the management and delivery of public services from the central and local state to private and voluntary sector providers, communities and individuals.

This latter point, of voluntary and community sector (VCS) providers along with the private and public sectors delivering reforms to the Criminal Justice System (CJS), appears to have been the conceptualisation of Big Society promoted in a Ministry of Justice Green Paper (MoJ, 2010a), in this case through:

- the market-testing of rehabilitation services to determine if the private sector or VCS can deliver these more effectively than statutory agencies;
- commissioning models to enable small and specialist VCS agencies to participate, particularly where these agencies 'can make a real difference with those offenders who are hardest to change' (MoJ, 2010a); and
- identifying specific barriers for small VCS providers in any Payment by Results (PbR) commissioning and finding ways to enable them to participate.

The policy intentions set out in the Green Paper appear to reinforce three competing narratives about VCS efficacy in the delivery of public services, which reflect the values and beliefs espoused by the sector: first, that the VCS can deliver services more cost effectively than public and private sector agencies – arguably, because they are value-driven, that is, they care more; second, that 'we're only a charity'[3] and therefore the VCS cannot deliver as well or as effectively as private and public sector agencies unless assisted to do so through capacity-building initiatives; and, third, the 'Heineken effect', that is, that the VCS can deliver niche services to individuals in ways that neither the public nor private sector can.

Taking the conceptualisation of 'Big Society' as the VCS and non-profit-making organisations (referring to them also as 'the third sector'), this chapter will examine the assumptions about VCS involvement in criminal justice service delivery (as contained in the Green Paper) and how their professed values and the public perceptions of these values may be impacted.

What contribution can the voluntary and community sector make?

As identified by Mills et al (2010), VCS organisations have had a long history of working in the CJS, specifically with offenders and their families. The origins of the probation service, traced back to Frederick Rainer in the 1870s, lie in voluntary sector activity (Probation Association, no date). In addition, they have also worked with the victims of crime and, more recently, in the delivery of justice for low-level offences through restorative justice processes (Meadows et al, 2012) and through volunteering in Community Justice Panels (Meadows et al, 2010). While there appears to be a new commitment to enlarging the role of the VCS in criminal justice through opening up the market for rehabilitation services, similar commitments have been made by past governments. The establishment of the National Offender Management Service (NOMS) under New Labour and commissioning under the principles of contestability failed to deliver the open market that VCS agencies expected. This was due primarily to limitations on the range of services that NOMS and their regional agents, Regional Offender Managers and then Regional Directors, were able to commission. Commissioning responsibilities for core services such as employment, training and education for offenders and accommodation lay with other government departments. The lack of opportunities (after the build-up to contestability for offender services) led to disillusionment among some VCS agencies who had prepared themselves for a widening market. In one area of England, this was particularly keenly felt after local VCS agencies were specifically supported by a NOMS-funded capacity-building initiative designed to enable the VCS to compete on a more equal footing with private and public sector providers (Wong, 2007).

While the current administration may intend to open up the market, at the same time, the Ministry of Justice is committed to cutting spending by a fifth from 2011 to 2015, a real-term reduction of £1.6 billion. The extent to which any 'new money' can be found from a reducing budget to pay for innovation or development is likely to be limited. The few exceptions to this include: the Innovations pilots, the one PbR initiative where the VCS have been encouraged to lead bids (Blunt, 2011); and grants awarded under the Ministry of Justice Victim and Witness General Fund (MoJ, 2011). The way in which VCS agencies are likely to be able to participate in the 'rehabilitation revolution' is through the market-testing of existing criminal justice services, signalled in the Green Paper and reinforced through the Probation Review (MoJ, 2012).

As noted by Mills et al (2010), opening up the criminal justice market to the VCS alongside the private sector could be described as 'privatising' criminal justice in a publicly acceptable way by commissioning providers who will not seek profit from punishment. They acknowledged that while ideological arguments against the policy remained, their research found a growing acceptance among public and voluntary sector providers that the quality of service provision and potentially improved outcomes for offenders are more important in determining service providers. However, they also noted that: 'this argument rather assumes that the voluntary sector will provide better, more effective services than the state; an assumption which is yet to be proved' (Mills et al, 2010).

The quality and effectiveness of service delivery by VCS agencies has seldom received the same level of scrutiny by the media, politicians and the public as public sector agencies such as the police, probation and prisons, which are regularly inspected by independent authorities. These bodies publish reports that are in the public domain and are reported on by the media. In contrast, VCS agencies are generally given a 'free pass'. This is in deference to their charitable status and an uncritical public perception of the VCS and their values, principally that of 'doing good'. The main line of 'public' accountability for the VCS is through their management board and their performance is made public through annual reports that tend to be promotional tools rather than providing a more critical review. VCS agencies with service-level agreements and commercial contracts are likely to be scrutinised by their commissioners. However, this scrutiny seldom receives media attention, if at all, even when a contract is withdrawn from a VCS provider. Thus, the efficacy of the VCS is not debated by the public or by politicians. If anything, the Cameron vision of a Big Society appears to have privileged the VCS in a way that neither the public nor private sector could ever hope to experience.

The debate around whether or not the VCS can deliver services more effectively than public or private providers is perhaps somewhat empty. Recent studies examining the involvement of the VCS in Integrated Offender Management (IOM) presents a more complex picture of VCS efficacy. In describing IOM, Senior et al (2011, p 3) noted that:

> IOM has emerged from a complex policy and practice agenda for jointly managing offenders across criminal justice agencies and wider community and government bodies. It has been characterised by 'bottom up' developments in local areas which have achieved a collective description of Integrated Offender Management.

In this developing area of offender management, Wong and Hartworth (2009) found that VCS agencies were involved at three levels:

- a service delivery level, in some instances co-located, with police and probation acting as lead professionals case-managing the offender;

- the operational management of IOM; and
- the strategic oversight and governance of IOM.

While there was variation across the study sites in the extent to which the VCS was involved at these levels, there were few reservations from public sector partners about VCS efficacy and the particular skills they brought to the IOM process. However, these were VCS agencies with a track record and experience of working with offenders. A later study by Wong et al (2012), examining the involvement of small VCS agencies with limited experience of working with offenders, found a more mixed picture (see later in this chapter).

The model of VCS engagement with IOM developed by Wong and Hartworth (2009) and refined following the study by Wong et al (2012) tracks the complexity and interdependency of local relationships between VCS and public sector agencies, which are often sidelined in a discourse on VCS versus other sectors. In part, this oppositional discourse is promoted by the VCS themselves and encouraged by government.

Figure 16.1: Revised model of voluntary and community sector engagement with Integrated Offender Management

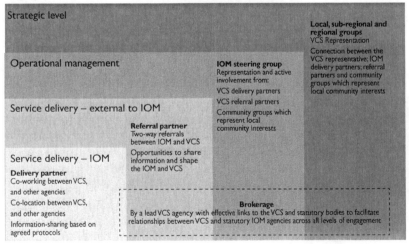

The voluntary and community sector as the 'underdog'?

A common narrative around VCS delivery of public services is that the VCS (as charities) has a more limited capacity than the public and private sector to bid for and deliver contracts. This tends to be a given, a notion that is regularly repeated in encounters between the VCS and government bodies. This is illustrated by minutes of the meeting between Crispin Blunt (a former minister at the Ministry of Justice) and VCS representatives, where it was noted that 'voluntary sector capacity overall is recognised as a barrier that needs addressing' (MoJ, 2010c, p 2). This is a notion that is generally unchallenged and plays into a convenient conceptualisation of the VCS as a perpetual underdog.

One way to assess the capacity and capability of the sector is to look at its structure. Using annual income as a proxy for size and charities registered with the Charity Commission (2011) as a proxy for the VCS, just over 1% of registered charities have an annual income of £5 milion and over. These charities have just over a two thirds share of the total annual income across all charities. At the other end of the scale, four out of 10 registered charities have annual income of less than £10,000. These charities only have a very small 0.4% of the share of the total annual income across all charities.

Taking income as a way of gauging capacity and capability, this suggests that there are, and will always be, differing levels of capacity and capability within the VCS. Large VCS organisations with incomes of £5 million and over are more likely to be able to compete with the public and private sector to deliver comparable, if not better, services. Small VCS organisations with an annual income of less than £10,000, and likely to be run purely by volunteers, are unlikely to have the same capacity or capability.

A more criminal justice-focused analysis of the income of VCS organisations (as a proxy for capacity and capability) has been conducted by Gojkovic et al (2011), who have estimated the annual income of third sector organisations (TSOs)[4] whose main beneficiaries were offenders, ex-offenders and their families. Using data from the National Survey of Third Sector Organisations, they found that 61% of organisations who responded to the survey had an annual income of £100,000 or less, compared with 80% of all TSOs. For those TSOs whose main beneficiaries were offenders, ex-offenders and their families, they found that 27% reported no income at all, compared with 17% of all TSOs. From this, they concluded that 'the income pattern for TSOs working with offenders is a rather uneven one, polarized between those with very little or no income and those with a more substantial income' (Gojkovic et al, 2011).

This finding appears to confirm the differences across the sector illustrated by the Charities Commission data. However, this pyramidal structure (based on numbers of agencies) found in the third sector and charities and the inverse pyramid in relation to income (and, by proxy, their capacity and capability) is partly mirrored elsewhere – in the private sector. Large businesses (employing 250 or more employees) make up 0.1% of all businesses. Medium-sized businesses (employing 50 to 249 employees) make up 0.7% of all businesses and small enterprises (employing fewer than 50 employees) comprise 99.2% of all businesses (Department for Business Innovation and Skills, 2011). There is a similar, albeit less polarised, apportionment of annual turnover between large and small private sector agencies compared to registered charities: large enterprises generate 51.2% of the total annual turnover of all enterprises, compared with the two thirds share of total annual charity income by the largest charities; with small enterprises generating 34.9% of the total annual turnover of all enterprises, compared with 0.4% of total annual charity income by the smallest charities.

Within the narrative of VCS 'incapacity' is a presumption, based on a general shared principle of inclusion, that all VCS agencies should have the opportunity to bid for all contracts regardless of size and capacity (Wong et al, 2012). This is unrealistic. A comparison from the private sector would be a neighbourhood corner store vying to set up a supermarket in competition with Tesco and suggesting that they needed assistance from the state to do this. As identified by Wong et al (2012), there needs to be a nuanced approach and expectation about what different parts of the VCS can deliver and the application of appropriate commissioning processes: 'service level agreements for volume services such as accommodation and drugs services, which attract competition, and smaller niche services required by a handful of offenders at any one time, which are purchased through small grants or spot purchasing' (Wong et al, 2012, p 25).

In terms of financial clout, the total annual income of registered charities in England and Wales (as a proxy for the VCS) was £55 billion in 2011. As a sector delivering services across a range of policy areas and therefore receiving income from a variety of government and non-government sources, they fared well in comparison with the annual budgets for the Ministry of Justice and the Home Office. In 2010/11 (prior to the financial cuts), the expenditure of both ministries totalled approximately £21 billion. However, placing these numbers in a commercial context, the total annual income of registered charities was some £13 billion short of the £68 billion annual turnover (over the same period) for Tesco, the UK and international supermarket giant, of which a modest 5.6% (£3.8 billion) was profit.

As noted in the NOMS (2008) third sector strategy, around half of the resources to support offender rehabilitation lie outside the CJS, much of it going through the third sector. This is illustrated by Fox (2012), who found the costs of managing an offender, (including all the necessary support services) totalled £60,806 over a 12-month period. The costs for each individual agency are set out in Table 16.1. By far the largest proportion of the costs was incurred by a VCS agency (55%), providing accommodation, followed by the Prison Service (17%), providing a different form of accommodation. It is worth noting that 71% of the offender management costs were for accommodation (in the community) and health and drug treatment – costs and services that lie outside the CJS.

Table 16.1: Costs of an offender to local agencies over 12 months

Agency	Cost over 12 months (£)
Probation Trust	2,356.36
Police	4,796.04
Magistrates' court	208.00
Voluntary sector run hostel	33,382.07
Third sector and NHS drug treatment services	3,785.45
Prison Service	10,384.62
NHS	5,893.00
Total	**60,805.55**

Does capacity-building work?

There have been various attempts by successive administrations to build the capacity of the VCS; aiming to create 'a 'fairer playing field', actively reducing barriers to diverse third sector involvement' (NOMS, 2008). The ChangeUp programme aimed to increase the capacity of VCS agencies who work with offenders to compete with private and public sector agencies for contracts. The Building Voluntary and Community Sector Involvement in Integrated Offender Management programme aimed to build the capacity of smaller VCS organisations (with little or no previous involvement in working with offenders) so that they can work with offenders and engage more effectively with criminal justice agencies.

Each of these programmes serves to reinforce the narrative of the VCS as the underdog. Arguably, this narrative tends to divert attention from questioning the rationale for VCS capacity-building programmes: 'Are they needed?' In addition, it diverts attention from applying more rigorous scrutiny of the efficacy and sustainability of these programmes: 'Are they effective?' and 'Are the benefits sustainable?'

Answering the second and third questions may help to answer the first. The £231 million ChangeUp programme aimed to improve *support services* for front-line TSOs. The National Audit Office (NAO, 2009) report found that ChangeUp had generally established better partnership-working between local support providers (ie those agencies providing support to front-line delivery agencies), although the impact of this improvement on front-line organisations was varied. Perhaps more importantly, the NAO found that it was not possible to assess the impact of this funding as there were no targets or baseline against which ChangeUp could be measured.

Future Builders operated a different model; a £215 million investment fund testing the idea that investing directly in TSOs that are financially viable, but unable to access commercial sources of finance, enables them to build their capacity to compete for and win public service delivery contracts. The NAO found that Future Builders funding had brought about positive change. Based on a sample of eight organisations, they found that the capacity of three out of the eight organisations had been developed such that the three organisations were able to secure just over £600,000 worth of contracts to deliver public services. However, the NAO also found that across the scheme as a whole, less than 50% of awards were actually drawn down and used by recipient agencies, concluding that this 'was not a satisfactory means of investing in the capacity of third sector organisations and of testing out a new approach to financing capacity building activities' (NAO, 2009, p 7).

The Nacro MOVE project (funded by the ChangeUp programme) aimed to build the capacity of VCS agencies in Leeds to engage effectively with the new commissioning arrangements (specifically contestability) arising from the establishment of the NOMS. The interim evaluation (Wong, 2006) found that some VCS agencies were reluctant to engage with MOVE because of disillusionment with past capacity-building initiatives that lacked sustainability. The final evaluation (Wong, 2007) concluded that the initiatives set up by the project were unlikely to be sustained, in particular, the VCS consortium that MOVE brought together, which was intended to enable agencies to collaborate on developing and delivering services within the NOMS, reducing reoffending pathways.

In their study of the Home Office-funded Building Voluntary and Community Sector Involvement in Integrated Offender Management programme, Wong et al (2012) found that the programme had consolidated local relationships between VCS and statutory agencies.

It had also been successful 'in positively influencing the views of those in the statutory sector on the value of the VCS sector. It had brought about a shift away from the VCS being viewed solely as "well-meaning amateurs"' (Wong et al, 2012, p ii).

Channelling grants through local VCS infrastructure organisations and providing seedcorn grants to small VCS agencies to work with offenders offered an alternative way to engage and build expertise within these agencies. However, they also found that despite the focus of the programme and specific events run by local VCS infrastructure organisations promoting IOM, there were mixed levels of understanding about IOM among these small VCS agencies. This carried through into service delivery.

This most recent programme appears to have learnt little from the previous programmes detailed earlier (Wong, 2006; NAO, 2009) in ensuring an adequate level of monitoring to assess impact. While the management of the programme was intended to be light-touch, no data was collected that would have enabled the programme management body (a national VCS infrastructure agency) and the Home Office to assess the extent to which the programme had met one of its aims – that of enabling small VCS agencies with no or limited experience of working with offenders to work with IOM statutory agencies and IOM offenders. It is unlikely that any government department would have applied such laissez-faire scrutiny to the public or private sectors. In contrast, during the time this programme was operating, from November 2010 to March 2011, the Ministry of Justice (MoJ, 2010b) set out its commitment to introduce a much more rigorous outcome-focused form of commissioning – PbR.

Do voluntary and community sector agencies collaborate or compete with each other?

While collaboration between VCS agencies is a commonly professed value/aim within the sector (Senior et al, 2005; Wong, 2006, 2007), the reality is different. One of the oft-mooted solutions to bridge the gap between large and small VCS agencies is the establishment of VCS consortia to share expertise in bidding for and delivering substantial contracts. In the current climate of decreasing resources and increasing competitiveness, VCS agencies are just as likely to join up with private sector and public sector agencies; for example, Catch 22 with Serco to deliver the Doncaster Prison PbR pilot and St Giles Trust with Sodexo to deliver the Peterborough Social Impact Bond PbR pilot.

More recently, VCS agencies have joined Probation Trusts to bid for the Innovation PbR pilots.

Where VCS consortia are established, their sustainability and efficacy is mixed. Establishing and maintaining a VCS consortium to be 'bid ready' in case contracts are let has inherent problems of sustainability. This requires: a bureaucracy to service it; someone to act as an 'honest broker' and/or an agreed protocol for deciding who among the consortium should bid or be part of the bid; and an investment of staff time from agencies to support it (Wong, 2007).

Wong et al (2012) found that while VCS organisations reported that the Building Voluntary and Community Sector Involvement in Integrated Offender Management initiative was effective in facilitating some progress in this area, there was a perception that the situation would never be fully resolved: "You will never get equality between [VCS] agencies, I don't think, but I think we're a little bit nearer to it" (VCS representative, cited in Wong et al, 2012, p 25).

The experience of VCS consortium-building from the community legal advice sector (which underwent a process of competitive tendering for contracts) is not promising. Fox et al (2010) found that the following factors were critical for effective consortium-building:

- *The need to accept compromise in order to succeed* – in one study site, it was reported that the trustees of local VCS organisations 'just couldn't get together and give up enough power between themselves to actually co-operate' (Fox et al, 2010, p 48).
- *The need for clear roles and responsibilities within the consortium* – in another study site, there was considerable confusion about which VCS agency was acting as the lead.
- *Overcoming organisational cultural issues* – rivalry was difficult to overcome; in one study site, two rival VCS agencies were forced into a consortium by the local authority, which may have been counterproductive, as suggested by this interviewee:

> "I think that partnership works well when probably it's chosen. ...it's going to work because we're all coming from the same place and we all want the best service. ...I think that there's a difference between choosing the right partners as opposed to being given a partner who might not be your choice." (Cited in Fox et al, 2012, p 49)

In another study site, differences in the size, capacity and capability of VCS agencies within the consortium made it difficult for them to work together to submit a bid and such disagreement made it difficult for them to work with a private sector provider in bidding.

- *Financial transparency* – in one study site, one of the VCS partners in the consortium went into liquidation shortly after the consortium secured the contract.
- *Good personal relationships* between key personnel from each of the agencies involved in the consortium – perhaps the most important factor.

Does the voluntary and community sector deliver more cost-effective services?

The new commissioning landscape challenges the efficacy of VCS service delivery – the notion that VCS agencies inherently deliver better (and more cost-effective) services than public and private sector agencies (arguably, because they care more). First, there is the challenge of financial viability. As noted by Mills et al (2010), VCS agencies may struggle to participate in PbR initiatives because they lack the requisite up-front funding.

Second, there is the challenge of VCS capacity and capability to monitor performance and live up to their claims to deliver better services. PbR appears to be creating an 'Iceberg illusion' (Syed, 2010) in relation to monitoring and evaluation. The focus of PbR is performance against a single outcome measure, such as whether an offender reoffends or not following discharge from prison in the HMP Doncaster pilot, or an agreed reduction in custody bed nights for the Youth Justice Reinvestment. These are the visible tips of the iceberg. While the Ministry of Justice is not requiring that PbR deliverers record and regularly report on management data, the providers themselves are having to establish sophisticated management information and monitoring systems (the less visible part of the iceberg under the water) in order to ensure that they are on target to meet the headline outcome.

A further test for VCS delivery is being posed by the whole place community budget pilots being trialled in four sites in England which offer the opportunity for joint investment between local agencies. In Greater Manchester, this includes a focus on reducing demand on the CJS, reducing dependency and supporting growth through investment in cost-effective services (Pleasant and Harriss, 2012). As noted by Senior et al (2005), Mills et al (2010) and Wong et al (2012), VCS agencies struggle quantitatively to evidence the impact of their services. Evidencing cost effectiveness is a sizeable step beyond this.

While VCS agencies have been keen to point to the shortcomings of public services delivered by the statutory and private sector, they have often been less ready to acknowledge that VCS agencies can also deliver poor-quality services. The Community Budget approach to both investment and disinvestment is sector-neutral, with commissioning based on how well a service is being provided rather than who is providing it, with a critical examination of existing models of service delivery.

Losing a commitment to inclusion

A key finding from the study into VCS involvement in IOM (Wong et al, 2012) was the challenge to the VCS commitment to inclusion. While this is not new, it does represent an inherent tension in working with offenders generally, and specifically in the context of IOM, which works on the principles of rigorous enforcement as well as effective coordination of support services. The dilemma for VCS agencies in contributing to enforcement activity is captured by this comment from a statutory stakeholder:

> "if I refer somebody to a voluntary sector partnership … and my offender causes a ruckus and punches somebody on the nose … I have to prosecute that person for failure to comply with his order, I need the voluntary sector person … to come to court and give evidence … that's what puts a lot of people off taking offenders because they don't want to engage with that side of the business." (Cited in Wong et al, 2012, p 22)

There were mixed views on this:

> Some VCS stakeholders indicated that such disclosure could potentially damage their working relationship with offenders and run counter to the VCS culture of inclusivity. Some interviewees in statutory bodies supported this view, regarding the role of VCS agencies as being quite separate to that of the statutory sector. However, other statutory stakeholders suggested that other VCS agencies, principally drugs and alcohol agencies, were already providing this kind of information to offender managers, for example, as part of [Prolific and Other Priority Offender] schemes. (Wong et al, 2012, p 22)

Perhaps the choice is a stark but simple one; if VCS agencies want to work in the CJS, then they need to decide to what extent they are willing to engage in contributing to enforcement activities and the extent to which this jeopardises their relationship with their clients. This necessarily involves a transparency in their role and relationships with statutory criminal justice agencies and with the offenders themselves.

Conclusion

Can Big Society deliver criminal justice? The short answer is 'Yes' and 'No'. While Big Society has generated much debate around definition and Coalition government intent, the reality, in practice, seems no more than a new iteration of the role of the VCS, other not-for-profit organisations and individual citizens as volunteers – an iteration to suit a time of austerity. If anything, it appears as more of a Conservative riposte to the purported Big Government and statism of the previous New Labour administration. In this sense, perhaps Big Society is nothing more than the Emperor's new clothes.

This chapter has used the VCS as a proxy for Big Society. The extent to which the professed values of the VCS and the ongoing narrative about VCS capacity and capability (which draws on this) are challenged by this new iteration of civil society appears to be limited. The sector as a whole (rather than individual agencies) has more financial clout than might be expected based on the rhetoric of the VCS and the government presumptions about the sector. The public finance cuts are having an impact on the VCS; the sector is shrinking, but then the same is true of public sector agencies.

Earlier in this chapter, the question was posed about whether or not the VCS needs capacity-building programmes. While the VCS rhetoric would suggest an unequivocal 'Yes', the efficacy of such programmes and the take-up of VCS capacity-building programmes indicate differently. There is variation in capacity and capability across the sector, as there is in both the public and private sectors. The cost effectiveness of investing in capacity-building for the VCS is largely unproven. It may deliver a feel-good factor for government – a tangible indicator of support for the sector. It may provide continued funding for a VCS service – that may or may not be effective. Before government or government departments commit funds for further capacity-building, they and the sector must accurately assess the need, target which agencies actually need it, assess the likely take-up, determine how best to deliver it and, above all, learn from past capacity-building programmes. Government departments have both a myopia about initiatives, declining the opportunity to learn from other government departments, and a policy amnesia, learning very little, if anything, from past initiatives. Borrowing a concept from the Greater Manchester Community Budget pilot, perhaps the principle underpinning any future capacity-building programme should be one of encouraging VCS self-reliance and reducing dependency.

The new challenges for the VCS and their professed values are in the new commissioning landscape, the need to form collaborations and alliances within and outside the sector, as well as in addressing the perennial challenges to the VCS principle of inclusivity inherent in greater involvement in criminal justice service delivery.

At a local operational level, public and private sector agencies appear to have a more realistic view of the capacity and capability of VCS providers, borne out of operational experience, compared with the somewhat naive perception of the VCS by the government and government departments, a perception that privileges the sector over the public and private sectors. Such realism is required if, during a prolonged period of austerity, the goal of delivering quality criminal justice services is to be fulfilled by whoever can deliver this most cost effectively.

Notes

[1] While the term 'Big Society' has become associated with Cameron, the concept of Big Society has been attributed to Steve Hinton, Cameron's policy advisor.

[2] http://healthyenvironmentsresearch.files.wordpress.com/2011/11/measuring_the_big_society_webbrief.pdf (accessed 3/06/2012).

[3] This has been a common sentiment expressed by small to medium VCS agencies encountered by the author when working with them on capacity-building initiatives.

[4] 'Third sector' is the terminology used by the authors of the report and in the survey from which the data has been drawn.

References

Blunt, C. (2011) 'Speech to the Youth Justice Convention'. Available at: http://www.justice.gov.uk/news/speeches/crispin-blunt/youth-justice-convention-021111/payment-by-results-innovation-pilots-110811 (accessed 25 August 2012).

Cameron, D. (2010) 'Speech to the Conservative Party Conference 2010'. Available at: http://www.conservatives.com/News/Speeches/2010/10/David_Cameron_Together_in_the_National_Interest.aspx (accessed 24 August 2012).

Department for Business, Innovation and Skills (2011) *Business population estimates for the UK and regions 2011*, London: Department for Business, Innovation and Skills.

Fox, C. (2012) *IOM Sussex evaluation – complex client costing*, Sheffield: Hallam Centre for Community Justice.

Fox, C., Moorhead, R., Sefton, M. and Wong, K. (2010) *Community legal advice centres and networks: a process evaluation*, London: Legal Services Commission.

Gojkovic, D., Mills, A. and Meek, R. (2011) 'Scoping the involvement of third sector organisations in the seven resettlement pathways for offenders', Working Paper 57, Third Sector Research Centre, University of Southampton, Southampton.

Meadows, L., Clamp, K., Culshaw, A., Wilkinson, K. and Davidson, J. (2010) *Evaluation of Sheffield City Council's Community Justice Panels project*, Sheffield: Hallam Centre for Community Justice.

Meadows, L., Albertson, K., Ellingworth, D. and Senior, P. (2012) *Evaluation of the South Yorkshire Restorative Justice Programme*, Sheffield: Hallam Centre for Community Justice.

Mills, A., Meek, R. and Gojkovic, D. (2010) 'Exploring the relationship between the voluntary sector and the state in criminal justice', paper delivered to the NCVO/VSSN Annual Research Conference, Third Sector Research Centre, University of Southampton, Southampton.

MoJ (Ministry of Justice) (2010a) *Breaking the cycle: effective punishment, rehabilitation and sentencing of offenders*, London: MoJ.

MoJ (2010b) *Business plan 2011–2015 November 2010*, London: MoJ.

MoJ (2010c) 'Meeting between Crispin Blunt and voluntary sector representatives to inform the sentencing and rehabilitation Green Paper 28 July 2010', MoJ.

MoJ (2011) *Organisations awarded funding under the Victim and Witness General Fund 2011–12*, London: MoJ.

MoJ (2012) 'Punishment and reform: effective probation services', Consultation Paper CP7/2012, March, London: MoJ.

NAO (National Audit Office) (2009) *Building the capacity of the third sector 2009*, London: NAO.

NOMS (National Offender Management Service) (2008) *Working with the third sector to reduce re-offending, securing effective partnerships 2008–2011*, London: MoJ.

Pleasant, S. and Harriss, S. (2012) 'Greater Manchester Community Budget pilot – progress report, Greater Manchester Combined Authority, 25th May 2012', Greater Manchester Combined Authority.

Probation Association (no date) 'A history of probation'. Available at: http://probationassociation.co.uk/about-us/history-of-probation. aspx (accessed 7 July 2011).

Senior, P., Meadows, L., Feasey, S. and Atkinson, J. (2005) *Enhancing the role of the voluntary and community sector – a case study of the Yorkshire and Humber Region*, Sheffield: Hallam Centre for Community Justice.

Senior, P., Wong, K., Culshaw, A., Ellingworth, D., O' Keeffe, C. and Meadows, L. (2011) *Process evaluation of five Integrated Offender Management Pioneer Areas, Research Series 4/11*, London: MoJ.

Syed, M. (2010) *Bounce – the myth of talent and the power of practice*, New York, NY: Harper Collins.

Wong, K. (2006) *Moving on an interim evaluation of Nacro MOVE April 2006*, London: Nacro.

Wong, K. (2007) *Move on final evaluation report for Nacro MOVE May 2007*, London: Nacro.

Wong, K. and Hartworth, C. (2009) *Integrated Offender Management and third sector engagement case studies of four pioneer sites, March 2009*, London: Nacro.

Wong, K., O'Keeffe, C., Meadows, L., Davidson, J., Bird, H., Wilkinson, K. and Senior, P. (2012) *Increasing the voluntary and community sector's involvement in Integrated Offender Management* , London: Home Office.

SEVENTEEN

What's valuable, what's valued in today's youth justice?

Anne Robinson

Introduction

New Labour, taking office in 1997, lost no time in setting out its plans for reform of the youth justice system (YJS) in England and Wales. Following the critical report, *Misspent youth* (Audit Commission, 1996), the *No more excuses* White Paper (Home Office, 1997) expressed dissatisfaction that the intervention offered to young people offending, or at risk of offending, was too little, too late or too ineffectual. The subsequent Crime and Disorder Act 1998 established a primary aim for the YJS of prevention of offending by children and young people, seeking to give coherence to a disparate range of agencies and activities. In section 39, this was bolstered by the requirement on local authorities to bring key partner agencies together in multi-agency Youth Offending Teams (YOTs) and management structures to support them.

It is now more than 10 years since New Labour's reforms and this is a timely point at which to examine what these reforms have meant, the values that informed them and how much has endured under the Coalition government. Becker (1967) suggested that sociological (and criminological) enquiry always takes one side or another, and this would seem to be true of social (and criminal justice) policy development as well. This chapter suggests that New Labour's reforms were on the side of adults, responding to fears and anxieties about young people, particularly those not in education, employment or training (pejoratively called NEETs). And New Labour was not alone, as authors have noted a common process of 'adulteration' across jurisdictions – a failure to distinguish children's particular needs in criminal justice policy and the application of sanctions (Muncie, 2006; Muncie and Goldson, 2006).

Structural reform, however, is not necessarily a single event and involves a much longer process of adjustment and evolution. Certainly, the new YJS in England and Wales has been characterised by change over the 'noughties', rather than stability, and there has been no inevitable uniformity in the ideas, values and beliefs that have motivated developments across this period. This chapter offers thoughts about how the YJS has worked with and absorbed conflict and contradictions, and where YOTs now find themselves in the Coalition world. How different is this to the youth justice arena of the 1990s and that of the early 2000s? Throughout these discussions, it is helpful to bear in mind a sense that 'Youth justice systems have never been solely devoted to reducing youth crime. They also convey a range of complex messages with regard to citizenship, individual autonomy and the boundaries of community morality' (McAra, 2010, p 305).

Dimensions of policymaking

Ross Fergusson (2007) explores the policy process in criminal justice and describes it as working at three distinct levels, with diverse stakeholders active and holding different priorities at each. First, there is the political rhetoric and associated discourses. Second, there is the way that these translate into specific legislation, policy and guidance, such as the *National Standards for Youth Justice Services 2009* (YJB, 2009b) – what Fergusson refers to as 'codification'. These are not necessarily discrete and policy developments might be associated with multiple strands of discourse, for instance, in terms of the rehabilitative punishment represented by accredited programmes (Robinson, 2007; Robinson and Crow, 2009). Similarly, the rationale for introducing the Youth Rehabilitation Order could simultaneously be argued as being an opportunity for more – and more responsive – welfare interventions, a mechanism to increase control over young people seen as problematic or simple punishment. The third and final element that Fergusson identifies is implementation, or the way that policy is interpreted and put into practice on the ground, in this case, within YOTs and associated partnership activities.

Fergusson's analytical framework is helpful when we look at values, because these also operate at these three levels and, indeed, underpin the political rhetoric, policy formulations and youth justice practices that he discusses. The focus here will be on policy and its implementation; in many respects, the political rhetoric has not changed a great deal, with punishment, personal and parental responsibility, remoralisation, and early intervention evident and still forming a powerful mix in *Breaking the cycle* (MoJ, 2010) and the government response to the consultation (MoJ, 2011). Although the Green Paper also talked about expanding restorative justice and opening up pre-court interventions, the tone is no more sympathetic to young people than New Labour's and still constructs them as a problem to be managed. Furthermore, the riots of August 2011 saw a return to the language of blame and the scapegoating of 'suspect populations' of young people and their parents:

> David Cameron announced a crackdown on 120,000 feckless families yesterday in a campaign to combat the moral decline which led to the riots.
> Declaring 'all out war' on gangs, the Prime Minister vowed to 'turn around' the most troubled families in the land and said he wants to see every 16-year-old complete a civilian version of National Service. (Shipman and Walker, 2011)

Such political rhetoric is powerful in the messages it conveys, and popular punitiveness of this kind will clearly influence the tone in which policy developments are presented. However, it does not necessarily inform the detail of policy, but has other purposes in terms of rallying opinion against particular groups in society, portraying the government as willing and able to take decisive action, and, often, reassuring a core constituency of supporters (see, for instance, Newburn, 2002). As illustrations, the tough speeches about law and order in the early days of the Thatcher government ran alongside developments in cautioning during the 1980s, which were generated by policymakers and practitioners on the ground to divert young people from the courts, and a reduction in youth custody (Smith, 2007; Muncie, 2009). In a similar vein, the focus of New Labour pre-election rhetoric on retribution and persistent young offenders gave way in 1997 to a more considered approach, highlighting evidence-based practice (Phoenix, 2010), managerial efficiencies and restorative justice as the government moved towards enacting legislation.

Fergusson (2007) notes that the process of 'codification' involves a different set of actors and stakeholders, in New Labour's case, including civil servants, academics, experts in the field and campaigning groups. The perspectives of these stakeholders were disparate, but in terms of influence, they collectively promoted a raft of policy characterised by:

- communitarian values;
- managerial techniques; and
- actuarial justice.

At the time, these were presented as a new departure, leaving behind the old penal–welfare debates associated with Right and Left political positions, respectively, and thus appearing at least superficially apolitical (Muncie, 2009). Examining each of these in turn, it is apparent that they are not so neutral in practice. In fact, if we consider Canton's (2007) precept that actions give expression to values, then specific structural reforms and practice directives – even the setting of a principal aim for the YJS in legislation – must be underpinned by values and beliefs (although these may not be clear or coherent). Such values, as they are realised in concrete measures, have political and practical implications, in this instance, in establishing youth justice machinery that justified increasing state intervention in young people's lives and in targeting those identified as persistent young offenders (Smith, 2007).

Drivers of reform

While managerial and administrative frameworks dominated the New Labour era (Newburn, 2002), the strand of communitarian thinking was also significant (Moore, 2008). This political philosophy highlights the salience of bonds and networks within communities – whether based on family, geography, occupation or interest – and the building of collective social capital, as explained by its US proponents such as Amitai Etzioni (1968) and David Putnam (2000). The focus on the experience of communities, and victims within communities, manifested itself in two main ways. First, it coalesced with Left realist concerns about the reality of anti-social behaviour and crime, particularly in 'hard-pressed' communities (Squires and Stephens, 2005), resulting in a range of multi-agency initiatives to prevent crime and tackle anti-social behaviour (Muncie, 2009). The Anti-Social Behaviour Order (ASBO) was developed as a tool to assist agencies in this endeavour. Second, communitarianism paved the way for the introduction of restorative justice (Rodger, 2008), through reparation orders initially and then the referral order scheme (Newburn, 2002).

The concept and structure of referral order schemes are of interest in that they are an explicit attempt to bring the community into the justice system through their participation in young offender panels. In this, they are attempting to empower communities and to increase awareness of the YJS. However, they are also consistent with the general hostility that New Labour showed towards professional groups and the blurring of professional boundaries, evident in any case in the creation of multi-disciplinary YOTs (see, for instance, Souhami, 2007). In particular, the referral order schemes appeared to be an attempt to destabilise the dominance of social work practice, which was associated with the previous main community disposal for young people, the supervision order. The young offender panel agrees the programme of intervention with the young person in the form of a contract, rather than YOT case managers negotiating a supervision plan. In theory, the items in the contract could be very creative and could extend beyond the interventions offered by the YOT and partner agencies itself (Earle, 2008). In practice, this potential has not been realised and research has shown that referral order contracts tend to draw on a familiar YOT repertoire (Crawford and Burden, 2005). Nevertheless, there was a symbolic significance in the attempted shift of power away from YOT case managers (who, at the stage when referral orders were first implemented in 2002, were mainly social workers).

Developing youth justice

The first period or phase in New Labour's youth justice lasted from the point where the first provisions of the Crime and Disorder Act 1998 came into force until roughly 2003. This phase, allowing space to *experiment and implement*, saw the establishment of YOTs, the introduction of the referral order system mentioned earlier and the setting up of Intensive Supervision and Surveillance Programmes (ISSPs) for young people whose offending matched certain criteria of seriousness or persistence. Outside core youth justice services, agencies came together to develop the anti-social behaviour agenda, which rapidly became an integral part of the youth justice landscape (Squires and Stephens, 2005). A range of preventive initiatives, such as Youth Inclusion Projects, Youth Inclusion and Support Panels and Positive Activities for Young People, burgeoned alongside, often resulting from pump-priming money from the Youth Justice Board (YJB) (Smith, 2007). At this stage, the YJB was a major generator of activity and enterprise, and it launched a series of research projects to assess the value and impact of new areas of practice, such as cognitive behavioural programmes, restorative justice and ISSPs in line with the precepts of evidence-based practice (Phoenix, 2010) and Left realist thinking (Muncie, 2009).

From the very outset, the YJB exercised control from the centre, balancing the autonomy of local multi-agency steering groups. The nature of this control changed in the second phase of New Labour's youth justice, characterised by the tendency to *routinise and discipline*. The performance framework for YOTs tightened, with 13 key performance indicators (KPIs), which entailed quarterly and annual reporting requirements, and an Effective Practice Quality Assurance process examining specific areas of practice (Graham, 2010). One of the effects of the KPIs was to mandate the completion of a standardised assessment tool, Asset, at set points in a young person's progress through the YJS, for instance, court appearance, sentence and release from custody (Stephenson et al, 2011). A similar form called Onset was subsequently introduced for young people who had not yet entered the court system (Smith, 2006). Both were based on assumptions about the relationship between risk and offending behaviour and operated on actuarial principles. As such, they have been consistently criticised for reducing risk assessment to a technical process (Case, 2010) – a totting up of risk and protective factors to produce a predicted probability of reoffending. Of course, this is not inevitably the case, and, recently, authors such as Whyte (2009) and Baker et al (2011) have explored the sophisticated use of standardised instruments to guide professional assessment. However, in this second phase, considerable pressure was placed on practitioners to complete Asset forms, with an emphasis on timeliness rather than quality. This coincided with a change in the demographic in the youth justice workforce involving the influx of large numbers of practitioners without the professional qualifications that had previously been required to work in this area.

The question of professional activity is highly pertinent to this period, where it could perhaps be seen as most under threat. A new and more prescriptive version of National Standards for Youth Justice Services was issued in 2004, described as:

> The required standards of practice which practitioners who provide youth justice services are expected to achieve. They provide
>
> • a basis for promoting effective work with children and young people who have offended or who are at risk of offending, and also their families and victims;
> • benchmarks against which the effectiveness of youth justice services can be measured and inspected. (YJB, 2004, p 3)

The YJB simultaneously developed a specialised youth justice qualification validated at Higher Education level, the Professional Certificate in Effective Practice. This was premised on 'what works' principles (see McGuire, 1995) and promoted an essentially positivist agenda, supported by a range of texts called Key Elements of Effective

Practice summarising the evidence base for specified areas, such as substance misuse, parenting and offending behaviour programmes. While offering guidance with the ostensible aim of improving practice, in fact, the nature of the evidence validated and authorised in this way was selective, with certain types of empirical knowledge privileged and others marginalised (Goldson, 2010). What was thus promoted was a pragmatic and, at worst, mechanical mode of practice not conducive to reflexivity or critical thinking. Moreover, the YJB's wider project to add to the research base and the understanding of impacts and effects was constrained within a utilitarian, administrative criminology 'defined by a narrow set of definitions, research problems and questions – and importantly one based on a fundamental inability to ask some of the far-reaching questions about criminal justice interventions into the lives of young law-breakers' (Phoenix, 2010, p 77).

Bill Whyte (2009) comments that the issue of effectiveness – what works best in practice – should be approached in an exploratory way rather than treated as a formula that can be applied in a routine way to children and young people. Sadly, the YJB seemed to lose sight of this during this phase, and attempted to direct and control the nature and the scale of interventions. Ironically, looking critically at the efficacy of youth justice interventions in England and Wales, performance measured in the YJB's own terms against its KPIs has been mixed; measured against wider indicators of fairness and justice, the YJS has fallen still further short (Graham, 2010).

So, this second phase of New Labour's youth justice involved disciplining the youth justice workforce, requiring adherence to a set of standardised rules and methods of practice, and limiting – although not eliminating – professional discretion. It was also characterised by a more authoritarian and disciplinary approach to young people, based more explicitly on Right realist thinking that conceives of offenders (including young people who offend) as calculating and rational actors (Squires and Stephens, 2005; Muncie, 2009). In wider social policy, the rhetoric of the 'something for something society' was strengthened, and rights were firmly coupled with responsibilities (disproportionately, the responsibilities of individuals to communities, not the other way round) (Rodger, 2008).

Within the youth justice arena, these trends were manifested in the Respect Action Plan, the emphasis on 'poor' parenting (Millie, 2009) and particular restorative justice practices that prioritised the need for the individual to take responsibility over reparation or actions to promote reintegration (Gray, 2005). Such restorative justice interventions have been criticised for taking little account of the age and development of the young person and therefore his or her ability to develop a sense of individual responsibility (Haines and O'Mahony, 2006). John Muncie (2009) identifies this as a 'responsibilisation' strategy and links the drive to promote individual responsibility for actions to more general neoliberal philosophies encouraging the private sector and communities to take opportunities to reduce crime and reducing the role and remit of larger state institutions (Muncie, 2008). This is evident in terms of the multiplicity of local groups active around anti-social behaviour under the broad umbrella of Community Safety Partnerships. Although there is a variety of support and enforcement mechanisms used in different proportions across local areas (Matthews and Briggs, 2008), policy in this second phase tended to be enforcement-led (Squires and Stephens, 2005). Significantly, the numbers of ASBOs imposed on young people under the age of 18 increased from 193 in 2001 to 628 in 2004, rising to 1,581 in 2006 (almost 40% of the total for that year) (MoJ, 2010). Unsurprisingly, the use of custody for young people also rose during this period, peaking at 3,012 placements in April 2008 (MoJ, 2011).

A third phase in developments

Youth justice, however, has not remained static and a third phase in New Labour's youth justice began to emerge from roughly 2007. Although this did not see a complete overturn of the established centralised and authoritarian tendencies, there has been a more explicit questioning of what were previously held to be certainties as policymakers started to *rethink and reformulate*. The decision to give the Department for Children, Schools and Families (DCSF) joint responsibility for youth justice in 2007 was emblematic of this shift (Graham, 2010) and it is significant that the Youth Crime Action Plan issued the following year (HM Government, 2008) was signed off by three government departments: the Home Office, the MoJ and the DCSF. Differences between these departments reflected essential ambiguities in government thinking about young people in trouble and their needs and vulnerabilities (Graham, 2010), but there seemed to be at least some welcome space for developing a more holistic range of responses.

The youth rehabilitation order became available to the courts in November 2009 and case management guidance (YJB, 2009a) was issued alongside a new version of the National Standards (YJB, 2010a) and a more structured system of risk classification. Although the 'Scaled Approach' has been criticised for its lack of evidence base and further erosion of professional judgement (Sutherland, 2009; Case, 2010), nevertheless, the case management guidance itself is constructive in that it seeks to bolster the central role of the case manager in ensuring that assessment and intervention is individualised and reaches out to other agencies and universal services as appropriate. While still advocating a bureaucratic approach, it does recognise the importance of relationships in promoting change, emphasising motivation and engagement as key tasks (YJB, 2009a). Related to this, indicators suggest that the YJB moved away from a strict 'what works' approach and became more open to looking at different types of evidence from practice, particularly around engagement and supervisory relationships (Prior and Mason, 2010; Stephenson et al, 2011).

More significant, however, are the drivers from outside the MoJ and YJB. These include unequivocal guidance from the Sentencing Guidelines Council's (2000) *Overarching principles – sentencing youths*, which restates the necessity of treating young people according to their age, maturity and stage of development, underlining both the aim of prevention of offending and the welfare principle dating back to section 44 of the Children and Young Persons Act 1933. Additionally, in 2008, the Independent Commission on Youth Crime and Anti-Social Behaviour was established to review existing services and make proposals for sustainable change. The Commission's report, *Time for a fresh start* (Police Foundation, 2010), was published in 2010, calling for youth justice services to be developed on the basis of three clear principles: restoration, prevention and integration.

The academic world has also galvanised and has moved on from critiquing New Labour policy to articulating new visions for youth justice. These advocate alternative approaches based on children's rights (Whyte, 2009), diversion and restoration (see the contributors in Smith, 2010), and a more reflective and reflexive practice (Taylor et al, 2010). Others call for policy to be informed by young people's perspectives (Barry, 2009; Hine, 2010) and for recognition of the salience of social capital for young people (Barry, 2006; Boeck, 2009). There is also a considerable momentum building around desistance approaches in the adult criminal justice world, which has not yet permeated youth justice (McNeill, 2009) but in due course must surely provide further impetus for change.

And what has happened in practice?

Of course, this begs the question of what has happened on the ground across the three phases of New Labour's youth justice and returns us to the third element of Fergusson's (2007) analytical framework: implementation and practice. Early research seemed to suggest that the social work ethos and values were stubbornly persisting even with a substantial change and diversification of youth justice personnel (Burnett and Appleton, 2004; Ellis and Boden, 2004; Field, 2007).Yet, Anna Souhami's (2007) ethnographic study of the formation of one YOT in the Midlands suggests that something more complicated was happening as occupational cultures were destabilised and professional roles and identities redrawn. Her account suggests fluidity, but also an initial tendency for YOT workers to cling to the security of well-known practices and ways of framing and conceptualising practice. Clearly, by the end of her study, there was a sense of altered allegiances and new cultures developing, with practitioners expressing less ambivalence about being part of the YOT enterprise. Rather than being threatened, YOT workers could then see the potential to extend the boundaries of practice and to increase their influence on external agencies during this phase of *experimentation and implementation*.

There has been significantly less attention to researching YOT culture and ethos during the second of New Labour's phases of youth justice: *routinise and discipline*. Nevertheless, some insights have emerged that give pause for thought. Christina Stahlkopf (2008) returned to the Oxfordshire YOT previously researched by Burnett and Appleton (2004) and found that the optimism evident among practitioners in the initial stages of the YOT had given way to a sense of disillusion due to workloads and the under-resourcing of core youth justice work. Sadly, performance targets, often linked to funding and status in the YOT performance league tables, had produced perverse incentives for compliance with basic requirements rather than promoting quality, thus risking the embedding of poor practice. This is a snapshot from one service and we should be cautious about generalising these findings, but they do resonate with my own experiences within the field. In a different vein, Anna Souhami's continued research with YOT senior practitioners also reveals tensions and suggests that YOTs are almost creating a new profession, ironically undermining the very value of diversity and creativity inherent in the early YOTs. She talks about the 'emergence of a new form of multi-agency profession, with its own knowledge base, training, values and skills' (Souhami, 2009, p 189).

The YJB-prescribed qualification, the Professional Certificate in Professional Practice, has contributed to this, but so too has the changing demographics of the YOT workforce, with fewer staff seconded from partner agencies and a growing number employed directly by the YOT (via the local authority). Table 17.1 illustrates changes in the workforce for full-time permanent employees.

Table 17.1: Secondments to youth offending teams

Employee status	2005/06	% of total	2009/10	% of total
Employed directly	1,684	35	3,230	54
Secondees social care	650	13	182	3
Secondees probation	216	4	202	3
Secondees police	316	7	320	5
Total	4,823		6,018	

Source: Data from YJB (2006, 2010)

What might this mean for the values and principles influencing practice? Two further studies shed some light on developments, particularly in relation to orientations towards welfare and punishment. First, Stewart Field's (2007) research in seven Welsh YOTs suggested that welfare still had a strong hold, but reconstituted by practitioners so that it was able to sit more comfortably alongside punishment, control and coercion within the new practice context. Social work practitioners in this study recognised the benefits of clearer boundaries for their work and, in different ways, had accommodated the more qualified voluntarism in their relationships with young people, influenced by their new practice requirements and dialogue with police and other YOT colleagues. What seemed to emerge was a more conditional approach to welfare. On the one hand, welfare issues were seen as intrinsically linked to offending and should therefore be prioritised. On the other hand, practitioners showed a greater willingness to accept the use of constraint and control for those not responding to community support and intervention or close to the custody threshold.

Second, Tim Bateman's (2011) discussion of enforcement practice is based on research in 2008 and similarly explores the increased willingness of practitioners to enforce orders and their acceptance of the use of custody for young people. Pre-1998, youth justice practitioners had been united in their hostility to custody and, at best, ambivalent about enforcement, so this represents a significant but not necessarily coherent shift. Bateman (2011, p 126) refers to 'a depiction of a qualitative break with the past, providing evidence of a fragmented workforce whose practice was no longer informed by a coherent value base'.

These studies suggest that practitioners have not necessarily become more punitive in any obvious or direct way. However, they have accepted the rationales for earlier and greater intervention, which, ironically, are often justified on welfare grounds. Paradoxically, more interventionist approaches, combined with an acquiescent approach to enforcement, may increase the amount of punishment and control to which young people are subject. As a result, practitioners are tolerating levels of punishment and control that would previously have met with concerted resistance, and have absorbed this into a reworked or reconstituted collection of values.

The phase of *rethink and reformulate* may not yet have impacted to any great extent in the practice world; there is likely to be a delay in any changes in approach at a policy level appearing on the ground in any case, but there is also no straightforward relationship with developments at a practice level, which may have their own drivers. Interestingly, during this latter period, the use of ASBOs has decreased as more creative use has been made of interventions such as Acceptable Behaviour Contracts, parenting initiatives and intensive family support (Pople, 2010). The number of young people under 18 in custody also significantly reduced and this trend has continued under the Coalition, down to 1,690 in June 2012 (YJB, 2012). This has happened without any great policy initiatives from the centre (Smith, 2011) and it is unclear what changes at a practice level have produced this outcome. Bateman (2011, 2012) suggests that it may be due to a decrease in first-time entrants to the YJS rather than a softer and more flexible approach to young people already in the system, but other factors may become apparent over time.

The Coalition government – some concluding thoughts

Of course, we are now in another era of youth justice under the Coalition administration. What is interesting – although entirely predictable – is how this government has presented its approach as a break with the past, just as New Labour did when coming into office in 1997. Naturally, there will be continuity as well as change, particularly in relation to the flexibility over performance targets that was already being introduced by the previous government as it left office. Clearly, YOTs themselves are valued and are here to stay, along with the multi-agency arrangements for their oversight and governance. The position of the YJB itself has been less clear: it was initially due to be abolished as part of the infamous 'bonfire of the quangos' in the autumn of 2010, but has since been reprieved, albeit with a lesser role operating from within the Ministry of Justice.

This new phase under the Coalition will see considerable *loosening and tightening*. The *loosening* is evident in the localism agenda, which will ease the controls from central government and allow individual areas to exercise greater autonomy in the use of their resources. Practitioner discretion is being promoted and the Asset/Onset assessment framework, so clearly linked to the risk factor paradigm, is being replaced by a more holistic assessment process. This creates opportunities, but also risks of fragmentation and inconsistency, in youth justice services, which may be compounded by the introduction of Payment by Results schemes (Morgan and Newburn, 2012).

Tightening relates to the current climate of austerity that inevitably means reduced resources, which will especially restrict the range of prevention projects associated with YOTs. This may have positive benefits in concentrating YOT activity on core functions – arguably, a disproportionate amount of energy has previously been spent on delivering a network of preventive services or inputting into their strategic management. However, austerity measures will also impact on the educational and social resources needed to provide a holistic response to the needs of troubled or troublesome young people and their families.

It is also worth noting the *loosening and tightening* impulses inherent in the rediscovery of diversion from the YJS and the attempts to reduce expenditure on custodial places, which are so costly in human and financial terms. Morgan and Newburn (2012, p 519) note the more cautious use of youth justice resources but comment that 'If parsimony is to be the new youth justice watchword, there has been a welcome retreat from the criminalising bonanza of New Labour's middle period, but if historic practice is any guide, the retreat could go considerably further'.

Ken Clarke, when he was Secretary of State for Justice, launched a 'rehabilitation revolution' and declared an intention to reduce the use of custody where offences are not sexual or violent (MoJ, 2010). It would be expected that this would influence the sentencing of young people in a positive direction because of the nature of their offences. Sadly, the impetus behind the 'rehabilitation revolution' was undermined by a punitive turn as the government responded to the *Breaking the cycle* consultation (MoJ, 2011). Nevertheless, greater discretion at the pre-court stage and restorative interventions rather than criminal justice processing will continue to reduce the numbers of young people caught up in the YJS.

Under Chris Grayling, the Ministry of Justice has stepped back from what Ken Clarke was attempting to portray as radical and daring, but which in reality was largely a return to the old penal–welfare philosophies associated with particular concepts of youth (Smith, 2011). Punishment/justice orientations tend to view young people as going through an inherently problematic life stage, with the focus on curbing and normalising behaviour so that the young person grows into a 'responsible adult'. Welfare orientations, on the other hand, recognise the young person's circumstances, seeking to redress problems and to promote positive well-being and fulfilment. What neither does is to conceive of young people as social actors (Smith, 2009). The New Labour era saw little acknowledgement of young people's perspectives or agency. It does not seem that the Coalition government is any more child-centred, although it may be more trusting and supportive of practitioners, the other important subordinate group in this arena.

Change at a governmental and a policy level looks as though it is taking an ambiguous direction, with both threats and opportunities. Over the forthcoming period, developments at a practice level may bring the most promise of positive transformation, as some of the more restrictive elements of the New Labour infrastructure are dismantled. Certainly, there will be pressure from the academic world to develop practice in ways that are more responsive to young people's experience of transitions and mobility within their social sphere. Whether bottom-up pressure will again be significant, as it was in the 1980s, remains to be seen, but there is increasing impetus for change incorporating new ideas and approaches into the best aspects of the New Labour reforms.

References

Audit Commission (1996) *Misspent youth: young people and crime*, London: Audit Commission.

Baker, K., Kelly, G. and Wilkinson, B. (2011) *Assessment in youth justice*, Bristol: Policy Press.

Barry, M. (2006) *Youth offending in transition: the search for social recognition*, London: Routledge.

Barry, M. (2009) 'Youth justice policy and its influence on desistance from crime', in M. Barry and F. McNeill (eds) *Youth offending and youth justice*, London: Jessica Kingsley, pp 78–94.

Bateman, T. (2011) 'We now breach more kids in a week than we used to in a whole year: the punitive turn and enforcement: the punitive turn, enforcement and custody', *Youth Justice*, vol 11, pp 115–33.

Bateman, T. (2012) 'Who pulled the plug? Towards an explanation of the fall in child imprisonment in England and Wales', *Youth Justice*, vol 12, no 1, pp 36–52.

Becker, H.S. (1967) 'Whose side are we on?', *Social Problems*, vol 14, no 3, pp 239–47.

Boeck, T. (2009) 'Social capital and young people', in J. Wood and J. Hine (eds) *Work with young people*, London: Sage, pp 88–103.

Burnett, R. and Appleton, C. (2004) 'Joined-up services to tackle youth crime: a case study in England', *British Journal of Criminology*, vol 44, no 1, pp 34–55.

Canton, R. (2007) 'Probation and the tragedy of punishment', *The Howard Journal of Criminal Justice*, vol 46, no 3, pp 236–54.

Case, S. (2010) 'Preventing and reducing risk', in W. Taylor, R. Earle and R. Hester (eds) *The youth justice handbook: theory, policy and practice*, Cullompton: Willan, pp 90–100.

Crawford, A. and Burden, T. (2005) 'Involving victims in referral orders and young offender panels: an evaluation of Leeds Youth Offending Service', in Centre for Criminal Justice Studies (ed) *Criminal justice review 2004–5*, Leeds: Centre for Criminal Justice Studies.

Earle, R. (2008) 'Referral orders', in B. Goldson (ed) *Dictionary of youth justice*, Cullompton: Willan, pp 283–5.

Ellis, T. and Boden, I. (2004) 'Is there a unifying professional culture in Youth Offending Teams? A research note', *British Society of Criminology 2004 Conference Proceedings*. Available at: britsoccrim.org/volume7/006.pdf

Etzioni, A. (1968) *The active society*, New York, NY: Free Press.

Fergusson, R. (2007) 'Making sense of the melting pot: multiple discourses in youth justice policy', *Youth Justice*, vol 7, pp 179–94.

Field, S. (2007) 'Practice cultures and the new youth justice in (England and) Wales', *British Journal of Criminology*, vol 47, pp 311–30.

Goldson, B. (2010) 'Research-informed youth justice?', in W. Taylor, R. Earle and R. Hester (eds) *The youth justice handbook: theory, policy and practice*, Cullompton: Willan, pp 64–72.

Graham, J. (2010) 'Responding to youth crime', in D. Smith (ed) *A new response to youth crime*, Cullompton: Willan, pp 104–42.

Gray, P. (2005) 'The politics of risk and young offenders' experiences of social exclusion and restorative justice', *The British Journal of Criminology*, vol 45, pp 938–57.

Haines, K. and O'Mahony, D. (2006) 'Restorative approaches, young people and youth justice', in B. Goldson and J. Muncie (eds) *Youth crime and justice*, London: Sage, pp 110–24.

Hine, J. (2010) 'Young people's "voices" as evidence', in W. Taylor, R. Earle and R. Hester (eds) *The youth justice handbook: theory, policy and practice*, Cullompton: Willan, pp 168–78.

HM Government (2008) *Youth crime action plan, 2008*, London: HM Government.

Home Office (1997) *No more excuses*, London: Home Office.

Matthews, R. and Briggs, D. (2008) 'Lost in translation: interpreting and implementing anti-social behaviour policies', in P. Squires (ed) *ASBO nation*, Bristol: The Policy Press, pp 87–100.

McAra, L. (2010) 'Models of youth justice', in D. Smith (ed) *A new response to youth crime*, Cullompton: Willan, pp 287–317.

McGuire, J. (1995) *What works: reducing re-offending*, London: Wiley.

McNeill, F. (2009) 'Supervising young offenders: what works and what's right', in M. Barry and F. McNeill (eds) *Youth offending and youth justice*, London: Jessica Kingsley.

Millie, A. (2009) *Anti-social behaviour*, Maidenhead: Open University Press.

MoJ (Ministry of Justice) (2010) *Breaking the cycle: effective punishment, rehabilitation and sentencing of offenders*, London: MoJ.

MoJ (2011) *Breaking the cycle: government response*, London: MoJ.

Moore, S. (2008) 'Street life, neighbourhood policing and the community', in P. Squires (ed) *ASBO nation: the criminalisation of nuisance*, Bristol: The Policy Press, pp 179–202.

Morgan, R. and Newburn, T. (2012) 'Youth crime and justice: rediscovering devolution, discretion and diversion?', in M. Maguire, R. Morgan and R. Reiner (eds) *The Oxford handbook of criminology* (5th edn), Oxford: Oxford University Press.

Muncie, J. (2006) 'Re-penalisation and rights: explorations in comparative youth criminology', *Howard Journal of Criminal Justice*, vol 45, no 1, pp 42–70.

Muncie, J. (2008) 'Responsibilisation', in B. Goldson (ed) *The dictionary of youth justice*, Cullompton: Willan, pp 299–300.

Muncie, J. (2009) *Youth and crime* (3rd edn), London: Sage.

Muncie, J. and Goldson, B. (eds) (2006) *Comparative youth justice*, London: Sage.

Newburn, T. (2002) 'The contemporary politics of youth crime prevention', in J. Muncie, E. McLaughlin and G. Hughes (eds) *Youth justice: critical readings*, London: Sage/Open University.

Phoenix, J. (2010) 'Whose account counts? Politics and research in youth justice', in W. Taylor, R. Earle and R. Hester (eds) *The youth justice handbook: theory, policy and practice*, Cullompton: Willan, pp 73–82.

Police Foundation (2010) *Time for a fresh start; the report of the Independent Commission on Youth Crime and Anti-social Behaviour*, London: Police Foundation.

Pople, L. (2010) 'Responding to anti-social behaviour', in D. Smith (ed) *A new response to youth crime*, Cullompton: Willan, pp 143–79.

Prior, D. and Mason, P. (2010) 'A different kind of evidence? Looking for "what works" in engaging young offenders', *Youth Justice*, vol 10, pp 210–26.

Putnam, D. (2000) *Bowling alone: collapse and revival of the American community*, New York, NY: Simon and Schuster.

Robinson, G. (2007) 'Rehabilitation', in R. Canton and D. Hancock (eds) *The dictionary of probation and offender management*, Cullompton: Willan.

Robinson, G. and Crow, I. (2009) *Rehabilitation: theory, research and practice*, London: Sage.

Rodger, J.J. (2008) *Criminalising social policy*, Cullompton: Willan.

Sentencing Guidelines Council (2000) *Over-arching principles – sentencing youths*, London: SGC.

Shipman, T. and Walker, K. (2011) 'Cameron's war on feckless families: PM attacks the human rights laws and backs national service', *The Daily Mail*, 16 August.

Smith, D. (ed) (2010) *A new response to youth crime*, Cullompton: Willan.

Smith, R. (2006) 'Actuarialism and early intervention in contemporary youth justice', in B. Goldson and J. Muncie (eds) *Youth crime and justice*, London: Sage, pp 92–109.

Smith, R. (2007) *Youth justice: ideas, policy and practice* (2nd edn), Cullompton: Willan.

Smith, R. (2009) 'Childhood, agency and youth justice', *Children and Society*, vol 23, pp 252–64.

Smith, R. (2011) 'Where now for youth justice?', *The British Journal of Community Justice*, vol 9, no 2, pp 69–80.

Souhami, A. (2007) *Transforming youth justice: occupational identity and cultural change*, Cullompton: Willan.

Souhami, A. (2009) 'Doing youth justice beyond boundaries?', in M. Barry and F. McNeill (eds) *Youth offending and youth justice*, London: Jessica Kingsley, pp 176–93.

Squires, P. and Stephens, D. (2005) *Rougher justice: anti-social behaviour and young people*, Cullompton: Willan.

Stahlkopf, C. (2008) 'Political, structural and cultural influences on England's Youth Offending Team practices', *International Criminal Justice Review*, vol 18, pp 455–72.

Stephenson, M., Giller, H. and Brown, S. (2011) *Effective practice in youth justice*, Abingdon: Routledge.

Sutherland, A. (2009) 'The scaled approach to youth justice: fools rush in …', *Youth Justice*, vol 9, pp 44–60.

Taylor, W., Earle, R. and Hester, R. (eds) (2010) *Youth justice handbook: theory, policy and practice*, Cullompton: Willan.

Whyte, B. (2009) *Youth justice in practice: making a difference*, Bristol: The Policy Press.

YJB (Youth Justice Board) (2004) *National Standards for Youth Justice Services 2004*, London: YJB.

YJB (2006) *Youth justice annual statistics 2005/6*, London: YJB.

YJB (2009a) *Case management guidance*, London: YJB.

YJB (2009b) *National Standards for Youth Justice Services 2009*, London: YJB.

YJB (2010) *Youth justice statistics 2009/10*, London: YJB.

YJB (2012) *Youth justice statistics 2011/12*, London: YJB.

EIGHTEEN

Economic values and evidence: evaluating criminal justice policy

Kevin Albertson, Katherine Albertson, Chris Fox and Dan Ellingworth

Introduction

The UK government is committed to reducing the costs of criminal justice. Specifically they aim to:

> Reform the sentencing framework so that it both punishes the guilty and rehabilitates offenders more effectively. These reforms will stem the unsustainable rise in the UK prison population. Proposals will be published in a Green Paper, and will include the use of tough community penalties where they are more effective than short prison sentences; using restorative justice; and paying private and voluntary providers by results for delivering reductions in reoffending. (HM Treasury, 2010, p 55)

This represents an explicit recognition of the budgetary and economic rationale of key criminal justice policy. It is, therefore, unsurprising that the skills and techniques from the discipline of economics have been increasingly used to address this challenge. At its core, economic theory seeks to determine the efficient application of resources to achieve a given goal. In other words, economics is a tool that is applied after the problem has been defined in a socio-political context. From this basic premise, the thrust of this chapter is to highlight the distinction between the morals and values of economics and the morals and values expressed in the way economics is used. Ultimately, we suggest that the choice of an economic approach is itself ideologically based. Notwithstanding, we conclude with a note of broad support for the use of economic evaluation in criminal justice policy – if thoughtfully and carefully applied.

The economic approach

The study of economics arises from the scarcity of resources (Robbins, 1945, p 15). Because resources are limited, it follows that we should use what is available to achieve the best effect. Thus, at its core, economic theory seeks simply to determine the efficient application of resources to achieve a given goal. There are two basic schools of thought within which the application of economic principles to policy decisions may be framed: normative and positivist (Keynes, 1891; Krauss, 2005).

The normative paradigm

Where the normative approach to economics is adopted, economic theory plays a dual role: both the validity of policy goals and the means by which these may be achieved are considered as part of the analysis. The 'norms' of society are both informed by and pursued through economic theory. For example, a normative economist would be prepared to comment on the validity of such issues as appropriate levels of minimum quality of life, social inclusion and social justice, as well as the means of pursuing these goals. In the context of policy, the values of the normative approach are, therefore, twofold: to discuss how closely the policy goal accords to an overarching social norm or moré and to investigate the most efficient means of pursuing the goal.

The approach has been much criticised (eg Robbins, 1952 [1935]; Freidman, 1953, 1955) for its supposed subjectivity. Although some (eg Gewirth, 1978) might argue that there is an objective basis for ethics (although McMahon [1986] is unconvinced), the practice of social norms is clearly context-specific. Because of this, two economic analyses might reach different conclusions based on the same data, depending on the analysts' conception of social morés.

The positivist paradigm

In contrast to the normative paradigm, the positivist approach limits itself to the efficient pursuit of predetermined goals without comment on their validity (Friedman, 1953). In this sense, it is held to be an 'objective approach'. It follows that the economist should no more comment on the validity of a policy goal than a nuclear physicist should comment on whether or not the development of a nuclear bomb is an 'appropriate' goal of physics.

Where economics is applied to policy analysis as an objective discipline, it is subordinate to the political process. In this sense, economics cannot be used to justify policy, merely to comment on the relative efficiency of different means of achieving predetermined policy goals. This approach to economic analysis is not without its critics; not least because there is little evidence that economic agents adopt a positivist approach in their own decision-making: 'Economic models describe the task that animals and humans face in any decision-making situation. They define how a problem should be solved. Real animals and real people deviate from these solutions' (Glimcher, 2003, p 334, quoted in Hands, 2010, p 14).[1]

Hands (2010) is not convinced that it is possible to separate the normative from the positive. In his opinion, 'as a practical matter among economists, knowing (positively) what is, tells us exactly what (normatively) ought to be' (Hands, 2010, p 16).

Efficiency

Whether normative or objective, the economic analyst is ultimately concerned with the measure of efficiency. In practice, however, efficiency is also a relative concept, requiring at least two means of achieving the desired end. Thus, any criminal justice intervention A will be considered to be more efficient than intervention B if (and only if) intervention A achieves a greater benefit for the same cost as B, and/or if A achieves the same benefit for a lesser cost than B. This determination of the ratio of costs to benefits for each potential intervention is termed cost–benefit analysis (CBA).

In sum, normative economics seeks to describe what ought to be, this may be compared to positivist economics, which seeks to describe what is (Levitt and Dubner, 2005). The choice between these outlooks reflects the values of the analyst. Objectively, we should not expect economists to tell us which policy objectives the government should adopt. In this case, all we can realistically ask of them is to determine the relative efficiency of different means to achieve politically determined social goals.

Defining the perimeters of the economic approach

In the following, we discuss the difficulties in realising the economic approach to intervention analysis and highlight how it is that value judgements inform the supposedly objective approach of efficiency analysis. In the first instance, the definition of a relevant 'benefit' and a relevant 'cost' is, by necessity, subjective, as analysts may consider the issues of relevance from different points of view. Further, the choice of a comparison case may also be made subjectively. If, for example, the government wishes merely to reduce the cost of incarceration, 'doing nothing' (ie neither detecting nor convicting offenders) will clearly have a cost–benefit ratio of zero – this is rather tautologically difficult to improve upon. For this reason, the comparison case is often determined by reference to what makes the most sense in the context of the policy goal. Indeed, it is in the selection of that policy goal that underpinning ideologies can often be identified most readily.

There is also, of course, the pragmatic observation that the costs of determining the benefits and costs of alternatives must be less than the extra benefit we expect to gain from carrying out CBA. Evaluation will take place only for those interventions where it is subjectively considered that significant savings might be made. As the prior experience of the analyst will suggest efficient means of evaluation, it seems reasonable to postulate that the choice of evaluation method is also subjective to some extent.

Applying economic analysis in the criminal justice sector

The application of economic analysis in the criminal justice sector can, and does, provide significant benefits by providing evaluation techniques with which we can estimate the costs of crime and evaluate the competing cost–benefit ratios of alternative approaches to criminal justice (Fox and Albertson, 2010; Albertson and Fox, 2012). We begin our discussion with a review of cost analysis. What follows is broadly based on a comprehensive review given by Albertson and Fox (2012, ch 6).

Defining and measuring costs

The viewpoint of any cost analysis sets the tone for the study (Drummond et al, 2005). In essence, the analyst must determine from whose budget the costs arise. Consider, for example, an intervention whereby the police identify offenders with substance misuse problems and refer them to an appropriate drug treatment programme operated by the National Health Service (NHS). From the point of view of the criminal justice system (CJS), the costs of the project involve the set-up and referral costs for the police. The additional costs of the drug treatment are not considered in the analysis. However, from the point of view of the state, we must also include the costs of the drug treatment programme, which is paid for out of the NHS budget.

In general, there are three viewpoints we may consider, and these must be established in consultation with the stakeholder who has commissioned the cost analysis. We may consider: a solely criminal justice perspective; a public sector (state) perspective; and a social/national perspective – where this latter includes both the costs to the state and the costs to society of the intervention, for example, we would also consider the costs incurred by unpaid volunteers, charities and other private sector service providers. Social costs might also include more subtle effects, such as the impact on a neighbourhood of a local probation office or substance misuse centre being opened – or closed. Thus, it is clear that there are several types of cost we may consider, as well as several points of view.

In practice, resources that would have been utilised whether or not the intervention is implemented are generally excluded from cost analyses (Dhiri and Brand, 1999). This forms the basis of the concept of 'additionality of costs' (Dhiri and Brand, 1999). Additional costs are those over and above existing or fixed costs, the value of which is unaffected by the intervention. For example, simply replacing one intervention with another, or where an intervention 'pays for itself' through increased efficiency, will involve no additional resource costs.

In addition, the time period over which the evaluation takes place may determine how we view costs (Cohen, 2000; Drummond et al, 2005). For example, where additional resources costs are based on a short time period they may be influenced by an atypical event or circumstance that might not occur if the intervention is rolled out more generally. Where evaluation takes place over the shorter time period than the natural life of the project, it may be that there is a reduced size in offender cohorts, meaning that the average cost might be overestimated. Alternatively, where a unit of treatment takes a long time to deliver, evaluation over a short time period might not take account of the full cost of implementation.

In sum, when gathering costs data, there will normally be a trade-off made between the time and effort required to gather data and the magnitude of the costs involved in data collection (Drummond et al, 2005, p 57). Clearly, the terms of reference of the study must be made clear. This is, to a greater or lesser extent, a subjective decision.

Defining benefits

To allow comparison of costs with benefits, the viewpoint from which we consider intervention costs defines the range of benefits we evaluate. For example, where we consider the costs of the intervention to fall on the state, the benefits we may realise are, in general, those that will accrue to the state. These might include reductions in the cost of responding to crime and reductions in the level of worklessness and therefore increases in taxes paid, or reductions in benefits required, by the client who benefits directly from the intervention. We might also consider reductions in the cost of hospital visits that might result from a successful decline in offenders' substance abuse. If the cost of the intervention is determined at the national/social level, we might also consider the improvement in the general well-being of the offender or ex-offender and the quality of life of their immediate family and society. Here, again, subjective judgements must be made by the analyst and the research-commissioning body so as to determine which outcomes may validly be termed outputs or benefits of the intervention. The valuation of such outputs is similarly by no means straightforward.

As costs are measured in monetary terms, so valuation of benefits is in also in monetary terms. That is to say, we may consider how much society or the state is willing to pay in order to reduce the incidence of crime. The willingness to pay may be taken to be equivalent to the financial burden placed on society or the state by criminal acts. In the UK, the standard source of such estimates is the Home Office (2005). These costs of crime are worked out by breaking them down into two elements: the physical and emotional impact on victims; and the direct monetary costs arising from the incidence of crime (Home Office, 2005).

This may sound simple enough; however, there are complex sets of considerations comprised of a mixture of public and private sector costs (eg the costs to the CJS in responding to crime and the cost to society of insurance). The Home Office's (2005) estimates of the costs of crime do not take account of the impact of crime on the 'quality of life' of non-victims. For example, there is the impact of crime on potential victims manifesting as fear of crime. Such fear may have a very real impact on some members of society, perhaps causing them to forgo leaving their homes after dark. While estimates for fear of crime have been calculated (Dolan and Peasgood, 2007), they are not included in the Home Office costs.

A further neglected issue is the broader impact on quality of life in a community. As Cornish and Clarke (1986) suggest, individuals are unlikely to become involved in crime simply through a rational one-step process. They may be drawn, incrementally, into such a decision through, for example, criminal friends and peers and the overall (lack of) social capacity of their neighbourhood. Where social norms are generally enforced, social capacity is greater; conversely, in a neighbourhood where social morés are weak, the potential perpetrator feels less pressure to conform to pro-social prescriptions. Such effects are well known in the criminology literature. For example, the suggestion that low-level criminality leads to more serious crime – the so-called 'broken windows hypothesis' (Wilson and Kelling, 1982) – formed the basis of William Bratton's approach to running the New York City Transit Police from 1990 to 1992 and the New York Police Department from 1994 to 1996 (Kelling and Bratton, 1993; Gladwell, 2000).

Any attempt to value the costs of crime without taking into account this feedback loop is likely to underestimate the savings that may be made from reducing seemingly trivial offences. Ultimately, it is clear that while costs of crime estimates focus on placing a fiscal cost for criminal justice agencies and individual victims, assessment of cost to the community will inevitably prove challenging and, as such, is effectively missing from the cost of crime estimates currently used (Cohen, 2007; Albertson and Fox, 2012).

Further, Home Office figures do not include the emotional costs that non-victims suffer through empathy with victims of crime. The classical model of economic thought postulates that all members of society are self-centred individuals who will not make any sacrifice of resources to a cause from which they receive no return. In practice, however, we see that members of society may contribute resources to charities that support complete strangers suffering, for example, from natural disaster, poverty or crime. That we are prepared to sacrifice to offset the impacts of such misfortune implies that we must place a value on its avoidance altogether; even if it does not impact directly on us. Home Office (2005) figures do not include this concern for others.

When once the terms of reference of cost savings arising from reduced criminality have been established, evaluation is further complicated by the that fact the costs of crime may not increase proportionally to the amount of crime (cf Becker, 1968; Gladwell, 2000). For example, the cost to society of two murders may be greater than twice the cost of a single murder. Similarly, criminal justice costs may not decline in proportion to a fall in reconviction rates. To rationalise the closing of a wing of a prison on the strength of a single individual's decision to refrain from crime – even if proven to be effective and financially sound – is realistically inconceivable. Thus, the saving to be made from a whole cohort of 100 offenders who cease to offend is not logically equivalent to 100 times the savings to be made from one individual ceasing to offend. From an economic perspective, the need to generate fiscal savings is a major challenge for the viability of any evidence-based policy model. Therefore, scale will always be an important factor, as delivering substantial changes in entrenched criminal behaviour in large cohorts and developing accurate measurement of such interventions and proving direct causation will always be challenging. It will also limit which interventions may be considered (Fox and Albertson, 2011).

This difficulty arising in evaluating the effect of the scale of an intervention may be exacerbated by the consideration that Home Office interventions may be required to be self-financing in terms of reducing the criminal justice budget (Fox and Albertson, 2011). The Home Office (2005) shows that the majority of the savings arising from a reduction in reoffending will accrue to society at large; however, it is only that part of savings that accrue to government agencies from which cost reductions to the state can be realised.

In sum, the benefits that arise from reductions in the level of offending may be estimated using the Home Office's (2005) values of the costs of crime. These include the fiscal and emotional costs suffered by the victim and the criminal justice costs of responding to crime. However, the estimated costs do not include: the impairment of the life of those non-victims frightened of crime; the impact on the community in general, and possible feedback into a more general atmosphere of criminality; and the cost imposed on one member of society when another is harmed. By definition, therefore, the Home Office's (2005) costs of crime are underestimated. Recall, it is the reduction of these costs that make up the estimated 'benefits' of the intervention we may evaluate. Therefore, we see that the economic approach to criminal justice is likely to underestimate the benefits of reducing crime. There may be little the analyst may do about this; however, it should be borne in mind. In short, Home Office (2005) figures remain the best we have.

Measuring benefits

More often than not, a simple outcome measure such as offending and reoffending rates is used as an indicator of the success of a criminal justice intervention (La Vigne et al, 2010). This outcome is usually evaluated over a one-year period, perhaps measured using rearrest or reconviction data. Such a datum is therefore better referred to as a measure of 'proven re-offending' (Ministry of Justice, 2011) and is likely to underestimate 'true' levels of reoffending.

The gold standard approach to evaluation of outcomes is that of experiments or techniques using comparisons with control groups. The effect of the intervention is measured in terms of comparing outcomes of the intervention cohort with outcomes observed in a cohort, in theory identical to that which receives the intervention. Indeed, the term 'evidence-based policy' has increasingly come to be understood to mean experimental-based policy (Sampson, 2010). This view is evident, as the Cabinet Office (the government department that supports the effective development, coordination and implementation of policy) has explicitly promoted the greater use of experiments (Government Social Research Unit, 2007). In reality, the 'policy cycle revolves quicker than the research cycle, with the result that "real time" evaluations often have little influence on policy making' (Pawson, 2002, p 157). So, policymakers with an interest in evidence-based decision-making have turned increasingly to systematic reviews of results of previous relevant analyses to inform future policy (Pawson, 2002).

For the reasons highlighted earlier, experimental evaluation implicitly tends to exclude interventions where the quantitative assessment of outcomes is difficult or impossible. At the least, it will tend to emphasise those interventions where outcomes are more easily measured and more easily monetised. Hence, the choice of intervention may be tailored not so much to the expected return, but to the ease of evaluating the return, which is not quite the same.

Irrespective of whether the evaluation of any criminal justice intervention itself is carried out in a value-neutral framework, the features of its construction are all subject to value judgements: the very choice of intervention studied; the outputs and/or outcomes selected for measurement or as triggers for payment; and the allocated time frames involved (short- or long-term outcomes). Further issues that impact on the supposed objectivity of economic analysis include: the resources made available for the evaluation; the choice of evaluator and evaluation commissioned; the ultimate decision whether to publish the results of the study; and any decision to roll out the intervention before the evaluation is complete. All these decisions are not made in a social vacuum; they are made in a particular political landscape and economic climate, where 'the aims of policy-makers are often limited to satisfying immediate public demands, not to maximising long-term social gains' (Stone et al, 2001, p 5).

The impact of prevailing economic thought on government policy

We have so far considered the impact of economic values on evaluation-specific interventions in criminal justice. At a more fundamental level, it may be that the range of criminal justice interventions that the government considers is informed by the adoption of a particular economic theory of the individual's role in society.

Individual incentive structures

The classical economic approach suggests that all members of society be considered as potential criminals whose self-serving tendencies are held in place only by the fear of detection and punishment (Becker, 1968). This paradigm, as Reiner (2005) notes, leads to an emphasis on individual deterrence, rather than social intervention, in seeking to create disincentives for crime. According to Garland (2001), the impact of this shift in perspective frames human failure in terms of an individual's shortcomings, rather than in terms of the failure of wider society to provide legitimate means for individuals to achieve reasonable aspirations. While previous approaches to crime suggested welfare and assistance as solutions, the acceptance of the market approach focuses systems in criminal justice on tightening controls and enforcing discipline (for more detail, see Garland, 2001, p 15).

Circumscribed role for government

Alongside an emphasis on the individual, classical economics provides a theoretical justification of a reduced role for the state in the provision of public services (McLaughlin et al, 2001). Broadly speaking, this has been realised through the emphasis on market systems and market competition as a lever for supposed efficiency in the provision of public goods and services. In practice, this involves central government: pushing budgetary pressure outwards to local government; setting clear and accountable priorities for public services; and introducing competitive tension into this sector (McLaughlin et al, 2001). Over the longer term, it is envisaged that this will reduce the role of the state in welfare provision and social interventions (McLaughlin et al, 2001). According to Gough (2012, p 20), this 'hollowed out state function in corrections may be conceptualised as merely a "market creator" rather than a service deliverer – or a regulator'.

Policymakers' acceptance of the classical economic discourse has led to a particular set of policy interventions that may be considered viable – those that address individual, rather than social, shortcomings – and the method of delivery of interventions – those that may most easily be 'marketised'. This political and ideological emphasis sets the context that frames the currently growing discourse of evidence-based practice.

The economic case for social justice

Although it has been the case that economic principles have supposedly provided the theoretical basis for interventions targeted at the individual, there is a school of thought that stresses the economic justification for social support as a complement to individual interventions. In the context of criminal justice, one such school is the Justice Reinvestment (JR) movement in the US (Tucker and Cadora, 2003; Cadora, 2007). The core motivating factor of JR arises from the observation that offenders are drawn disproportionally from areas experiencing social exclusion. Symptoms of social exclusion include: high rates of poverty; high rates of unemployment; health inequalities; lack of infrastructure and investment; and lower than average educational attainment.

In their seminal work, Tucker and Cadora (2003) suggest that JR involves establishing programmes to redirect resources that would otherwise be spent on imprisoning offenders into community-based alternatives that tackle the causes of crime on a geographically targeted basis. In this sense, a high level of criminality is not presented as the root cause of a problem that society seeks to address, it is suggested that (a large proportion of) criminality is a symptom of outstanding social needs. In a JR construct, economic analysis is employed to determine where it is most efficient to address the social cause of criminality.

JR is a holistic approach, in that authorities and agencies outside the CJS must play a part in reducing the numbers of those coming into the CJS. The purpose of JR is to manage and allocate criminal justice spending more cost-effectively. At its broadest, the ideology of JR is that reducing crime through robustly evaluated social justice interventions will generate savings that can be 'reinvested' in further evidence-based strategies (for an in-depth discussion and further references, see Fox et al, 2013).

In sum, although the tenets of economics have been said to support individual interventions and marketised services in the criminal justice sector, they could just as easily have been used to justify state provision and social intervention.

Conclusion

The UK government has committed itself to the adoption of evidence-based policy based on economic analysis. We suggest that these form, at best, a selected set of values – positivist (that is to say, supposedly value-neutral), rather than normative – and are informed by an approach to economic policy that emphasises the individual over society. In practice, the chosen subset of economic values informs the theoretical basis of, among other things, the marketisation of social interventions, where the state plays the role of market-maker and procurement agent, rather than provider, of social services. As we cannot appeal to economic values to justify the adoption of economic values, this underlying approach must logically result from a policy decision.

Whatever interventions are considered, however, it is clear that such schemes require robust evaluation. Evaluation requires a definition of 'outcome', which, in the case of current criminal justice policy, amounts to punishment of the guilty, crimes averted and prison places closed. For economic purposes, these outcomes must be monetised (although no attempt has been made to value 'punishing the guilty'). We suggest that government evaluations of crimes averted underestimate societal savings. Similarly, the savings arising from reduced imprisonment may be difficult to realise.

Irrespective of whether the evaluation of any criminal justice intervention itself is carried out in a value-neutral framework, the features of its construction are all subject to value judgements: the very choice of intervention studied (whether individual or social); the outputs and/or outcomes selected for measurement or as triggers for payment; the allocated time frames involved (short- or long-term outcomes); the resources made available for the evaluation; the choice of evaluator and evaluation commissioned; the ultimate decision whether to roll out the intervention – these are all beyond the role of economics to determine. All these decisions are not made in a social vacuum; they are made in a particular political landscape and economic climate.

The appeal to an economic approach is justified if decision-makers will be persuaded by the most accurate or scientifically plausible option. In practice, it has been suggested that 'the aims of policy-makers are often limited to satisfying immediate public demands, not to maximising long-term social gains' (Stone et al, 2001, p 5). These issues indicate that policy may be less evidence-based than we might suppose. In some instances, so-called evidence-based policy may be, rather, a policy seeking an evidence base.

In sum, we suggest that the choice of an economic approach is itself ideologically based. As this chapter has highlighted, the distinction between the morals of economics and the morals and values expressed in the way economics is used must be acknowledged. Criminal justice policy should be informed by, but cannot logically be based on, economic values.

Economics is an indispensable tool, like a carpenter's hammer. Policymakers, however, require a complete tool kit. At the risk of overextending our metaphor, we cannot resist pointing out: to a person with only a hammer, everything looks like a nail.

Note

[1] The page number refers to the online version of Hands (2010). Available at: www.fea.usp.br/feaecon//media/fck/File/P7_Hands_Positive_Normative_ Dichotomy.pdf

References

Albertson, K. and Fox, C. (2012) *Crime and economics: an introduction*, Oxford: Routledge.

Becker, G.S. (1968) 'Crime and punishment: an economic approach', *Journal of Political Economy*, vol 76, pp 169–217.

Cadora, E. (2007) 'Justice Reinvestment in the US', in R. Allen and V. Stern (eds) *Justice Reinvestment – a new approach to crime and justice*, London: International Centre for Prison Studies, King's College.

Cohen, M.A. (2000) 'Measuring the costs and benefits of crime and justice', in Office of Justice Programs, US Dept of Justice (2000) *Measurement and Analysis of Crime and Justice, Criminal Justice 2000, Vol 4*, Washington, DC: US Dept of Justice, pp 263–315.

Cohen, M.A. (2007) 'Valuing crime control benefits using stated preference approaches', paper prepared for a workshop on 'Cost–Benefit Analysis and Crime Control', 20 November, sponsored by the National Institute of Justice, Home Office, Urban Institute Justice Policy Center and Matrix Research and Consultancy.

Cornish, D. and Clarke, R. (eds) (1986) *The reasoning criminal*, New York, NY: Springer-Verlag.

Dhiri, S. and Brand, S. (1999) *Analysis of costs and benefits: guidance for evaluators, crime reduction programme – guidance note 1*, London: Home Office.

Dolan, P. and Peasgood, T. (2007) 'Estimating the economic and social costs of the fear of crime', *The British Journal of Criminology*, vol 47, pp 121–32.

Drummond, M., Sculpher, M., Torrance, G., O'Brien, B. and Stoddart, G. (2005) *Methods for the economic evaluation of health care programmes* (3rd edn), Oxford: Oxford University Press.

Fox, C. and Albertson, A. (2010) 'Could economics solve the prisons crisis?', *The Probation Journal*, vol 57, no 3, pp 263–80.

Fox, C. and Albertson, K. (2011) 'Payment by results and social impact bonds in the criminal justice sector: new challenges for the concept of evidence-based policy?', *Criminology and Criminal Justice*, vol 11, no 5, pp 395–413.

Fox, C., Albertson, K. and Wong, K. (2013) *Justice Reinvestment: can the criminal justice system deliver more for less?*, Oxford: Routledge.

Friedman, M. (1953) 'The methodology of positive economics', in M. Friedman (ed) *Essays in Positive Economics*, Chicago, IL: University of Chicago Press, pp 3–43.

Friedman, M. (1955) 'What all is utility?', *The Economic Journal*, vol 65, pp 405–9.

Garland, D. (2001) *The culture of control: crime and social order in contemporary society*, Oxford: Oxford University Press.

Gewirth, A. (1978) *Reason and morality*, Chicago, IL: University of Chicago Press.

Gladwell, M. (2000) *The tipping point: how little things can make a big difference*, Abacus: Little, Brown Book Group.

Glimcher, P.W. (2003) *Decisions, uncertainty, and the brain: the science of neuroeconomics*, Cambridge, MA: MIT Press.

Gough, D. (2012) '"Revolution": marketisation, the penal system and the voluntary sector', in A. Silvestri (ed) *Critical reflections: social and criminal justice in the first year of Coalition government*, London: Centre for Crime and Justice Studies. Available at: www.crimeandjustice.org. uk/opus1931/Critical_reflections_FULL.pdf

Government Social Research Unit (2007) *Background paper 7 – why do social experiments? Experiments and quasi-experiments for evaluating government policies and programmes*, London: Cabinet Office.

Hands, D.W. (2010) 'The positive–normative dichotomy and economics', in U. Maki (ed) *Philosophy of economics*, Volume 13 of D. Gabbay, P. Thagard, and J. Woods (eds) *Handbook of the philosophy of science*, Amsterdam: Elsevier.

HM Treasury (2010) 'Spending review 2010', The Stationery Office. Available at: http://cdn.hm-treasury.gov.uk/sr2010_completereport. pdf (accessed 3 January 2013).

Home Office (2005) *The economic and social costs of crime against individuals and households 2003/04, Home Office online report 30/05*, London: Home Office.

Kelling, G.L. and Bratton, W.J. (1993) 'Implementing community policing: the administrative problem, perspectives on policing 17', National Institute of Justice, US Department of Justice and the Program in Criminal Justice Policy and Management, John F. Kennedy School of Government, Harvard University.

Keynes, J. (1891) *The scope and method of political economy*, London: MacMillan.

Krauss, S.E. (2005) 'Research paradigms and meaning making: a primer', *The Qualitative Report*, vol 10, no 4, pp 758–70.

La Vigne, N.G., Neusteter, R.S., Lachman, P., Dwyer, A. and Nadeau, C.A., (2010) *Justice Reinvestment at the local level, planning and implementation guide*, Washington: Urban Institute, Justice Policy Center. Available at: www.urban.org/UploadedPDF/412233-Justice-Reinvestment.pdf (accessed 2 November 2012).

Levitt, S.D. and Dubner, S.J. (2005) *Freakonomics: a rogue economist explores the hidden side of everything*, New York, NY: William Morrow/HarperCollins.

McLaughlin, E., Muncie, J. and Hughes, G. (2001) 'The permanent revolution, New Labour, New Public Management and the modernisation of criminal justice', *Criminal Justice*, vol 1, no 3, pp 301–17.

McMahon, C. (1986) 'Gewirth's justification of morality', *Philosophical Studies*, vol 50, no 2, pp 261–81.

Ministry of Justice (2011) *Proven re-offending statistics quarterly bulletin January to December 2009, England and Wales*, London: Ministry of Justice.

Pawson, R. (2002) 'Evidence-based policy: in search of a method', *Evaluation*, vol 8, no 2, pp 157–81.

Reiner, R. (2005) 'Be tough on a crucial cause of crime – neoliberalism', *The Guardian*, 24 November. Available at: www.guardian.co.uk/politics/2005/nov/24/ukcrime.uk (accessed 2 November 2012).

Robbins, L. (1945) *An essay on the nature & significance of economic science* (2nd edn), London: Macmillan.

Robbins, L. (1952 [1935]) *An essay on the nature and significance of economic science* (2nd edn), London: Macmillan and Co.

Sampson, R.J. (2010) 'Gold standard myths: observations on the experimental turn in quantitative criminology', *Journal of Quantitative Criminology*, vol 26, no 4, pp 489–500.

Stone, D., Maxwell, S. and Keating, M. (2001) 'Bridging research and policy', paper for an international workshop funded by DfID at Warwick University, 16–17 July. Available at: www2.warwick.ac.uk/fac/soc/csgr/research/keytopic/other/bridging.pdf (accessed 9 November 2012).

Tucker, S. and Cadora, E. (2003) 'Justice Reinvestment: to invest in public safety by reallocating justice dollars to refinance education, housing, healthcare, and jobs', *Ideas for an Open Society*, 3. Available at: http://www.soros.org/publications/ideas-open-society-justice-reinvestment

Wilson, J.Q. and Kelling, G.L. (1982) 'Broken windows', *The Atlantic Monthly*, (March), pp 29–38.

NINETEEN

Reflections on values and ethics in narrative inquiry with (ex-)offenders

Paula Hamilton and Katherine Albertson

Introduction

This chapter reflects upon value and ethical issues raised by narrative inquiry within criminological research, particularly in its use with vulnerable and marginalised populations, in this case, (ex-)offenders. Drawing upon experiences of undertaking two desistance-focused research projects, we explore the contours of debates around taking 'sides', sympathy, bias and values in narrative inquiry in this area, as well as the ethical issues relating to consent, ownership and interpretive authority raised by its use.

The field of narrative inquiry is complex and diverse. Researchers employ a number of different approaches, strategies and methods, which reflect subtle differences in ontological and epistemological understandings and assumptions about what is being studied (Clandinin, 2007). Notwithstanding, narrative inquiry is based on a number of central propositions: that people ascribe sense and meaning to their experiences and to their lives by grasping them as stories or narratives; that identity or the self is essentially a storied concept; and that people's stories therefore offer insights about their subjective experiences of the world and identities. Common threads in narrative inquiry thus include an interest in people's lived experiences, in the self and representations of the self, and change over time, as well as a desire to empower research participants to contribute to the most salient themes in the area of research (Elliot, 2005).

The fundamental ontological and epistemological differences between traditional 'scientific' research and narrative inquiry are summarised by Bruner (1986). What he terms the 'logical scientific' mode of research centres on the epistemological question of how to know the 'truth' and the search for a universal truth condition, whereas narrative inquiry looks for particular conditions and centres on the broader question of the meaning of experience. His summary highlights how traditional notions of objectivity, validity and supposed truth in research are arguably reframed in narrative inquiry. Such inquiry often explicitly attempts to engage with the researched, to reconstitute the research relationship and to view people's stories not as an accurate representation of the 'truth' of what really happened or as works of fiction, but as accounts of participants' truth in the sense of how they interpret and attach meaning to their experiences and how they construct and reconstruct their identity. As highlighted by Somers (1994), narrative, with its association with the humanities and literary studies, has long been deemed the epistemological 'other' in the social sciences. However, reflecting a move to more interpretivist or constructivist positions, narrative inquiry is becoming a more common approach in a range of disciplines, including the social sciences. However, this work predominantly remains non-narrative, based on quantitative data and informed by positivist assumptions about cause, effect and proof (Pinnegar and Daynes, 2007, p 3).

Criminology (or at least mainstream criminology) has arguably been particularly slow to embrace the narrative approach compared to other social science disciplines. Offenders' accounts of their criminality have been used to shed light upon various aspects of criminality for some time; however, it is argued that the discipline has largely, at least until recently, failed to engage with narrative as an explanatory variable (Presser, 2009). Criminology's apparent reluctance to engage with narrative inquiry may be due in part to the so-called positivist, scientific assumptions on which it is founded (Walklate, 2004) and the enduring commitment to what Garland (2002) terms the Lombrosian and governmental projects that result; namely, the search for (universal) 'causes' of crime and research concerned with the efficient administration of justice.

Understood in these terms, much mainstream or administrative criminological research can be construed as more closely allied with, and reflective of, the views and interests of the government and policymakers (to use Becker's [1967, p 239] terminology, the views of 'superordinate' parties) in criminal justice; those at the 'top' of a hierarchy of credibility, who are regarded as having a more complete picture of 'what is going on' in criminal justice, rather than with the views and experiences of offenders, as offered in their own accounts.

The notion of a hierarchy of credibility (Becker, 1967, p 241) – who has the right to be heard and define 'how things are' in criminal justice – is reflected in the field of what can be broadly termed 'offender change'. Policy and practice in this field, particularly in the last few decades, has been driven by the findings of empirical (largely quantitative) and ostensibly value-neutral research concerned with establishing an evidence base for the effectiveness of various criminal justice interventions or 'programmes' to reduce reoffending; very much a top-down approach.

The desistance research agenda, on the other hand, starts from the bottom up in exploring with (ex-)offenders individual-level accounts of the complex change processes involved in desistance. In this endeavour, many researchers have turned to narrative inquiry as a means of understanding the lives of (ex-)offenders in their biographical and historical context, or, in other words, the 'lived experience' of desistance (Maruna, 2001). It has been argued that a core feature of narrative inquiry, particularly when framed by feminist or critical theory, is that it aims to describe the meaning of experience for those who are frequently marginalised or oppressed (Marshall and Rossman, 2006). So, the use of narrative inquiry in exploring desistance with (ex-)offenders can be seen as an attempt to challenge the hierarchy of credibility within criminal justice and criminal justice policy by giving a voice to those who have been traditionally silenced: 'subordinate' (ex-)offenders.

Nevertheless, it must be acknowledged that potential for exploitation remains in narrative inquiry, although this takes a different shape than in more traditional research approaches. This potential is particularly pertinent in the use of narrative inquiry with vulnerable populations and where respondents' ontological narratives are regarded not simply as a description of 'a world already made' (Elliot, 2005, p 140), but as constitutive of self and identity. Narrative inquiry raises particular ethical issues around consent, 'ownership', confidentiality and interpretive authority, which necessitate a reflexive approach to the ethics of data collection and analysis. The following discussion explores the nature of the ethical issues raised by the use of narrative inquiry in two studies with (ex-)offenders, and explores how the debate about 'taking sides' in criminological research is arguably reframed in such research.

Experience of narrative inquiry with (ex-)offenders

The (ex-)offenders participating in the Desistance Study were identified from a group of 20 men previously involved in an evaluation of a counselling service in custody in 2006. The study took five of the original sample and explored their transition from criminal activity to desistance, focusing on respondents' understandings and interpretations of the factors and experiences related to their own 'journey'. Specifically, the study sought to examine the relationship between their desistance and services designed to support their routes to desistance. The work was funded by a local Safer Neighbourhood Partnership Group, who wished to gauge the impact of the original counselling service years after offenders had engaged, and to identify, from a user perspective, which local support services had provided the most effective support for their desistance.

The Probationers' Stories of Desistance (PSD) doctoral research aimed to build upon the findings from previous qualitative research to further explore and understand the psychosocial aspects of the desistance process and to explore within this the meaning of contemporary rehabilitative efforts (primarily probation supervision) to desisters. A series of three narrative interviews was conducted with each of a cohort of eight participants recruited via a probation service in the north-west of England. The study focused exclusively on male offenders (based on emerging research findings suggesting that the process of desistance for women and for men may be significantly different) and on those with histories of 'conventional' offences (based on the premise that sexual and domestic abuse offences have particular antecedents and therefore possibly particular pathways to desistance).

The empirical materials that researchers study can take a variety of forms and can be gathered using a variety of methods, reflecting the diverse field of narrative inquiry (Chase, 2008). However, the narrative interview used in both these studies is a common method employed by researchers in the field. It is argued that even in loosely structured, flexible, qualitative interviewing, it is the researcher who 'sets the agenda' and who remains in control of the information produced through the selection of the thematic areas and issues to be explored, and through the ordering and wording of questions (Hollway and Jefferson, 2000, p 96). In narrative interviewing, in contrast, narrative responsibility shifts to the interviewee. In telling the story about his or her subjective experiences, the interviewee determines the terms of reference and focus of the research. It is thus argued that narrative interviewing enables researchers to 'tap into' the subjective experiences and meaning frames of respondents and so to gain a better understanding of the perspective and 'life world' of their research subjects, particularly, in these cases, of their desistance 'journeys'.

Although both studies employed narrative interviewing, the approaches to the interviews and the form of narratives sought were quite different. In the Desistance Study, a life history approach (McAdams, 1997) was adopted. Participants were encouraged to think about their life as a series of book chapters. Participants were asked to identify what they saw as significant events and relationships in each 'chapter' of their life, and to focus on the events, relationships and services (if any) impacting on their desistance 'journey'. While attempting to ensure that participants retained control of the narrative telling of their lives, it was recognised that the temporal constraints of a single two-hour interview needed some degree of guidance from the researcher. In this way, the pragmatic, real-world constraints of the research project necessitated much more structure than many narrative approaches.

The PSD study was much less time-constrained. Fieldwork involving three interviews took place over a three-month period. There were fewer restrictions on the time taken over each interview. This allowed the researcher to adopt a much more 'free-flowing' approach, where participants were asked simply to tell their story of their involvement in, and later desistance from, crime.

The two studies also took different approaches to analysing the narratives. The Desistance Study conducted a content and thematic analysis across the five life stories and presented them to illustrate the contexts and events that participants saw as having had the most significant impact on their entry to offending and their later desistance. Within these stories, similarities were identified in terms of initial disruptions in formative relationships, attribution and redemption scripts, and transformative experiences (Maruna, 2001). In the PSD study, ongoing analysis focused on the *holistic* content of the entire narratives and also on the form or structure of the narratives; the ways in which desisters told their stories.

Despite notable differences between the two studies in their governance, focus and methodological approach, both shared a commitment to using narrative inquiry as a way of giving a voice to (ex-)offenders and their subjective experiences of desistance, in terms of defining 'how things are' and in influencing the future direction of desistance-supportive policy.

Through the narrative approaches used in these studies, it could be argued that both pieces of work sought to promote the world view of 'subordinates' in Becker's 'hierarchy of credibility' (Becker, 1967, p 240). In these cases, making judgements on the individual interviewee's story was not considered the research task, rather the task was 'about respect, empathy and exploring the interviewees' world from their perspective' (Liebling, 2001, p 473). It was to understand someone else's world, not only to 'generate intellectual insight' (Liebling, 2001, p 478), but also to ensure that these traditionally silent voices were heard and captured in order to inform policy and funding priorities. In this way, the experiences of the very people who have been through the system can have an impact in the political arena, and assist in the development of practical provision (see Rumgay, 2004; Bird and Albertson, 2011). Within this framework, narrative interviewing was used in both studies not only as a way to explore respondents' subjective lived experiences, but also as a way of helping redress some of the power differentials inherent in the research enterprise, including research interviews. Narrative inquiry centres on notions of a reconstituted research relationship in that shifting narrative responsibility to respondents and allowing them to structure the interview and determine its focus offers a 'space for less dominating and more relational modes that reflect and respect participants' ways of organising meaning in their lives' (Reissman, 2002, p 332).

Informed consent

A core ethical principle of any social science research is gaining participants' genuinely informed consent to participate. We were both concerned about the extent to which individuals with extensive experience of mandatory engagement in criminal justice system activities would feel able to freely consent, and whether they would decline to participate. We therefore took particular pains to explain to interviewees that taking part in the research was entirely voluntary and that their participation would in no way affect any future contact with the criminal justice system. In both studies, some individuals declined to take part, which, although disappointing, provided some reassurance. However, this also led to another consent-related issue associated with the violation of role expectations and expectations of an interview situation involved in narrative interviewing (Flick, 2002). In other words, using narrative interviewing as opposed to the traditional question-and-answer interview format raised questions for us about how far potential participants were able to give consent to something of which they had no experience. In order to address this, efforts were made to communicate the nature and purpose of narrative interviewing in some detail during the initial 'recruitment' stages. The PSD study communicated these details during the first of the three interview series and periodically revisited consent issues, while the Desistance Study relied on an initial letter and telephone conversation to provide an overview of what to expect.

Confidentiality and anonymity

The use of narrative inquiry also raised difficult issues around the core ethical principles of confidentiality and anonymity. In narrative inquiry, there is often a focus on the individual and on the close study of lives and experience, and a commitment to understanding and representing individuals' stories as holistically as possible, often through the provision of life histories. This was certainly the case in the PSD study, and, as Elliot (2005, p 142) notes, 'once a combination of attributes and experiences is ascribed to a particular case in a research report it can be very difficult to ensure that the case does not become recognizable'. As scholars in the field of narrative inquiry attest, there is no easy way to resolve these issues (Lieblich et al, 1998; Elliot, 2005). In the PSD study, participants were assured that every possible effort would be made to protect their anonymity, but were explicitly made aware of the potential risks once the research was written up. It was also agreed with participants that the researcher would seek their explicit approval if their story was going to be presented in a case study format in print. These issues were less pertinent for the Desistance Study as participants were informed that their stories were to be presented in an abridged format that would be arrived at as the researcher looked for themes across the five interviews. This approach to analysis and report presentation reduced the likelihood of vicarious identification.

Interpretive authority

Traditional research often regards participants as repositories of data and information that they consent to give away to the researcher. In contrast, the narrative approach used here views people's narratives as vehicles for active and ongoing identity work. The ethical issues about ownership of participants' narratives and interpretive authority are not easily resolved and we both struggled with these issues. As a consequence, we felt that it was important to be as open and transparent as possible with (potential) participants at the early 'recruitment' stages, making it clear that their stories would not simply be repeated, but would be interpreted and analysed, guided by the theoretical concerns of the study.

Despite this, difficulties arose when beginning preparation for writing up findings. We both experienced some level of discomfort about layering our interpretations and analysis onto participants' personal narratives. One way we sought to minimise this discomfort was to check out emerging interpretations with participants. This member-checking is regarded as good ethical practice and as an important validation strategy in qualitative research, but this is less straightforward in narrative research, where participants may feel resistant to, or resentful about, their stories being (re)interpreted by the researcher. For instance, Chase (1996) cites a number of examples where sharing work in progress and interpretations of narratives elicited angry and critical responses from participants. Chase goes on to explain how she reconciled her commitment to feminist methodological principles and her decision not to share her interpretations with her participants based on the idea of interpretive authority. In other words, she felt that there was a distinction between what she would wish to communicate through her interpretations of what was said and what her participants wanted to communicate through narration of their experiences. This approach to interpretive authority was, to some extent, adopted in these studies, although we both felt that it was ethically important to check out at least our emerging interpretations with participants. Despite some initial concerns, this turned out to be a wholly positive experience, with participants broadly agreeing with interpretations in a process that often prompted further fruitful and insightful collaborative exchanges. Furthermore, we both found that participants appeared to value and welcome the opportunity to collaborate and share in this process.

Ethics and values issues in situ

Conducting narrative, as opposed to more traditional forms of research interviews, also necessitates a certain set of skills. Some authors in the field have suggested that interviewees are likely to spontaneously offer narratives about their experience given a suitably narratised question, and that the structure of the interview itself and/or the questioning style of the interviewer do not serve to suppress such stories (Mishler, 1986; Reissman, 1990). Other scholars have suggested that some interviewees from vulnerable or marginalised populations may be less able to give narrative accounts of their lives and experiences. This was reflected in both of these studies; some participants were readily able to give lengthy and comprehensive narrative accounts, whereas others were far more reticent.

In more traditional interview interactions, any interruption in the flow of the interview would be treated as a time for the researcher to ask further probing or prompting questions. In the narrative interview situation, however, we found that we had to keep additional questioning to a minimum in an effort not to take control of the interview interaction and further suppress narratives. Being comfortable with periods of silence was often followed by a more spontaneous narrative. It has been widely noted that successful narrative interviewing necessitates good listening skills and efforts to signal empathy, for example, through the use of encouraging body language and phrases, and that it is important not to interrupt participants' narratives. Not interrupting was something that we both rather struggled with. In the PSD study, the researcher was an ex-probation officer and it took a conscious effort to resist the temptation to interrupt to reframe what participants were saying more positively, to motivate them and to offer advice.

Dealing with emotion

In telling life stories that may be troubled and harrowing, participants often became emotional and sometimes this resulted in tears and expressions of anger. During our research, we both became acutely conscious of how much we were asking of participants in terms of telling these stories to us, essentially, to strangers. Perhaps rather naively, we did not at first expect this level of emotional response based on the premise that (ex-)offenders would be used to discussing their backgrounds and experiences with a range of professional 'strangers', such as probation officers and prison psychologists. However, what became apparent was that by asking (ex-)offenders to tell their own stories, as opposed to answering questions, this involved them actively making sense of their own experiences and doing the 'identity work' *in* the interview encounter, and that this was a significantly different experience to what they were used to. Some participants reflected openly that their narrative interview was a much different and far more emotionally demanding experience than anything they had encountered before. Lieblich et al (1998, p 177, cited in Elliot, 2005, p 137) describe an experience of narrative interviewing with members of a kibbutz as similar to 'opening a Pandora's box' of painful accounts of past experiences and how she was 'tormented' by the idea of opening old wounds and leaving them in pain. Similarly, our experiences raised concerns for us about whether we were in danger of causing emotional or psychological harm. On reflection, however, we recognised that in being asked to tell their stories, participants had some control and choice over what they talked about and could therefore 'protect' themselves to some extent. However, committed to minimising emotional or psychological harm, we sought to address these concerns in our research design. The interview composition in both studies therefore included a debrief section that afforded participants an opportunity to 're-acclimatise'. Participants were also provided with contact details of local support services that they could access post-interview.

Conversely, by affording participants time and a safe space to talk about troubling or upsetting experiences and events in their lives, narrative interviewing may also be therapeutic or reassuring (Elliot, 2005, p 137). This was borne out in both studies. Some participants reflected that although they had found the research very emotionally demanding, they had also found it beneficial in terms of affording them new insights and increased motivation to sustain the changes that they had made in their lives. Narrative interviewing can therefore be described as somewhat akin to a therapeutic encounter, which means that it is even more important that the researcher is experienced enough to manage the interaction and ensure that any negative effects are minimised. We both found that we often needed to draw on basic counselling skills that we had developed, either through many years of qualitative interviewing or through previous professional experience, such as the appropriate use of empathy and unconditional positive regard.

Discussion

These observations, however, bring us back to Becker's (1967) question about researchers' sympathy undermining professional integrity, and to Liebling's (2001, p 473) question: 'Can we simply sympathise with everyone?' Our answers would be 'Yes, possibly' to Becker and 'No' to Liebling, but not for the reasons one might imagine. Providing genuine rapport with an individual in terms of the 'suspension of value judgements ... openness, warmth and devotion to the task' (Liebling, 2001, p 474) is the research task. However, in working so closely with individuals, there is always the risk that the feelings of intimacy that this type of interviewing can create could easily be confused in this research situation – potentially by researcher and subject alike. It is the researcher's responsibility to manage these expectations carefully, both for themselves and the safety and well-being of the respondent. For a researcher, this is where the distinction between unconditional empathy must not be confused with unconditional sympathy. The distinction needs to be clearly made, because if we wholeheartedly sympathise, we are in danger of emotional eclipse as researchers, as we unreservedly not only enter, but also accept, another person's world view as our own: 'The attempt to empathise with research subjects is not equivalent to sympathising; to empathise means that the researcher understands the nature of the belief system, while to sympathise conveys acceptance of the ideology' (Jipson and Litten, 2000, pp 154–5).

We are not trying to say that showing signs of sympathy may be inappropriate in the interview situation, but expecting to be able to genuinely sympathise with everyone has both patronising and potentially collusive connotations. Using narrative methodologies demonstrates a commitment to reconstituting the traditional power relations in research in terms of reducing them as much as possible, but we cannot pretend that they no longer exist. Indeed, with regard to the research participants, one wonders what side they saw us, the researchers, as being on. Wherever positioned on the hierarchy of credibility, however, individuals post-interview related their enjoyment of the opportunity to simply 'participate in the account' and reported that they felt that their accounts had been or would be 'treated kindly' (Liebling, 2001, p 476). Narrative interviewing involves a large investment of emotional work on the behalf of the researcher. While accepting that building rapport and suspending value judgements is appropriate, researchers must develop genuine empathy with those they interview. Genuine empathy, not sympathy, is the armour against falling into such a deep sympathy 'with the people we are studying' (Becker, 1967, p 239) that we begin to engage in the right/wronged morality paradigm that Becker goes on to cite as demanded by the hierarchy of credibility (Becker, 1967, pp 239–40).

Conclusion

This chapter has drawn on two different narrative studies to illustrate the continuing challenges around the contours of the debate about taking sides, sympathy and values in criminological research. As this approach gains in popularity in criminology, particularly with the growth in interest in the desistence agenda, we have illustrated that, in terms of issues of subjectivity, bias, validity and truth, the narrative inquiry approach may offer an opportunity to reframe the debate. We argue that narrative inquiry, with its explicit commitment to exploring participants' subjective experiences and identities – their 'truth' – inherently and unapologetically involves 'taking the side' of those we research in the sense of entering and seeking to better understand their world view or perspective. Indeed, the same can be said of adopting narrative approaches with superordinate groups, for example, Czarniawska's (1998) work around a narrative approach to organisational studies.

Becker's article alerted researchers to the dangers of 'doing' research to serve a political cause and of the accusations of conducting partisan and 'underdog' sociology that may follow. Again, we argue that this issue is reframed in narrative inquiry, where, particularly when framed by feminist and/or critical theory, there is a clear value position in terms of the aim to give a voice to those who are frequently oppressed or marginalised – the 'subordinates' whose voices are seldom heard. In terms of understanding desistance, we would argue that it is imperative that these voices are heard if we are to better understand the complex processes involved in desistance and so develop informed criminal justice policies and practices that can sensitively and meaningfully facilitate and support people in their efforts to change.

References

Becker, H.S. (1967) 'Whose side are we on?', *Social Problems*, vol 14, pp 329–47.

Bird, H. and Albertson, K.E. (2011) 'Prisoners as citizens, Big Society and the rehabilitation revolution: truly revolutionary?', *British Journal of Community Justice*, vol 9, nos 1/2, pp 93–109.

Bruner, J. (1986) *Actual minds, possible worlds*, Cambridge, MA: Harvard University Press.

Chase, S.E. (1996) 'Personal vulnerability and interpretive authority in narrative research', in R. Josselson (ed) *Ethics and process in the narrative study of lives* (vol 4), London: Sage.

Chase, S.E. (2008) 'Narrative inquiry. Multiple lenses, approaches, voices', in N.K. Denzin and Y.S. Lincoln (eds) *Collecting and interpreting qualitative materials*, Thousand Oaks, CA: Sage.

Clandinin, D.J. (2007) *Handbook of narrative inquiry: mapping a methodology*, Thousand Oaks, CA: Sage.

Czarniawska, B. (1998) *A narrative approach to organization studies*, A Sage University Paper, Qualitative Research Methods Series 43, Thousand Oaks, CA: Sage.

Elliot, J. (2005) *Using narrative in social research: qualitative and quantitative approaches*, London: Sage.

Flick, U. (2002) *An introduction to qualitative research* (2nd edn), London: Sage.

Garland, D. (2002) 'Of crimes and criminals: the development of criminology in Britain', in M. Maguire, R. Morgan and R. Reiner (eds) *The Oxford Handbook of Criminology* (2nd edn), Oxford: Oxford University Press.

Hollway, W. and Jefferson, T. (2000) *Doing qualitative research differently: free association, narrative and the interview method*, London: Sage.

Jipson, A.J. and Litten, C.E. (2000) 'Body, career and community', in G. Lee-Treweek and S. Linkogle (eds) *Danger in the field: risk and ethics in social research*, London: Routledge.

Liebling, A. (2001) 'Whose side are we on? Theory, practice and allegiances in prisons research', *British Journal of Criminology*, vol 41, pp 472–84.

Lieblich, A., Tuval-Mashiach, R. and Zilber, T. (1998) *Narrative research: reading, analysis and interpretation*, Thousand Oaks, CA: Sage.

Marshall, C. and Rossman, G.B. (2006) *Designing qualitative research* (4th edn), Thousand Oaks, CA: Sage.

Maruna, S. (2001) *Making good. How ex-convicts reform and rebuild their lives*, Washington, DC: American Psychological Association.

McAdams, D. (1997) *The stories we live by: personal myths and the making of the self*, New York, NY: The Guilford Press.

Mishler, E.G. (1986) *Research interviewing: context and narrative*, Cambridge, MA: Harvard University Press.

Pinnegar, S. and Daynes, J.G. (2007) 'Locating narrative inquiry historically: thematics in the turn to narrative', in D.J. Clandinin (ed) *Handbook of narrative inquiry: mapping a methodology*, Thousand Oaks, CA: Sage.

Presser, L. (2009) 'The narratives of offenders', *Theoretical Criminology*, vol 13, pp 177–200.

Reissman, C.K. (1990) 'Strategic uses of narrative in presentation of self and illness: a research note', *Social Sciences and Medicine*, vol 30, no 11, pp 1195–200.

Reissman, C.K. (2002) 'Analysis of personal narratives', in J.G. Gubrium and J.A. Holstein (eds) *Handbook of interview research*, Thousand Oaks, CA: Sage.

Rumgay, J. (2004) 'Scripts for safer survival: pathways out of female crime', *The Howard Journal*, vol 43, no 4, pp 405–19.

Somers, M.R. (1994) 'The narrative construction of identity: a relational and network approach', *Theory and Society*, vol 22, pp 605–49.

Walklate, S. (2004) *Gender, crime and criminal justice* (2nd edn), Cullompton: Willan.

TWENTY

Working with different values: extremism, hate and sex crimes

Malcolm Cowburn, Marian Duggan and Ed Pollock

Introduction

This chapter addresses dilemmas and conflicts in research with people who hold different opinions and values to the researcher. The chapter draws on three research experiences: a female researcher directly and indirectly interacting with members of a recognised group targeted for identity-based victimisation who do not necessarily identify as 'victims'; a male researcher indirectly interacting with people of undisclosed or 'virtual' identities demonstrating extremist ideologies; and a male researcher directly interacting with convicted male sexual offenders. There is a tension in each case between researcher standpoint (interpretive framework) and research participant standpoint. In each case, the viewpoint of the research participant presents problems for the researcher in acknowledging 'whose side' she or he is on, while also retaining a commitment to listen to and present data from participants in a way that respects their own 'truth'.

Qualitative research with marginalised people can allow the expression of 'difficult' or sensitive issues; on occasions, this is problematic. According to the epistemological standpoint of the researcher, the purpose of empirical investigation may be to obtain the objective 'truth' about particular events or it may be to understand how researchers and research participants co-construct and interpret their stories (Franklin, 1997). Data from qualitative research may be construed as more or less accurately representing the experiences under examination, or as a current narrative *of value in itself* (Miller, 2000). Whatever standpoint is taken, presentation of data involves choices and is inevitably some form of *interpretation*. However, choices about presentation are not value-free.

'Values' is a problematic concept; Banks (2006, p 6) offers this working definition: '"values" can be regarded as particular types of belief that people hold about what is regarded worthy or valuable'. This brings together issues of both ethics and epistemology – 'good' conduct and 'good' knowledge underpin the values that orientate a researcher to her/his research task (of course, issues of what is 'good' in either case may be contested). 'Values', however, often initiate and drive qualitative research; in this chapter, feminist values influence the shape and conduct of the homophobia and sex offenders studies, and anti-racist values underpin the internet study. Moreover, all of the studies share values that consider interpersonal violence and the threat of interpersonal violence to be morally wrong.

The chapter outlines the three areas of research. In each case, issues relating to *preparation* and the *process* of research are explored. Preparation addresses issues that need consideration prior to starting empirical work. Process considers the management of the dynamics of the empirical activity. The final section of the chapter considers issues of interpretation and dissemination; it considers the challenge of giving voice (in publications and presentations) to 'difficult' attitudes and experiences. This sharply brings into focus, again, the issue of taking sides in research.

Researching homophobia in Northern Ireland (Marian Duggan)

This section considers research into homophobia in Northern Ireland, particularly during the 30 years of violent ethno-political conflict known as the 'Troubles' (1968–98) (see McKittrick and McVea, 2001). Using a feminist-inspired grounded theory approach, 24 lesbians and gay men shared their stories of growing up gay during the conflict (Duggan, 2012). The analysis illustrates the value-based tensions involved in discovering and presenting how lesbians and gay men interpret their experiences of homophobia without enhancing their feelings of victimisation.

The premise driving the research was that the life stories would unwittingly provide evidence of the ways in which biblical, moral, legal, social and political discourses construct ideologies of homosexuality as negative, harmful and dangerous. However, there was a presumption that these experiences, at the time, may have been minimised or normalised by the participants and those around them in line with the wider culture of anti-homosexual sentiments. Yet, as a result of significant socio-legal changes, it was envisaged that these stories may have been reconceptualised in the intervening period as evidence of discriminatory experiences (aided by awareness of legal, social and political advancements in sexual minority rights). Thus, a specific approach was taken that gave weight to the reassessment of previously unremarkable experiences as 'evidence' of naturalised, or hegemonised, socio-political homophobia. In effect, this was taking an anti-homophobic 'side' in conducting the research. However, Becker's (1967) suggestion that researchers take 'sides' is particularly complex in Northern Ireland, where there are continual attempts to 'place' people in relation to identity and affiliation: republican–loyalist; nationalist–unionist; catholic–protestant (Mitchell, 2006). However, in relation to these specific 'sides', the researcher is not from Northern Ireland and therefore issues of allegiance did not arise.

Preparation

The qualitative methodology employed was underpinned by a poststructuralist feminist approach to research (Weedon, 1987). Poststructuralism involves questioning, dismantling and problematising socially constructed identities (Shütz, 1962). Feminist research eschews claims to neutrality and objectivity, favouring instead a research paradigm that exposes and explores gendered power relationships (Roberts, 1981; Maynard and Purvis, 1994). Amalgamating these two approaches allows the researcher to question the social and power relations involved in research design, conduct and outcomes (Reinharz, 1992).

Feminist research situates the researcher in her study in order to account for the relationship between the researcher and the researched, and how this affects the findings (Alcoff and Gray, 1993; Reay, 1996). The underlying reasons for such considerations are transparency and reflexivity in critical social research (Harvey, 1990; Stanley and Wise, 1990). These issues are all important for the present research given that the interviewees involved were describing personal experiences that, at times, may have been particularly difficult to discuss, especially with a stranger. Therefore, the poststructuralist feminist insistence on the primacy of interviewees' interpretations of their experiences was particularly relevant to the analysis.

In identifying people to interview, it was important not to appear to be seeking 'victims' of 'homophobia' or hate crime. This was too limiting in a society where many homophobic responses were (and, in some cases, still are; see Duggan, 2010, 2012) normalised as hegemonic responses to expressions of sexual difference. Instead, men and women were recruited who had been aware of their sexual orientation for a significant amount of time and who were able to illustrate how living in a society openly opposed to homosexuality during a specific time period had impacted on them. Potential participants were made aware of this requirement so that they were able to provide life histories that illustrated the impact of their sexual orientation on the shape of their lives, and how homophobia was informed and sustained in Northern Ireland during the period of the 'Troubles'.

However, it was also important to ensure that the sample was balanced by gender and faith in order to reduce inferences of (political) bias. In giving voice to this group of people, it was important to ensure that research participants were not characterised as speaking *for* their particular demographic (ie Catholic lesbians or Protestant gay men), but as speaking *from* that specific background in theorising their own experiences.

Feminist, sensitive and ethical research methodologies strive to ensure that those involved in the research process do not come to harm as a result of their participation (Lee, 1993). Efforts were taken to ensure that informed consent, anonymity and confidentiality processes were explained, understood and adhered to. However, Northern Ireland is a small society with a population of fewer than 2 million people and only two major cities. The interpersonal nature of traditionally close-knit communities is still the norm in Northern Ireland. While this came up as an issue in many interviewees' stories as constraining what they could do, with whom and where, it also proved problematic in ensuring anonymity among participants. The snowball sampling method adopted meant that many participants knew of others involved in the research. Some participants had advertised it among their social networks, so were aware of potential or actual interviewees in the research process. Furthermore, at times, references were made to other interviewees, as they had been involved in pivotal events (particularly concerning the campaign for decriminalisation of homosexuality). Interviewees often recommended their partners as potential participants and, in one case, a couple requested to be interviewed in a joint session as they had spent three decades of their lives together so many of their experiences were shared.

Process

Process issues in this project are primarily concerned with avoiding causing harm to the research participants. The potential tension between the researcher's standpoint in relation to homophobia and participants' need to tell a story with which they were happy was constantly managed during the interviews. Key to this were the efforts taken with the language used and awareness of, and sensitivity to, power dynamics within the research process, where measures were taken to respect those power dynamics and not infer a victimised identity where it was not acknowledged.

Allowing research participants to determine what stories they wish to tell (within the remit of the brief they had been given regarding the nature and purpose of the research being undertaken) shifts the power relationship in their favour during the data-collection process. Some direction was given regarding specific moments that may have demonstrated similarities in terms of importance for participants (the 'coming out' process, meeting a partner, moving in with a partner, negotiating childcare, etc), but the overall narrative was decided by the person him- or herself. Recollections of key definitive moments in their life histories where they were made uncomfortably aware of the non-conformity of their sexual orientation were used as the basis for determining how, when, where and by whom homophobia was demonstrated and used as a tool of oppression in people's lives.

However, exploring uncomfortable experiences brought with it potential for repeat victimisation of those sharing their experiences through recalling them within a framework of identifying pejorative attitudes. For example, one interviewee recalled how he struggled with whether or not to continue teaching music to children in his neighbourhood once he realised what his sexual orientation 'meant' to those around him (at the time, homosexuality and paedophilia were incorrectly linked). He had to make a decision then as to whether other elements of his life (not having a female partner, appearing – in his words – 'quite effeminate'), coupled with his close proximity to children and teaching of a 'softer' subject such as music, would enhance his exposure to victimisation. Thus, his 'choices' were founded on self-preservation but determined by the wider social culture around him. In recalling this, he had to relive the negative emotions he went through at the time.

Qualitative (observation) research with Far Right racists (Ed Pollock)

This section concerns ethical dilemmas and values in conducting observation research of racist hate speech in internet newsgroups. Newsgroups, one of the oldest components of the internet, are open discussion areas that allow like-minded individuals to discuss topics of shared interest. Newsgroups are provided by Internet Service Providers (ISPs) via news servers, which contain a list of every newsgroup that a given ISP offers. Messages sent to newsgroups are termed 'posts' and are listed for anyone who enters the newsgroup to read. When a 'post' is clicked upon and 'opened', it is downloaded from the news server to be read in the same way as an email. Members can then reply to any message in the same way as they would reply to an email, knowing that all newsgroup subscribers may read it. However, it is relatively easy to conceal a contributor's identity and it is very difficult to control the content of material posted to newsgroups. Consequently, some newsgroups have become a means for generating and disseminating material that some people find harmful, offensive or obscene (Mann and Sutton, 1998). The present study concerns such newsgroups.

This discussion draws on a study of three Internet newsgroups where contributors posted racist messages and disseminated racist hate speech. The suggestion here is that the nature of the research renders irrelevant or unnecessary many of the ethical and emotional dilemmas associated with traditional qualitative research.

Although observation, as a research method, has been employed to examine the behaviour of individuals or groups in a variety of social settings (see, eg, Ditton, 1977; Humphreys, 1970; Parker, 1974), Covert, Invisible, Non-Participatory Observation (CIN-PO) is a qualitative research method that can be used to observe subjects in any 'virtual' setting (ie a setting where a researcher has no physical presence at the scene they are observing), such as newsgroups, chat rooms and web forums. The method is *Covert* because the researcher does not disclose his or her role to the researched, *Invisible* because the researcher is not in the same space or social setting as the researched and so is not visible to them and *Non-Participatory* because the researcher does not engage in any activity, such as 'posting' messages to the newsgroups, or conversation with the research subjects. In research where CIN-PO is used, the researched are not aware that they are being studied, this enables research on groups or individuals who are usually hard to reach or who, typically, may not allow 'outsiders' to infiltrate their social world.

Preparation

Key issues in preparing for qualitative research are informed consent, confidentiality and the minimisation of harm. Traditionally, the management of these issues has to be resolved before identifying and recruiting participants takes place. However, the British Society for Criminology (BSC) notes that in all but *exceptional circumstances*, researchers must gain the freely given informed consent of their research participants (British Society of Criminology, 2006). In

CIN-PO research, this is not possible. However, the BSC guidelines state that *exceptional circumstances* relate to the importance of the topic rather than the difficulty of gaining access to participants. Despite the ethical challenges posed by the research methodology, the research was considered to be necessary for the purpose of academic advancement and the contribution to knowledge of a previously largely under-researched social world (Pollock, 2010). The University Research Ethics Committee thus approved it.

In relation to confidentiality, newsgroups are publicly accessible and, as such, their conversations are already in the public domain. Issues of confidentiality and anonymity are, therefore, not relevant. All newsgroup participants are aware that they should not post messages that they would not like another member of the public to see and that anything posted to the newsgroup can be viewed by anybody else at any time throughout the period it is posted online.

The selection of the newsgroups was, therefore, based solely on demographic rather than ethical issues. The aim of selecting newsgroups to study was not to identify specific research *participants* as the source of data, but to choose *settings* (ie newsgroups) that could be observed over a long period of time in order to collect the required data. The *settings* (ie newsgroups) were chosen according to the number of contributors and the number of messages. However, additionally, in order to collect rich and useful data, the selected newsgroups needed to be 'actively racist'. Three newsgroups were chosen: two hosted hate speech towards a variety of racial and ethnic groups and the third was largely an advertising forum for racist merchandise, such as racist podcasts broadcast on racist websites, subscriptions to racist magazines, meetings of hate groups like the British National Party or National Front, clothing endorsing particular racist ideologies (eg links to Nazism), racist computer games and racist literature.

In considering potential harms, the impact on the researcher of undertaking this type of research must also be considered. The researcher who conducted the research was a white, heterosexual, male without religious affiliation and so was, to some extent, detached from the personal emotional effect of the racist language disseminated in the newsgroups. However, the newsgroups also attracted those who appeared to have been targets of racist victimisation (emotionally and physically) and contributed to the newsgroup in order to attempt to reproach disseminators of hate speech and to also convey their experiences of abuse. So, although the researcher appeared, at first, to be detached from the impact of the discourse, he found that he was not necessarily unaffected by the impact upon him of the lived experiences of the victims. Nonetheless, the virtual world of the internet allows for the creation of a physical distance between those who use it, which does enable the researcher to be sheltered somewhat from the emotional impact of what he was reading.

Process

The focus of the research is upon the organisation, structure and social dynamics of the newsgroups. The research process involves the collection and storage of data. Collecting data from newsgroups allows for the collection of very rich and unsanitised data because it is written directly by the research participants themselves.

Researching those who hold or engage in racially obscene, offensive or indecent views or behaviour is often difficult, largely because of the possible emotional impact upon the researcher. However, a CIN-PO methodology can reduce this emotional impact as the internet provides spatial and physical distance between the researcher and the researched. Being in a dialogue with someone expressing hate is very different to seeing his or her words as script. So, if one reads a *transcript* of an *interview* with a contributor to a racist chat room, then it is possible that the impact on the reader would be similar to if they were to read material written directly into that chat room by a contributor. Hence, the emotional impact is not only dependent upon the *content* of what is heard or observed from respondents, but also the *process* by which the data is collected and transcribed. Similarly, the spatial and physical distance between the researcher and participant significantly reduced the need for consideration of the safety of both parties during the data-collection stage of the research process. As a complete observer (and not contributor), there was no risk of any respondents detecting that the researcher was observing the groups or determining the location of the researcher.

Preparing transcripts for publication of findings is easy because there is no need for the researcher to transcribe the data as the messages posted to the newsgroup by the newsgroup contributors represent the data transcripts (once the newsgroup data is saved electronically or printed and stored). Additionally, newsgroup data can be saved directly from source, so, once recalled, its accuracy is relatively unquestionable and can be checked or confirmed by simply finding the appropriate conversation within the specific newsgroup again (Pollock, 2010). Therefore, there is little doubt that everything seen by the researcher is authentic in respect of the accuracy of the data collected.

Qualitative research with male sex offenders (Malcolm Cowburn)

Qualitative research with sex offenders requires researchers to *engage* with men who have seriously harmed others. The researcher may be required to listen to accounts that may cause horror, anger and distress. Research participants may express attitudes and values that the researcher finds difficult to hear or to leave unchallenged. Moreover, the research participant may become unguarded in what he discloses or he may become very distressed as he looks back on the events of his life. These challenges are considered in this section of the chapter.

Preparation

Preparation for research with sex offenders involves consideration of the physical, psychological and emotional safety of the research participant, the researcher and significant identified other people. This involves thinking, in advance, about how the following issues will be dealt with:

- the nature of the offences;
- the manner in which the offender attributes responsibility and recognises harm in relation to their offences;
- the disclosure of unreported offending by the research participant or other identified people;
- the intention to harm self or other people;
- the distress of research participants;
- the way in which the sex offender behaves towards the interviewer;
- the (cumulative) impact of hearing accounts of harms and distress (both experienced by and inflicted by the offender) on the researcher; and
- the nature of support available to the researcher.

In relation to the offences, the researcher may be able to discover some details about the criminal convictions and the victims (age, relationship to offender) before the interview; this will help to prepare for hearing fuller details.

The manner in which the research participant talks about his offences may present some difficulties. Dependent on how the researcher *understands* sex offending, he or she may need to reflect on how he or she will deal with hearing repeated denials of responsibility and harm.

Disclosure of unreported offending or the intention to harm self or identified others is primarily managed through the nature of confidentiality that is offered to research participants. Complete confidentiality, potentially, leaves a variety of individuals at risk of harm, as such, ethically, this is not an option (see Cowburn, 2005). Key to managing these issues is the preparation of a clear 'participant information sheet' that outlines the boundaries of confidentiality and identifies actions that will be taken in response to disclosure of unreported offending or expressed intentions to harm self or others.

Managing how a research participant behaves during an interview, including becoming distressed, requires preparation and planning. In relation to distress, before consent is given, the researcher can identify with the research participant sources of support that he or the researcher may contact if he becomes distressed. These should then be named within the consent form. Additionally, if the research is occurring in an institution (eg a prison or a hospital), the researcher needs to acknowledge, again on the consent form, that specific identified people (agreed with the research participant) within the establishment will be informed should the research participant become distressed. In relation to managing the distressed research participant, Cowburn (2010) highlights the importance of reflecting on how the epistemological underpinnings of the research approach may facilitate or inhibit a caring response.

Other behaviours that may occur in an interview that need to be considered *prior* to the interview are sexualised conversation and 'grooming' behaviour. Anticipating the possibility that a research participant may seek to sexualise the research interview through his answers to research questions and through body language during the interview is the starting point for developing a response to such behaviour.

Interview-based research with this group of people is emotionally demanding and may be potentially harmful; early recognition of this allows appropriate support mechanisms to be in place. This may involve the use of colleagues, co-researchers, counsellors or supervisors before, during and after the interview has been completed.

Process

Understanding what is *happening* during an interview, rather than just what is being said, is important both in understanding the dynamic of the interview and in recognising what feelings the process generates for the researcher. Three issues are highlighted in the case study: dealing with invitations to collude with offensive attitudes and behaviours;

responding to offence accounts that minimise harm and offender responsibility; and managing disclosures of harm to identified others.

In relation to dealing with offensive attitudes, to adopt an openly conflictual stance presents many problems, not least the termination of the interview and possibly the research project (see Cowburn, 2007). Moreover, to challenge directly the (implicit) attitudes and values of the research respondent is to shift radically the focus of the research interview. An alternative strategy of explicitly not colluding with an offensive comment and following this with an ingenuous question *opens up* data-collection possibilities rather than closing them. The research respondent is invited to express his views more fully, but without expectations of endorsement from the interviewer. Any information forthcoming is germane to understanding the wider social values of the particular research participant.

Listening to offence accounts may be problematic: the stark detail of offences is in many cases very difficult to hear. Additionally, in a long interview, continual denial of both responsibility for the offending and of the harm done by the offending can be very difficult to leave unchallenged.

Disclosure of harm to self or others is likely to occur unannounced in interviews with sex offenders. Despite carefully worded consent documents that clearly identify the parameters of confidentiality, research participants engaged in (long) interviews are likely to forget the conditions under which the interview is being conducted. It is essential that researchers remain vigilant to possible disclosures and forewarn participants of the implications of what they are about to say.

Interpreting and disseminating research

The studies in this chapter have outlined issues pertinent to preparing for and undertaking qualitative research where the researcher and the researched may view the world and their experiences differently. These differences require researchers to prepare for empirical work thoughtfully and regularly to reflect upon their practice. Two problematic issues remain to be discussed: interpretation and dissemination. It is in these two activities that the potential differences between researcher and researched become most marked. However, whatever epistemological standpoint is taken at the outset of the research, presentation of data is inevitably some form of *interpretation*. Of the studies presented in this chapter, Marian's work highlights most graphically the dilemmas faced by the researcher.

The aim of the research was to identify how homophobia suppressed individual actions or choices. Thus, data were analysed and coded to elicit where opposition to homosexuality was evident in the narratives, and how this indicated wider social, political and legal forces at work to suppress or disparage homosexuality. In order to assess how homophobia was informed and sustained, interviewees' experiences were considered within a Foucauldian (Foucault, 1976) theoretical framework, exploring how sexual subjugation was used as a tool to protect the interests of the powerful (in this case, politicians in a politically divided, conflict-torn society) at the expense of the powerless (homosexuals). This necessarily situated the interviewees and their experiences as disadvantaged. Analysis concentrated upon evidence of unequal power relationships, social control, identity subjugation and the construction and marginalisation of the demarcated 'other' in society. Thus, while interviewees may not have seen homophobia as functioning in particular decisions or events, the analysis of the data may have considered this to be the case.

There was a tension in whether to present interviewees as 'victims' when they did not see themselves as such. This involved balancing values when reading interviewees' otherwise 'everyday' experiences as rooted in a deep-seated and dangerous prejudice. For example, some interviewees recalled moving from small, rural villages to larger, urban areas on the premise of enhanced educational or employment opportunities. In hindsight, they also recognised that they were more likely to be able to seek out same-sex partners with greater anonymity than would have been possible had they remained at home, where they were reduced to conforming to heterosexuality or celibacy (which may also have raised suspicions). They did not see this as a constraint of a heterosexist, or homophobic, society at the time as that was the norm and they were the anomaly. At the time of the interview, however, many recognised that such constraints directly link to negative constructions applied to lesbian and gay identities, and that these may have impacted on life choices.

Plummer (1995) suggests that interpretation and presentation of data is primarily the province of the researcher. Interpretation of the participants' narratives in Marian's study shifted the balance of power to the researcher, who, in effect, reconfigured individuals' experiences as symptomatic of wider cultural responses informed by negative ideologies towards homosexuality directed by particular moral discourses. What a participant might perceive as a natural response to homosexuality was interpreted as an element of the culturally dominant homophobia.

Disseminating research that explores sensitive and controversial subjects raises a number of issues that need consideration. Some of these issues require reflection on ethical issues, particularly relating to confidentiality, anonymity and the presentation of data. In Ed's study, these issues presented no difficulties because his data was already available in the public domain and the identities of 'participants' were not publically identifiable.

In this latter case, citing the pseudonyms of the chat-room participants did not jeopardise anyone's safety. In Marian's study, the issue was more complex, but also easily resolved. Although interviewees were informed that their identities would be anonymised in any publications, the activist nature of many interviewees meant that, among their social cohorts, it would be possible that they could be identified. Interviewees recognised this risk but consented to their data being included in publications, often stating that they placed greater importance on disseminating the information than adhering to a strict level of anonymity. Malcolm's research with convicted sex offenders is more problematic; however, all participants are given assurance that if their words are used in publications, they will not be identifiable. This requires not only the use of pseudonyms, but also changing any details that may enable the research participant to be identified (eg the town where they committed their offences, their employment or community position).

Another issue that requires consideration in preparing data for publication is the potential impact of the content of the material. This is most marked in Ed's and Malcolm's work.

The development of the Internet has increased the opportunities for racists to disseminate offensive, harmful and obscene racist material to a wider global audience. Giving a voice to those with racist views or values both in publication and conference presentations is troubling. However, such views and attitudes are not presented without comment or in a favourable light. The views are in the public domain and by presenting them in academic publications and presentation, they can be brought to the attention of a wider audience, who may be critical of the attitudes and values being expressed, and subjected to rigorous academic critique.

In relation to presenting material from research with sex offenders, there is a danger of presenting the words of the offender in such a way that the victim-survivors of sex offences may feel re-victimised. This is particularly the case where data from offence accounts is used: without adequate explanation and justification, explicit descriptions of sexual offences may be experienced as offensive or distressing. The researcher has to balance what particular data say about the research participant, his offences and his victims; merely to reproduce an offender's account of his offences runs the risk of erasing the experience and pain of the victim–survivor(s).

Conclusion

In my experience, it is possible to take more than one side seriously, to find merit in more than one perspective, and to do this without causing outrage on the side of officials or prisoners, but this is a precarious position with a high emotional price to pay (Liebling, 2001, p 473).

This chapter considered issues in undertaking research with populations that present challenges either because of how they interpret their experiences, the nature of their offending behaviour or their expressed attitudes. Each of the areas illustrate that it is not only possible, but *necessary*, to take more than one side in researching difficult and contentious areas. However, the *sides* may not be clearly defined. It is important to understand the *detail* of the experience of research participants, but to represent this accurately without reproducing the harms described. This inevitably requires researchers to give due consideration to the various interpretive communities in which they wish to be heard.

References

Alcoff, L. and Gray, L. (1993) 'Survivor discourse: transgression or recuperation?', *Signs: Journal of Women in Culture and Society*, vol 18, pp 260–90.

Banks, S. (2006) *Ethics and values in social work* (3rd edn), Basingstoke: Palgrave Macmillan.

Becker, H. (1967) 'Whose side are we on?', *Social Problems*, vol 14, no 3, pp 234–47.

British Society of Criminology (2006) Code of *ethics for researchers in the field of criminology*. Available at: www.britsoccrim.org/ethical.htm

Cowburn, M. (2005) 'Confidentiality and public protection: ethical dilemmas in qualitative research with adult male sex offenders', *Journal of Sexual Aggression*, vol 11, no 1, pp 49–63.

Cowburn, M. (2007) 'Men researching men in prison: the challenges for profeminist research', *Howard Journal*, vol 46, no 3, pp 276–88.

Cowburn, M. (2010) 'Principles, virtues and care: ethical dilemmas in research with male sex offenders', *Psychology Crime & Law*, vol 16, nos 1/2, pp 65–74.

Ditton, J. (1977) *Part-time crime: an ethnography of fiddling and pilferage*, London: Macmillan.

Duggan, M. (2010) 'The politics of pride: representing relegated sexual identities in Northern Ireland', *Northern Ireland Legal Quarterly*, vol 61, no 2, pp 163–78.

Duggan, M. (2012) *Queering conflict: examining lesbians' and gay men's experiences of homophobia in Northern Ireland*, Surrey: Ashgate.

Foucault, M. (1976) *The history of sexuality*, London: Penguin Books.

Franklin, M.B. (1997) 'Making sense: interviewing and narrative representation', in M.M. Gergen and S.N. Davis (eds) *Toward a new psychology of gender*, London: Routledge.

Harvey, L. (1990) *Critical social research*, London: Unwin Hyman.

Humphreys, L. (1970) *Tearoom trade: a study of homosexual encounters in public places*, London: Duckworth.

Lee, R. (1993) *Doing research on sensitive topics*, London: Sage.

Liebling, A. (2001) 'Whose side are we on? Theory, practice and allegiances in prisons research', *British Journal of Criminology*, vol 41, pp 472–84.

Mann, D. and Sutton, M. (1998) 'NetCrime: more change in the organisation of thieving', *The British Journal of Criminology*, vol 38, pp 201–29.

Maynard, M. and Purvis, J. (1994) *Researching women's lives from a feminist perspective*, Oxford: Taylor and Francis.

McKittrick, D. and McVea, D. (2001) *Making sense of the Troubles*, Belfast: Blackstaff Press.

Miller, R.L. (2000) *Researching life stories and family histories*, London: Sage.

Mitchell, C. (2006) *Religion, identity and politics in Northern Ireland: boundaries of belonging and belief*, Aldershot: Ashgate.

Parker, H.J. (1974) *View from the boys*, Newton Abbot: David and Charles.

Plummer, K. (1995) 'Life story research', in J. Smith, R. Harré and L. Van Langenhove (eds) *Rethinking methods in psychology*, London: Sage.

Pollock, E. (2010) 'Researching white supremacists online: methodological concerns of researching "'speech'"', *Internet Journal of Criminology*. Available at: www.internetjournalofcriminology.com

Reay, D. (1996) 'Insider perspectives or stealing the words out of women's mouths: interpretation in the research process', *Feminist Review*, special issue, *Speaking Out: Researching and Representing Women*, no 53 (Summer), pp 57–73.

Reinharz, S. (1992) *Feminist methods in social research*, New York, NY: Oxford University.

Roberts, H. (1981) *Doing feminist research*, London: Routledge.

Shütz, A. (1962) *The problem of social reality*, The Hague: Martinus Nifhoff Publishers.

Stanley, L. and Wise, S. (1990) 'Method, methodology and epistemology in feminist research processes', in L. Stanley (ed) *Feminist praxis: research, theory, and epistemology in feminist sociology*, New York, NY: Routledge.

Weedon, C. (1987) *Feminist practice and poststructuralist theory*, London: Blackwell.

TWENTY-ONE

Value for money? The politics of contract research

Paul Senior

Introduction

In research contracts, the relationship between funders, those being evaluated and commissioned researchers is a complex one and differentially impacts upon the outcome of research according to the focus, and sometimes whims, of the funder, the reaction of those sites subject to the research, the service users, the policy context, and the perspectives and theories of change of the researchers themselves. It is a complex and mixed picture with lots of pinch points where the objectivity of the research process may be compromised (Walters, 2003a, 2003b, 2005).

Arguably, all commissioned research potentially involves a contract between the funder and the researcher but there is often a conventional distinction made between basic or pure research and applied or contract research. The former is typically commissioned via research council funding and taking place within an academic context ostensibly in pursuance of knowledge for its own sake, and the latter may be commissioned via local and national government, individual organisations, and other charitable sources with a problem–oriented approach designed to impact in a more immediate way upon policy and practice. This chapter focuses on the latter, so-called 'contract research', where, typically, the agenda for the focus of the research is set beyond the initial control of the researcher. The regulation of research in this context is discussed but rarely acted upon (Khoshnood, 2006; Miller et al, 2006). The research is undertaken by way of a contractual agreement that can circumscribe the extent and nature of the research. The outcomes are usually explicitly linked to an aspect of policy analysis, change, implementation or development. The policy context dominates the focus of the research and predetermines to a considerable extent the agenda, approach, methods chosen and outcomes to be achieved within an inevitably constrained, and usually inadequate, budget.

Commentators have shown that following the election of New Labour in 1997, and throughout subsequent Labour administrations, there was a growth in contract research opportunities along with demand for 'evidence-led' policies (Parsons, 2002; Walters, 2009; Widmer, 2009; Smith 2010). As Loader (2006, p 580) states:

> Since 1997, however, respondents note a move, as one criminologist put it, 'from an era where nothing was evaluated to an era where everything is evaluated' – one that has seen a surfeit of government funding for certain styles of criminological work – what two former civil servants in turn called 'quick and dirty' research whose job is to justify what has been funded rather than contribute to open-ended debate.

Indeed, an expansion of funding was noted by Hillyard et al (2004), who reported that between 1998/99 and 2000/01, the budget went from being £2,754,000 to £17,013,000 – a 500% increase.

Initially, the nature of the research engagement was more akin to research council funding with large programmes of work such as the Crime Reduction Programme (see Maguire, 2004). The different aims of policymakers, practitioners and researchers soon became evident, with the former requiring that programmes remain broadly 'on track', with feedback on 'quick wins' in the form of reductions in crime. According to Maguire (2004), the researchers could have worked harder to warn the Home Office that expectations were too high with regard to the potential achievements and timescales of projects. Programmes were being started, if not completed, before the researchers produced substantive feedback on results of initiatives and suggestions for pragmatic improvements (Hope, 2004, 2008). These ambitious programmes have been curtailed in the last decade. As Maguire (2004, p 233) presciently suggested:

> Given this, and given all the problems described earlier, it is tempting to conclude that the ideal of 'evidence-based policy' may be more effectively pursued as a series of quiet iterative processes in individual corners of the criminal justice arena, than through one large-scale and high profile 'programme'.

In recent years, contract research has been commissioned through more tightly prescribed, one-off procurements, as Maguire predicted, and the funding has become more restrictive and focused on specific policy goals. This is the context within which the work of one contract research centre, which this chapter draws upon, currently takes place. It is beyond the scope of this chapter to consider the argument that all such 'administrative criminology' is 'atheoretical' and merely buttresses the already prescribed policy journey of government (Young et al, 2002; Matthews, 2009). This critique has been well rehearsed elsewhere (Hope, 2004; Maguire, 2004; Matthews, 2009). Rather, this chapter explores the questions Becker (1967) raises in his seminal article 'Whose side are we on?' by reflecting on the detail of the processes of engagement in this 'quick and dirty' research.

There has been comparatively little attention paid to the contract researchers themselves and the dilemmas and tensions that inform their experiences of conducting research (Allen-Collinson, 2000; Collinson, 2003). How do researchers manage the competing pressures of a range of 'superordinates' in this process, maintain their own ethical integrity and also ensure the voice of the 'subordinate' – usually service users – is heard above all the noise of policy directions?

Drawing empirically on a range of 50 contracted research projects in the research centre, including large-scale multi-site projects as well as smaller local projects, this chapter explores this cache of policy-oriented contract research, where researchers seek to negotiate the challenges of what Becker would perceive as 'multiple sides'. These include contested terrains, including those:

- between researchers and policy analysts in government;
- between government research project managers, the pilot sites under investigation, civil servants and politicians;
- between outcomes envisaged by the funder as client and the observed impact on those who are normally at the receiving end of such reports in criminal justice – the subordinates;
- between the service user, victim or offender; and
- between bureaucracies, ethics and Ethics Committees, appraising ethics as points of resistance, and obligations to research participants.

Going further, the chapter locates these tensions within debates on the nature of criminology as a discipline and the production of 'truth' in reporting the outcomes of this more pragmatic arena for research endeavour. It will be argued that the researcher's own potential theoretical bias is but one 'side' in a multi-sided endeavour where competing claims on the veracity of outcomes emerge from the positional relationships of the various participants in the contract. This can leave the researcher vulnerable to multiple pressures to preserve a 'truth' maybe at odds with the value positions of 'superordinate' players in this complex modality.

The nature of contract research

There are usually three distinct elements that distinguish contract research: the funding arrangement, the focus of the research and the intended recipients. In this analysis, it will be noted that five types of funder have been identified. First, central government departments, particularly for crime-related matters: the Ministry of Justice, Home Office, Department of Work and Pensions and related departments for health and children services, but also including national organisations such as the National Offender Management Service (NOMS) and the Youth Justice Board, for instance. Local government is a second funder through local authority or city council budgets. A third funder is through charitable sources; this can be a national grant-making body, a local charity or voluntary sector organisation, or an infrastructural organisation such as Clinks. The fourth type of funder is an area/regional criminal justice organisation; typically, this would include the main criminal justice organisations such as the police, probation trusts, prisons, local criminal justice boards, community safety partnerships and so on. Finally, European sources of funding are identified and in the studies discussed here, this is European Social Funding (ESF) EQUAL Initiative funding and could typically include some of the above-mentioned funders as joint participants in the projects.

The second aspect relates to focus, including the core aims and objectives defined by the funders, sometimes in liaison with the project leads, for the research. Typically, in pure research, the research questions are first identified by the researcher and refined and elaborated in the 'Case for Support'. While the focus might have policy relevance, it is defined more by the primary interests of the researcher, who seeks to persuade research councils to fund. In contrast, the objectives of contract research are defined by the funder in advance of engaging a researcher, typically in a tender document. This document starts the engagement process and determines the focus. Tenders are usually competitively advertised to a range of potential suppliers, although sometimes this is restricted to a group of 'preferred bidders'. In previous years, there was often a more direct approach made to individual researchers chosen on the basis of previous relationships and perceived expertise, but the procurement culture has formalised this procedure in recent years, possibly reducing the nepotism implied in the former process. The costs of such tender processes are rarely calculated as part of the opportunity costs of engagement in the research process. However, preparing bids, attending interviews and a likely failure rate of one in five bids, plus the extensive time taken by funders to prepare the tender documents, assess bids, conduct interviews, prepare contracts and oversee projects, suggests that this is a somewhat uneconomic way of commissioning research (see Spurgeon and Hicks, 2003). Furthermore, the pace of such competitive procurement processes, alongside locating it in a competition, reduces the opportunity to engage in a dialogue and refinement of the aims of the research. It could be argued that the capacity to start work immediately and respond to short timescales and deadlines and a minimalist budget is as significant in the selection process as is the quality and expertise of the research team. Does such an investment lead to ethically appropriate, methodologically sound and independent research findings? This issue is analysed and addressed as the chapter develops.

The third aspect of contract research relates to its essentially instrumental emphasis. It has been commissioned not to investigate a criminological concern, though the research may do so, but rather to seek answers to a policy or implementation concern or problem. Such research asks the researcher to evaluate the intervention, policy process or project under investigation to test its efficacy and capacity for further policy development and to assess its impact on the recipients. This is somewhat negatively badged by some criminologists: 'These bodies of criminological research are representative of what I shall term "jobbing criminology"' (Loader and Sparks, 2011).

All parties – funders, participating organisations, the consumers/service users, the wider government and the criminal justice system – have a vested interest in the outcomes. There are literally many players of which the researcher is but one, theoretically acting as the surrogate for these vested interests. However, as Becker (1967) would identify, the researcher may have his or her own perspective/bias, which might dictate the way the research is conducted.

Unpacking the detailed processes of contract research will help in explicating the way in which the outcomes challenge the value neutrality of the researchers and the ability to present 'truth' in the output reports. Unlike researcher-initiated research more typical of pure research, the researcher is commissioned to work on outcomes defined and determined by others. The processes within which this engagement takes place acts to constrain independent thinking and action emerging from the research findings themselves. Ultimately, this raises a key question of whether the resultant findings are defensible and helpful evidence to guide future policy. In other words, does this process enable the development of a rich library of evidence-based research outputs that can guide policy and practice in criminal justice? Or does the process itself, buffeted by so many vested interests, produce 'policy-based' evidence that merely validates the direction of policy originally desired by the superordinate players in the system, serving neither the interests of the pursuance of truth, the desires of the subordinate players nor the predilections of the researcher?

The study analysed 50 different contracts run by a university-based contract research centre over a 12-year period from 2000. The diagram shows their distribution over different funders and different amounts of award made. Many took place over a very short period, often as little as six months, but a proportion, around 10%, operated over one, two or three years. Some operated during a change of government, where the pressure to respond to a changing policy environment was particularly acute.

Figure 21.1: Distribution of projects undertaken by monetary value and type of funder

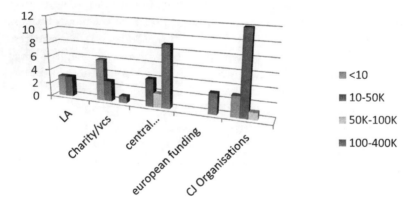

There are routine frustrations in every contract research engagement, what might be termed contingent factors, and these, in no priority order, include:

- inadequate preparation time for bid writing;
- immediate start to the work post-award;
- redefining of aims not agreed at the tendering stage;

- preparation of interview schedules;
- ill-prepared sites;
- the projects not actually producing researchable activity;
- poor or non-existent data sets;
- insufficient numbers to meet the research specification;
- delays attendant on data security issues;
- sites being unwilling to agree fieldwork dates;
- refusals to allow access to key institutions such as prisons; and
- other day-to-day management headaches.

In examining the 50 projects,[1] five interrelated and substantive themes were identified where risks to the integrity of the research were potentially crucial and significant. These five themes were: validation or evaluation; interference in report writing; warring between superordinates; establishing the voice of the subordinate; and ensuring a fit between policy and the research.

Validation or evaluation

The language used in the tender documents is primarily concerned with establishing whether a particular identified project or programme is 'working', often defined in unrealistic terms such as reducing reoffending. However, establishing this seemingly simple goal was compromised by a number of variables, including the circumstances in which the research was being commissioned, the timescale and resources allowed, and the overarching external policy priority. Contract research was often commissioned in response to an external need to validate the ongoing project work. This could be particularly the case in small voluntary and community sector (VCS) projects, where the uncertainty of project funding often required an independent piece of research to validate how successful the programme had been before further funding would be allocated. The pressure to produce a piece of work that was descriptive of the project but did not essentially challenge the aims was acute. Researchers often fed back on the pressure to provide a report that showed unconditional support for the programme under evaluation. The researchers reported the very different attitudes of the funder when the report challenged the efficacy of the work to any degree. Sometimes, this could be couched in terms of the quality of the report writing or a misunderstanding of the project itself. In multi-site projects, there was sometimes pressure from the project leaders on each site to push the researchers into defining whose was the 'best' project and providing their own 'evidence' to dispute any seemingly negative conclusions drawn. Project leaders could welcome reports that offered insights into improving their practice, but this was as commonly disputed as welcomed. Openness to critique was such an erratic response by project leaders. Where the contract research included an element of action research, the researcher could engage the projects in their developing thinking, producing a shared vision in the final report. One example offers a cautionary remark, however, about this approach.

In one multi-site government-funded project, it was clear that one site lead could not accept any critique of his project. This led to numerous tactics to ensure that his views predominated:

- detailed questioning of evidence presented;
- questioning the researchers' understanding of the local context;
- comparing 'inappropriately compiled' statistics from their site to the other two sites;
- delays in providing necessary data;
- cancelling of research interviews;
- refusing to allow certain workers to be interviewed without the project leader's presence; and
- dismissing the views of the subordinate player, the service users, by claiming that they were an unrepresentative sample, despite providing the sample themselves.

In this case example, the researcher had to spend considerable extra time to answer queries, to respond to spurious information and to be bold enough not to simply give in to this tactical barrage of criticisms.

Interference in report writing

The researcher often does not feel the weight of funder or project leader disagreement until a draft report is prepared. This is particularly so where the methodology does not involve an element of action research. In government-funded reports, both the shape of the report itself and the content can be battlegrounds for disagreement. The report format is known as the 1:3:25 format, requiring a one-page headline, a three-page executive summary and a 25-page report. This format is applied no matter whether the project is a small, one-site, single issue evaluation or a seven-site national comparative evaluation over two years, the same strictures apply. This forces the report to be compressed into those pages before it is assessed. Much useful explanatory material is therefore relegated to appendices or not included at all. At a certain stage before publication, the report will also be subject to independent peer review. Feedback from these reviews frequently request additional material and development of key ideas, originally excluded only because of the limits of space. The reports themselves are subject to several layers of scrutiny. The nature of this scrutiny can be of three types: grammatical, technical or policy compliance.

There will always be debates about the use of plain English, the construction of sentences and appropriate language. While much of this is a matter of personal preference and the degree to which spilt infinitives are allowable, on occasions, this can mask more subtle intents to prescribe the direction of the report. Two brief examples illustrate this point. On one report, the researcher was repeatedly told to use a particular description of the project name. The researcher had been told by the project itself that it preferred to be called by another name, indicating its geographical reach more accurately, a clear nod to the local city council who wanted its central engagement appropriately labelled. However, the funder wanted to create a different perspective and pursued a name change on successive drafts reflecting a county-wide designation. A more serious linguistic debate relates to the use of the word '*offender*' to describe service users, the subordinate, in the research. Becker would have pointed to this, and the use of other such negative labels, as examples of the process by which deviance is amplified (Becker, 1973). This has become a seriously contested issue in the world of 'offender' management.

A second concern relates to more technical questions about methodological rigour. Often, key issues are only drawn to the attention of the researcher once a report is submitted. These discussions are sometimes easily resolved; at other times, they represent fundamental questions about the efficacy of the research itself and the conclusions drawn. The difficulty for the researcher is the power imbalance between the research officer representing the funder and the researcher's own data. At the end of the day, control of the report's publication is in the hands of the funder. These can be uncomfortable discussions where researchers believe strongly that the research methods used are appropriately constructed, planned and delivered and they have adhered to appropriate research standards. There is clearly a tension where the researcher believes that their research is of the highest standard and the dispute over it is hiding more subtle debates about the conclusions drawn. Where the funder does not agree with the defence of the research work, the report is not published. As intellectual property rests with the funder, the capacity to publish independently can be severely restricted, if not forbidden entirely. Sometimes, the reports are published with a time delay, another way of controlling the impact by publishing when the policy relevance may have simply disappeared.

Demanding policy compliance is a much more overt attempt by funders, usually represented by government civil servants, to ensure that the report outcomes reflect government policy priorities. Here, there is a real risk to the researcher, where suggestions for change are resisted, of the non-publication of the report. There are constant pressures reported by researchers to produce recommendations that do not always easily flow from the research undertaken but reflect the policy direction (Hope, 2005). One particularly acute example of this will illustrate the dilemma. A five-site national evaluation was undertaken during the final stages of the previous New Labour government. The report was subject to four drafts and the peer review. Each draft did not necessarily constitute progression but sometimes the researchers were asked to revert to some of the initial thinking that showed tension between three superordinates in the process, that is, the project research manager concerned about research rigour, the site senior project leads and the policy-driven civil servants. However, eventually, the researchers were able to reach agreement on a final draft.

At this point, the country went to an election and 'purdah' or pre-election period (House of Commons Library, 2010) occurred, which meant that civil servants could not engage in any discussions about ongoing commissioned work. The publication of this work was stalled at this point. Following the election of the Coalition government, further discussion on this report and two others prepared from the same piece of research was not reignited for over eight months. At this point, the researchers received a revised draft of the report containing a number of significant changes which illustrated that policy on the topic area was now subject to new government policy priorities. For instance, all mentions of regionalisation were expunged from the report, in keeping with the abandonment of a regional tier of government. In other subtle and not-so-subtle ways, new government policy was incorporated into a piece of research that had been conducted over 18 months previously. Subsequently, this revised report was published 14 months after the original final draft had been prepared. Two further reports on the same research were never published.

Warring between superordinates

The more complex the piece of research, the more disputed is control of the outcome between stakeholders. From the previous five-site evaluation discussed earlier, the following stakeholders were identified as seeking to influence the outcome: the government research manager, government policy analysts/civil servants, representatives of key national organisations, each site senior project manager, staff on each site, peer reviewers, and, of course, control of publication ultimately rests with government ministers. With this range of stakeholders, disputes can arise at a number of levels, which the researcher can record in their field notes but which may not be appropriate to include in analysing the project. Examples of this can include disputes:

- between local site leaders and central government perspectives;
- between the research manager and policy leads;
- between staff on the project and their managers;
- between different sites; and
- between external stakeholders, such as professional associations developing agency policy, and the site project staff themselves.

Researchers have to handle these disputes, sometimes just as observer, but there can be pressure to 'take sides', to reflect one particular point of view. Response to this pressure is often calculative – what are the consequences of supporting one view over the other? How far do such disputes enable the researcher to assert their own perspective and maintain the integrity of the fieldwork data and does accommodation, as distinct from challenge or disagreement, enable the researcher to ensure that the work is completed and, to some extent, justify a compliant approach to challenge? A couple of examples illustrate the tensions here, one in a large multi-site national evaluation, the other in a small VCS evaluation.

In the first example, researchers became conscious of a strong disagreement between a site leader and the organisation's project lead. These disputes were evident both in formal meetings and in individual discussions where 'confidential' views were expressed. This was difficult for the researcher to resolve and demanded diplomacy and conciliation skills not necessarily in the armoury of the researcher. In the second example, the pressures exerted by the VCS organisation leaders on the scope of the work caused the researcher major difficulty. Individual elements of the research were hijacked by these leaders, turning up to workshops and individual interviews without invite with a view to controlling the contributions of their staff members and trying to shape the research towards their perspective. The researcher in this situation was placed under intolerable pressure, which led to the research centre temporarily withdrawing from the work until a protocol could be established.

Establishing the voice of the subordinate

Criminal justice research has a number of customers. The researcher has a number of clients to satisfy. Becker (1967) had identified how the radical sociology researcher may see themselves as identifying with the subordinate in the research engagement, and this particular 'taking of sides' was central to Becker's initial thesis. Contract research identifies the funder as the primary client, with other superordinates also having a claim upon the ear of the researcher. The subject of the research is often the service user. A high proportion of the 50 studies analysed here would have involved some aspect of service user research – focus groups, observations, semi-structured interviews, narrative interviews, workshops, data analysis of trends in reoffending – and yet the nature of the contract does not make the subject the client and therefore their voice may not be seen as the paramount one. Indeed, although many projects in criminal justice are seeking to demonstrate a reduction in reoffending, the service user is merely the object of this goal and a 'dummy player' in the project. Following Becker, researchers will wish to ensure that the voice of the subordinate is properly represented in the research report. However, the nature of the contract frequently can set the researcher up to fail in achieving this goal. Data management within agencies is often inadequate for the task set:

- often researchers are provided with data sets that cannot be exported for analysis in SPSS (SPSS Statistics is a software package used for statistical analysis);
- the data itself can be inconsistently coded;
- comparative data from the Police National Computer (PNC) can be unavailable or so delayed that it cannot be completed within the timescales allowed for the research and the numbers involved; and
- once data cleaning has taken place, it is frequently inadequate for establishing statistical significance.

Yet, there is considerable pressure on researchers to produce quantifiable data that demonstrate reducing reoffending, the current policy obsession. This is reflected in contracts that require researchers to demonstrate such reductions whether or not there is adequate time, resource, data or appropriate methods, such as Randomised Control Trials (RCTs) (Widmer, 2009), to demonstrate such an outcome. This can be particularly evident in small-scale VCS-funded projects, where the resource is woefully inadequate for such a task. Qualitative research that can add meaning to the experience of the subordinate is then unjustly criticised for failing to produce outcomes that it is structurally ill-equipped to provide.

Ensuring a fit between policy and the research

Walters addresses this concern simply: 'Conducting research commissioned by the Home Office is a frustrating, one-sided arm-wrestle – where the Home Office always ensures that it will almost always "cherry-pick" the answer it wants' (Walters, 2009, p 207). This issue is a constant headache for policy-oriented contract researchers. As discussed in the introduction, the apparent commitment to evidence-based practice is regarded as paramount in many areas of policy development and this is strongly the case for criminal justice research. Yet, it can be seen how government policy can shift rapidly over individual issues, which confounds research direction and independence and suggests that policy decisions are regarded as overriding rather than awaiting the advice from the research itself (Parsons, 2002; Wyatt, 2002). This is unsurprising.

> Policy changes for reasons other than the discovery of new knowledge: for example, because of shifts in the public mood, the political commitments of new administrations, crises and cock-ups, the personal ambitions of politicians, the obvious failure of past policies. (Solesbury, 2008, p 22)

The recent announcement by the Justice Secretary, Chris Grayling, of the privatisation of up to 70% of the public probation service (Ministry of Justice, 2013) was met with much criticism both from within the Probation Trusts and from academic researchers, primarily because it ignored strong evidence of the success of the Probation Trusts at reducing reoffending, and ascribed failure to the Probation Trusts in an area where they were not responsible for supervision. In a succession of blogs posted at the time, strong evidence was repeatedly mounted to illustrate that Grayling's pronouncements were driven more by ideological and policy preference than a selfless commitment to evidence. This can lead, in contract research, to the production of what can be described as 'politically inconvenient' research. Research prepared with appropriate rigour but produced at a time when the policy direction has changed can suffer either from non-publication, delayed publication or 'quiet' publication – a regulatory device noted by Miller, Moore and Strang (2006).

This is not a new phenomenon. Two historical examples illustrate the point. Research on restorative justice as a pre-sentence, post-conviction measure, then known as victim–offender mediation, was undertaken in three sites in 1985. Political concern grew over the perceived manipulation of the sentencing process by offenders engaging in the mediation but not demonstrating remorse. The experiment was deemed politically risky and quietly shelved and the subsequent Home Office research was not published until 1990 (Marshall and Merry, 1990). Another concerning example of policy over evidence was, yet again, from the Home Office's own psychology research department, who were asked to research the impact of the short sharp shock detention regime inspired by Willie Whitelaw in the early 1980s. Before the research was even completed, Leon Brittain, who had replaced Whitelaw and who was inspired by the hawkish Right, announced that the regime would be extended to all detention centres across England and Wales. Some while later, the research, showing little in the way of effectiveness of such regimes, was quietly placed in the Home Office library without any announcement of its 'publication' (Thornton et al, 1984).

Examples of this phenomenon can be found in the 50 studies. As intellectual property rests with the funder and is carefully prescribed in contracts, non-publication of the report prevents the researcher from producing intellectual capital in the form of articles and chapters based on the original research. It must also be noted that there are more pragmatic considerations. Even when a report is published and therefore in the public domain and an article can be scoped, no staff time is usually attributed in the budgets for such dissemination activities and, in most instances, permission will still be required before independent publication is undertaken. Of course, the researcher can challenge such onerous authority but there is a power dynamic here. The researcher may be looking to that funder for future work and there is a strong risk associated with oppositional behaviour. There are a number of risks to the researcher from asserting independence throughout the research engagement and this will be considered further in the section on implications for practice later.

Suffice it to note here that there were a number of tensions experienced over publication during these 50 studies:

- major reports produced for the government and pronounced acceptable following peer review but unpublicised without explanation;

- reluctance of small funders to fund publication, which forces the researcher to spend to produce a hard copy report or settle for a pdf version;
- refusal to publish outright or report on the findings at all;
- delayed publication beyond the policy–relevant period for impact;
- summary publication only;
- refusal to support article publication;
- organisation comments on the report findings in press releases and so on that distort said findings; and
- outcome reports badged as the organisation's output and not that of the researcher who has written the report.

Implications for good practice in contract research

The tensions of contract research, as described earlier, have been identified and can present as depressing reading for the budding researcher. However, a good researcher, if he or she is to survive and prosper in contract research, must work effectively with these tensions and 'multiple sides' to steer an ethically defensible and methodologically rigorous research encounter. What strategies can be identified to make this outcome more likely to be achieved, remembering that such is the power invested in the superordinates that this will not always be possible? Five strategies are highlighted here: high–quality bid documents; utilising aspects of action research; methodological rigour; policy intelligence; and a strong, 'calculative' will.

High-quality bid documents

Setting out precisely and clearly what you can achieve in the research drawn from the project specification within budget limits and methodological requirements sets the initial contractual engagement on a footing that can be returned to when disputes occur. A clear statement of ethical standards can also be an essential bargaining tool when disputes occur. Having a process where ethics are assured through an internal independent procedure buttresses this approach and can structure debates with the superordinates in cases where there is dispute. One example relates to the use of incentives to engage service users in participating in fieldwork activity. The funders were reluctant to support this element in the budget, not on cost grounds (as it was such a small element of the total budget), but rather due to the potential for awkward political questions regarding rewarding service users for participating. This was strongly resisted on ethical grounds and in that case, at least, successfully resisted.

There will always be compromises in bid documents as budgets become increasingly tight and costs of staff time continue to escalate, but at least clarity of expectations will minimise the risks of inappropriate demands being placed on the researcher at the outset. A clear statement regarding how the particular policy context is viewed should also be included but there are obvious risks to winning a bid if you hit an oppositional tone to the funders' preferred policy direction.

Utilising aspects of action research

One of the main themes articulated in this chapter is an acceptance that 'multiple sides' do exist in contract research. Rehearsing the direction of the research, sharing insights with the sites and with policy leads as the results begin to emerge, can enable a productive debate to take place and help avoid a potential major disagreement at the draft report stage. Among the 50 studies, there are a number where difficult issues have been identified during the research that have been highly charged and confrontational. But, when complex outcomes are rehearsed in an atmosphere of mutual engagement, acceptable compromises can be found. The researcher may still find their perspective challenged, as discussed earlier, but will find ways of using the research itself to debate outcomes and achieve a consensus.

Methodological rigour

The rigorous researcher should possess an in-depth appreciation of the nuances of the research methods chosen to enable a robust and substantive defence when in dispute with sites where the latter challenge the findings, using their positional power as superordinates to assert dominance. Tim Hope (2005, p 4) writes:

> Given the power of politics, it is not rocket science to predict what will happen when evidence gets in the way of a good policy. Recently, Tony Bottoms has written that 'methodology matters' (Bottoms, 2005). It matters because methodology, complicated and tedious though it may appear, is the only way in which science can rescue, defend and indeed empower evidence within the political claim-making about 'what works'.

Practitioners and managers normally do not have a detailed understanding of research methods and respond to conclusions more out of disappointment that their preferred policy outcome or project appreciation is not being achieved than an in-depth dissection of the limitations on inferred outcomes that the research method has demonstrated. This can be very different in government-funded research, where the research manager often has a thorough knowledge of research methods and also a commitment to the so-called 'gold standard' of research methods with, at times, an instinctive dislike of qualitative methods.

It is beyond the scope of this chapter to debate the value positions implicated in the qualitative versus quantitative research method debate (Young, 2011). However, this is not irrelevant to previous discussions on policy-based evidence. Current preoccupations with economic modelling of outcomes based on statistically sophisticated research or so regarded puts strong pressure on contract bidders to foreground quantitative methodologies in their bids as a policy preference, whether or not the budget or the circumstances of the project will enable such methodologies to be attempted (Government Social Research Unit, 2007). One reflection from researchers is that the 'bar for evidence' has risen in recent years, and in the future, outcome data may become the only data of interest to funders. This preoccupation, though, is not supported with the wherewithal to achieve this – resources, robust data sets, access to PNC, information-sharing protocols, clarity over measurements, ethical probity of RCTs and so on have not been provided along with this policy trend.

Policy intelligence

Each contract research centre needs to have an in-depth understanding of the policy context and, ideally, have staff who, in previous roles, have undertaken policy development or implementation. Although the researcher is engaging ostensibly in routine research tasks, in fact, they are attempting this work in the more charged environment of policy development. The research will always be mediated through this context and the researcher has to appreciate the pressures on sites and on policy leads to deliver projects that meet policy priorities. If policy priorities change during the life of the research, the researcher needs to offer positive solutions, possibly amending fieldwork priorities, to reflect this new direction. This requires a level of contextual familiarity and methodological flexibility that would be less important, and, possibly, less legitimated, in pure research.

Strong, 'calculative' will

In recommending this final characteristic, it is argued that merely being 'strong willed' may not be a sufficient or appropriate stance to protect the researcher from dispute and, ultimately, from exclusion from the contract and potentially future contracts. Researchers need to be calculative, that is, to assess the appropriate times at which a dispute is so fundamental to the integrity of the research as to warrant a firm stance but to do so in ways that will not derail the outcome. Experience of working in these contexts is vital here and there is always a delicate balance to be maintained. Policy leads and site leads will push their perceptions to the limits, but when the facts of the research findings are robust and defensible and with diplomatic aplomb, resistance to these pressures will produce positive outcomes, though not in all situations.

Conclusion

The argument rendered in this chapter is that contract research presents the researcher with multiple sides and vested interests, and, at times, the researcher voice might feel like the least significant of these. Research is surely not the predominate element in the crowded arena of policymaking (Locock and Boaz, 2004), but those who undertake it are seeking a role in policy that can be regarded as 'embedded criminology' (Petersilia, 2008). There is little doubt that where researchers can work alongside policymakers in an action research, co-production model, research can play a more substantial part in the process of policy change. As Becker (1967) would contend, the researcher may associate with the 'subordinate', who, in so much criminal justice research, is both the object and the subject of the research. What makes sense to the service user may not be the same as the funder. This engagement, therefore, is rarely straightforward, buffered by the many pressures to conform to funders' and project leads' steer. In seeking to protect a criminological 'truth', the researcher has to manage all those sides and do so, as far as is possible, through ethical integrity, methodological rigour and the ability to articulate contrary views when the fieldwork reveals it. This is not to pretend that it is an easy or uncontroversial place to operate.

Acknowledgement

I would like to thank the work of one of my researchers, Dr Hayden Bird, who undertook some invaluable background literature reviews to support the academic underpinning of this chapter.

Note

[1] I have observed and discussed issues with all my researchers in the field through individual and group investigations to identify key concerns where the research enterprise was compromised by the process itself. The discussion in this chapter draws on key recurring themes in those discussions. Examples used are all drawn from real case examples but anonymised to protect all parties.

References

Allen-Collinson, J. (2000) 'Social science contract researchers in higher education: perceptions of craft knowledge', *Work, Employment & Society*, vol 14, no 1, pp 159–71.

Becker, H.S. (1967) 'Whose side are we on?', *Social Problems*, vol 14, pp 239–47.

Becker, H.S. (1973) *Outsiders: studies in the sociology of deviance* (2nd edn), New York, NY: Free Press.

Bottoms, A. (2005) 'Methodology matters', *Safer Society*, vol 25, Summer, pp 10–12.

Collinson, J.A. (2003) 'Working at a marginal "career": the case of UK social science contract researchers', *The Sociological Review*, vol 51, pp 405–22.

Government Social Research Unit (2007) *Background paper 7 – why do social experiments? Experiments and quasi-experiments for evaluating government policies and programmes*, London: Cabinet Office.

Hillyard, P., Sim, J., Tombs, S. and Whyte, D. (2004) 'Leaving a "stain upon the silence": contemporary criminology and the politics of dissent', *The British Journal of Criminology*, vol 44, pp 369–90.

Hope, T. (2004) 'Pretend it works: evidence and governance in the evaluation of the Reducing Burglary Initiative', *Criminal Justice*, vol 4, no 3, pp 287–308.

Hope, T. (2005) 'Things can only get better', *Criminal Justice Matters*, vol 62, no 1, pp 4–39.

Hope, T. (2008) 'The first casualty: evidence and governance in a war against crime', in P. Carlen (ed) *Imaginary penalties*, Collompton: Willan.

House of Commons Library (2010) 'Purdah, or the pre-election period', HoC Library, Standard Note: SN/PC/05262, 4 January.

Khoshnood, K. (2006) 'The regulation of research by funding bodies: a wake-up call', *International Journal of Drug Policy*, vol 17, pp 246–7.

Loader, I. (2006) 'Fall of the "platonic guardians": liberalism, criminology and political responses to crime in England and Wales', *British Journal of Criminology*, vol 46, pp 561–86.

Loader, I. and Sparks, R. (2011) *Public criminology?*, Oxon: Routledge.

Locock, L. and Boaz, A. (2004) 'Research, policy and practice – worlds apart?', *Social Policy and Society*, vol 3, no 4, pp 375–84.

Maguire, M. (2004) 'The Crime Reduction Programme in England and Wales: reflections on the vision and the reality', *Criminal Justice*, vol 4, no 3, pp 213–37.

Marshall, T.F. and Merry, S. (1990) *Crime and accountability: victim/offender mediation in practice*, London: HMSO.

Matthews, R. (2009) 'Beyond "So what?" criminology: rediscovering realism', *Theoretical Criminology*, vol 13, no 3, pp 341–62.

Miller, P., Moore, D. and Strang, J. (2006) 'The regulation of research by funding bodies: an emerging ethical issue for the alcohol and other drug sector?', *International Journal of Drug Policy*, vol 17, pp 12–16.

Ministry of Justice (2013) 'Transforming rehabilitation – a revolution in the way we manage offenders', Consultation Paper CP1/2013.

Parsons, W. (2002) 'From muddling through to muddling up – evidence based policy making and the modernisation of british government', *Public Policy and Administration*, vol 17, no 3 pp 43–60.

Petersilia, J. (2008) 'Influencing public policy: an embedded criminologist reflects on California prison reform', *Journal of Experimental Criminology*, vol 4, pp 335–56.

Smith, K. (2010) 'Research, policy and funding – academic treadmills and the squeeze on intellectual spaces', *The British Journal of Sociology*, vol 61, no 1, pp 176–195.

Solesbury, W. (2008) 'Research and policy change: the power of opportunism', *Criminal Justice Matters*, vol 72, no 1, pp 22–3.

Spurgeon, P. and Hicks, C. (2003) 'The tendering process: flaws and all', *Health Services Management Research*, vol 16, pp 188–93.

Thornton, D., Curran, L., Grayson, D. and Holloway, V. (1984) *Tougher regimes in detention centres: a report of an evaluation by the Young Offender Psychology Unit*, London: HMSO.

Walters, R. (2003a) 'New modes of governance and the commodification of criminological knowledge', *Social and Legal Studies*, vol 12, no 1, pp 5–26.

Walters, R. (2003b) *Deviant knowledge: criminology, politics and practice*, Devon: Willan.

Walters, R. (2005) 'Boycott, resistance and the role of the deviant voice', *Criminal Justice Matters*, vol 62, no 1, pp 2–27.

Walters, R. (2009) 'The state, knowledge production and criminology', in R. Coleman, J. Sim, S. Tombs and D. Whyte (eds) *State, power, crime: readings in critical criminology*, London: Sage.

Widmer, T. (2009) 'The contribution of evidence-based policy to the output-oriented legitimacy of the state', *Evidence and Policy*, vol 5, no 4, pp 351–72.

Wyatt, A. (2002) 'Evidence based policy making: the view from a centre', *Public Policy and Administration*, vol 17, no 3, pp12–28.

Young, J. (2011) *The criminological imagination*, Cambridge, UK and Malden, MA: Polity.

Young, K., Ashby, D., Boaz, A. and Grayson, L. (2002) 'Social science and the evidence-based policy movement', *Social Policy and Society*, vol 1, no 3, pp 215–24.

Index

Y

Z